# You are cordially invited to

# Weddings

## Dating & Love Customs of

## Cultures Worldwide

# Including Royalty

## by Carolyn Mordecai

# Acknowledgments

*Special thanks to my son, Leonard Mordecai, for his thoughtful and generous support and to my daughter, Diane Mordecai, for her understanding and advice.*
*Special thanks to my brother, Elliot Stein, and his wife, Eileen, for their kind support.*
*My thanks also to my cousins Marla and Stuart Levine.*

*In memory of my father Lewis Stein*

**Dust Cover Design by Kellogg Cirino**

**Copyeditors**
*Jackson White, Ph.D., Mignon Parker, Vicki Kunzelman, Jerry Eaton*

*Macintosh technical advisor, Laurie Breagle of Thompson-Shore, Inc.*

**Photographs on the cover are the courtesy of the following:**
**India wedding**. *Mrs. Rashmi Singh as Hindu bride (front cover) and Mr. Yagyadeep Singh Gaur as Hindu bridegroom (back cover). Rashmi Singh, Mr. Yagyadeep Singh Gaur, and Sumitra Singh.*
**Nigerian-style United States wedding.** *Sylvia Small, UJAMAA Fashions,*
*Photography: Stann Golden of Golden Studios.*
**Heart Wedding Cake.** *The Wilton School of Cake Decorating and Confectionery Art. ©Wilton Enterprises*
**Austrian Folk Wedding**. *Austrian Cultural Institute, New York*
**President and Mrs. John F. Kennedy**. *John F. Kennedy Library*
**Greek Orthodox Wedding**. *Jim and Christina Speros*

© 1999 by Carolyn Mordecai

**Library of Congress Cataloging-in-Publication Data**
Mordecai, Carolyn
   Weddings, dating, and love customs of cultures worldwide,
   including royalty
      p. cm
   Includes bibliographical reference and index.
   ISBN 0-9613823-2-5
   1. Marriage customs and rites 2. Weddings 3. Love and dating 4. Religion
   GT 2665.M76
   392.5 Mordecai 1999
   Printed in the United States of America by Thompson-Shore, Inc.
   First Edition

# Contents

## 1 RELIGIOUS WEDDINGS

*includes philosophy of marriage for each religion*

## 2 AFRICA

## 3 NORTH AMERICA

## 4 CENTRAL AMERICA

### 104 Introduction to Latin America

## 5 SOUTH AMERICA

## 6 ASIA

## 7 EUROPE

## 8 MIDDLE-EAST

## 9 OCEANIA

## 10 ROYALTY

# Acknowledgments

**I wish to thank the following people for their help in making the informational contents of this book a reality:**

Reiko Minatoya, Japan • Sumitra Singh, India • Stanley Levine, United States • Julio Gomez, Cuba
Reverend Theos Anastas, Greece and United States • Stann Golden, Photographer, United States
Reverend Michelle and Lonnie Whittington, Religious Science • Ghada Abdullatif, Jordan and Jerusalem
Phyliss Towner, United States • Orville Allison, United States • Bhapakamile Gongo, South Africa
Reverend Peggy Conger, Religious Science • Andrew V. Dorko, China • Daphne Kartchev, Bulgaria
Michael Le Tourneau, Associated Press • Sonia Voyles, Belgium • Alexandra Levaditis, Greece
Martin Ottenheimer, Ph.D., Domoni • Henry Muonoweshuro, Zimbabwe • Lilian Tsappa, Cyprus
Aye Hla Bu, Myanmar • Margriet Willems, Netherlands • Sharon D. Ringen, Germany
Teresa Quesada, Peru • Warren H. Stewart, Sr., D.Min., United States • Helen Fisher, Ph.D., Anthropologist
Jerry Smallidge, Publisher of *Wedding Day Magazine* • Roger Axford, Ph.D., United States
Martin Ottenheimer, Ph.D., Anjouan • C. Buttigieg, Malta • Anne E. Audem, Mexican Government Tourist Office
Sylvia Small, United States and Africa • Ambassador Park & David A. Parker, Korea
Father Antonio Sotelo, Mexico and United States • Friederike Zeitlhofer, Austria
Joyce Etu-Mantey, Ghana • Liana Eglitis, Latvia • Karen E. Curry, United States
Johndennis Govert, Roshi, Zen Buddhism • Volkmar Kurt Wentzel, National Geographic Society
Jorge G. Argarin, Philippines • Phyllis Towner, American Indians
Rabbi Mark Schaffel, Orthodox Judiasm • Meredith Pillon, Cypress • Rabbi Maynard Bell, Reformed Judiasm
Teresa Buswell, Houghton Mifflin Company • Ximena Prudant, Chile • Eqrat Shaeulian Entern, Israel Ministry
of Tourism • Alexandra Brodie, French Government Tourist Office • Meredith Pillon, Cypress
C. Buttigieg, Malta • Beverly Renwick, Grenada • Kinga Skorek, Poland
Margriet Willems, Netherlands • Amina Elaissami, Morocco
Tove U. Lange, Norway • Susanne Fischer, Austria • Roberta & Fredric S. Goldberg, United States
Patrice M. Wilke & D. Gail Saunders, Ph.D, Bahamas
Ellen Pittman, Royal Danish Embassy • Esther A. Koch, Technical advisor, United States
K. Brakstad, Royal Palace, Norway • Mimi Dornack, National Geographic Society

*Princess Grace studies a prayer book during Mass following the religious wedding ceremony uniting the American actress and Prince Rainier at Monaco Cathedral. The sixty-three minute ceremony was held on April 19, 1956 following an April 18th civil ceremony.*
*AP/WIDE WORLD PHOTOS.*

# Introduction

Anthropologists have rarely reported a functional society that lacked the concept of men and women getting married. People marry in every country. Even though many couples choose to live together prior to marriage, especially in certain Northern European countries, marriage is usually regarded as mandatory when children are involved. Regardless of the country and its political systems, religions or lack thereof, marriage, historically, is a rite of passage and weddings are generally the cause for celebration. Couples throughout the world have similar characteristics and motivations for marrying.

### ❤ Reasons why men and women marry:

1. For the belief that marriage has traditional, religious and moral value
2. For love, companionship, psychological, and physical fulfillment
3. To have children or to legalize their children conceived prior to marriage
4. Notice that their friends are marrying and do not want to remain single (social pressure)
5. For the sake of their parents desires
6. To acquire wealth or financial support
7. To escape a difficult family situation
8. To be sanctioned by society to have sexual relations
9. To prevent loneliness
10. To increase their prestige by marrying into a wealthy and socially elite family
11. To have the hand of someone who possesses prestige and beauty
12. To elevate the husband and wife into a position of maturity and responsibility
13. To provide a secure foundation for nurturing children
14. To acquire the financial and domestic advantages of chore sharing
15. For the longing desire to live an entire life time with a particular person
16. For emotional security and mutual protection and to care for each other in times of illness and disaster
17. To strengthen kinship ties and keep financial resources within the family
18. To obtain beneficial rights as far as taxes, legal documents, and wills are concerned.
19. To avoid sexually transmitted diseases

Everywhere on this planet, friends and relatives gather for the festive occasion of marriage marked by a feast and by an exchange of gifts. The bride wears a special costume designed for the occasion. Her head is usually veiled or she wears a crown or wreath. Throwing rice, other grains, candy, or floral petals over the newlyweds are also world customs. A wedding is an emotional occasion for all involved, especially the parents, who have raised their children into adulthood and sometimes feel they are losing their children to a spouse.

### ❤ Reasons couples who love each other do not commit to marriage or delay marriages:

1. Differences in religions, race, class, or value system
2. Their families move away while the couple is too young to marry
3. Desire to finish college or post-graduate education
4. Lack of well-paying employment or job loss
5. Parents believe the couple too young to marry; or else the parents do not like their child's choice of partner
6. Hurt due to the couple's own misunderstandings or interference by others
7. Military service
8. Mourning the death of a parent
9. Not yet attaining the legal age to marry
10. Mental or physical problems
11. Difficulty obtaining visas when marrying someone from a different country

### ❤ Arranged marriages or freedom of choice

Actually, freedom of spousal choice is a new phenomenon in the long evolution of marriage in world history. Arranged marriages, especially among the Jews, are a relic of a not-so-distant past. Many Hindu, as well as Islamic marriages, are still arranged by parents. The Hindus, who have had a caste system for generations, are obliged to marry within the class into which they were born. Both African and Native American tribal marriage customs have changed. As a result of Christian colonization by Eastern European countries, freedom of spousal choice is now the norm.

Today in many countries of the Western world, especially those predominantly populated by Christians and Jews, young people choose their spouses based on romantic love, similar views, and physical attraction. Though couples have the opportunity to marry outside their class, education, and status, they usually are attracted to those with a similar background. Their marriages hopefully are sanctioned by their parents prior to the wedding, but this is not always the case.

On the other hand, marriages continue to be arranged by parents or intermediary representatives in many Muslim and Hindu countries. In certain countries where these religions prevail, young people may marry their own relatives, particularly their cousins, to maintain family ties, to improve social and financial status, or to keep their material wealth within their clan. Unions are arranged by parents or go-betweens who look into the backgrounds of perspective spouses. Often the bride and groom do not meet each other before their wedding. It is hoped that love develops after marriage.

Arranged marriages in certain Muslim and Hindu countries are yielding to free choice, especially when children leave home to receive a higher education and meet their spouses at the university. Increasingly, they meet, inform their parents, then ask for parental approval. Alternatively, many from such cultures are beginning to appreciate their past and try to incorporate traditions into their weddings. Whether the marriage is arranged or not, factors universally thought important to conjugal success are love and affection, a similar value system, a good disposition, a high education, and a good family background.

### ❤ Types of marriages

Varied types of marriages exist throughout the world. *Monogamy*, a marriage between one man and one woman, is most prevalent; however, in Western countries with a high divorce rate, *serial monogamy* often occurs. Legally divorced or widowed individuals may marry two or more marriage partners over a lifetime. Because of an increase in longevity, elderly Western men and women may even find lost sweethearts of their youth and marry again late in life.

*Polygamy* occurs when a man marries two or more women. The Muslim religion permits *polygamy,* allowing a man to have up to four wives simultaneously.

*Polyandry*, the marriage between one woman and several men, is rare. *Polyandry*, a form of arranged marriage, was prevalent in Tibet. Polyandry actually occurs in only one percent of the population throughout the world. According to anthropologist Helen Fisher, Ph.D., *Over 80 percent of world cultures permit a man to have more than one wife.* She says that men of high position particularly tend to have more than one spouse;

yet, for the majority of individuals throughout the globe, monogamy is the most prevalent reproductive strategy. A monogamous individual, however, may or may not necessarily be faithful to a spouse.

### ❤ Similarities throughout the world

1. Marriage rites and ceremonies are used throughout world history to unite couples.
2. The marital state is utilized to control society and provide harmony.
3. Except for a certain minority of indigenous tribes or some religious nonbelievers, marriages throughout the ages and in all countries have had religious significance and incorporate religious rites.
4. Rates of marriage are higher for the rich than for the poor.
5. Dating, marriage, and related customs are continually in a state of transition.
6. The payment of the brideprice was common in tribal cultures, such as Native Americans (in the past), and still is common among Muslims and African tribes.
7. Most families desire that their children have an education before marriage.
8. The higher the level of education, the longer the individuals delay marriage.
9. Most families feel a couple should wait until they are financially secure before the marriage takes place.
10. Most males and females live together in a monogamous relationship.
11. Wedding celebrations and feasts with relatives and friends follow the wedding or contractual agreements
12. The most universal feature of weddings is the occurrence of a wedding feast.
13. Men commonly desire physical attractiveness in a woman and women desire financial security in men.
14. Older marriage traditions and customs tend to remain longer in the country than in the cities, where unfamiliar people are less likely to pass judgment or to control their actions.
15. In regions where people remain generation after generation, marriages are more likely to retain a common heritage or include elements of ancient marriage rites.
16. Marriages differ slightly from one region to another and often take on the

Reference: **Guest Helen Fisher, Ph.D., on April 7th, 1997 PBS** *Straight Talk with Derek McGinty.*

viii

character of adjacent countries.

17. Immigrant families usually retain the established dating and marriage traditions of their place of origin. The next generation is likely take on the norms of their surroundings, unless they have settled into their own ethnic or religious ghetto.

18. Today, marriage customs in many nations are influenced by the borrowing of traditions seen in global mass media, publications and television, especially traditions from the Western countries.

19. Past traditions of Native American tribes had similar marriage customs to the past and present tribal cultures of Africa. A brideprice, particularly in the form of livestock, was given to the bride's family.

20. Throughout the world, desirable qualifications for bridegroom are:
    - High education
    - Gainful employment
    - Income to support a family
    - Good health
    - Decent temperament
    - Good family background

21. Throughout the world, desirable qualifications for a bride are:
    - Beauty
    - Good character and conduct
    - Mental and physical health
    - Good family background

22. Marriage is a business involving monetary and psychological transactions.

23. Because of computer internet services, people worldwide with access to computers can look for spouses locally, regionally, nationally, and internationally.

24. Marriage is not a rigid institution and is in a continuous state of transition. In cultures where changes occur rapidly, societal changes are influenced by mass marketing through the media or by war.

Throughout history, the celebration of marriage between men and women has been a universal experience, except for a few tribal cultures where an accepted marriage simply takes place upon the individual's living together. Marriage is significant because of the fulfillment resulting from a mutual bond of loyalty and faithfulness and it is highly valued to establish a meaningful family life. Public weddings and celebrations permit the community to take part in the joyful spirit of the occasion and to acknowledge the new status of a married couple.

ix

## Note from the Author

Information for this book was obtained through anthropological journals, clergy, contributing embassy personnel, wedding magazines and guides, interlibrary loans, and by interviews with knowledgeable individuals. Although *Weddings* is an anthropological-sociological attempt to cover the entire world, differences in customs vary within families and regions. All possibilities cannot be presented in this volume. The book simply offers a glimpse into reality. You are welcome to write to Nittany Publishers or send e-mail with information to consider for a second edition.

I began this book when I was a child, not actually knowing I was going to write it. Having lived in the central Pennsylvania town of Philipsburg, I, of Jewish faith, wanted to attend churches with my Protestant friends. My father, Lewis Stein, who secretly harbored the same altruistic views of the world religions, made arrangements with his Christian minister friend, Reverend MacClay, so that I could attend the Presbyterian church. When President Roosevelt died, we did not have a rabbi for our little synagogue, so my family was warmly welcomed at the church. Having received such a positive feeling towards the goodness in other religions, I have been investigating religious history ever since.

Such inquiry into various religions and cultures became a lifelong quest. Because I am a romantic, I was pleased that this research evolved into a history of love and family, rather than a history of war. As I researched further, I questioned why some of the meaningful and colorful marriage customs of past cultures disappeared. It soon became apparent that marriage would always be in the state of change as the result of political takeovers of regimes, trends in mass media, and increased travel and migration.

Though some people judge other cultures by standards of the culture in which they live, it seems to me that people all over the world share the same humanity and the same basic underlying truths, values, vulnerabilities, and innate goodness. My hope is that this book will contribute to world peace and appreciation of the many beautiful customs of different world cultures.

# MAJOR WORLD RELIGIONS, THEIR CUSTOMS AND WEDDING CEREMONIES

Traditional marriage ceremonies throughout the globe have their origin in particular religious beliefs, customs, and rituals. Most weddings involve a lawfully signed marriage contract, a religious wedding ceremony (or recognition of unity), and celebration and feasting with relatives and friends. The following are the major world religions throughout our planet:

### Number of people

| | |
|---|---|
| Roman Catholic | 1,058,069,000 |
| Protestant | +391,143,000 |
| Total Christian | 1,449,212,000 |
| | |
| Muslim | 1,035,453,000 |
| Hindu | 764,000,000 |
| Buddhist | 338,621,000 |

**Source:** *1996 World Almanac*

### ❤ Wedding apparel

Western brides of Judeo-Christian European and American origin usually wear white or cream wedding gowns as a symbol of purity. More recently, some wear gowns of other colors, even black. Years ago, the Netherlands and Spanish brides wore elegant black wedding gowns which could be worn later at funerals.

Traditionally, Asian Hindu and Buddhist brides wear decorative red silk as a symbol of happiness, and Hindu brides profusely adorn themselves with valuable decorative jewelry. In China, Buddhist brides may also wear white Western-style gowns, but they carry a bright red umbrella and red roses as accessories to celebrate their joy and passion. In Japan, brides often wear a Shinto wedding kimono which is white on the outside and lined with red on the inside. Later, the brides change into white Western-style gowns for the reception.

The Yemen people *(p. 217)* and the Laplanders *(p. 203)* wear decorative and unique wedding apparel.

### ❤ Reasons for marriage

Most major and minor religions throughout history extolled marriage as an arrangement for the birth of children. If the woman was unable to bear children, among certain religions a divorce was inevitable. This phenomenon still exists in some areas of the world.

In many cultures, couples make a conscious decision to marry for love and companionship, whether they have children or not. Other loving couples wish to have a second wedding ceremony later in life to reaffirm their vows. *(See more reasons for marriage in the Preface, page vi.)*

### ❤ Wedding vows

Western-style wedding vows originated in and evolved from the early civilizations of Rome, Italy, and Greece. Wedding vows are promises of commitment that a bride and groom make to each other during Jewish and Christian wedding ceremonies, but vows have not always been part of their marriage ceremonies. In ancient times when marriages were arranged by parents for financial, social, and political advantages, there did not appear to be a need for vows. *(See the ancient Greek ceremony on page 187.)*

Today, as well as in the past, many Muslim cultures do not say vows, since couples are committed by a written marital contract and separate celebrations are held for males and females.

### ❤ Variations of wedding ceremonies

Wedding ceremonies may differ within one religion. For example, some Islamic countries and cultures have religious wedding ceremonies while others do not. Buddhist ceremonies differ widely depending on the country and the type of Buddhism. Jewish Reform, Conservative, and Orthodox ceremonies vary. Regions of the country that have the same religious faith may incorporate their own unique customary marriage rituals or combine their own marriage rituals with those of neighboring cultures.

Clergy also may change or add special words to the accepted traditional wording of formal ceremonies printed in standard prayer books. In addition, the bride and groom and/or their parents may make special requests and the officiator may abide by their wishes.

Today, contemporary Western couples, who have children when married for the second time, may change their vows and other ceremonial rituals to include their children so that all immediate family members make promises of commitment.

Couples of different faiths may satisfy both sides of the family and themselves by having an interfaith wedding ceremony which includes selected readings, prayers, and vows from both religions. Clergymen must be consulted in advance as to whether they wish to officiate in an interfaith wedding ceremony.

Some creative individuals, especially members of the Unitarian, Religious Science, and Baha'i faiths, simply prefer to write their own ceremonies. For Unitarians, there is no exact liturgy. Unitarian couples incorporate their beliefs and ideals through their readings which are most likely, but not always, from the Judeo-Christian heritage. Couples who are world-oriented may include meaningful readings, music, and lyrics from many religions.

**Reference:** *Complete Book of Wedding Vows* by Diane Warner.

*The following wedding ceremonies throughout this book are typical, not literal, examples that show the different ways humankind weds throughout the world.*

# *Baha'i*

This religious faith was founded during the 19th century in Iran by Bara'u'llah, who desired to start a universal religion which would spiritually unite the world. Today, Baha'i is a world religion which is spread over two hundred countries. Baha'ists believe in the unity, harmony, and agreement of all mankind. Since outwardly perceived differences tend to separate peoples and sometimes cause conflict, Bara'u'llah developed these fundamental unities to unify all mankind:

- ❤ *The Earth is but one country and mankind its citizens.* (from the *Gleanings from the Writings of Baha'ullah*) In other words, only one race exists and that is the human race.

- ❤ There is but one God, the God of all religions, even though God is called by various names.

- ❤ The practices of religions differ and their outward observances vary, but the reality of truth and human virtue is the same for all people.

- ❤ All religions evolve from a Divine origin.

Baha'ists believe in the elimination of prejudice, extreme wealth and poverty, the equality of the sexes, universal knowledge, and global peace.

### ❤ Baha'i Philosophy of love and marriage

Baha'ists are free to choose their own spouses; however, they must receive consent of their parents, and even their extended family. They believe family support is essential to a successful marriage. The couple must have written parental consent which they are required to give to their local assembly of nine elected individuals. Sometimes, the consent takes the form of a letter; otherwise, the parents simply state they approve their daughter or son marrying the intended partner and specify their names. Witnesses may be selected by the assembly to attend the wedding or the couple may choose their own, then friends and relatives are invited to the wedding.

# Baha'i Wedding

❤ **Public statement.** The couple gives the following public statement before two witnesses:

*We will all verily abide by the will of God.*

❤ The couple may choose a traditional ceremony or devise their own, with much personal thought going into it. Because there are no prescribed rituals or order of service, the couple usually has an explanation printed on the wedding program or an oral explanation is given to guests. In order to provide a background for public understanding, their commentary includes what readings and songs they chose and why.

❤ The couple also freely select their own style of wedding attire. The bride usually selects the white Western-style gown.

❤ **Readings.** Readings from Baha'i Scriptures and other religious faiths may be incorporated into the ceremony, for their faith accepts the wisdom of all prophets.

❤ **Inclusions.** Music by singers and instrumentalists, meaningful secular readings, or self-written poetry and prose are included. Saying their vows and signing their marriage certificate may also be part of the bride and groom's nuptials.

---

**References:** *Bride's All New Book of Etiquette* by the Editors of Bride's Magazine and *An Introduction of the Baha'i Faith prepared by Kamran Hakim and Mike Register* from the Soc. Religion. Baha'i usenet news service on the WWW, July 1995.

# Buddhism

❤ **Buddhism, its history and philosophy.**

Buddha, meaning Enlightened One, is an honorary title for all those who reach the peak of transcendental wisdom. As Kenneth W. Morgan states in his book *The Path of the Buddha*, Buddha is a true friend, philosopher, and guide.

Buddhism was founded by Gautama Siddhartha, the Buddha or "enlightened one," born about 563 B.C. in Nepal. He began to meditate under a tree and there discovered the "Middle Way," a path which resisted extremes of pleasure and pain. Buddha wrote a collection of teachings and commentaries, many labeled sutras, in the sacred text called the *Tripitaka*. He preached that individuals' lives involved the following aspects:

❤ Suffering
❤ Desire
❤ Selfish craving

He believed people suffer misery and unnecessary attachment to people and to things in the world where nothing is permanent. To put an end to suffering, called *dukkah*, is to adhere to Buddhist doctrine *Dharma*, the cessation of desire in order to attain quality existence and reach *nirvana*. To alleviate desire and do away with suffering, Buddha provided the Eight-fold Path as the way out of captivity.

### ❤ Eightfold Path

1. Right understanding
2. Right morality
3. Right speech
4. Right action
5. Right livelihood
6. Right effort
7. Right mindfulness
8. Right concentration

Buddha also believed that a human's essence is always changing, that people are in a cycle of rebirth which involves their *karma*. *Karma* is the cause and effect according to a person's good and evil deeds. Good actions bring reward and bad actions bring disaster on both universal and individual levels. The *karma* also applies to those who are reincarnated.

Buddha and his teachings are highly respected, even though he is not considered God in a supernatural or material sense. Buddha now represents all Enlightened ones.

Throughout the centuries Buddhism spread from India to other countries: Sri Lanka, Burma, Thailand, Laos, Kampuchea, Indonesia, China, Korea, Japan, Tibet, Mongolia, Russia, and the United States.

### ❤ Types of Buddhism

1. *Theravada*, native to South Asia, emphasizes pure thought and deed. Its Noble Virtues are loving kindness, understanding, serenity, and satisfaction for others' well-being.

2. *Mahyana*, (Zen and Soka-gakkai) believes in the saving grace of higher beings, ritualistic practices, and meditative disciplines. Followers do not believe in forming an attachment, for what is truly real comes and goes. They think a couple must work to attain wisdom and compassion.

3. *Tantrism* is a combination of Buddhist rituals and philosophy.

4. *Vajrayana,* the Diamond Vehicle, stresses transformation of emotional energies for the betterment of self and those around this person. He or she works on the energies of the mind and emotions to achieve balance, including the balance of male and female in their relationships. *Vajrayana Buddhists* believe that partners should also attain balance in marriage.

### ❤ Buddhist concepts of love in a relationship

John Stevens, author of *Lust for Enlightenment*, explains that sexual relations between partners should be consummated selflessly and with understanding and compassion. It should be an enriching act for both parties and should deepen Buddhist understanding by promoting spiritual emancipation. Mainly, if the uniting is beneficial to the parties involved, it is considered a virtuous act. If, on the other hand, sex is the result of animalistic passion originating from pleasurable physical desire to possess, manipulate, dominate, or diminish the other person, it is considered evil. In other words, neither male nor female should be misled or harmed. If their love is pure, their union fits the Buddhist concept of enlightenment.

According to the book *Living Faiths: Marriage and the Family* by Pricket, Buddha did not prescribe any age at which followers should marry or whether or not they should be monogamous or polygamous. No endeavor was made to designate the correct marriage for lay Buddhists. In Tibet, monogamy, polygamy, and polyandry (a woman with more than one husband) were permitted. Since marriages in Tibet were arranged in the past when more were polyandrous, the woman years ago simply accepted the husbands selected by her parents.

Though Buddha did not prescribe the style of marriage, he taught the virtues that man and woman should not harm each other, commit adultery, or lie. These virtues were actually ethical qualities basic to society. Being understanding, respectful, and loyal to one another created security for a good marital relationship, benefited both parties, and provided balance. Buddha believed that the husband should place his spouse as number one in his life, and both husband and wife should work diligently to fulfill the goals of their partnership. As far as balance was concerned, Buddha believed that the wife, as her husband's best friend, should hold her husband with respect while he earns a living and she performs her duties. Buddhist instruction concerning marriage reflects the sense of each other's welfare brought about by each other's every word, thought, and action.

Before Western influences, Buddhist marriages in Asia were arranged and many still are. Buddhist marriage is of such importance that families on both sides should be compatible. Because no one desires anyone in the family to be hurt by the union, feelings of the prospective bride and groom are often subordinated to the group. Those steeped in Buddhist culture believe that the couple will fall in love after they are married; therefore, the bride or groom's family hires a professional marriage consultant, a go-between, to make recommendation of a prospective spouse for their eligible child. Sometimes, relatives or friends suggest a suitable spouse. In Vietnam and China, the more well-to-do the parents are, the more people they will consult.

Parents confer with astrologers and other supernatural consultants who decide whether or not the couple is compatible and when is the best time for the marriage to take place.

The go-between takes into consideration the qualities of the prospective bride and plans a formal meeting in which gifts are given between the families. After a spouse is selected, the couple meets in the presence of the group. Afterward, the parents may or may not consider the child's wishes. Actually, the children often are obliged to marry the selection out of respect for their parents, for they wish to honor them. Marriage is a way for the couple to repay their debt to society and to their parents for their own lives; it is a debt to the sages who provided wise Buddhist sayings on which their enlightenment depends.

Go-betweens, respected by the family, are given the responsibility to act as mediators between the couple after their wedding. They are expected to take an interest in the marriage, find out what is wrong, and assist in solving the couple's problems.

### ❤ History of Buddhist ceremonies

Marriage for Buddhists throughout Asia was originally a secular affair; however, over the centuries many followers felt Buddhists needed a ceremonial occasion with religious elements to satisfy the need to celebrate the occasion of marriage. Couples and the relatives asked monks to chant sutras after a civil ceremony or at their home, but Buddhist monks and nuns were not permitted to marry.

Various types of Buddhist marriage ceremonies, often contingent on the type of Buddhism, eventually evolved in many countries of the world. Depending on the Asian region, Buddhism is often bound in different ways with combinations of Taoism, Confucianism, Animism, and Shintoism. In Japan, Buddhism is thought to reflect the philosophy of death, and Shintoism, the philosophy of life, including marriage; therefore, in Japan Shinto marriages are often performed. In the United States, Buddhist Churches of America have incorporated twentieth century Christian Methodist rites into their marriage ceremonies.

During a Buddhist wedding, the bride and groom promise to be considerate, loving, respectful, and faithful to each other. Often, the groom indicates that he will bestow gifts and will please his wife. In turn, the bride vows to be hospitable towards the groom's family and friends. When a monk officiates, the bride and groom promise to be faithful and keep the Buddhist precepts that teach ways to happiness: no stealing, no falsehoods, and abstinence from alcohol. Weddings often take place in a garden in order to be surrounded by divine nature since Buddha believed that the garden has no artificiality.

*Also see Laos, Myanmar (Burma), and Mongolia under Asia.*

❤ **5**

# *Zen Buddhist Wedding*

*Zen marriage vows entail that the husband look after his own enlightenment, his promise to work extensively, and to assist his family to do likewise– with the hope that he and his family will succeed.*

❤ **Tea ceremony.** The couple, accompanied by a third party host, meet at a ritualistic tea ceremony a week prior to the wedding. There, the couple can share a quiet time alone.

❤ **Wedding.** The bride arrives for the wedding with her parents. Her father accompanies her to the altar where the ceremony with the groom takes place. An offering of floral incense, symbol of a person's potential, activates their ceremony which starts by the chanting of the *Heart of Wisdom Sutra*. A confession, an acknowledgment of past life things that need forgiveness or things unknowingly done that also require forgiveness, takes place. The officiator inserts a fresh leaf into a container of water and puts three drops of water on the foreheads of the bride and groom. The officiator then cleanses the water off their foreheads with a dull knife to symbolize the cleansing of the mind. The refuges introduced are:

❤ The refuge of Buddha as the Enlightened nature.
❤ The refuge of *Dahrama*, which involves the teachings of Buddha

# Zen Buddhist Wedding Ceremony

❤ The refuge Sangha relates to the community which practices the realization of enlightenment. The priest who performs the ceremony offers incense, then presents the bride and groom a circle of Ojuzu or Mala beads which symbolizes the circle of all life. While the bride and groom recite their vows, they and the priest hold onto the beads with one hand. After the couple returns the beads to the priest, they exchange rings. Later, the priest gives them another set of Ojuzu beads for a keepsake, and he announces that the couple is married in the sight of Buddha, the Enlightened One. Finally, the priest congratulates the newlyweds and presents them with a gift. Dinner follows.

# United States Buddhist Wedding

❤ An American-style Buddhist wedding ceremony, originating in Hawaii, has spread through other regions of the United States where Buddhist culture continued among Japanese, Chinese, and other Asian immigrants. Surrounded by the Western-Style Judeo-Christian majority, their wedding ceremonies often take on aspects of that culture. Because of their varied Buddhist backgrounds, American Buddhists do not have a standard ceremonial format.

❤ Generally, the Western-style Buddhist wedding ceremony begins with the priest chanting the Buddhist philosophy. The vows, the exchange of rings, the words pronouncing the couple husband and wife, and final blessing are all similar to those in Judeo-Christian weddings. As with some Christian ceremonies, the priest even asks if anyone is aware of any impediment to their marriage. During the ceremony, Buddhist duties of the wife and husband are spelled out. For example, the wife is to be patient, gentle, and faithful, and the husband is responsible for the care of his wife. Both need to support and cherish each other under any and all circumstances.

❤ The ceremony ends when the priest joins the couple's right hands and places a string of beads around them. Each bead symbolizes a step towards Enlightenment. The ceremony concludes with the truths taught by the Buddha. The truths denote the compassion which leads from both illusion and sorrow towards Enlightenment and Peace. Finally, the bride and groom offer incense to the Buddha as an offering of respect for his teachings.

# Another United States Buddhist Wedding

❤ The wedding ceremony occurs in a *poruwa*, a platform beneath a white silk canopy. The canopy is covered with flowers, and the platform has flowerpots in each corner.

❤ The priest or elder sings religious chants, then the bride and groom share betel leaves symbolizing a display of honor both to each other and to their parents.

❤ After the bride and groom give each other wedding rings, the priest pours water over their hands which are tied together with gold thread.

❤ The services then end with religious chants and blessings.

**Reference for the above wedding:** *Bride's Book of Etiquette* by the Editors of *Bride's Magazine*.

# Christianity

The New Testament of the Christian bible includes the teachings of Jesus Christ, their Lord and Messiah. Christians believe Jesus Christ was the Messiah who came to earth to save people from their sins. *(Matthew 1:21)* They believe that Jesus, Son of God, was sent to earth to save humanity and open a way to eternal life. In other words, Jesus was the fulfillment of God's promise to the Jewish people that a Messiah would come to save the world.

Son of Joseph and the virgin Mary, Jesus, born a Jew, went to Galilee to teach at synagogues and preach the gospel of the kingdom. He healed people of disease. Such miracles, according to the New Testament, gave relief to suffering people and revealed that God gave Jesus the power to perform good works. He had crowds of followers, many who believed he was God in the flesh. He went upon a mountain where he gave the famous Sermon on the Mount. Here is an excerpt from this sermon:

## ❤ The Beatitudes

1. *Blessed are the poor in spirit, for theirs is the kingdom of heaven.*
2. *Blessed are those who mourn, for they shall be comforted.*
3. *Blessed are the meek, for they shall inherit the earth.*
4. *Blessed are those who hunger and thirst after righteousness, for they shall be satisfied.*
5. *Blessed are the merciful, for they shall have mercy.*
6. *Blessed are the pure in heart, for they shall see God.*
7. *Blessed are the peacemakers, for they shall be called sons of God.*
8. *Blessed are those who are persecuted for righteousness' sake, for theirs is the kingdom of heaven.*
9. *Love your enemies and pray for those who persecute you.*
10. *Judge not, that you be not judged.*
11. *Ask, and it will be given you; seek, and you will find; knock, and it will be opened to you.*
12. *Golden Rule: So whatever you wish that men would do to you, do so to them.*

Christians believe that Jesus, who was crucified by nonbelievers, was resurrected from the dead three days after he was nailed to the cross. Three centuries after Christ's birth the ecumenical council met in Nicea, Turkey where the Credo (Creed) of the Holy Trinity:

1. The Father
2. The son Jesus
3. Holy Spirit

was adopted. During the next century, the Virgin Mary was held in high regard as a nourishing, caring, gentle mother figure of Jesus. Mary, given the title "Mother of God," is highly regarded in the Catholic church.

Today, the Christian biblical text is mainly New Testament, but Protestant ministers and Catholic priests quote from the Old Testament during ceremonies.

## ❤ Locations of Christian populations

According the book titled *Atlas of the Christian Church* by Henry Chadwick and G.R. Evans, Christians comprise over 80 percent of the population of the following countries:

- ❤ North and South American countries and Greenland.
- ❤ European countries (Portugal, Spain, France, Belgium, Netherlands, Germany, Poland Norway, Denmark, United Kingdom, Italy, Romania, Hungary, Austria and Poland.)
- ❤ Australia, New Zealand, the Philippines, Papua-New Guinea, and the Solomon Islands

African countries which have over 60 percent Christian faith population are South Africa and Zambia, Tanzania, Ethiopia, Nigeria, and Botswana. Zimbabwe is well over 40 percent Christian.

There are many denominations of Christian churches reflecting a wide variety of Christian beliefs that has developed in various countries since the death of Jesus Christ. The major Christian religious denominations covering a wide range of religious practices and interpretations are:

- ❤ **Protestant.** Baptist, Church of Christ, Church of England (Episcopalian and Anglican), Lutheran, Methodist, Mormon, Orthodox Christian, Pentecostal, Jehovah's Witnesses, and Presbyterian.

- ❤ **Roman Catholic.** Many Orthodox Christian churches have similar beliefs.

Since the English, throughout history, have colonized so many countries, many Christian wedding ceremonies, particularly the Anglican and Episcopalian, are modeled after the British Church of England. *(See the Church of England's wedding ceremony described in the European chapter under The United Kingdom).*

### ❤ Christian philosophy of love and marriage.

According to William J. Fielding, who wrote *Strange Customs of Courtship and Marriage,* ancient text indicates the following Christian thought pertaining to the desirability of marriage:

*Nevertheless to avoid fornication, let each man have his own wife, and let each woman have her own husband, for it is better to marry than to burn.* (New Testament, Corinthians I, vii, 2)

Christians ideally believe in premarital chastity and that intercourse is reserved for marriage. Sexual relations between a man and women are permitted as the ultimate expression of love and should only occur after a public commitment during a marriage ceremony. The bride wears a white gown to her wedding to signify that she is pure. Christian marriages are ordained by God, to be honored by everyone, and are life-long unions. Life-long commitment is expressed in the text of their wedding ceremony by the words *until death do us part.* Thus, Christians believe in a monogamous state of lifelong faithfulness. Widowed or divorced women who marry for the second time are encouraged to wear a dress of color.

The Protestant ceremony is usually performed by an ordained clergyman (minister), and a Catholic wedding is performed by a priest. At a wedding, Jesus is the third party and the bride and groom are considered the remaining two parties in the marital arrangement. The following biblical passage from St. Paul in Ephesians 5:25-29 explains how husbands should treat their wives during their marriage:

*Husbands, love your wives, as Christ loved the church and gave himself up for her....For no man ever hates his own flesh, but nourishes and cherishes it, as Christ does the Church.*

Reasons for marriage are for the procreation of children, for the right to have sexual relations, and for companionship.

The following quote from the New Testament is often read at Protestant weddings:

*Love is patient and kind; love is not jealous or boastful; it is not arrogant or rude. Love does not insist on its own way; it is not irritable or resentful; it does not rejoice at wrong, but rejoices in the right. Love bears all things, believes all things, hopes all things, endures all things.. . So faith, hope, love abide, these three; but the greatest of these is love.* (*Corinthians I, 3.4*) **Reference: *Harper Study Bible*.**

### ❤ Types of weddings

Most active Christians, both Protestant and Catholic, marry in church. Weddings are not held during Holy Week between Palm Sunday and Easter. The weddings may range from extremely formal to informal, depending on the financial capabilities of the families, especially the bride's family who is usually expected to pay the expenses of the wedding. Elaborate formal weddings are followed by a reception and banquet costing several thousand dollars. These usually occur at a church, ballroom, large home or country club. One to two hundred invited guests may enjoy a stately dinner with music. At very formal or royal weddings, the bride wears a white gown with a long train, often with gloves and veil. The standard dress for a first time bride is white; however, more recently, brides wear colored wedding dresses. Less formal weddings may be held anywhere, and the reception may be more simple, with or without music. Not as many guests are invited, and the bride may wear a suit or more casual clothing.

### ❤ The wedding ceremony

Traditionally, brides promised to obey their husbands during their wedding ceremony, but today, the word "obey" is often omitted so that the woman does not have to accept a submissive role. Other Christians still wish to keep "obey" in their wedding vows.

A Western-style Protestant wedding is preceded by a wedding rehearsal the night before. The service may differ according to the desires of the couple, clergyman, or by religious denomination.

The following wedding ceremony displays the format that most Protestant weddings take:

# Protestant Episcopal Wedding

*(For a formal wedding, a white runner is unrolled and placed over the aisle prior to the processional.) The following order of service is typical for Episcopalian and other Protestant wedding ceremonies.*

❤ **Musical prelude**

❤ **Solos.** Songs, accompanied by musical instruments, are sung as guests are seated by the ushers.

❤ **Lighting of Candles.** Sometimes the bride and groom carry a lit candle, then hold the flames from them onto an unlit candle which rests on the altar. The lighting of one candle represents the union of the bride and groom. (This may also occur later in the ceremony)

❤ **Pre-processional.** After the ushers lead the guests to their seats, an usher takes the grandparents down the aisle to the family pew in the front of the sanctuary. A groomsman then escorts the groom's mother down the aisle while her husband follows. She and her husband sit on the right side of the sanctuary with the groom's relatives. Lastly, a brother or son ushers the bride's mother, the hostess, to her pew on the left side of the sanctuary where the bride's relatives and friends are seated.

    The minister often enters the sanctuary from a side entrance near the altar or he walks down the side aisle. The groom and best man follow, then the groomsmen (or ushers) take their standing positions near the altar of the church.

❤ **Processional.** The processional is the announcement of the bride's arrival. The bridesmaids, one at a time, walk down the aisle towards the altar. Next, the Maid or Matron of Honor, usually a sister or the bride's best friend, approaches the altar. The Matron of Honor stands to the right of the altar so that she can assist the bride. Next, the little flower girl, tossing rose petals, and a young boy ring bearer proceed down the aisle. The bride's mother stands while the organist plays the *Wedding March* from *Lohengrin* by Wagner, then all present usually rise. As the *Wedding March* begins, the bride, holding her father's right arm, enters the sanctuary and approaches the altar where the groom waits for his beloved. (A bride may be escorted down the aisle by a brother, friend, or other if her father is not available. Both the father and mother may escort their daughter down the aisle.)

❤ **Giving away of the bride.** The father "gives the bride away" near the altar. He may take the bride by the right hand, give her hand to the minister who, in turn, passes her hand to the groom. Afterward, the father sits in the pew next to the bride's mother. The bride, traditionally *wearing something old, something new, something borrowed and something blue*, stands next to the groom at his left while a minister officiates. If the bride or groom have children from the first marriage, the children may participate in the wedding as well.

❤ **Opening words.** According to the *Book of Common Prayer* based on the Church of England and the Episcopal Protestant Church in the United States, the traditional wedding ceremony begins with the following opening words on the next page:

# Protestant Episcopal Wedding

*Dearly beloved: We have come together in the presence of God to witness and bless the joining together of _____(first name of woman) and _____(first name of man) or this man and this woman in Holy Matrimony. The bond and covenant of marriage was established by God in creation, and our Lord Jesus Christ adorned this manner of life by His presence and first miracle at a wedding in Cana of Galilee. It signifies to us the mystery of the union between Christ and his Church, and Holy Scripture commends it to be honored among all people.*

*The union of husband and wife in heart, body, and mind is intended by God for their mutual joy; for the help and comfort given one another in prosperity and adversity; and, when it is God's will, for the procreation of children and their nurture in the knowledge and love of the Lord. Therefore, marriage is not to be entered into unadvisedly or lightly, but reverently, deliberately, and in accordance with the purposes for which it was instituted by God.*

Other Protestant opening words are---

*We have come together today in the presence of God to witness the joining of _____ and _____ in Holy Matrimony. This is a time of joyful celebration you will always remember.* Otherwise, the minister may begin with the following words: *Dearly beloved, we are gathered together in the sight of God...*

❤ **Invocation.** The invocation includes words of welcome, biblical scriptures from the Old or New Testament of the Bible, and a homily or sermon stressing the Christian aspect of marriage and its responsibilities.

❤ **Consent or blessing of the parents.** (sometimes omitted) The minister asks, *Who gives this woman to be married to this man?* The bride's father or brother, whoever accompanies her down the aisle, or her mother and father both say, *I do.*

❤ **Question of intent.** The marriage from the *Episcopalian Book of Common Prayer* is as follows:

The minister asks the bride and groom, Will you take _____ (name) or_____ (name) in the covenant of *marriage? Will you love her (him), comfort her (him), honor her and keep her (him) in sickness and in health; forsaking all others, be faithful to her (him) as long as you both shall live?* Otherwise, the bride and groom say that they promise *to love each other for better or worse, for richer or poorer, in sickness and in health till death do us part.* Other contemporary statements regarding questions of intent are also performed in other Protestant weddings; for example, the couples may be asked to indicate their intentions and if they will accept their marital responsibilities.

❤ **Wedding vows and response.** Or, Protestant ministers ask the bride and groom, *Do you promise to have and to hold from this day forward, for better or for worse, for richer or poorer, in sickness and health, to love and to cherish, as long as you both shall live?* The bride and groom may simply respond, *I do.* Otherwise they repeat the minister's words:

*I, _____ take you, _____ to be my wife, to have and to hold from this day forward, for better or for worse, for richer or poorer, in sickness and health, to love and to cherish, until we are parted by death .*

*In the Name of God, I_____(name) take you, _____(name), to be my (wife, then husband) to have and to hold from this day forward, for better for worse, for richer for poorer, in sickness and in health, to love and to cherish, until we are parted by death. This is my solemn vow.*

❤ **Blessing of the rings.** The minister says the following: *Bless, O Lord, this ring to be a sign of the vows*

# Protestant Episcopal Wedding

*by which this man and this woman have bound themselves to each other; through Jesus Christ our Lord, Amen. (The Book of Common Prayer)*

❤ **Exchange of rings.** *I, _____, give you this ring as a symbol of my vow, and with all that I am, all that I have, I honor you, in the Name of the Father and of the Son, and of the Holy Spirit (or in the Name of God).* After each places a ring on each other's third finger of the left hand, the bride and groom repeat the minister's words: *I give you this ring as a sign of our marriage with my body I honor you. All that I am I give to you. All that I have I share with you within the love of God.*

❤ **Pronouncement of Marriage.** The Priest then joins the right hands of the husband and wife and says the following words: *Now that ____ and ____ have given themselves to each other by solemn vows, with the joining of hands and the giving and receiving of a ring, I pronounce that you are husband and wife, in the Name of the Father, and of the Son, and of the Holy Spirit. Those whom God has joined together let no one put asunder.* (The Book of Common Prayer).

❤ **Blessing of the couple and closing words.** The congregation stands and the husband and wife may kneel as the minister says the Blessing of the Marriage: *Most gracious God, we give you thanks for your tender love in sending Jesus Christ to come among us, to be born of a human mother, and to make the way of the cross to be the way of life. We thank you, also, for consecrating the union of man and woman in His Name. By the power of your Holy Spirit, pour out the abundance of your blessing upon this man and this woman. Defend them from every enemy. Lead them into all peace. Let their love for each other be a seal upon their hearts, a mantle about their shoulders, and a crown upon their foreheads Bless them in their work and in their companionship; in their sleeping and in their waking; in their joys and in their sorrows; in their life and in their death. ...(The Book of Common Prayer).*

*The Wilton School of Cake Decorating and Confectionery Art. ©Wilton Enterprises*

❤ **Thanksgiving prayer or Lord's Prayer** may then be followed by Holy Communion and an agape meal. (This prayer may given later at the wedding feast, then it is followed by a benediction.)

Other Protestant closing prayers express thanks to Jesus Christ. They may include blessings for abundance, safety, a joyful, faithful companionship, and that married couple will eventually feast in heaven through the Lord Jesus Christ, the Holy Spirit and the one reigning God.

# *Protestant Episcopal Wedding*

❤ **Recessional.** The most popular music for the recession is Mendlessohn's *Wedding March* from *A Midsummer Night's Dream.* As the song is played, the bride and groom turn and hurry back toward the entrance of the church, then the bridal party follows with the men and women pairing. The bride and groom, often with their attendants, parents, and grandparents, form a receiving line at the church entrance where the departing guests congratulate them. Then, guests wait outside the church so that they can throw rice, a symbol of fertility, over the newlyweds.

❤ **Reception and festivities.** While the guests sit at linen-covered tables at the banquet, the best man toasts the bride and groom to wish them happiness. Sometimes, he gives a meaningful and/or amusing short speech. After dining, the newlyweds cut the first piece of wedding cake with a knife decorated with ribbons and flowers. They place a bit of cake in each other's mouth. They might take a large piece and shove it into each other's mouths for amusement. All enjoy the wedding cake and ice cream, followed by music and dancing. The bride dances the first dance with her new husband, then with her father. Then her father dances with the bride's mother. Afterward, the guests join in and dance as well.

The groom removes the bride's garter from her leg and tosses it over his shoulder to the crowd. Then the bride throws the bridal bouquet to eligible single girls. The lucky girl who catches the bouquet is believed to be the next to marry. After thanking their parents, the newlyweds finally leave for their honeymoon in their decorated car.

**Reference:** *The Book of Common Prayer*

**12**

❤ **Variations of Protestant wedding ceremonies**

Contemporary forms of Christian ceremonies often vary. Some denominations do not include secular music and only use music that makes reference to the glory of God. Sometimes the minister may say, *if there is any just reason why the couple may not be married, speak now, or else forever hold your peace.* The couple's fathers or mothers may be involved in the ceremony by saying a few words for the couple. Even children from the bride and/or groom's former marriage may do likewise.

The bride and groom may publicly say thoughtful words to the parents and stepparent(s) prior to the formal ceremony, then give each a hug and a flower. A minority of couples make up their own ceremony. The signing of the church register is a matter of personal choice. Wedding bells may ring at the close of the ceremony.

Married life often begins with a vacation or honeymoon before settling into a home or an apartment. When the couple arrive at their residence, the husband carries the bride over the threshold. Years later, some couples have a renewal of marriage vows.

See the Protestant

*Church of England's*

weddings under the United Kingdom.
Both the Anglican and Episcopalian
have their roots in the Church of England.

❤

*Episcopal Church*

The United States Episcopal church, a
branch of the Anglican Communion, became an
independent denomination after the American
Revolution. Today, the Episcopalian
Church has almost three million members
in the United States, Mexico, and Central America.
There are also Anglican churches in the U.S.

❤

*Anglican Church*

Canada, Australia, and certain countries
of Africa have a large Anglican population.
*The Book of Common Prayer's*
basic liturgical structure common to all
three churches is slightly changed to meet
various cultural and language differences.

# Lutheran

The Lutheran religion is the state religion of Denmark, Iceland, Norway, and Sweden. Many live in Germany and the United States. The Evangelical Lutheran churches have written services, but wedding ceremonies vary according to the cultures in the various nations. Some services include the Eucharist, while others do not. Some cultures use a "unity candle" during the wedding and others do not. Certain wedding ceremonies are quite sophisticated, with evening rites and classical music played by string quartets. Other weddings are extremely informal.

Generally, Lutheran Christians believe that marriage is a gift from God to the entire human community throughout the world. To the Lutherans, marriage is more than the couple's promise to love one another. It is a covenant of fidelity and a faithful commitment to share all that life brings. The vows that a husband and wife make to each other and the ability to keep them are given strength by God's faithful love for the couple as revealed in Jesus Christ, the Lord.

## Evangelistic Lutheran Wedding

*Thanks to All Saints Lutheran Church in Phoenix, Arizona*

Musical solos and the processional precede the Lutheran marriage ceremony.

❤ **Invocation.** *The grace of our Lord Jesus Christ, the love of God and the communion of the Holy Spirit be with you all. And also with you.*

❤ **Prayer.** *Eternal God, our Creator and Redeemer, as you gladdened the wedding at Cana in Galilee by the presence of your Son, so by His presence now bring your joy to this wedding. Look in favor upon _____(bride) and _____(groom), and grant that they, rejoicing in all your gifts, may at length celebrate with Christ the marriage feast which has no end. Amen.*

❤ **Charge to the Couple.** _____(bride) and _____(groom), *you have come together in this place to join yourselves as husband and wife and to ask for God's continued presence and blessing on your life together. Christ abundantly blesses this union of mutual and lasting fidelity.*

*It is appropriate that you be reminded today of the enormity of what you are about to undertake with these vows. Because you are human and, therefore, subject to error and temptation, as all humans are, and because you have no idea what the future holds for you - what joys and sorrows await you - your decision to marry requires tremendous faith on each of your parts. You must have faith in yourselves as individuals and in what you have to give to each other; faith in your relationship as a couple and in what you can be and do together; and most of all, faith in God and God's presence with you to face whatever the future holds. Never forget that the marriage vows are not just vows in love, but they are vows of fidelity for each other grounded in God's love for you both.*

❤ **Passages from the Bible: lessons.**

❤ **Solo or hymn.**

❤ **Sermon by the minister.**

13

# Lutheran Wedding Ceremony

❤ **Statement of Intention.** _____(bride) and _____(groom), *if it is your intention to share with each other your joys and your sorrows, and all the years will bring, with your promises bind yourselves to each other as husband and wife.*

❤ **Wedding vows.** The couple has several choices of vows. Here are two:

*1. I give myself to you _____ as my wife/husband, to have and to hold from this day forth, through all the changing experiences of life...to love, cherish and respect so long as we both shall live. This I pledge to you as a solemn promise and trust before God.*

*2. I receive you _____ as my wife/husband, and these things I promise you: I will be faithful to you and honest with you; I will respect, trust, help and care for you; I will share my life with you; I will forgive you as we have been forgiven; and I will try with you better to understand ourselves, the world, and God: through the best and worst of what is to come as long as we live.*

❤ **Ring ceremony.** Bride and groom say, *I give you this ring as a sign of my love and faithfulness.*

❤ **Pronouncement of Marriage.** _____(bride) and _____(groom), *by their promises before God and in the presence of this congregation, have bound themselves to one another as husband and wife. Those whom God has joined together let no one put asunder.*

❤ **Blessings.** In some Lutheran churches, there are blessings given by children and step-children of the couple when they marry for the second time and form a blended family. Bride's and groom's families and friends may bless the bride and groom as well.

❤ **Prayers.** The minister gives words of thanks: *Let us bless God for all the gifts in which we rejoice today.*

*Lord God, constant in mercy, great in faithfulness: With high praise we recall your act of unfailing love for the human family, for the house of Israel, and for your people the Church. We bless you for the joy which your servants, _____ and _____ have found in each other, and pray that you give to us such a sense of your constant love that we may employ all our strength in a life of praise of you, whose work alone holds true and endures forever.*

*Faithful Lord, source of love, pour down your grace upon _____ and _____ , that they may fulfill the vows they have made this day and reflect your steadfast love in their life-long faithfulness to each other. As members with them of the body of Christ, use us to support their life together; and from your great store of strength give them power and patience, affection and understanding, courage and love toward you, toward each other, and toward the world, that they may continue together in mutual growth according to your will in Jesus Christ our Lord.*

*Gracious God, You bless the family and renew Your people. Enrich husbands and wives, parents and children more and more with your grace, that, strengthening and supporting each other, they may serve those in need and be a sign of the fulfillment of your perfect kingdom, where, with your Son Jesus Christ and the Holy Spirit, you live and reign, one God through all ages of ages. Amen.*

❤ **Celebration of the Eucharist.**
❤ **Lord's Prayer.**
❤ **Benediction.** *Almighty God, Father, Son and Holy Spirit, keep you in his light and truth and love now and forever. Amen.*
❤ **Introduction of the wedded couple.** *Dear friends in Christ, I present to you _____ husband and wife.*
❤ **Recessional.**

14

# Roman Catholic

The largest numbers of Roman Catholic people reside in Southern Europe and in Central and South America. Many reside in Ireland, the Philippines, and North America.

### ❤ Philosophy of love and marriage

The Roman Catholic Church regards marriage as a monogamous, lifelong, sacred union that can only be broken by the death of a spouse. The Catholic church views the communal event of marriage as a sacrament. This sacrament is an inner expression of Christ's grace and love as symbolized in the union of the man and woman. The love of each partner is to emulate the way Christ loves them. Both know that they are loved by God and, therefore, are in touch with the character of God's love. Faith in Jesus Christ and the indissolubility of marriage is assumed, and the bride and groom promise to be committed to each other forever.

Roman Catholicism holds marriage to be an indissoluble sacrament, but has nullifying procedures for marriages. The Roman Catholic Church has always discouraged its people from marrying people who were not Catholic, unless the non-Catholic party converted to Catholicism. Their belief is that mixed marriages may weaken the faith and create problems in raising children. To obtain dispensations for an interfaith marriage, the Catholic partner must promise that the children resulting from their marriage be baptized and raised as Catholics.

Ideally, the couple has an interview with the priest nine months to a year before the wedding date. Documents that are required for marriage in the church are the Baptismal Certificates, letters of freedom stating neither has ever been married, and letters of permission from parents. Also necessary is an investigative data sheet stating the couple's names, family backgrounds, and religious thought.

Usually the wedding takes place in the bride's parish, and the groom will make certain a notice of intended marriage is made at his church. Notices of an upcoming marriage are called banns which are published or "called" in his church three times prior to the wedding. If the wedding is to take place at any church other than the bride's church, she will be responsible for the banns.

Catholic wedding rituals vary in different localities and countries.

# Roman Catholic Wedding

The liturgical part of the wedding is often celebrated during Nuptial Mass; otherwise, the couple may chose to have a simple wedding ceremony.

❤ **Pre-processional.** The marriage rites begin after the priest greets the couple at the entrance of the church or at the altar. Once the family and guests are seated, the procession of wedding attendants walks to the altar of the sanctuary while organ music is played. The bride's father, friend, or relative escorts the bride down the aisle to her future husband. (In South American countries there are usually no bridesmaids or Matron of Honor. The Godparents are the attendees.)

Or else, the priest leads the bride, groom, their families, and witnesses from the entrance of the church to the altar to display a feeling of family solidarity. The bride is not given away by her father, but he simply accompanies his daughter as she goes toward the altar to meet the groom.

❤ **Mass begins with an opening prayer**. The opening prayer by the priest includes a reference to the couple's bond in marriage, for God to hear their prayers on their wedding day, and the request for God's blessing through the Lord.

# Roman Catholic Wedding

❤ **Biblical readings.** Some readings are read by a family friend. The priest or deacon then recites scriptures from the Old Testament, the New Testament, and the Gospel.

❤ **Sermon.**

❤ **Vows.** Option #1. The entire congregation stands during the rite of marriage when the couple takes their vows, their intention of commitment. The book *Rite of Marriage* indicates the Catholic vows as: *I_____ take you_____ to be my (husband or wife). I promise to be true to you in good times and in both sickness and in health. I will love you and honor you all the days of my life.* The Priest expresses the seal of their love in the presence of the church and the community. Then, he announces Christ's blessings as the couple assume the sacrament of marriage so that they embrace their marriage duties with lifetime fidelity. Then, the priest may ask if there is any lawful reason that they should not be joined in matrimony as husband and wife.

    The bride and groom then join hands and the priest asks, *Do you take this (name) for your lawful wife/ husband, to have and to hold, from this day forward, for better, for worse, for richer or for poorer, in sickness and in health, to love and to cherish until death do you part?* Other wording for the vows may be used, such as, *Do you freely accept without reservation giving yourselves to each other in marriage?*

Otherwise, the Priest says:
*My dear friends, you have come together in this church so that the Lord may seal and strengthen your love in the presence of the church's minister and this community. In this way you will be strengthened to keep mutual and lasting faith with each other and to carry out other duties of the marriage. And so, in the presence of the church, I ask you to state your intentions.*

*_____ and _____, have you come together freely and without reservation to give yourselves to each other in marriage? Will you honor each other as man and wife for the rest of your lives? Will you accept children lovingly from God, and bring them up according to the laws of Christ and his church?* The couple responds, *yes.*

*I____, take you,_____, to be my (wife, husband). I promise to be true to you in good times and in bad, in sickness and in health. I will love you and honor you all the days of my life.*

The bride and groom drink from the same goblet signifying that they will share their lives together during happiness and sadness.

❤ **Exchange of rings.** After the bride and groom respond *I do* to the inquiries, they exchange rings. Each says, *I take this ring as a sign of my love and fidelity in the name of the Father, Son, and Holy Spirit.*

❤ **Prayers of petition and Nuptial blessing.** The prayers of petition end by expressions depicting Jesus Christ and his Holy Mother Mary. There are also prayers of nuptial blessings.

❤ **The Lord's Prayer.**

❤ **Final blessing.** After the priest gives the final blessing, he dismisses the congregation by saying, *Go*

16

# Roman Catholic Wedding

*in peace with Christ . . .* to which the congregation responds, *Thanks be to God.* Otherwise, the priest may say the following words: *May the Holy Spirit of God always fill your hearts with His love.* The congregation responds, *May God, the almighty Father give you His joy and bless you. May the Son of God have mercy on you and help you in good times and in bad. And may almighty God bless you all, the Father, and the Son and the Holy Spirit. Amen.* (from the *Rite of Marriage*)

The continuation of the Mass includes Prayer of the Faithful and the Liturgy of the Eucharist used to depict Jesus Christ's Last Supper and death. Afterward, the priest says a Nuptial Blessing petitioning for the Lord's strength and protection. Marriage ceremonies may also include communion for the bride and groom, along with the congregation and wedding party. During some Catholic ceremonies, the bride and groom each carry a lighted wedding candle. One large wedding candle is lit from both candles to signify the unifying grace of the Sacrament. Gifts are sometimes presented to the couple during the ceremony. Another traditional option is for the bride to place a bouquet of flowers on the shrine of the Blessed Virgin Mary and ask for her blessings while the song *Ave Maria* is played. The placement of the floral bouquet may occur either before the processional or after her husband escorts her up the aisle.

**References:** *Your Catholic Wedding* **Rev. Chris Aridas and** *Weddings* **by Abraham J. Klausner.**

# Eastern Orthodox Weddings

The Eastern Orthodox Church, which broke from the Roman Catholic Church in 1054, has about 250 million communicants. Orthodox teachings are still very much the same as the Roman Catholic Church.

During Christian Albanian, Greek, Bulgarian, Romanian, Serbian, Russian, and other Eastern Orthodox wedding ceremonies, wedding customs involve:

- ❤ The bride and groom carrying lighted candles denoting the Light of the Lord.
- ❤ The betrothal which is the exchange of rings.
- ❤ Crowning of the bride and groom.
- ❤ Sipping wine from a common goblet.
- ❤ Sometimes the binding of the couple's hands together.
- ❤ While the bride and groom hold hands, they encircle a table with sacred items on it.

**Reference:** *The World's Religions* **by Huston Smith.**

*Victorian Charm Wedding Cake with "I Do" Ornament. The Wilton School of Cake Decorating and Confectionery Art. ©Wilton Enterprises*

❤ 17

*Mrs. Rashmi Singh, Hindu bride and Mr. Yagyadeep Singh Gaur as Hindu bridegroom.. Courtesy of Mrs. Rashmi Singh , Mr. Yagyadeep Singh Gaur, and Sumitra Singh.*

# *Hindu*

**Special thanks and credit to Sumitra Singh, Librarian**
**Embassy of India, Washington, D.C.**

The world's third largest religion, Hinduism began about 1,000 years ago in India. Hinduism, a polytheistic religion also known as Brahmanism, is rich in ceremony and the smell of sweet incense. Hindus have magnificent temples with abundant carvings and roadside shrines. Though over two-thirds of the Hindu population now reside in India, their religion has spread to Indonesia, Thailand, and Malaysia where its influence is felt today. Small Hindu populations are scattered throughout Europe, North America, Africa, and the West Indies. Even though customs and the people's languages in different countries vary, Hindu followers still maintain the same fundamental beliefs.

Hindus base their way of life on sacred laws from books illuminating their duties or *dharma*. Hinduism has many gods and goddesses to worship, but each of them is part of the Supreme God, then beyond, only One. Two major Hindu sects have a different, but sig-nificant major God, as well as lesser gods whom are divine. The major Gods from each sect are--

- ❤ *Shiva,* the Lord of the Dance, symbolizes the world's eternal energy. It causes patterns and cycles, and through its dance, the universe will be created over again though an endless cycle.
- ❤ *Vishnu* who comes to the aid of people.

Obedience to Gods' laws and placation through ritual are part of the Hindu's everyday life. The *tikka*, the divine eye, is represented by a dark sandalwood paste applied to the middle of the forehead. It is a sacred symbol to aid in the search for God.

Because of their belief that all existence is comprised of earth, water, fire, wind and aksha (ether), Hindu people make ritualistic offerings, symbolizing each element, at dawn or dusk at Hindu temples. Their offerings are made to the accompaniment of drum beating, bugle-blowing, bell ringing, and the chanting of *Vedas*.

Present-day Hindus often feel existence and the reality of life are too complicated and broad to be encompassed into a creed. Their beliefs contain many metaphysical ideas and viewpoints; therefore, an individual can choose his beliefs, practices, and rituals according to his understanding. Annually, *shraadam*, a day long ceremony with feasting takes place to honor their Hindu ancestors.

The Hindu's sacred text is the *Veda* which includes the *Upanishads*, a collection of rituals and mythological and philosophical commentaries. The most significant belief is that the soul is reborn many times; that the body grows old and dies, but the soul lives on. This soul is then reborn within a human form or another living form. Should the person's action in his life be one of good deeds, the person will be reborn to a higher level. Conversely, if his or her bad characteristics outweigh the good, the rebirth would will be in a lower form. The law of *karma*, cause and effect, is thereby based on one's deeds which determine one's next life. Their birthright is the reward or punishment for how they lived in their prior life and the events taking place in their lives are predestined.

Hindus believe that people start on a *Path of Desire* by wanting pleasure, wealth, fame, and power. Such wants are considered legitimate as long as people do not no injure others or act stupidly. Most people eventually tire of such pleasures and finally embark on a *Path of Renunciation*. They simply realize that truth goes beyond self-aggrandizement. What people truly desire is what they already possess within their own bodies: their true hidden self composed of their conscious being and their own personality buried beneath distractions, false assumptions, and untruths. Hindus believe that all peoples are linked to the God-creator *Brahma*. The goal after seeking pleasure is to achieve oneness with *Brahma*, the World Soul, who is in an eternal state of perfect knowledge and bliss. Hinduism offers the following paths to salvation to obtain bliss:

❤ Psychophysical exercise. Insight and spiritual knowledge gained from meditation and yoga until a state of enlightenment is attained.

❤ Total devotion to the ultimate God. The way to God is through knowledge.

❤ Work. Unselfishly serving others and striving for a good society.

❤ **Philosophy of love and marriage**

According to Dr. Krishna Nath Chatterjuee, author of the *Hindu Marriage Past and Present*, "The purpose of the Hindu marriage is to have sexual relations, continuity of the race, and discharging of religious, and social duties." The *Path of Desire,* consisting of achieving religious duty, attaining prosperity, worldly pleasures, and salvation, are the goals of marriage. The Hindu marriage is a sacred institution with the couple becoming one in spirit. A Hindu man has not attained his complete self unless he is married and has the cooperation of his wife. Among the Hindus, begetting a son is important.

❤ **Selecting a spouse**

Hindu marriages are arranged by parents. They select mates best suited for their children by examining personal qualities, education, and social status of a prospective partner. Because their concepts of reincarnation and *karma* keep the Hindu caste system alive, the people accept their station in life and thereby marry within their caste.

For many Hindus the caste system remains strong, especially in Indian villages where 75 percent of the population resides. Castes are related to the traditional occupations which are passed from father to son and influence who a Hindu marries, even with whom a person shares food. The castes are---

1. The *Brahmans* who are priests and philosophers.
2. The *Kshatriyas* who are the warriors responsible for military service and sustaining the law.
3. The *Vaishyas* are those responsible for trade and commerce.
4. The *Shudras* are manual laborers.
5. The low-caste masses called "untouchables."

The higher the caste, the greater the purity. If a person from a higher caste accidentally touches an untouchable, he must bathe and perform a ritual to regain purity. More achievements are expected from the higher castes than from the lower ones.

Years ago, parents arranged marriages for their children while they were babies or very young. Compatibility between the two families was of primary concern, for a young daughter had to live with her husband's extended family. They believed if young people grew up together, they could learn over time how to understand and adjust to each other's manners. The girl did not have to leave her parents to live with her husband and in-laws until she matured. In that case, she just visited them. Because the wedding occurred before puberty, the girl was a virgin and her parents did not have to be concerned about their daughter having a child out of wedlock.

Today, child marriages are forbidden, and girls can marry only after they are 14 years of age. Young girls are not permitted to have any other boyfriends prior to marriage and are expected to remain virgins. Marriages are arranged by parents, but now with the consent of their son or daughter. (Some parents consider whether or not their children's horoscopes are compatible.) Marriages are arranged with the expectation that love will grow and blossom throughout a lifetime. *(Please see India for more details.)*

### ❤ The Hindu Marriage

During the Hindu wedding ceremony, the bride and groom take the *sapta-padi* or seven steps together, promises led by a priest or Brahmin. The couple takes the *sapta-padi* before God, the Radiant One, symbolized by fire and light. Thus, their promises are witnessed by God's wisdom, truth, and justice.

### ❤ Hindu wedding.

Today's Hindu weddings are celebrated lavishly by family and friends. They also provide an opportunity for the parents to observe prospective eligible prospects for their other unmarried children.

The wedding usually takes place at the bride's home with the bride wearing a beautiful sari. Usually a large tent is erected and filled with beautiful interior decor: flowers, colorful personal adornment, and jewelry. Other places for the wedding are a garden, courtyard of the bride's house, a blocked-off street or square. Weddings are elaborate celebrations with about 100 relatives gathering for the occasion. Guests enjoy dining and lunch on their three-day visit. Sumitra Singh's father was so pleased on the occasion of his daughter's wedding that he had roses thrown to the earth from an airplane.

Because people's wealth and status differ and every state within India has its own customs, language, and manner of dress, Indian marriage customs and ceremonies vary.

**20** **References:** *Living Faiths: Marriage and the Family* by John Prickett, *Hinduism and India, Collier's Encyclopedia, Marriage Customs* by Anita Compton, *The Encyclopedia of Religion* by Mircea Elilade, *Hindu Marriage Past and Present* by Dr. Krishna Nath Chatterjuee, and *The World's Religions* by Huston Smith.

## *Hindu Wedding Ceremony*

❤ **Pre-wedding customs.** When the groom, his relatives, and friends arrive at the bride's town, the bride's parents hold a welcome ceremony. After the groom dines at the bride's home, the bride and groom stand on a decorated wood plank as priests hold a curtain between them. While the bride's bridal party (maternal uncle and bridesmaids) stand behind the bride, the priests chant marriage songs and the guests shower rice and other grains over the couple.

❤ **Wedding ceremony.** The priest or Brahmin officiates at the wedding ceremony. The wedding begins when the curtain is removed and garlands of sandalwood chips are placed around the necks of the bride and groom.

❤ **Bridal upliftment of *Dharma*.** The bride's father gives his daughter to the groom for the upliftment of *Dharma*. The father includes his daughter in the three *Purusharthas*: *Dharma* for right conduct, *Artha* for prosperity, and *Karma* for the enjoyment of legitimate gratification.

# Hindu Wedding

❤ **Marriage symbols.** After the bride applies sandalwood paste to the groom's forehead, he makes a round red mark on her forehead for her to display as long as they are married. The offerings of puffed rice and purified butter from the hands of the bride and groom are thrown into the fire, representing the *Radiant One*, while the priest removes the darkness by chanting more mantras, which are blessings.

❤ **Vows.** Vows in a Hindu marriage are made before a fire that represents the deity, the *Radiant One*; thus vows are witnessed by the God's wisdom, truth, and justice. The husband accepts his wife as a token of good fortune so they can assume their Hindu life together. The groom vows to always include his bride and to consult her. While the groom takes the bride's hand and leads her around the fire, mantras are said. These mantras include accepting the responsibilities of fidelity, love, mutual respect, and procreation for as long as they live. As the priest chants the seven steps, the bride and groom step closer to each other. The couples start walking where the rice is heaped on one side. Holding hands, they take the *sapta-padi,* seven steps symbolic of their common journey through life. As they circle around the sacred fire pot, they agree to do the following:

- ❤ Earn a living for their family and respect their abundance.
- ❤ Live a healthy lifestyle for each other.
- ❤ Be concerned for the partner's welfare.
- ❤ Enhance each other's pleasure and live together as friends.  Enjoy happiness and friendship throughout their religious-centered lives.
- ❤ Eat and drink together and be with each other on special occasions.
- ❤ Desire children for whom they will be responsible and love.
- ❤ Adapt to the other person at any given time and place.

Then, the bridegroom recites the traditional *mantras* to the bride, including:

*I am the words and you are the melody, I am the melody and you are the words.*

❤ **Blessings.** The bride's parents present gifts to the groom.  Cotton is tied around the bride and groom while blessings for a long and happy life are given. The bride washes her hands, then bride and groom pray that their prosperity, success, and *Dharma* will be fulfilled.

❤ **Placing of the floral love necklace.** The bridegroom places a floral love necklace around his bride's neck while he asks her to accompany him in his Hindu activities.  Another wedding necklace, a gold or silver chain with gold semicircles and black beads from both families, symbolic of the union of the two families, is also worn.

# Islam

Eighty percent of the world's Muslims, followers of Islam, are Sunni Muslim and the remaining are Shia and Druze Muslim. The Islamic socio-political system defines marriages and political administrations, and is a total way of life. Countries where Islam is practiced by more than 90 percent of the population are:

*North African:* Mauritania, Morocco, Algeria, Tunisia, Libya, Egypt.
*Middle Eastern:* Jordan, Iraq, Saudi Arabia, Yemen, South Yemen, Somalia, Oman, Turkey, Iran, Kuwait, Afghanistan, and Pakistan.

The following countries have a 50 to 90 percent of the Muslim population:

*North African:* Mali, Niger, Chad, and Sudan

Other nations with a large percentage of Muslims include Bulgaria, the former Soviet Central region, Singapore, Borneo, India, and China. Islam has several million followers in the United States, and Canada has an Islamic population as well.

Often, the state and religious community are one. The *Cambridge Factfinder* indicates Islam is the state religion in the following countries: Afghanistan, Algeria, Bahrain, Bangladesh, Egypt, Iran, Iraq, Jordan, Kuwait, Libya, Malaysia, Mauritania, Maldives, Morocco, Oman, Pakistan, Qatar, Saudi Arabia, Somalia, Sudan, Tunisia, United Arab Emirates, and Yemen. Some Muslim countries are totally ruled by Islamic law, but in other countries, where family law is not always enforced, many adhere to tradition as a matter of religious principle.

### ❤ Islamic religion

Islam, one of the world's monotheistic religions, espouses the belief in the oneness of God, *Allah*. Muslims, followers of Islam, believe that Mohammad is *Allah's* Prophet and that God's words are revealed by Mohammad, the prophet, as His messenger. The *Holy Quar'an* (also spelled the Koran), the sacred scripture, is believed to be the word of *Allah* revealed by the Prophet Mohammad, and the *Hadith* is the foundation of the legal systems in Muslim countries. Muslims have duties, the *Five Pillars of Islam,* which they follow:

- ❤ *Shahadah*, the profession of the faith.
- ❤ *Salah*, praying five times a day toward the Ka'abah in Makkah (Mecca) located in Saudi. Arabia.
- ❤ *Zakat* or almsgiving (giving to charity).
- ❤ *Sawm*, fasting during the month of Ramadan.
- ❤ *Hajj*, the pilgrimage to Makkah at least once in a lifetime.

The *Holy Quar'an* (Koran) and the *Sunnah*, the foundation of the legal system in Muslim countries, provide the framework for *Shari'ah*, the sacred law of Islam, called the straight path. The sacred law governs public and private, social, religious, and political life of every Muslim. No structure of church hierarchy exists as in Christianity.

Simply, Muslims believe in the direct communication with God and total submission to His will.

### ❤ Muslim philosophy of love and marriage

Muslims believe that marriage is a religious duty. Under Islamic law, purity and chastity prior to

marriage are the same for both male and female. Historically, women are protected by body-covering robes to help keep the male's honor intact. *Purdah* has been the means of maintaining moral standards. This practice requires women to wear the veil and greatly limits socialization between men and women. Because of higher education, influences from other countries, and the fact that professional middle and upper class women are increasingly in the work force, certain countries have relaxed these standards. Egypt gave up *purdah* years ago.

In Muslim countries marriages are most often arranged by parents. Young people are united by parents with the intent of strengthening families socially, monetarily, and politically. Historically, it is not proper for a girl to display an interest in a future marriage with a member of the opposite sex, for Islamic parents believe romantic love will grow after the successful union of two congenial, personable people.

According to Geraldine Borrs's *Cosmopolitan* article "Nine Parts Desire," written about Iraq, a committee of Islamic scholars more recently ruled that young women could meet their intended spouses unveiled before the wedding. Yet some women who have family-arranged marriages do not take advantage of this concession.

Islamic law in Muslim countries permits a man to have up to four wives, but he must receive the consent of his other wives. If he has only one, he can spend as much time with her as he wishes; however, if the man has more than one, he must be committed to spend every fourth night, in turn, with each wife. He is expected to treat them equally. Historically, men are granted authority over women as their protector and provider. According to the *Quar'an*, he must also divide his finances and his time equally among them. The husband must support each wife as long as she is living with him and is dutiful.

A Muslim man can legally marry a Christian or Jewish (a monotheist) woman. Yet, a Muslim woman must marry a Muslim man because belief in Islam is passed through the paternal line and the non-Muslim fathers would not possess the faith. A non-Muslim man must convert to Islam before he can marry a Muslim woman.

### ❤ Wedding contract

Throughout most of the Islamic world, marriages are arranged by parents. Each family acts in its own interest or through agents. Muslim marriage contracts are often signed weeks before the wedding celebrations, but can be signed on the day the celebrations occur. Depending on location, there are different customs regarding signing the contract. The *Holy Quar'an* says, *If the intention of a husband is not to pay the dower, the marriage is void.* Once the terms of the contract are agreed upon and witnessed, the couple is bound by canonical law. The *maher,* security for the wife, is sometimes provided by the husband, so the *maher* may be part of the marriage contract. When it is not practical, it becomes a superficial formality.

A wedding contract is often signed by representatives of both families with or without the bride and groom's consent. The ceremony and festivities often take place at a later date. Either the groom or his father may sign the civil contract in the presence of an *Imam*, a recognized Muslim religious leader, plus two witnesses from each family. A representative from the bride's family, usually her father, signs the contract. In some locations, a representative takes the contract to

the bride for her signature, and thus the bride and the groom separately sign the contract. In that case, the bride must repeat three times before witnesses that she agrees to marry the groom to show that she does not marry against her will. A woman may or may not be consulted depending on the region where she and her family reside.

**Reference: Anita Compton's book**
***Marriage Customs.***

### ❤ Marriage customs

In most places, Islamic weddings do not take place in a Mosque, since Islamic marriages are effected by a civil contract and men and women must remain separate. Not all Muslim cultures have a wedding ceremony because couples are considered married by the signing of the marriage contract. Marriages are ceremonially confirmed at the bride's and groom's receptions and banquet given by the family. Receptions are usually held separately for men and women, and women attendees may be veiled or unveiled. The bride may wear a Western style wedding gown for the reception.

When the marriage ceremony is held at a mosque, the wedding is officiated by a *ma'dhun*. In such regions there are no restrictions on choosing other places for the ceremony, like a home or a judge's office. At a mosque wedding, where both parties are Muslim, witnesses must be of the Muslim faith. Before the wedding, the groom informs his prospective bride's father of his intentions for marriage and asks for permission to visit. The *Khitbah*, the formal betrothal, takes place with friends and family in attendance. The betrothal ceremony starts with prayers praising *Allah*, seeking His forgiveness, and asking His protection against evil. Prayers include the words *God is God and Mohammed His messenger.*

At the betrothal, a relative or friend of the groom makes a statement of the groom's intent. If the bride's family approves of the man, the bride's family representative acknowledges the request. Then, a prayer is recited and the bride's father formally accepts the man as his daughter's future husband. An engagement ring and presents are given to the bride. In Egypt, the wedding ring is given to the bride during the engagement party. The wedding feast is called the *walimah*.

In some parts of the Islamic world, a procession of guests may arrive with bridal gifts which are then displayed at receptions. A celebration for the bride may occur in the new home. During that time, the bride is adorned in elaborate costumes and jewelry. The groom, followed by friends and well-wishers, may celebrate by riding a horse through the streets. Family and friends feast for a day or more.

❤ **Henna ceremonies.** In regions where there is a wedding ceremony, an evening *henna* ceremony precedes it. At that time *henna* paste is applied to the bride's and groom's hands and feet.

*(See Israel and Jordan for additional information about Muslim marriages.)*

# Muslim Wedding Ceremony

*Not all Muslim cultures have a wedding ceremony.*

❤ **Mutual meal.** The bride and groom do not celebrate with family and friends, but are secluded in their quarters where they partake of a mutual meal in which special foods are sent to them.

❤ **Wedding Ceremony.** The next day the following rituals may take place: The bride and groom, facing each other, clasp hands. A white cloth is placed over them. The *Faihah*, the first part of the *Quar'an*, is recited.

❤ **Inquiries.** The opening prayer offered by the officiator is followed by inquiries to the bride and groom. The bride responds, *I _____, offer you myself in marriage in accordance with the instructions of the Holy Quar'an and the Holy Prophet, peace and blessing be upon Him.*

❤ **Pledge.** Then, the officiator asks them to pledge their *honesty, sincerity, obedience and faithfulness,* and finally, he conveys his good wishes.

❤ **Wellwishes of guests.** As the bride is escorted to her husband's residence, candy and rice are showered upon her. The couple receive gifts of candy or eggs.

**References:** *Concise Encylopaedia of Islam* by Cyril Glasse, *A Complete Guide to All Religious* and *Interfaith Marriage Services* by Abraham J. Kausner.

# Jewish

The Jewish people are scattered through nations all over world. Except for Israel, they are generally a small minority in most countries. According to *The Historical Atlas of the Jewish People*, 29 percent of the total world population of Jews lives in Israel, 45 percent in the United States and Canada, 10 percent in the Soviet Union, and 8 percent in Europe. The remaining number are in other countries like Argentina, Uruguay, and Australia. A high Jewish population resides in the cities of New York and Los Angeles in the United States. Since the Jews have moved to and from so many countries and have liberal to orthodox views, wedding customs differ. Yet, many essential traditional religious philosophies, prayers, and viewpoints remain the same.

## ❤ Jewish Religious Philosophy

The Jewish religion is monotheistic, for Jewish people believe that God, as revealed through Abraham, is the creator and sole ruler of the universe. The Old Testament of the Bible, particularly the first five books, constitute the *Torah*. The *Torah*, along with *The Ten Commandments*, which Moses received from God on Mount Sinai, emphasize the ethical behavior Jews should have as true worshipers of God. Judaic laws cover almost every aspect of Jewish life. Many major commandments were revealed to the Jewish people as they fled from Egypt during biblical times:

## ❤ Ten Commandments
1. *You shalt have no other gods before me.*
2. *You shalt not make yourself graven images.*
3. *You shalt not take the name of the Lord, your God, in vain.*
4. *Observe the Sabbath day and keep it holy. Six days you shalt labor, and do all your work; but the seventh day is a Sabbath to the Lord your God.*
5. *Honor your father and your mother.*
6. *You shalt not kill.*
7. *You shalt not commit adultery.*
8. *You shalt not steal.*
9. *You shalt not bear false witness against your neighbor.*
10. *You shalt not covet your neighbor's house, wife, or manservant or his other belongings.*

The Jews traditionally believe that the Messiah, a savior of humanity, is yet to come.

## ❤ Traditional Jewish world marriages

According to the *Encyclopedia of World Cultures*, years ago Jewish marriages in European and Asian countries were arranged. In Russia, Uzbekistan, Tajikistan of Central Asia, and surrounding Mideastern countries, the boys' fathers used to send matchmakers to the prospective brides' parents to make a settlement. The process was often carried out even when the children were very young. When an agreement containing a brideprice was made, a ceremonial betrothal meeting between the bride and groom's parents took place. There, the bride unveiled her face and the bride and groom saw each other for the first time. Seven days before the wedding date, the bride's dowry was displayed and a party for the bride was given. Closer to the wedding, the bride was cleansed at a bathing pool called a *mikvah*. The bride's hands were often painted with henna, and her marriage contract was signed.

*Russia.* In the past, Russian Jewish wedding procedures were held separately in the groom's home and in the bride's home after the matchmaker matched the young couple. The bride brought clothing, ornaments, and pastry (called *likakh*) to her engagement party. The marriage contract was negotiated between families prior to the wedding. As the bride was about to leave for her future husband's home, her friends would sing farewell songs to her at her family home. She was beautifully dressed, her head covered by a silk kerchief when the groomsmen came for her. The brideprice was accepted by the bride's friends before the groomsmen could take her to the groom's home. Holding burning lamps, candles, and torches, the groomsmen sang, played music, and danced as they led her to the groom's residence. Groomsmen threw candies and rice over her for good luck and fruitfulness. *(See more about Russian Jews of Southwest Mountains on page 199.)*

In the more recent past, when Jewish Russian couples were married, either outside or indoors, the

25

family and Jewish community would be present. Guests watched the wedding ceremony and later, one by one, each publicly announced their wedding gift and presented it to the bride and groom. Men performed line dances. During the celebration, some men lifted bride and groom on separate chairs, as depicted in the Hollywood movie *Fiddler on the Roof.*

Today, a wedding is usually held jointly with both families involved. Relatives, neighbors, and friends are invited to one sumptuous affair. They bring envelopes filled with money and give them to a special collector. After the wedding, a banquet is held and wedding cake is served. Otherwise, tables are filled with appetizers, Jewish foods, and drinks. Festivities, led by designated toastmasters, are followed by music, singing, and dancing. While the bride dances with guests, her dancing partners give her money. Sweets and tea are enjoyed by all at the end of the celebration.

*Western Russia.* Many Jews who live in the mountains of western Russia are now nonbelievers as the result of the anti-Semitic pressure they faced, partially because of their link with Zionism. They no longer follow the Jewish wedding customs.

*Algeria and Arabia.* Before the wedding, an Algerian Jewish bride and groom with their families eat bread, symbolizing the sustenance of life, and honey, for sweetness. Jewish women sing high pitched songs to show their happiness for the bride.

*Hassidic customs.* Orthodox Hassidic Jewish customs vary according to sects and occur in many nations throughout the world. In some sects, a Jewish male over the age of nine cannot touch a member of the opposite sex, except for medical reasons or unless he is married to the woman. He cannot touch his wife in public. Men dance in line dances with other men. In certain sects, the woman shaves her head after she is married and her head is kept covered so that she does not tempt other men, though she is permitted to wear a wig in public. Shaving is not common today.

Married couples of some Hassidic sects sleep in bed with a sheet between them. There is a hole in the sheet to facilitate marital relations.

*Western countries.* Western Jewish weddings have evolved in various ways. They usually take place at times other than the Sabbath (Friday nights and Saturdays), a holy day, or on other special days of the year. The ceremony is celebrated at synagogues, temples, hotels, at home or outdoors. The wedding ceremony differs depending on whether the wedding is held in an Orthodox (strict religious beliefs) synagogue or a Conservative (moderate beliefs) synagogue, or a Reform (liberal beliefs) Temple. In countries where English is spoken, most blessings during the wedding are first spoken in Hebrew, then repeated in English.

❤ **Jewish philosophy of love and marriage**

The purposes of Jewish marriages are procreation, companionship, and maintenance of family life. Only at Reform temples is there a tolerance of mixed marriage, especially when the non-Jewish member studies in order to convert.

To bring good luck to a marriage, the bride and groom do not see one other until the veil ceremony. The bride usually wears a white or cream wedding dress as a sign of purity, and she wears the veil over her head. During most wedding ceremonies, the groom lifts the bride's veil after he has tasted the wine. The groom wears a skull cap, called a *yarmulke,* and a white prayer shawl, called a *tallith,* over a suit or formal attire. While the ceremony is performed, the bride *(kallah)* and groom *(choson)* stand beneath the *chuppah.,* or canopy, which represents a lifetime home of sweetness. A Rabbi (teacher) is the officiator. The *cantor,* or singer, usually provides the music and chants the prayers in the Hebrew language for the ceremony. Traditionally, the wedding ring for the bride is a simple gold band. A glass or cup may be used during the service to sanctify the family's life-cycle and another, the loving cup, is used for the couple who are establishing a new home.

Many of the logistics of the wedding ceremony, such as the father giving the bride away, are similar to Christian weddings.

*Victorian Charm Wedding Cake with "I Do" Ornament. The Wilton School of Cake Decorating and Confectionery Art.* ©*Wilton Enterprises*

***Ketubah by Sara Glaser © 1993.*** *Water color. Collection of Lisa and Mel Tranter Sibony. Sara Glaser Design, Oakland, California. (510) 595-7779.*

## The Seven Benedictions spoken at a Jewish Wedding

1. *Blessed art Thou, O Lord our God, King of the Universe who hast created the fruit of the vine.*

2. *Blessed art Thou, O Lord our God, King of the Universe who has created all things for His glory.*

3. *Blessed art Thou, O Lord our God, King of the universe, creator of man.*

4. *Blessed art Thou, O Lord our God, King of the universe who hast made man in His image, after His likeness, and hast prepared for him out of his very self, a perpetual fabric. Blessed art Thou, O Lord, creator of man.*

5. *May she who was barren be exceedingly glad and rejoice when her children are united in her midst in joy. Blessed art Thou, O Lord, who makes Zion joyful*

*through her children.*

6. *O Lord, make these beloved companions greatly rejoice even as Thou didst rejoice at Thy creation in the Garden of Eden as of old. Blessed art Thou, O Lord, who makest bridegroom and bride to rejoice.*

7. *Blessed art Thou, O Lord our God, King of the universe, who has created joy and gladness, bridegroom and bride, mirth and exultation, pleasure and delight, love, brotherhood, peace and fellowship. Soon may there be heard in the cities of Judah and in the streets of Jerusalem, the voice of joy and gladness, the voice of the bridegroom and the voice of the bride, the jubilant voice of the bridegrooms from the canopies, and of youths from their feasts of song. Blessed art Thou, O Lord who makest the bridegroom to rejoice with the bride.*

27

♥ **Rituals common to most Jewish weddings**

The rabbi reads the invocation. Then, the rabbi recites the betrothal benediction over a glass of wine, a symbol of sanctification in which the praise to the one and only God is voiced. The prayer is, *We praise you, Adonai our God, Ruler of the universe, Creator of the fruit of the vine.* The bride and the groom sip the wine. The groom places the ring on the bride's finger while reciting in Hebrew, *Thou art consecrated unto me with this ring as my wife, according to the law of Moses and Israel.* At the very end of the ceremony, a glass or goblet, usually wrapped in cloth, is placed on the floor.

The groom smashes it with his foot. To some, the breaking of the glass symbolizes the destruction of the Temple in Jerusalem centuries ago. To others, it may symbolize the husband and wife sharing a marriage in which no one else can partake. After the wedding, joyous guests wish the couple *mazel tov*, meaning good luck.

The *Ketubah*, the marriage contract, traditionally written in Aramaic, is read during an Orthodox ceremony. Signed by the couple at the beginning or end of the ceremony, it contains promises and duties to each other according to the tradition of Moses and Israel.

# Orthodox Jewish Wedding

*My thanks to Rabbi Mark Schaffel, Executive Director of the Torah Foundation of Milwaukee, Wisconsin, U.S.A. for the Orthodox Jewish Wedding Ceremony*

❤ **Pre-wedding customs.** The bride and groom usually fast all day and say a special prayer during the afternoon prayers. In *Ashkenazi* (European Jewish) communities, the *chuppah*, a canopy, is held or constructed outdoors under the open sky to recall God's blessing to Abraham that his children will be *as the stars of Heaven* (Genesis 15:5). Many sects still observe the custom of placing ashes on the groom's forehead. The *Talmud* mentions this practice to recall the destruction of the Jewish Holy Temple,

❤ **Wedding procession.** When the bride and groom are about to marry, the groom is escorted down the aisle by his father, father-in-law, Roshei ha Yeshiva, Rabbi, and friends of the bride. The bride awaits the groom's arrival under the *chuppah*. The veil covers the bride's face, reminiscent of Rachel's deception when Jacob married Leah in the Old Testament of the Bible.

The Orthodox ceremony is composed of two parts: the betrothal and the marriage.

❤ **Vows.** The Rabbi asks if the bride and groom *will take each other, promise to cherish and protect ____(her) ____ (him), whether in good fortune or in adversity and to seek together with her (him) a life hallowed by the faith of Israel. (Rabbi's Manual)*

❤ **Betrothal.** The betrothal process, completed before witnesses, signifies that the couple are thereby sanctified to each other. The groom places the gold ring on the index finger of the bride's right hand. The ring is symbolic of the groom encircling himself around the bride to provide her with protection, When placing the ring on the bride's finger he may say, *By this you are consecrated to me according to the law of Moses and Israel.* She accepts the ring and together they say, *We praise You, Adonai our God, Ruler of the universe, who hallows us with mitzvot (blessing) and consecrates this marriage. We praise You, Adonai, who sanctifies our people Israel through kiddushin, the sacred rite of marriage at the chuppah. (Rabbi's Manual)*

❤ **Reading of the Ketubah.** To separate the two parts of the ceremony, the Rabbi reads the *ketubah* aloud. To activate the contract, the groom hands the *ketubah* to his bride before the witnesses.

❤ **Reading of the Seven Blessings.** The Seven Blessings are recited by the honored guests and closest relatives. *(See the Seven Blessings, listed on page 27.)* Finally, the blessings celebrating joy and gladness for the bride and groom, along with jubilation, cheer, delight, love, friendship, harmony and fellowship, are given.

❤ **Breaking of the glass.** The ceremony concludes with the groom breaking a glass. This action serves as a reminder that even at the height of joy, Jews still mourn the destruction of their Holy Temple in Jerusalem over 2,000 years ago.

# Orthodox Jewish Wedding

♥ **Circling the groom.** The bride walks around the groom seven times. One explanation is that there were seven revolutions of the earth during the seven days of the earth's creation.

♥ **Closing words.** *May God bless you and keep you.*
*May God's presence shine upon you and be gracious unto you.*
*May God's Presence be with you and give you peace.*

♥ **Private meeting.** When the ceremony is over, the couple is escorted to a private room where they have an opportunity for a few minutes of privacy to enjoy their new relationship undisturbed. In the past, the bride and groom fed food to each other to symbolize the support they would have for one another during their relationship. The bride takes on her husband's last name.

♥ **Reception.** There is a special Jewish commandment that the new husband and his wife should be entertained at their reception. To accomplish this blessing, the band plays, dinner is served, and all are invited to dance after the married couple make their first entrance as Mr. and Mrs.____. This reception is held at a home or in a hall with line dancing and merriment. Traditionally, the men and women dance in separate circles to Jewish folk music. The line dance, the *hora* is performed by all who wish to participate. During the excitement, the bride and groom, while seated on chairs, are lifted into the air by the guests.

♥ **Post-wedding customs.** For the next seven days, the couple eat a meal at a *minyan* (a quorum of 10 men). The same Seven Blessings that were recited during the wedding are then repeated.

# Reformed Jewish Wedding

*Courtesy of Rabbi Maynard Bell of Temple Solel serving Phoenix and Scottsdale, Arizona*
*Dee Lomax, Rabbinic Secretary*

♥ **Rabbi's blessing for the couple about to be married.** *Mekor haChayim, Source of all life: We ask Your blessing for ____ (bride) and ____ (groom). We pray that the sacred commitments of their wedding day will sustain them all the days of their lives. May the love that binds them be strong and lasting, and their hearts be filled with patience and understanding for one another. May their home be a Mikadash Me-at, a sanctuary built on the devotion to God, Torah, and Israel.*

*May they be blessed with health, courage, and good fortune, their love and friendship deepening through the years. We pray that they will find* **shalom** *(peace) together. Amen.*

♥ **Signing of the *Ketuba* before the wedding service.** The couple, their immediate families, and witnesses go into the rabbi's study or in a private room where the bride and groom recite together or separately the following words:

# Reform Jewish Wedding

*You are about to be sanctified to me as my wife/husband according to the traditions of Moses and Israel. I will love, honor, and respect you. I will provide for you and sustain you as is proper for a Jewish wife/husband to do.* After the couple and witnesses sign the *ketuba*, the parents or others hand the *ketubah* to the couple.

Here is one example of the many types of Reformed Jewish wedding services:
Hebrew verses may be sung: *Blessed are you who have come here in the name of God. Serve Adonai with joy; come into God's presence with song.*

❤ **Opening words.** *We rejoice that _____ and _____ join in marriage in the presence of God and loved ones. O most awesome, glorious, and blessed God, grant Your blessings to the bride and groom.*
*Surrounded by loved ones whose joy and prayers are with you here, you stand at this chuppah, symbol of the Jewish home. May your home be a shelter against the storm, a haven of peace, a stronghold of faith and love.*

❤ **Prayer of gratitude.** The rabbi and the congregation join in saying: *We praise You, Adoinai our God, Ruler of the Universe, who has kept us in life, sustained us, and brought us to this joyous time.*

❤ **God joining the couple.** Rabbi says, *In this union, the sacred work of creation goes on: God joining man and woman; God planting the divine likeness within them. Man and woman were created in the divine image. Male and female God created them. May the union of _____ and _____ animate the divine in each of them, and may each help the other to grow in God's likeness.*

❤ **Praising God by rabbi.** While lifting the wine cup, the rabbi says, *We praise you, Adonai our God, Ruler of the universe, creator of the fruit of the vine.* Other praises follow, including *We praise You, Adonai our God, who causes bride and groom to rejoice. May these loving companions rejoice as have Your creatures since the days of creation.*

❤ **Praising God by all.** *We praise You, Adonai our God, Ruler of the universe, Creator of joy and gladness, bride and groom, love and kinship, peace and friendship. O God, may there always be heard in the cities of Israel and in the streets of Jerusalem: the sounds of joy and of happiness, the voice of the groom and the voice of the bride, the shouts of young people celebrating, the songs of children at play. We praise You, our God, who causes the bride and groom to rejoice together.*

❤ **Sipping the wine.** As the bride and groom drink wine from the same Kiddish cup, the rabbi says,
*As you have shared the wine from a single cup, so may you, under God's guidance, share contentment, peace, and fulfillment from the cup of life. May you find life's joys heightened, its bitterness sweetened, and each of its moments hallowed by true companionship and love.*

❤ **Vows.** The rabbi continues, *And now I ask you, in the presence of God and this assembly: do you, _____, take _____ to be your wife, to love, to honor, and to cherish. And do you, _____, take _____ to be your husband, to love, to honor, and to cherish?* (Each responds, "Yes.") *_____, as you place the ring on the finger of the one you love, recite the words that formally unite you in marriage.*
As the bride and groom face each other each says, *Be wedded to me with this ring as my wife/husband in keeping with the religion of the Jewish people. "I betroth you to me forever; I betroth you to me with steadfast love and compassion, I betroth you to me in faithfulness."* (Hosea 2:21-22.)

# Reform Jewish Wedding

❤ **Rabbi's remarks or the reading of the ketuba.**

❤ **Closing statements and silent prayer.** *In the presence of these witnesses and in keeping with our tradition, you have spoken the words and performed the rites that unite your lives. _____ and _____, you are now husband and wife in the sight of God, the Jewish community, and all people. I ask you and all who are gathered here to pray in silence, seeking God's blessings upon your marriage and your home.*

❤ **Closing prayer.** *May God bless you and keep you, May God's light shine upon you and be gracious to you. May God's presence be with you and give you peace.*

❤ **Breaking of the glass.** The groom breaks the glass with his foot.

# Shinto

*Shinto Wedding Attire*

❤ **Shinto philosophy**

Shinto, the way of the *Kami* practiced in Japan, means the "way of the gods." The superior object of worship is the *kami*, indicating fertility and aesthetic wonder of nature's bounty. Thus, *kami* can mean anything that inspires wonderment, reverence, or mystification in mankind. For example, Japanese receive their bountiful diet and ritualistic bathing from the sea which has a *kami*-nature. The freshness of the ocean and the reflected light of the sun create the principle of *kami*, the Sun Goddess symbolizing purity. Because water, being pure and clear in rivers and waterfalls shows endless change, renewal, and freshness, Shintos conclude that life is a succession of change and renewal.

Throughout early Japanese history to the present, the concern of the Shinto religion is with ritual purity, which includes the Japanese love of bathing. Death is considered impure; thus, Shinto rituals reflect belief in nonvisual spiritual energies that power the future of human beings. In Japan, Buddhism often deals with death and Shintoism only concerns itself with marriage, though some people practice Buddhist marriage customs in their original form.

❤ **Shrines**

Because purity is very important to the Japanese people, all important events of life are celebrated by a visit to the local or family shrine. Shintos worship at a *Miya*, a Shinto shrine or palace. Shrines with a variety of architectural styles are found everywhere throughout Japan. The architecture may be a simple structure consisting mainly of two columns with a horizontal shape resting over them or be a beautiful curved roof building where Japanese people can feel a sense of renewal energizing their bodies and minds. Shrines, involving the *kami* nature of the Japanese culture, are associated with creativity, fertility, and productivity. The weather, territorial geographical phenomena, and animals are also enshrined and venerated, as are ancestral spirits which involve the imperial family.

People not only pray at their local shrines, but many celebrations, such as marriage, take place at shrines. When Shinto wedding ceremonies are conducted at shrines, foods are made for the *kami*. Following the flow of life, the priest gives thanks to the *kami* when a baby is welcomed into the world.

### ❤ Ordering of human affairs

Shintoism covers people's relationship to the world and one another. People are born of nature and should be appreciated. There are no particular ethics, but everything goes along with the flow of life. Their mythology features the Sun Goddess, who possesses dual identities, one for the sun and the other for the ancestral *kami* of the Imperial family which symbolizes power. Embracing the manifold *kami* of nature, the Shinto religion thereby grants the imperial family the honor of descending from the supreme Sun Goddess. The Sun Goddess is consulted during important events. The prime minister and cabinet usually visit Ise after a new government is inaugurated, since traditionally the ordering of human affairs is supervised by sacred leaders. Government and religion are considered one and the same.

### ❤ Arranged marriage

The *nakodo*, or honored go-between, is the representative who usually makes the match. He is always a respected person who, along with his wife, accompanies the bride and groom throughout the Shinto wedding ceremonies. Usually an older, respected, and wiser married man, the *nakodo* acts as a counsel should the couple have marital problems later.

### ❤ Philosophy of marriage

According to Shinto thinking, the newly married couple will be prosperous if they revere the way of the *kami*. Even though life may be difficult, people should not possess a fatalistic pessimism.

**Reference:** ***Shinto: Japan's Spiritual Roots* by Stuart D.B. Picken.**

### ❤ The wedding

The Shinto wedding ceremony may take place near a shrine, though often it is held at a wedding palace. At the White Crane Palace, an employee makes certain that all proceedings for the wedding ceremony go smoothly. A shrine, dedicated to a deity, and an altar are in the room where the wedding takes place. Two priests and young females adorned as shrine maidens are present.

When a Japanese bride follows the traditional custom, she wears traditional kimonos, and often changes them during the course of the wedding ceremony and reception which occurs afterward. The brief, dignified ceremony takes place as the couple sit before the priest in the presence of their family and friends. The priest offers prayers that the couple may be blessed and free from ill fortune. Then the priest waves his *haraigushi*, a sacred tree having white linen or paper streamers attached, as a symbol of purification. All share rice wine, called *sake*, which symbolizes that the protective *kami* has been invoked.

*The following wedding ceremony was held at the shrine of the White Crane Palace in Japan:*

❤ **Procession.** The wedding party enters to the sound of a large drum and flute music. The bride and groom are seated at a small table in the front of the room near an altar. The *nakodo* and his wife are seated at another table directly behind them. The groom's party stands near the groom's parents, and the bride's party, next to the bride. Cameras are suspended from the ceiling to take videos of the wedding.

❤ **Wedding rituals.** Shinto rituals are performed along with current customs: purification, a prayer, an invocation, and an offering. Then, wedding rings are exchanged during the recitation of the wedding vows and the sharing of *sake*. Those invited only to the reception await in another room until the wedding ceremony is over. The assistant, an employee of the White Crane Palace, begins the ceremony by stating its

# Shinto Wedding

purpose: to solemnly unite the man and woman before the *kami* (deity) through the auspices of the *nakodo*.

❤ **Purification.** All present stand and bow toward the altar. A priest utters a short prayer, then picks up an instrument for purification (*harai-gushi*), a long stick with a great number of strips of white paper attached to one end. Jerking the stick quickly left, right, and left again, he produces a loud "Whoosh! Whoosh! Whoosh!" to purify the room and its participants.

❤ **Prayer.** The priest then chants an invocation (*norito*). He addresses several deities (including Izanagi and Izanami, the primal couple credited in myth with procreating the universe), proclaims the bride and groom united through the auspices of the *nakodo*, and prays for their happiness and prosperity.

❤ *Sake* **ceremony.** The assistant then announces the first of three *sakazukigoto*, the ritual sharing of *sake* that creates or reinforces social bonds. The second priest plays high-pitched, wailing notes on a wooden flute. Then, the *miko* brings a vessel filled with sake and a tray holding three nested cups to the principals' table. The groom takes a cup and drinks the sake with a series of three sipping motions. Afterward, the tray is offered to the bride and she drinks from the same cup in similar fashion. This procedure is repeated with a second and third cups.

While flute music is played, the *miko* serves *sake* to the groom's father and mother and bride's father and mother. Finally, the two groups of relatives share *sake*, together with the *nakodo*. Once the *miko* pours *sake* into the small cups set for each person, all present drink together and proclaim *"Omedeto gozaimasu"* (congratulations).

❤ **Wedding vows.** At the assistants's instructions, the groom picks up a text from the table in front of him and reads the wedding vows: *We have now become united as husband and wife for all ages before the kami at White Crane Palace. We respectfully pledge from here on to make our hearts as one, give mutual help and support, faithfully execute our marital duties and responsibilities, and spend all the days of our lives together with unchanging trust and eternal affection.*

❤ **Offerings.** The assistant closes by reading the wedding date and the groom's full name; the bride adds her first name only. The couple then make a traditional offering of *tamagushi* to the *kami*. The *miko* brings the bride and groom these items and leads them to the altar. Cued verbally by the assistant and visually by the exaggerated movements of the *miko*, everyone bows twice, claps their hands two times, then bows.

❤ **Ring exchange.** The couple returns to their places for the ring exchange. The *miko* brings the box holding the rings and extends it to the groom for him to take the bride's ring, which he places on her finger. When the bride completes the exchange, the audience applauds. The other *miko* presents items from White Crane Palace: an album for keeping wedding memorabilia and an amulet from the hall's famous parent shrine. Then, all bow towards the altar. The priest recites the invocation, announces the successful completion of the ceremony, and offers his congratulations. He instructs the newlyweds to build a harmonious home. *(For more details concerning Japanese wedding customs, see Japan on page 139.)*

33

**Adaptation from reprint of the book *Modern Japan Through Its Weddings***
**by Walter Drew Edwards with permission of the publishers, Stanford University Press.**
**© by the Board of Trustees of the Leland Stanford Junior University.**

# Sikhism

Sikhism, founded in northwestern India by Nanak Sahib, has approximately 16 million global followers. Sikhs believe in a supreme formless God and in the Hindu concept of birth, death and rebirth. Because of Islamic influences, Sikhs reject Hindu divine incarnations *(avatars)*, the caste system, worshipping of images, and the sanctity of the *Vedas*. Sikhs are guided by a Guru, a spiritual leader, and by God's way.

According to Rahul Singh's book *The Sikhs Today*, the traditional Eastern Indian Sikh marriage ceremony begins when the groom gallantly rides a horse from his house to the bride's family home. His friends and relatives form a procession, accompanied by music, and go with the groom. They are greeted by the men of the bride's family. As they enter the home, the groom is teased by the bride's sisters and girlfriends. If the marriage is traditionally arranged, the bride and groom might be seeing one another for the first time.

The Sikh Wedding Ceremony is called *Anand Karaj*, ceremony of bliss. Originating in India, it is officiated by any Sikh man or woman who is strongly religious, knowledgeable, and highly respected in the community. The ceremony may be conducted at a Sikh temple or at the bride's home in the early hours before dawn. During that time, professional singers sing hymns customarily used at morning worship. Otherwise, the wedding may take an entire day and last until the small hours of the morning.

The bride often wears red attire decorated with gold designs. The bridegroom's face is covered with a *kalgri* or face mask and he often wears a decorated dark red turban over his head. One lengthy scarf is shared by both as they make their wedding vows.

## Sikh Wedding Ceremony

The groom sits before the *Granth*, the Sikh holy book, and then the bride comes to sit next to him. A respected person requests that the bride, groom, and the parents stand, then invokes a blessing of God on the couple's marriage and informs them of their Sikh marital obligations. Duties stated during the service include:

- ❤ Being faithful and loyal to each other
- ❤ Being good to one another during times of sorrow or pain
- ❤ Celebrating each other's joys
- ❤ Being respectful of relatives in both families

A person reads parts of the *Granth* while singers sing the identical words. The officiator often states the high regard that Sikhs have for marriage, that the purpose is to unite their souls so that they become one spiritually, physically, intellectually, and emotionally. As the person officiates, the bride and groom say their vows and accept the duties of a Sikh marriage.

After they are pronounced husband and wife, the bride's father places floral garlands around the necks of the bride and groom. He also inserts the tip of a colored sash in the groom's hand. The groom steps forward as he holds one end of the sash, then gives the other end of the sash to his bride. Clasping the other end, the bride follows the groom while they walk four times clockwise around the *Granth,* with the bride's male relatives assisting her. Reverence for the holy book symbolizes the couple seeking God's help, grace, and blessings. The musicians then play hymns while the couple are walking clockwise around the holy book to indicate that they accept their responsibilities towards each other. At that time, a hymn is sung and a verse from the *Lavan* is stated, then sung. While walking around the holy book for the final time, the guests spray colorful flowers and petals over the couple. When the couple complete their turns, they bow respectfully and are seated until the final verse is read. More flowers are showered over the couple. The singing of more marriage hymns follows, then a Sikh prayer is voiced by all. *(Refer to page 134 which covers Sikh weddings in India for more details).*

**References:** *Marriage Customs* **by Anita Compton and the Encylopaedia Britannica and** *The World's Religions* **by Huston Smith.**

# *Western-Style Wedding Customs*

## ❤ History

Western countries of North, Central, and South America, and other countries, such as Australia and certain African nations, have a history of Judeo-Christian colonization and have marriage customs from Western Europe. Historically, Western-style wedding customs have evolved from British, French, Spanish, and Portuguese colonial influences. These countries have been instrumental in forming Western customs going into the next century. Presently, in Western-style cultures, Catholic, Protestant, and Jewish unmarried individuals generally make their own decisions about whom they will marry, usually on the basis of love, then resolve to spend the rest of their lives with that person. Their decision to marry thus relies on friendship, romantic attraction, hopes and dreams, and usually, the similarity of social and educational backgrounds.

In the United States, women almost always adopt their husband's last name when they are married. In countries of South America, the men add the last name of the woman to their own.

## ❤ Dating

Dating, also called courting, is a time when couples meet and get to know each other's character to decide whether or not they want to make a marital commitment. There is usually a period of unchaperoned dating before marriage; however, chaperoned dating still occurs in some South American countries.

Couples meet through introductions by friends, at social gatherings or work, at schools and colleges, while traveling, through a variety of dating services, and through personal advertisements in newspapers and online computer services. While dating, the couple goes to the movies, to dinner at a restaurant, to each other's residence, or to amusement parks. Dating mainly takes place after work hours in the evenings or on weekends when the opportunity is greatest.

In many Western countries, dating may or may not lead to romance and marriage. To some, convictions of abstaining from sex before marriage appear unimportant and thus, dating may evolve into brief affairs or trial marriages.

## ❤ Engagement

When the couple decide to marry, the man usually gives the woman an engagement ring with a diamond or another type of stone. Traditionally, the groom asks the bride's father for his daughter's hand in marriage. The man generally seeks the parent's approval prior to ring's purchase, but not always. When the couple do not receive parental permission, they often resort to eloping by having a civil ceremony before a judge or magistrate. Otherwise, they may be married in a wedding chapel, resembling a traditional atmosphere, with a nonreligious officiator who specializes in weddings presiding. When the couple's marriage is sanctioned by their parents, an engagement party with friends and relatives takes place usually at the bride's home to celebrate the announcement.

## ❤ Pre-wedding customs

Immediate families, especially those on the bride's side who generally pay for the wedding, become involved in planning the date of ceremony, the guest list, and the actual wedding itself. Female friends of the bride hold a shower for her at a friend's or relative's home or at her residence, where they bring household gifts. Showers are sometimes planned as a surprise party for the bride. Usually, wedding gifts are of more value than the shower gifts. For the male, a bachelor party with his male friends is usually held the night before the wedding.

## ❤ Other pre-wedding customs

Prior to the wedding, invitations printed with names, dates, and location of the wedding are sent to friends and relatives. A smaller response card is enclosed with a self-addressed stamped envelope for a reply. Sometimes the bride utilizes the services of a bridal gifts registry at a department store to let family and friends know what kinds of household gifts she and the groom desire. The registry keeps track of how many pieces of silver or china are needed and the record is usually computerized.

## ❤ The wedding

Western-style wedding ceremonies usually are held in churches and synagogues, although other locations include hotels, banquet halls, private clubs, public sites, homes (where a staircase can be used for the bride's entrance), outdoors, or on ships. Music is selected for both the wedding ceremony and for the celebration afterward.

Western weddings can be either formal, semiformal or informal. The bride selects the color and style of the bridesmaid's and matron of honor's dresses or gowns. During a formal wedding, the bride most often wears a white gown, and the groom and his best man and ushers wear rented tuxedos or black suits. Less formal weddings only require the men to wear navy, gray, or ivory suits, while the bride might wear a suit or a dress. During the wedding, the bride and her attendants hold floral bouquets. Flowers are also used to decorate the altar, the pews of the church, and as centerpieces for the banquet table. Most families of the bride will have a photographer taking pictures or a person taking videos to document all the events as they occur. After the church or synagogue wedding or after the reception, the newlyweds are showered with rice, symbolizing prosperity and fruitfulness.

❤ **Reception and honeymoon**

Usually a reception or formal banquet, held at a hotel ballroom, church reception room, or at a home, takes place immediately following the formal ceremony. The reception is often followed by music and dancing. Financially able families often choose a sit-down dinner. Others may have a buffet dinner using caterers to serve food and drinks. Parents who hold the wedding and reception at home are able to minimize their expenses.

At the reception, an ornately decorated wedding cake is served. *(See the Wilton wedding cakes on pages 26 and 11.* Chocolate, yellow, or white cakes are decorated with white icing. For large weddings, cakes are layered or set on pillars in graduated tiers. The smallest, the top layer of the cake may be removed before serving, then frozen, and saved for the couple's first wedding anniversary. The couple formally cuts the first piece of cake and stuffs it into each other's mouths for the audience's amusement. Although traditionally the wedding expenses are born by the bride's family, the groom's family or else the bride and groom may contribute to the expenses of their wedding.

The bride throws her bouquet to the eligible maidens and the one who catches it is said to be the next to marry. While music is played, the bride dances first with her husband, then with her father.

The groom is expected to pay for the honeymoon, a vacation trip often taken by the newlyweds. Once the wedding ceremony and festivities are over, the couple leave in their decorated car or limousine for their honeymoon. In some places, the bride and groom are transported by horse and carriage before and after wedding festivities. Of course, western-style wedding customs may vary according to the couple's or immediate families' desires, traditions from the regions from which they come, and altered by unexpected amusing or catastrophic events. Some couple renew their vows later in life.

**References: Martin King White's article** *Choosing Mates —The American Way, I Do: A Guide to Creating Your Own Unique Wedding Ceremony* **by Sydney Barbara Metric**

# Interfaith Religious Ceremonies

Interracial and interreligious marriages are increasing. Such marriages encourage creative personalized weddings in which traditions and prayers may be modified and adapted to please the couple, family, or clergy. Some parts of the traditional wedding service may be omitted altogether. The innovative bride and groom may write or edit the service and include personally meaningful selections. Hymns that are familiar to the religions of both may be included, as well as scriptures from both participants' holy books. When the bride and groom are Christian and Jewish, sometimes the clergy of both denominations may be asked by the family to officiate. However, orthodox clergy from many faiths refuse to marry people who are not of their religion.

# Other Wedding Ceremonies

Couples may choose to wed at civil ceremonies held in state offices where a state official or a Justice of the Peace officiates. Such wedding ceremonies may be brief and nonreligious in order to include all people who wish to marry under such circumstances.

Couples who elect to marry this way may be adventurous and decide to marry at the spur of the moment, those who wish to elope because they do not have parental approval, and those who want to save money because of the high cost of a wedding and reception.

Some couples choose to be wed at a Unitarian Church or other interdenominational church where couples are free to change the text of their ceremonies according to their beliefs.

# Religious Science

**Thanks to Reverend Michele and Lonnie Whittington and toReverend Peggy Conger**

Religious Science recognizes that there is one great Power which is called God and that we are all unified with God. God is a loving and forgiving God and is not to be feared. Individuals are expressions of God, created in God's image. Followers of Religious Science believe our lives are ruled through the *Law of Attraction* which is - *Whatever we hold in consciousness, that is what we think, feel, and believe, we are attracting into our lives at any given time. We therefore can change our lives by changing our thinking.*

Religious Science weddings are similar to traditional Christian church weddings, except that they include more about the individual's need to be strong to make a strong marriage and that each support the other's unfolding development. This idea is usually demonstrated by quoting Kahlil Gibran in *The Prophet*. *(See page 38.)* Followers do not use the word "obey" in their ceremonies. The majority of Religious Science weddings are double-ring ceremonies.

*The Wedding of Michele and Lonnie Whittington*

## Religious Science Wedding

**Courtesy of Michele Whittington,**
**Minister of Creative Living Fellowship in Phoenix, Arizona**

❤ **Opening words by the minister.** *We have come together here today to honor the desire of _____and _____to commit themselves to a long-lasting partnership within a marriage. To this moment, they bring the dreams which bind them together; they bring the fullness of their hearts to share with each other; and they bring that particular personality and spirit which is uniquely their own and out of which will grow the reality of their life together . . .*

❤ **Giving away the bride.** (Optional) *Who presents this woman to be married to his man?* The father of the bride says, *Her mother and I do,* then is seated.

❤ **Minister's message.** . . . *The marriage of two people is the closest of all earthly relationships — an event to be entered into thoughtfully, reverently, and with a full understanding of its sacred nature. I know you enter into it with love and respect. Love is the strongest and the most powerful emotion in the world. Loving someone means that you want to be with that one person more than any other. Love is wanting to see that person happy and helping him or her to grow emotionally, mentally and spiritually. But most of all, love is allowing each other the freedom to grow and express your individual personalities and accepting and encouraging this growth without jealousy or envy. . . You must each allow the other the freedom to grow into that divine potential which makes each expression of God an individual one. . . .* The optional passage from *The Prophet* by Kahlil Gibran may be included here. *(See page 38.)* *There is no human institution more sacred than the one you are forming now, as husband and wife. . . . A sharing of not just the material things, but also sharing comfort in times of need; joy in times of happiness and empathy at all times. . .*

❤ **Vows.** Minister says, *Now, will you please join right hands* and the vows are accomplished according to a standard western-style Christian weddings in this chapter.

❤ **Advisory**. . . . *First, love each other with an all-encompassing spectrum of love. Next, have a nurturing*

# Religious Science Wedding

*concern for each other's happiness and well-being. Be mindful of each other's needs, making a true effort to find out what those needs are and then doing your best to satisfy them. Understand the need for solitude and honor each other's need for it. Understand and make provisions for each other's humanness with both its strengths and weaknesses.*

*And finally, and of greatest importance, open yourselves up to the realization that you are each an individual expression of God, created in God's image and likeness. Open yourselves to the Divinity that is within you and realize that the infinite Creator wants to express Itself through you. Know that there is no limit to the Good which God has for you if you will but open yourselves to receive it through right thinking. As the Master Teacher Jesus said, "It is done unto you as you believe." Believe in God's love, believe in God's guidance, believe in God's grace in your lives and in your marriage..*

♥ **Ring ceremony.** The ring ceremony is similar to that of a Protestant wedding.( A song or special music is inserted here, if that is to be part of the ceremony. )

♥ **Candle Lighting Ceremony.** (Optional) The minister says, *Behind me are three candles — two are lighted and one is left to be lighted. Because of the universal force of Love, your paths have crossed and now, together, you will each take a lighted candle which represents your former individual pathways and you will light the central candle symbolizing the Power of that Universal Love which expresses through you individually and as a partnership. In blowing out your individual candles, you symbolize your willingness to be committed to this new experience of walking through life together.*

♥ **Option A.** *Corinthians I, 3.4* of the *New Testament.* See page 8.

♥ **Option B.** *. . . Infinite, Father/Mother/God, we know your blessings are bestowed on_____ and _____ here today as they begin their walk through life together. We affirm and accept that their pathway of happiness unfolds in harmony, good health, material abundance and satisfying self expression. We know that their home, wherever they choose to make it, will radiate such a consciousness of love and harmony that all who cross their threshold will be uplifted and encouraged for having known them. Today, we recognize the presence of Universal Love and we accept for_____ and _____the commitment and love to honor and cherish the vows they have made here today; therefore, through the word that I now speak, we believe that they live in the midst of love, in peace, good health, and security now and forever more. Amen!*
*Inasmuch as _____ (groom ) and _____ (bride ) have consented together in the vows of marriage before God and these witnesses, it is my very real pleasure and privilege to pronounce that you are husband and wife, according to the laws of the State of Arizona and in harmony with the authority vested in me as a Minister. Amen. You may seal your bond with a kiss.*

♥ **Pronouncement by the minister.** *Mr. and Mrs. _____, to the audience, assuming bride takes groom's* last name. If not, minister introduces_____ and _____as husband and wife.

♥ **Passage by Kahlil Gabron.** *Love one another, but make not a bond of love: Let it rather be a moving sea between the shores of your souls. Fill each other's cup but drink not from one cup Give one another of your bread but eat not from the same loaf. Sing and dance together and be joyous, but let each one of you be alone, Even as the strings of a lute are alone though they quiver with the same music. Give your hearts, but not into each other's keeping. For only the hand of Life can contain your hearts. And stand together yet not too near together: For the pillars of the temple stand apart, And the oak tree and the cypress grow not in each other's shadow.*

**Reference: © 1923. *The Prophet* by Kahlil Gibran, Alfred A Knopf, Incorporated, Publisher.**
**Permission granted by Random House, Inc.**

# African Countries

The Islamic religion is dominant in Northern Africa (Sahara region) and Somalia as the result of former colonization by Muslims from Mideastern countries. Yet, both ethnic religions and Christianity from British colonization are prevalent in the southern two thirds of Africa, including the island of Madagascar. Therefore, Christian weddings are prevalent in some parts of Africa. Overall, marriage throughout Africa is looked on as a God-commanded sacred obligation. In Africa's basic ethnic religion, marriage is a meeting place for those who are departed, the living, and those who are yet to come. All who are able are expected to get married. Since there are over 1,000 African tribes, marriage customs usually differ from tribe to tribe.

## ❤ African marriages, a family affair

Historically, African marriages are a union of two family lineages. Family relationships are so important that when a couple marries, the two families are married to each other. Many marriages are still arranged by a parent, relatives, or go-betweens who are appointed by families to negotiate terms between both sides. In some regions where tribal traditions still exist, parents or relatives choose spouses for their children, sometimes prior to the child's birth. For the most part, the uniting of a couple also requires the positive affirmation of the bride or groom.

To take a bride, traditionally the groom and/or his family pay a negotiated brideprice to the bride's family. The brideprice in terms of goods and/or services for the bride's family is settled between the two families. Post-marital residence may be either at the husband's or wife's village, depending on tribal patterns. If the wife turns out to be a poor worker or barren, the husband can end the marriage.

For people who leave the rural areas for the cities,

social patterns have changed. There nuclear families, having only the father, mother, and child within the household, have replaced the extended family. Because of such changes in lifestyle and increasing educational opportunities, legislation in the Congo, Gambon, Cameroon, Mali and Zaire gives individuals the power to choose their mates, though those under 21 years of age must have parental consent.

## ❤ Initiation and preparation for marriage

Traditional practices for becoming an adult, which include a circumcision for the boy and clitoridectomy for the girl, are still practiced yearly or biannually in many regions of Africa. Female circumcision before the age of 20 continues in countries such as Togo, Tanzania, and Kenya. If a person has not gone through this part of their initiation, he or she is considered a child, no matter what the age might be. Because the young girl is given status after a clitoridectomy, she feels proud once the painful procedure is done. This initiation is a gateway to marriage.

The night before the circumcision or clitoridectomy is done, people enjoy a drinking celebration. It is a time when the families bring gifts. In preparation for the girl's clitoridectomy, the hair from the young girl's head is sheared off and she is painted with red ochre by the other females. The following day she is held down on the ground while a woman circumcises her with a knife or razor blade. The blood she sheds during the initiation binds the girl to her people and to her departed ancestors and represents the flow of life. If the girl does not live, the parents think she is meant to die.

**Reference: May 2, 1996 United States televised *Nightline* show with Ted Koppel.**

39

# African Indigenous Religion

Indigenous African religious beliefs encompass the existence of the following:

- God.
- Life of the people.
- Remembering and respecting their ancestors whose features can be reborn within the family.
- Spirits that explain the mysteries of the universe.
- Magic.

Man is the center of the universe since he is the beneficiary and user, but the Creator, God, ruler of the universe, sustains and controls the universe and is everywhere. Some think of God as the Father and give him human attributes. Those subscribing to the African religion believe that God is good, merciful, and holy. The name and description of God changes from country to country.

The African religion involves praying, giving offerings to God at sacred places, and performing ceremonial rites. Places, including shrines, hills, rivers, and other natural locations, are considered sacred, and are, therefore, used for religious purposes. While performing ceremonial rites, they use objects, such as masks and charms, each having meaningful connotations. These objects are sometimes given spiritial attributes and character of human beings. Music, dance, and singing are expressions at all ceremonies. Musical instruments used to play rhythmic music are drums, gourd rattles, gourds with beads woven over the exterior, flutes, string instruments, and trumpets.

The goal is for people to live in harmony with nature by living a harmonious existence with the universe. In that way, people abide by the precepts of natural, moral, and mystical order.

As far as magic is concerned, they believe that there is a universal force which can be secured by certain people to be used for good or evil towards others. Sickness, misfortune, or wrong doing are caused by magic and witchcraft. Such misfortune may be breached by proper conduct. Evil spirits, some caused by the newly dead, must be chased away.

The indigenous African religion has no sacred scriptures in a bible, but instead has a variety of wise sayings, proverbs, and legends passed from generation to generation. Their values of morality are ---

- Honesty.
- Love.
- Justice.

Responsibilities of an individual and his community are carried out for each generation by leaders: tribal elders, priests, medicine men and those who help maintain the religious way of life.

Rituals and ceremonies celebrate important occasions, like circumcision and ceremonies initiating children into adulthood and marriage. Announcing the marriage and seeking guidance and blessings from ancestors is an integral part of the marriage process.

Marriage and childbearing in Africa are looked on as natural God-commanded sacred obligations for the entire population.

**Reference:** *Introduction to African Religion* **by John S. Mbiti.**

*(Continued from page 48)*
Initiation also means that the girl is prepared for marriage by entering a period of seclusion. She is taught about her history, culture, and the beliefs of her people, and is mainly provided with instruction on raising a family. Historically, no one is permitted to be married without going through initiation rites.

### ❤ Polygamy vs monogamy

Polygamy has always permeated Africa within indigenous populations as well as with the Islamic people who are permitted to have up to four wives at one time. A Muslim man could always inherit his deceased brother's wife or make arrangements to have the wives of impotent or absent husbands. Historically, such arrangements were well accepted since being wed and having children were of such prime importance that no one should be left out. Furthermore, the rich or royalty, who make political ties with other influential families, would most often have many wives to increase their power and advance their lifestyles.

The increase in the number of monogamous marriages is the result of post-colonial Christian influence and the institution of the Western nuclear family caused by changing economies and urbanization. Even where monogamy is morally and legally acceptable, the alternative to polygamy with some Sub-Saharan men is to have concubines or outside wives. The polygamous patterns are so ingrained in some African cultures that present marriage patterns do not always follow the predicted road toward the Western prototype. While polygamy is decreasing, the newer practice of keeping outside wives exists. Not having enough means to support more than one wife is a major reason that polygamy has decreased.

Despite the cultural tradition of polygamy, educated women in most urban areas of Islamic countries long for, and often demand, monogamy. An educated woman is most likely to resist polygamy and demand to be the only wife her husband will have; therefore, among younger men and women with more education, plural marriages are declining. At the same time, older economically successful men still practice polygamy.

Although Muslim men are permitted to have as many as four wives, some African countries have banned polygamy altogether in favor of monogamy. The exceptions are those nations whose state religion is Islam.

African traditions are in constant change. As a result, tension exists between those who desire traditional polygamy and those influenced by Christianity. Western monogamy continues to change the peoples' destiny, because the elite, held as ideally successful, often adopt the Christian marriage ceremony and a family life similar to that of the Western world.

❤ **Selecting a spouse**

Basically, traditional African people acquire spouses through arrangements and negotiations by the parents or relatives. Young people may choose marital partners themselves and then seek permission to marry. Young people meet their future spouses at dances, at school or work, or in their own neighborhoods. No matter how the selection of a mate occurs, families and relatives exchange visits and presents. Once the rela-

tionship is serious, the girl's parents usually request certain marriage gifts, including a negotiated brideprice from her future spouse.

Changes from tradition occur more in cities than in rural areas, but in some nations the rural areas are much more extensive and include more people. Those who reside in the countryside tend to live in extended families and are more likely to retain more traditional customs. Those who move to the cities live in Western-style nuclear families away from the family group; therefore, obligations of city people toward their extended family group decrease. Being away from family supports independent thought and the concept of romantic love as a motive for marriage.

❤ **Traditional African marriages**

Historically, in small villages people announced the news of future marriages by word of mouth. The announcer might shake a large hardshelled gourd rattle as she goes from house to house. Now couples often invite guests by sending friends to deliver printed scrolls tied with raffia.

African marriages possessing an indigenous tribal flavor often have a series of steps, a process which takes a lengthy time to complete. The phases involve visits between families, the negotiation and payment of a brideprice, then a progression from engagement to marriage. That period may or may not include sexual intimacy. Some tribes value female virginity prior to marriage while in other tribes, cohabitation and sexual relations occur prior to the completion of marriage. As for the latter, only after the couple's engagement, the granting of sexual rights, and the beginning of cohabitation, does their final union with a ceremony occur. If any one of the phases does not work out, the marriage does not take place.

The first few years of marriage are often a trial period. It is considered complete once the brideprice or service by the groom is totally paid or else when children are born. A wait of two years may occur between having sexual relations and the giving of the final ceremonial drinks or kola which fully legalizes the marriage. In Africa, various drinks, such as liquor, gin, or beer, are associated with all of the various stages of ethnic marriages.

Even though the elite find the imported civil and Christian religious marriage with a prestigious ceremony more legitimate than their former marriage customs, many marriages retain an indigenous flavor along with their Christian rites.

**References:** *Nuptiality in Sub-Saharan Africa* by Bledsoe and Pison, *Polygamy and Economy in Sub-Saharan Africa* by Mabare Ngom for the *Cuadernos-de-Realidades-Sociales* in 1991, and Melanet on the WWW.

# Algeria

Islam, Algeria's official religion, traditionally permits a man to have up to four wives. Marriages are a family affair arranged by the couple's parents with the aid of a matchmaker or personal contacts. When parents on both sides approve of their selection, a negotiated civil contract is signed by representatives of the bride and bridegroom.

Because the family's honor is at stake, female virginity is vital prior to marriage. Concern for women's purity limits female activities so much that the sexes do not mingle socially. Girls are punished if their indiscretion is discovered. Young men and women are aware of marriages based on romantic love, but they rarely have opportunities to meet.

The legal marriage age for males is twenty-one; it is eighteen for females. After marriage, the bride usually goes to the house or region where the bridegroom's parents and relatives reside. The trend in urban areas and among the better educated is towards a nuclear family in which the married couple and their unmarried children live apart from their extended family

Personal ads from single people looking for spouses have been published in Algeria since 1989. Though personal ads remain taboo in most of the Muslim Arab world, such ads have survived censorship in Algeria. These advertisements are placed by a range of individuals from the illiterate to the highly educated. The advertisements are considered beneficial for people who have difficulty finding someone, especially for divorced men and women, handicapped individuals, and the elderly.

*(See Islamic religion and weddings in Chapter 1.)*

**References:** *Algeria: A Country Study, New York Times* **article "Looking for Love (Shh!) in ads"
by Chris Hedges.**

# Angola

Angola has a 68 percent Catholic population due to Portuguese colonization. This country also has many native tribes.

*Eumbo* (or *Ambo*) people. Traditionally, the highest form of *Eumbo* matrimonial life is polygamy. Men who practice monogamy are considered inferior. Although nobility is permitted to rotate regularly among wives at will, the average husband is obliged to visit his wives equally. As a general rule, the husband visits each wife's hut or she comes to his abode once every four nights.

When a boy makes a marriage proposal to a girl, she may not accept at first, although she may admit to villagers that she is pleased with his proposal. If she is interested, the suitor then meets with the girl's brothers and sisters to discusses the prospect of marriage. The girl's siblings thereby become mediators between the suitor and the girl's mother, for the suitor does not become directly involved with the girl's parents.

When the girl's mother eventually approves of the suitor, he and his family will work in the mother's fields. Traditionally, this is the way his family displays their eagerness to have the daughter as his wife. His family may also bring firewood, construct a grain bin, and weave a mat for the future mother-in-law. The suitor's mother even may carry a basket, beads, and money to his future in-laws to reinforce that her son desires to marry their daughter.

While the suitor works for the girl's mother in the fields, the mother and her daughter prepare porridge and fowl for the suitor's family. First, the suitor gives the girl a string of beads, then he partakes of a meal with his future in-laws. He refuses to eat all of the porridge for fear his future in-laws would think he would rather devour the porridge than take their daughter for his wife.

The girl's mother continues to invite the suitor to dinner or sends him porridge. When the girl and her mother visit the boy's mother, they bring her a lubango basket of meal, fowl, money, and strings of beads. The wedding takes place once the suitor has the amount of goods required to be a supportive husband. Then, he selects an instructress, his paternal grandmother or his father's sister, to give the bride training to become a good wife.

Today, when the suitor is employed and does not work for the girl's parents, he sends clothing for his future bride.

# Eumbo Wedding

❤ **Presenting of gifts.** The groom gives the instructress money and/or beads to present to the bride's mother. On the evening of the wedding the instructress carries the bride on her back to the entrance of the groom's dwelling. If the instructress is unable to carry the girl, she simply takes her by the hand and they walk together to the boy's home.

❤ **Consummation.** As the groom makes the marital bed, the instructress spreads it with leaves of a negwelulu tree believed to intensify the sensual excitement. Later at night, the groom finds his bride in the hut and they have sexual relations. When the intructress knocks on the door the next day, he boastfully lets her know the culmination of marriage has taken place successfully. Afterward, the instructress relates the joyous news to the villagers.

❤ **Symbolic rituals and rites.** First, the instructress provides hot water so the couple can bathe, then she shows the bride how to wash the floor. Then the instructress hands a cigarette to the groom and to the bride to symbolize the belief that the couple will not give a lung disease to anyone to whom they give tobacco.

❤ While the instructress warms the water for the porridge, the bride holds the intructress's left hand and the bridegroom holds the bride's right hand. The purpose of this ritual is to purify the bride. The same rites are repeated when the instructress pours salt into the fowl relish.

❤ **Reception.** At the wedding festival for the villagers, the couple eat porridge together. Porridge has been prepared separately and served to the members of the community. When the meal is finished, the guests place strings of beads on their empty plates, and the bride's mother gathers them.

The son-in-law and the brides's mother are not allowed to meet until after the couple's first child is born.

**Reference:** *The Ethnography of Southwest Angola by* **Carlos Estermann.**

# Bennin

*Edo.* The *Edo* are also in Angola. Traditionally, the birth of a girl attracted the notice of the young boy's father. He would approach her parents about a marital alliance while his son was still young. The boy's father would bring wooden logs and yams to the girl's parents to pave the way for his son's marriage. The father would often make the betrothal arrangement himself to assure a future spouse for his son when he matures. As the girl approached puberty, the suitor then offered more gifts to the girl's ancestors to let them know about the impending marriage. He also made appeals to them to make certain their marriage would be fruitful and prosperous; then, he gave presents to the girl's parents.

If the girl's father, after consulting his father or brother, approved of the marriage, he notified the prospective husband of his formal betrothal date. The suitor then carried gifts of palm wine, coconut, and kola nuts to the altar of the bride's patrilineal ancestor informing him of their betrothal. In the past, the suitor worked for his future in-laws and gave them gifts of yams at periodic intervals, but today he is more likely to give his fiancee's parents money and fabric, and the marriage contact is finalized by a payment of money.

# Bennin Edo Wedding

♥ **The procession.** On the day of the wedding, the groom's side of the family and his friends dance and sing at his house. Then a procession, consisting of the bride, her brothers, sisters, and friends go to the groom's dwelling. Since her parents are saddened by the loss of their daughter, they are not present at the ceremony. Upon the shy bride's arrival, she is lifted onto the groom's lap.

♥ **Rituals and rites.** A female member of the groom's family, perhaps the senior wife, comes with a container of water with money and cowry shells inside to cleanse the bride's hands. The act of cleansing symbolizes fertility and shows that she is accepted into her new husband's family. Afterward, she must dine alone.

♥ **Reception.** The new husband provides entertainment and food for all the guests and gives them gifts, including presents for the bride's relatives to take back to his in-laws. As the bride's party returns to their homes, the husband and his party continue feasting and dancing.

♥ **Visitations.** A couple of days after this celebration, the husband visits and eats with the bride's parents to show his gratitude. After a few more days pass, the girl's father visits the groom and his family.

♥ **Consummation.** The bride's mother visits her daughter one week after the wedding. Her mother asks to see a cloth from the bridal bed where they consummated their marriage. If blood appears on the cloth, the bride is given cash for having been a virgin. The wife's mother is then treated to a meal by her son-in-law.

**44**

*Northern Edo.* The suitor gives a full or partial marriage payment, along with service to the bride's parents. The payment is later divided among close kin. Their marriage ceremony simply consists of the exchanging of gifts between families.

*Urihbob and Isoko.* Among these tribes who live on the Niger delta, marriage rituals occurred over a lengthy period of time. In the past, the boy and girl were betrothed to each other when the girl was young, and their marriage was then arranged by their parents. The betrothal process continued when families used special names for each other and exchanged presents. When the bride reached puberty, she was circumcised, and a bridal reception was held at her fiancé's home. The marriage was complete when the bride left her parental abode for her husband's home.

Today, young people usually choose their own spouses. The suitor will see his future spouse privately for a significant amount of time prior to paying a visit to her parents. Once the girl's parents meet the suitor, they will make inquiries concerning his character and his family's wealth. Her family prays to identical ancestor spirits for guidance. Later, the suitor sends his older brothers to ask the girl's father for her hand in marriage. During the first couple of visits, the father usually refuses the proposals. By the third visit, the brothers are given gin and palm wine. At that time, the girl's father finally gives the brothers an answer in the presence of his wife and members of his family. After he agrees, the marriage payment, *emu aye*, is negotiated. Then, the contract is finalized by drinking palm wine. Those witnessing the agreement make the contract binding.

The groom gives at least a partial payment to the bride's father. In addition, the bride receives a small part of the *emu aye* in gifts. Partial payment is advantageous to the groom's side in case the bride must be returned. Once the groom gives at least partial payment, the girl is his wife.

*Itsekiri.* While the couple are courting, the suitor gives gifts of gin and kola nuts to the girl and her parents for the family head to use later to invoke and receive the blessing from the ancestors. The suitor gives imported gin to the bride's parents when they are married. He presents the second unit of gin and a cash payment to her parents when the bride proves to be a virgin.

**Reference:** *Benin Kingdom* **by R.E. Bradbury and P.C. Lloyd.**

# Burinka Faso

Forty-three percent of Burinka Faso's population is Muslim and 45 percent of the entire population maintain traditional beliefs.

*Fulani.* Among the Muslim Fulani in Jelogji, marriage, or *koowga*, occurs when the representatives of the man and girl meet and agree on the amount of cattle that the groom is to present to the bride's parents. This brideprice is publicly designated and the contractual ceremony sanctioned by the Muslim religion. Often, the bride and groom have never been together before.

Many customs surrounding Fulani marriages deviate from customs in other Muslim countries. Once the young man's friends find out that his *kabbal* has taken place, they tease and insult him until he gives them a goat which they slaughter and roast. The bride may be taken on a horse immediately after the *kabbal* to the husband's village at sunset; otherwise, up to two years may pass before the *bangal* ceremonial, when the bride, along with her girlfriends, goes to the husband's home.

If his new wife was never married, the women from the man's village hold a welcome ceremony. The village women encircle her while they blow a mist of milk from their mouths. When they enter the in-law's dwelling, they find no one is present. The bride and her friends remain inside, while outside, young village women sing welcoming songs and playfully dance. The bride and her friends dance and sing spontaneously as well, but when the husband finally arrives, no one is in the hut! His bride, with her companions, have gone back to her village to hide at a friend's house or with a relative. The same evening, the husband's friends go to her village to search for the bride. The bride may escape many times before his friends can capture her.

In the end, the husband and wife do not reside together, for they do not have their own hut. In fact, on initial occasions when they have sexual relations, they hide in the bushes. The bride stays at her mother-in-law's or with her husband's brother's wife until a hut is built by the husband's family. The process of completing the house takes a year or so. At the same time, the new wife and her friends make the conjugal bed with matting supplied by the wife's mother. The wood is provided by her father.

After the hut is constructed and furnished, it is the husband who runs and hides! His friends must bring him back. The couple then reside together. As a result, all involved slowly recognize the reality of the couple's marriage.

**Reference:** *Freedom in Fulani Social Life* **by Paul Riesman.**

# Cameroon

Cameroon has a Catholic, Protestant, Muslim, and traditional African religious population.

Today, the younger generation desires the right to choose their partners based on romantic love. In fact, sometimes they are pitted against the wishes of their parents and tribal chiefs because of different philosophical views between generations.

### Traditional tribal marriage customs

*Bamenda Tikar.* After the suitor gave required marriage payments to his spouse's parents, the new husband provided repeated gifts and services to her parents throughout his wife's life. As the brideprice, he gave his wife's family goats, farm implements, fabric, and drums filled with oil. After 1954, he provided mostly cash payments. The richer men turned over higher payments to their in-laws.

*Tikar* girls were wed at 16 years of age. When a suitor wanted to marry, he asked the girl's father for his consent. If the father approved, the suitor, along with his friends and family, brought her father a present that week. After they met with the girl and her family, their engagement was announced. The father then decided the amount of the marriage payment and set the date of the marriage. After the wedding feast and ceremony, the new husband returned to his home. Several days later his new wife, cleansed, then covered with camwood, was given to him by her mother and close female relatives.

*Bamum*. After the girl was betrothed at five or six years of age, she was sent to reside with her future husband. By age 12, she had the rights and responsibilities of a wedded wife. A father could give his daughter to a slave, but he would only receive a small brideprice for her by comparison to that offered by a free man. When a king gave his daughter in matrimony, the groom provided the present for the royal family. Marriage celebrations lasted for several days. If the wife died without bearing his children, her father gave her husband another daughter as a replacement.

*Bamileke*. Parents could arrange a betrothal of their children a few months after birth. A girl was usually 15 when she married. The boy married after his circumcision between the ages of 14 and 18. When the girl's parents chose a young man for their daughter, she was not forced to marry him later if she was displeased with their selection.

The suitor could also ask his future father-in-law for his approval to marry his daughter. If he was accepted, he gave goats to the girl's parents and grandparents. The girl's mother and her daughter thereafter brought him prepared food regularly and, in turn, he gave his intended bride a gift. When the brideprice was settled by her suitor and her father, the bride, her relatives, and friends went to the home of the groom's parents. They gleefully sang and danced outside the bridegroom's home. Then, the bride's escort sang the marriage song. Once they all entered the hut, everyone danced. The next day when they went to the groom's home, the bride and groom faced each other with their feet together at the doorway, and the groom's father threw water over their feet.

The girl's parents decided the date of the wedding. On the eve of the wedding, the bride, her parents, friends, and relatives went to the groom's home. When they arrived, the groom's friends then asked the bride and the brothers what they needed. They responded with silence. The bridegroom's friends informed the groom that the bride and her party were nearby. After the groom's brothers handed cash to the bride's brothers, they entered the dwelling where all partook of a feast. Later, the bride tried to leave with her relatives, but could not until her brothers received another present from the groom's relatives. A week later, the brides's mother and her friends returned carrying large food baskets of yams. These gifts of food provided by the bride's mother and her friends finalized the marriage.

*Banen*. Historically, two families exchanged brides; however, since the 1930's marriage exchanges have been illegal. Only the bridewealth payment, officially registered, remains as a remnant of the past. Formerly, the girl resided with her young husband's kin when she was still a child. Because the men were polygamous, the husband or his senior wife took responsibility for the girl. The girl's new presence in her husband's dwelling was celebrated with dancing by both sides of the family, and songs symbolizing a happy and fruitful life were sung. Consummation of their marriage took place after the girl's puberty ceremony. Today, the Banen are Christian, but the puberty ceremony may still occur.

*Bafia*. Marriage by capture (theft of a woman) used to constitute marriage. In fact, the girl's father or even her former husband, if she was married, would not try to find her and take her back. In return, however, her husband or father could capture one of the captor's wives. If the girl was not married before she was stolen, the captor was obliged to get along with her parents. Some women who were stolen from other villages could have many husbands. Marriage by capture gradually disappeared. *Bafian* marriages still involve a suitor's payment to the bride's family.

**References: Margaret Littlewood's chapter "The Bamileke" in the book *Peoples of the Central Cameroon: Tikar* by Marran McCulloch, *Bamum and Bimileke* by Margaret Litttlewood, *Banen and Bafiia* by I. Dugast, *Cameroon* by Mark W. DeLancey.**

# *Chad*

Chad's Muslim social units consist of several male generations. Their families use marriage to strengthen kinship ties among families. Unions between cousins are common. Senior males make initial contacts with other families to negotiate a marriage contract that reinforces their social status and wealth. An exchange of gifts by both families constitute the bridewealth. Today, money is given in place of cattle. After a ceremony is held in presence of a *faqih*, a Muslim religious official, delighted neighbors, relatives, and friends accompany the bride to her husband's house.

*Toubou.* In the Sudanian zone, *Toubou* marriages reflect a broad scope from temporary to traditional alliances. Even though the family influences the choice of marriage partners, parents take individual preference into account. Bride stealing, a process of pretending the brides are pirated from their families, is common. Her family is expected to respond by displaying sorrow and anger.

**Reference: Thomas Collelo's** *Chad: A Country Study.*

# Cote d'Ivoire (Ivory Coast)

Ivorians practice local religions combined with features of Christianity and Islam. Only a quarter of the people are Muslim and one eighth of the population is Christian. Because 65 percent of the people profess traditional beliefs, the population has never fully embraced any major world religion.

### ❤ Past marriage customs

As with many other African countries, the Ivorian past tribal traditions placed high significance on polygamy, a brideprice, and the collective nature of the family. Lineage elders always enforced standards of etiquette and marriage. Drinks and kola nuts were historically used to celebrate and establish a legal marriage. Today, different types of European schnapps, brandy, rum or gin serve the same function.

### ❤ Present marriage customs

In 1939, their government's Mandel Decree permitted the minimum age for marriage to be 14 and made mutual consent of both parties necessary before marriage. By 1951, the Jacquinot decree stipulated that in-law's claims to the brideprice paid to a woman's family were invalid. This decree also specified that monogamy was to be the only legal form of marriage in the Ivory Coast and that couples should not wed without parental consent. In order for a religious marriage to be legal, the couple must show proof of a prior civil marriage.

*Baoulé.* Traditionally, parents arranged marriages, often at birth. Three out of four *Baoulé* tribes circumcised their girls, while others cleansed them according to traditional rites. The brideprice and traditional presents, like palm wine, offered to the bride's family were not considered as a bridal purchase. Rather, the brideprice was only given as compensation to the bride's parents for the loss of their daughter. The man also provided the bride's trousseau.

Sometimes, marriage by capture occurred. The seizure took place with the assistance of a friend or the man's first spouse. When the bride returned home with her husband, the head of the extended kin would bless her and provide counsel. After the brideprice was turned over to the bride's father, the marriage was pronounced as binding. More recently however, young people are more free to choose their spouses.

According the *Baoulé* norms, brothers cannot court the same girl and sisters cannot go after the same young men.

Currently, girls are in no rush to marry. Many couples go through a period of cohabitation before discussing marriage. Even though free unions are quite permissible, couples are teased mercilessly if they display any love for each other, even by chatting intimately, or by kissing. Many *Baoulé* insult or hurt the ones they love so the victim realizes that they are truly loved. Sucking the beloved's arm until the blood comes to the surface of the skin symbolizes great love.

*Agni.* Historically, polygamy was extremely common with *Agni* males, who were supposed to treat their spouses equally. Generally, the senior wife, chosen on the basis of family proprieties, had the power to control her husband's successive wives. Brideprices were low since they believed higher prices indicated female subjugation.

*Bete.* Two-thirds of the *Bete* male population practiced polygamy throughout the twentieth century in order to increase their status and sexual access, and to have many children. The *Bete* historically required consent of both parties, consummation, and a high brideprice.

**Reference:** *Cote d'Ivoire: A Country Study*

# Egypt

*My thanks to Prof. Abdul-Monem Al-Mashat and Ihssan Wali, Cultural Attache
at the Embassy of The Arab Republic of Egypt Cultural and Education Bureau*

Egypt's population is 94 percent Sunni Muslim, a religion which influences Egyptian traditions, customs, and the type of relationships possible between man and woman. A small percentage of Egyptian who are Coptic Christians marry in church. Since most of the people are Islamic, the following information pertains to the Muslim population:

They do not condone dating or any type of sexual interactions prior to marriage. Males and females enjoy social communication without being involved in sexual relationships. A love marriage is uncommon in their society although it does exist.

## ❤ Types of Muslim marriages

❤ **Love marriage.** A love relationship often grows out of friendship when a boy meets a girl either at school or at work. After graduation, the boy proposes to the girl's family. Most families oppose this kind of marriage, for parents believe their daughter is inexperienced and too young to choose the right husband. In the end, the parents generally approve and give their blessings to the marriage when the two are of the same social and educational status. The love marriage is not totally exclusive to urban areas.

❤ **Traditional marriage.** The traditional or prearranged marriage occurs in the city as well as in the villages. Because the prospective partner's family background, education, social status and reputation are of great concern to both families, both sides make inquiries. Relatives, friends and neighbors assist in obtaining such information. Once the young couple are introduced to each other, they may start visiting, and chatting. The bridegroom with his family visit the bride at her house or at a meeting which is often held at a country club or in the house of a friend or relative. If the boy and girl like each other, they meet in the presence of others several times to become better acquainted. The second step is the engagement period during which time preparations for the marriage occur. The groom gives the bride a wedding ring during the engagement party.

# Egyptian Marriage Customs

❤ **Wedding celebrations.** When the couple marries, the bridegroom signs the contract with the bride's father in the presence of members from each family. Since the bride sits in another room, a member of the family will come to her to obtain her approval. The signing of the contract takes place either at the bride's house or at the mosque, whichever the family prefers. All family members extend their congratulations and wishes to the bride and the bridegroom. There is generally a ceremony and a reception, usually with men and women socializing together. The size and ambiance depend on the social and economic standing of the family. Middle and upper class families celebrate weddings in the ballrooms of hotels with singing and dancing. When the wedding is at a hotel, the bride and the bridegroom walk together hand in hand to the strains of the *Wedding March* while hotel hosts, carrying torches, stand in two lines to form a path for the couple to walk through. The couple cuts the cake, which may have as many as 10 tiers; it is lowered from an opening in the ceiling. In addition, the bride and groom change their rings from their right to left hands. All kinds of meats, rice, nuts, salads, sweets and pastry are served in abundance. Like the Western-style wedding, the bride throws the bouquet to the maidens and there is dancing and music. If they are not too religious, they may have belly dancing as entertainment. Other families celebrate the wedding by having small parties at their homes.

❤ In rural areas and in families from upper Egypt, separate celebrations for men and women are commonly held. A country bride is very shy and covers her face with a veil during the traditional wedding. Sweets and tea are served. Once the couple is married, it is extremely difficult for the husband and wife to separate. Though not prohibited, divorce is highly disliked both socially and religiously. Egyptians couples adore their home and consider it their main source of status and prestige.

**Reference: Prof. Abdul-Monem Al-Mashat, Embassy of The Arab Republic of Egypt**

49

# Ethiopia

Ethiopia is almost half Muslim and 40 percent Ethiopian Orthodox. Ten percent hold traditional beliefs. Most marriages still represent the union of two families. Though the families involved decide on a suitable spouse for their son or daughter and arrange the marriage, most parents permit their daughters and sons to decide if they wish to marry the selected partner. Marriages endure well.

*Ethiopian Jews.* A minority of Jews live in Ethiopia, many of whom immigrated to Israel during this past decade.

After a Jewish boy reaches the age of 18, his parents look for a suitable girl no more than 13 years of age. The fathers on both sides handle the matchmaking and the initial contact. When successful, the boy's family gives jewels to the bride's family, who are then blessed by the *cahenat* (rabbi) and the elders. In turn, the bride's parents present the groom with cattle.

# Ethiopian Jewish Wedding

❤ **Building the wedding hut.** The wedding celebration lasts for seven days. Before the wedding ceremony both families celebrate separately for three days in their respective villages. Meanwhile, the groom and his family build a wedding hut which is blessed by the *cahenet*.

❤ **Purity ceremony.** First the *kesherah* ceremony begins with a congregation present. (The *kesherah* is a cord or cords painted white for the purity of the groom and red for the bride's virginity.) The *cahenet* places the *kesherah* at the groom's feet, then leads it upward, tying it to the groom's forehead. Afterward, the *cahanet* and the congregation honor the groom by singing and dancing.

❤ **Pre-wedding customs.** On the eve of the wedding, the bride colors her fingernails, palms, and feet with red dye. During another ceremony, sheep are slaughtered. Bearing gifts, the groom's entourage and the groom, on a horse or mule, go to the bride's village where a large hut is erected. The bride and her entourage leave her home and go to the hut where the groom and guests wait for the wedding ceremony.

❤ **Wedding ceremony.** The *cahenet* delivers the sermon and blesses the couple by saying: *Be fruitful and multiply.* After the ceremony, three witnesses, the bride and groom, respected individuals, and the officiating *cahanet* sign three copies of the marriage certificate. The father then accepts gifts from the groom. Once the bride's parents say goodbye to their daughter, the couple the leaves for the groom's village.

❤ **Purity.** If the bride proves not to be a virgin, the marriage documents are torn into shreds. The authorities give the woman a writ of divorce or she is shunned by others.

**References: *Ethiopian Jewry (Beta Israel, Falasha, Jews of Ethiopia): Halacha, Customs and Traditions*, from the World Wide Web.**

50

# Gambia

**Thanks to Abdoulie Mbye, First Secretary, Embassy of the Gambia**

Ninety percent of the population is Muslim and less than 10 percent is Christian.

The Gambian people regard marriage as a sacred institution. In the past, marriages were arranged by parents. Negotiations for traditional marriage were concluded by the parents as well. After the signing of the contract, drumming and dancing marked the occasion. A group of elderly women then accompanied the girl to the house of the man's family.

Today, the girl is required to stay in her home to help her parents with the chores until a man approaches her as a potential wife through her parents or guardian.

A young girl is not expected to seek a partner if she is under the age of 16. When girls and boys reach age 16, they can date freely and have a boyfriend or girlfriend. They must consult their parents when the courtship becomes serious, for they cannot enter into a marital contract without the knowledge of their parents.

With the encroachment of Western culture at schools and colleges, girls attend schools like their male counterparts. Even though boys and girls have more opportunities to choose a spouse, they are still expected to involve the parents when a meaningful relationship looms.

The initial step in asking for a girl's hand in marriage is for the suitor to have the community elders offer a kola nut to the girl's family. The second step is to send the brideprice. Then, a date is set for the wedding and accompanying festivities. The ceremony involves the slaughtering of cattle as a symbol of triumph and manhood.

# Ghana

*Thanks to the Embassy of Ghana*

Ghana's population is about 40 percent native culture, 38 percent Muslim, and 25 percent Christian.

### ❤ Selecting a spouse

Arrangement by the parents and introductions by friends are two types of premarital customs usually practiced by Ghanans. Parents arrange marriages for their children after first having sisters and an elder look into the background of a potential spouse. The elder or elders determine the reputation of a marriage candidate, taking into consideration his or her health, wealth, and family heritage. To express an interest in a woman, the young man's family delegation, composed of elders, parents, aunts and uncles, make an initial visit to the home of the young woman's family. They will ask about her accomplishments or failures; then, the girl's family will do a background check on the groom. When an agreement is reached, the young man's delegation visits the prospective bride's family again to solicit a union. If the communications of both families result in an engagement, female relatives enjoy the role of helping arrange the details of the couple's courtship and marriage ceremony. Marriage often takes place approximately three weeks after the agreement. In Ghana, the joining of both families is as important as the uniting of the bride and groom.

### ❤ Types of weddings

The groom pays a brideprice of money, cloth, and other goods to the bride's parents, plus additional gifts to the bride's elders. After a libation is poured for the ancestors, the bride and groom kiss. An alcoholic drink, schnapps or gin, imported from Europe, is usually served.

The second type of marriage occurs when a stranger takes a fancy to a lady. The suitor must be introduced by friends and spend time with the girl's family in order to pursue her. Thereafter, the suitor gives gifts to display love toward the woman and her family. To win permission to marry from the girl's parents, the suitor offers a beverage to the girl's parents and asks them if they would welcome him as their son-in-law. This procedures is called "knocking on the door" and is notably done in the *Asante* tribe. An *Asante* suitor sends his mother and her brother to "knock on the door" of the girl's family. If her parents accept him, the suitor brings drinks to the parents and their relatives. When the betrothal takes place, the man gives presents to her parents and relatives to show his gratitude. This presentation means that he appreciates the parents having raised a daughter of high moral character. Once he provides money for clothing, cooking supplies, and other gifts for his fiancée, the couple is married.

Christian weddings in Ghana are similar to those in Western countries. Muslim wedding customs generally adhere to those of the Islamic faith.

Typically, the groom wears a toga at the wedding. The bride wears a long skirt with a decorative white shirt top, a sash around her waist, and a head wrap.

## Ghanan Akans Marriage

❤ **Prewedding customs.** Before the date of the wedding ceremony is set, the following gifts are sent by the groom to his future wife: funds for the bridal clothing and adornments, blouses with head scarves to match, a mat, a traditional stool, and a trunk. The groom provides the bride's parents and other close relatives with presents and tokens of good will. Parents, relatives, and friends deliver money, livestock, food, jewelry and cooking fuel to the bride and groom. On the wedding day, the groom's delegates, carrying beverages and money for the girl's family, go to the bride's house to escort her to the groom's home. As the bride's family and relatives join together to watch her go, the bride's elderly relatives offer her last minute advice about marriage. To invoke the gods and souls of the departed, a libation is poured to protect the bride and grant her a peaceful, happy life with her husband. When she is about to leave her father's home, her brothers cheerfully bar the entrance to their home from the groom's delegates. Her brothers demand a "brother-in-law's knife," which is another fee permitted by custom. After the groom's brothers provide the fee, the bride, who is accompanied by maids and female attendants, is permitted to leave for her wedding at the groom's home.

# Akans Wedding

♥ **Wedding.** As the bride approaches the bridegroom's home, his family greets her with shouts such as, "Here she is! Lovely angel from a good home!" While the bride and her party are served drinks, the elderly people from the groom's family also advise the couple on how to have a successful marriage. The head of the groom's family then fills a calabash, a hardshelled gourd which is a symbol of the home, with palm wine and sets it in the center of the gathering. He blesses the couple with a prayer that evil departs, that only good come to them, and that they have children. He also prays for their long life with honor.

♥ **Celebration.** Early the next day, the bridegroom's friends and family bring rum and other drinks to the bride's parents. The people wear their best traditional attire. The *kente,* attire worn to the feast, is white. The wedding feast climaxes in the marriage ceremony. The bride, helped by her female attendants and relations, prepares delicious food: lamb, chicken, yams, vegetables, and drinks. Traditional drumming and dancing takes place until very late in the evening. Sometimes, a brass band is also invited. The newlyweds are seated on a dais, and as the guests depart, they wish the couple a successful married life by shaking their hands.

*Ashanti.* This tribe formalized their marriages with two bottles of gin or a sum of money. The head of the groom's family gave gifts to the bride's guardian. This payment, transferred before the couple lived together, gave the husband the sole sexual privilege of his wife and legal fatherhood of their children. The clothing worn at weddings was made of fabric decorated with special symbols having distinct meanings.

*Anlo Ewe.* The bride stayed away from the groom and all others, except for a few elderly women, for several months prior to marriage. After her seclusion, a huge feast was held. The bride's family formally gave the bride to the groom's parents after she was powdered, an act symbolizing her allegiance to her future spouse.

52

**References:** Harriett Cole's books *Jumping the Broom and Jumping the Broom Wedding Workbook, Nuptiality in the Sub-Saharan Africa, Ghana: The Enchantment of the World Series* by Martin Hintz.

# Kenya

The Kenyan population is about 66 percent Christian with more Protestants than Roman Catholics. Twenty percent hold indigenous beliefs, and a small percentage of people are Muslim.

♥ **Circumcision**

Historically, when boys and girls reached puberty, most tribes circumcised both sexes. Boys from ages 12 to 15 went through circumcision. Prior to being circumcised, young men and women left the village for a while, then returned as adults. While the young girls were secluded, they received instruction from older women. On the day of circumcision, girls rubbed chalk over their faces and concealed themselves by wearing robes. Boys were also secluded at which time they wore women's clothing. Later they returned as warriors with their heads shaved. The warriors then departed from their homes to reside in rough compounds with other young males their age. When they became engaged, they presented their fiancee with colored beaded necklaces.

Because circumcision for girls is potentially damaging, the government and international women's groups have tried to end the practice. Yet, many people who reside in the countryside tend to value tradition.

♥ **Polygamy**

Formerly, polygamy was thought to be beneficial since each wife separately could watch some of her husband's animal herds. Kenyans accepted polygamy until the Christians denounced the practice. Occasionally, a Kenyan man still takes more than one wife when he can afford to give each a separate dwelling. The first wife usually has enough authority that she is consulted when he chooses other wives. Presently, only wealthy men can support more than one wife.

### ❤ Choice of spouses and weddings

Sometimes, parents still arrange a marriage, and the boy's family pays the brideprice to the bride's family. In that case, the young people may or may not be consulted. When the girl approves of the selected spouse, the two fathers discuss the brideprice. The boy's family later prepares a feast at which time the bride and groom are recognized as married.

Educated women now question traditional customs of polygamy and arranged marriages, so they are less likely to accept traditional practices. Young people in Kenya today may choose their own partners. When a man finds a woman he wishes to marry, he simply enters into negotiations with her father. Today, the brideprice may be in the form of money or electrical goods, rather than a number of cattle or goats, as was the custom in the past. The groom pays the full amount when the bride's father gives his daughter to him in ceremonial dress. After the brideprice is paid, a feast commemorating the marriage is given at the groom's house.

Protestants and Catholics have Christian church weddings similar to those celebrated in Western countries. They advocate monogamy.

*Gabra Nomads.* In northern Kenya, the *Gabra* made establishing a new house a important part of their wedding rituals. Having a wife is so significant for the welfare of the man that they select a lunar date on which to transfer the bride to the groom's family and construct their home in the bride's village.

*Iteso.* Transference of the brideprice did not always precede the couple's living together. While the girl was betrothed by an agreement made by her father, the girl could be kidnapped by young men representing the bridegroom, even while negotiations for the brideprice were in progress.

Today, the girl often lives with her lover without her father's consent, and her family will try to learn her whereabouts after the fact. Upon discovering her residence, they often remain silent for a year or two until they know the relationship is serious. If the parents discover that the cohabitation is successful, marriage negotiations and settlement of the brideprice begins. The brideprice takes two forms: full payment, prior to or within a short time after cohabitation, or in small payments transferred over the duration of many years. Cash may be involved in the brideprice as well as the traditional cattle and goats.

*Pokot.* A young man may notice a girl and woo her at a dance or while she does her daily chores. When a young man decides he wants to wed, he and his male companions carry beer to the prospective bride's father. If her father keeps the beer, that means he desires to have the suitor as his son-in-law.

First, the elders investigate the groom's ancestry to learn whether or not the clan has produced males of worth. The clan's elders from both sides of the family then negotiate the amount of bridewealth, in the form of cattle, that the groom must give to the bride's father. Even though a young couple may run away together, most marriages are the result of negotiation with the bride's father. After the groom fulfills his payment obligations, the young man's family invites the entire neighborhood and holds the wedding at their homestead.

## *Kenyan Pokot Wedding*

❤ While the couple stand next to each other inside the house, the groom ties a leather wedding band around the bride's right wrist. People say prayers petitioning for blessings.

❤ Following the wedding, the village celebrates by drinking, singing, and dancing. The words of wedding songs remind the young couple about their responsibilities as husband and wife.

*Rendille.* In the desert of central Kenya, when a man wishes to marry, he has his representative deliver beads to the girl's mother. At first the girl may not know who is wooing her. Once she is aware of the young man and accepts the beads, she and the suitor are engaged to be married. A wood ornament is then placed over the beads by the bride's mother.

Prior to her marriage, the girl's earlobes are pierced and tatoos are applied to her body. The groom then gives bridewealth of male and female camels to the girl's family. He gives other camels to relatives of the bride and one is slaughtered for the wedding feast.

Before a girl marries, she dons white necklaces. After her wedding, she wears spectacular jewelry created from glass and metal. During the conclusion of the wedding ceremony, the men in the family form two parallel lines and the couple walk between them. As they do, the family holds up sticks in diagonal fashion, similar to a Western military wedding.

*Kipsigis.* The *Kipsigis* of Western Kenya impress upon a young girl that she must be a virgin prior to marriage. When a *Kipsigis* man marries, he gives three cattle and three sheep or goats to the bride's parents as bridewealth. Though the transference of bridewealth is not necessary, the gift helps cement both families. The girl's family must return the bridewealth if she is not able to produce children. If this occurs, the man can marry another woman.

Today, the man provides bridewealth in terms of money for a daughter's education. As a result, men very often cannot marry when they are young. Young women tend to marry older men who are more affluent.

The *Kipsigis* man marries as many spouses as he can afford to support. The first wife must approve before he takes on succeeding wives. Each wife then resides in her own separate home. Efforts to Christianize the *Kipsigis* are less successful than in other cultures in Africa.

*Akamba.* The *Akamba* of the Kilimanjaro region are increasingly Christian and tend to marry in church. Men are less likely to be polygamous. Before the influence of Christianity, the man presented the bride's parents with livestock. He needed his father's and his first wife's permission to take on another wife.

**References:** *Enchantment of the World: Kenya* **by R. Conrad Stein,** *Transformations of African Marriage* **by Harriet Ngubanem, Melanet Home page on the World Wide Web,** *The Heritage Library of African Peoples: Rendille:* **by Ciarunji Chesaina Swinimer, Ph.D., Ronald Parris, Ph.D., Karim Bangura, Ph.D., and Tiyambe Zeleza, Ph.D.**

# *Libya*

Libya's state religion is Islam. Parents arrange marriages with the help of social contacts or through professional matchmakers. Ideally, cousins are preferred spouses for their children. When the marriage is arranged, parents usually ask the couple if they agree to the match.

If their children select their own spouses, each family must approve of their son's or daughter's choice. Marriage thereafter unites both families once representatives make the civil contract.

The Libyan *Tuareg* nomads always permitted their young people courtship and the freedom to choose their mates. If a father forbids his daughter to marry a man she has selected, the girl can petition the court for permission when she is 21 years or older.

Today in Libya the groom's family pays a large brideprice equivalent to approximately $10,000. Because the man must wait many years to accumulate this money, men tend to be much older than the women they marry. Though Muslim men are permitted as many as four wives, most Libyan men wed only once unless the wife cannot bear a child. The ceremony, officiated by a local *imam*, and signing of the marriage contract are usually held in the bride's home.

*Bedouin.* The desert *Bedouin* believe every man must wed to produce children, for the more children he has, the more powerful his tribe will be.

**References:** *Libya: A Country Study, Libya: A Country Study, The Cultures of the World.*

# Madagascar

Grandparents may arrange the marriage when the children are young; otherwise, families arrange the marriage when their children become of age. Cousins on the father's side and other female relatives are considered as possible marriage prospects. When the boy's father asks for a sister's daughter to be wedded to his son, his desire is rarely refused because the sister would not wish to offend her brother. One impediment may be numerous claims on the same girl. Unrelated people may choose each other, cohabit, then eventually marry.

As a boy matures, he looks for a girl. Once he makes his selection, the boy's father presents the proposal to the girl's family. Because all adult relatives from the girl's family must consent, the suitor must take great effort to persuade all members. When her family accepts the proposal, an astrologer is consulted for the best date for the marriage. Occasionally, a member of a family objects, and the marriage is in jeopardy until the last minute. In that case, one last council takes place with the girl's family, the boy, and his father present. If all goes well, they enjoy a meat dinner.

## Traditional Madagascar Wedding

♥ Older wives bring their children and often nurse their babies during the wedding. The girl's father, or representatives from both sides, invoke the gods and ancestors. They announce the marriage between the bride and groom. After the groom kills a cow and presents the knife to a representative, all drink a combination of blood and water. Should the couple be first cousins, they perform a separate ritual to nullify the incest taboo. A few weeks after the marriage takes place, the bride goes to her husband's hamlet where they consummate their union. Since another gift from the husband to the girl's family solidifies the marriage even more, the husband gives a cow to his in-laws when he is sure that his bride will continue to reside with him. A minimum gift from the tribal *Bara* man to the woman's family to establish a marriage is only one cow; however, if he is able, a herd of 30 to 100 cattle is most welcomed.

**Reference:** *Gender and Social Structure of Madagascar* **by Richard Huntington.**

55

# Mauritania

The Mauritanian population is mostly Sunni Muslim. Traditionally, fathers and mothers prepared their daughters for marriage by emphasizing homemaking skills and ensuring their physical beauty. Force feeding of their preteen daughters with large quantities of food and milk was required to insure their daughters would be attractive enough to form marital alliances. Parents arranged marriages when their children were 8 to 10 years of age. An agreed brideprice was in their contractual arrangement. Those who remained unmarried as teenagers were subject to ostracism.

Now, a minority of women attend secondary schools and college and more are entering professions. Women who were from the rural interior find their childhood customs challenged by urbanization.

*Maure. Maure* males and females usually marry members of the same clan who have the same lineage. The preferred Islamic marriage pattern is to unite first cousins to insure that lineage, social level, and wealth will continue within the family. Very few *Maure* men have more than one spouse, though under Islamic law they are permitted to have as many as four wives. Serial monogamy is common, especially among the elite.

Though levirate marriages are allowed, wives whose husbands have died usually live with a son rather than marry their husband's brother.

**Reference:** *Mauritania: A Country Study.*

# Morocco

*Thanks to Embassy of the Kingdom of Morocco*

Morocco has a high Sunni Muslim population, yet is multi-cultural.

### ❤ Traditional customs

Parents arranged marriages, which were highly celebrated, lavish occasions. Since arranged marriages were traditionally the norm, the sexes did not mix socially prior to marrage. Couples could marry only after parents consulted their friends or a professional matchmaker for the best spouse for their child. The family group showed a keen interest and everyone took part.

A representative from each family signed the marriage document without the couple's presence. After the signing of the contract, the mother planned the wedding. Then the bridegroom and his family made a large monetary payment to the bride's family. A man paid extra when his bride was a virgin. A portion of the brideprice could be held to pay on demand to the wife if a divorce should occur. Should the wife fail to produce a son, a divorce could be granted or else the hus-

band might take on a second wife. The wedding celebration could last from three days to one week, depending on the wealth of the couple and their families.

### ❤ Present marriage customs

Males and females have the opportunity to meet in secondary schools and universities. Whereas most unmarried women formerly were chaperoned when they were with men, educational settings provide an avenue for them to meet without supervision. The male may now suggest to his parents his preference as to whom he wishes to marry. The bride and groom mutually consent to the negotiated civil marriage contract.

Presently, the four stages of Moroccan marriages are the engagement ceremony, the signing of the marriage contract, separate celebrations for men and women, and the bride's departure.

The bride and groom are carried separately by participants during some wedding celebrations at which both men and woman are present. The bride changes into various garments during the process. Women dance to music while men watch.

## Moroccan Wedding

❤ **Engagement ceremony.** The bride's family holds the engagement ceremony at their home where they have a small reception. There the groom-to-be, or a member of his family, asks for the woman's hand in matrimony. After receiving the consent of family and the girl, the *Fatiha* from the Koran is presented. The fiancé then offers his future bride gifts of jewelry, cloth, cookies, or flowers. During the engagement, which may last from six months to two years, the groom sends his fiancée other gifts on Muslim feast days.

❤ **Henna ceremony.** Before the signing of the marriage contract, a ritual bath and henna ceremony take place. The henna ceremony is attended by female members of the woman's family and some of her closest friends. A woman, called a *Nakasha*, draws henna designs on the hands and feet of the bride.

❤ **Marriage contract.** The bride and groom sign the marriage contract at her home in the presence of two notaries. The groom then blesses his bride with valuable gifts of jewelry, fabrics, and perfumes at a reception or banquet held to celebrate the occasion. The groom also gives his bride a dowry, and the date of the wedding ceremony is settled.

❤ **Celebration and departure of the bride.** On the wedding day, there are two separate receptions:

56

# Moroccan Wedding

one at the bride's parents' house with family, friends, and neighbors, and another at the groom's parents' home. The bride, assisted by two to four female attendants called *neggafa*, is dressed in a traditional long and brightly colored silk under-gown covered with a transparent over-gown. The over-gown has gold thread embroidery. She is garnished with jewelry and her hands and feet are decorated with henna.

❤ **Mida session.** A veil covers the bride's face. A *neggafa* leads the bride, followed by finely dressed women carrying candles, as they slowly proceed around the patio. The bride sits on a round table. The *neggafa* and women raise her up on their shoulders and sing.

❤ **Men's reception.** Meanwhile, the groom is busy with his own reception at his parent's house. It echoes with music and songs which entertain a large group of his relations, friends and neighbors. About nine or ten in the evening, the groom, accompanied by members of his family, leaves for the bride's reception. Later, he takes his bride to his parents residence where the celebration continues until morning. Their guests shower the newlyweds with dates, figs, and raisins, which symbolize fertility.

**Reference:** *Morocco: A Country Study*

# Nigeria

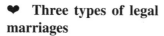

Nigeria is 50 percent Muslim and about 40 percent Christian.

❤ **Three types of legal marriages**

*1. Indigenous or traditional marriages.* They consist of the couple's public announcement, consent of the parents, and a marriage payment to the bride's parents. Traditional tribal marriages include libation rituals at the bride's home. Polygamy is permitted.

*2. Ordinance or State marriages.* The civil marriage permits a man to have one wife and is held in a registry office. Since divorce is permitted, serial monogamy may ensue.

*3. Religious marriages.* Religious marriages are mostly Muslim, which involve a marriage contract and a brideprice. The monogamous Christian marriage is preceded by romance and is supposed to last a lifetime. A certificate of registration from a government agency is obtained. Christian weddings are so expensive that they are more common among high society.

The urban Nigerian family is increasingly monogamous as the result of Christian influence and Ordinance marriages, which provide more freedom and security to the wife. Though urbanization results in the European type of monogamous family, strong former traditional customs and extended family ties are still maintained on the countryside. Because there are many more rural than urban families, traditional marriages compose at least 75 percent of marital unions. Even though marriage customs are continuously changing, the transference of the brideprice, the payment to the bride's family, is common in all types marriages.

❤ **Inside and outside wives**

*Inside wives.* In Lagos, the *"inside"* or the *"ring" wife* is regarded as an elite woman who has a Christian church or civil wedding (or both). Living in a nuclear family with her husband and children, she holds tenaciously to the Western concept of love, companionship, and fidelity. A Lagos woman usually regards personal fulfillment as having a legal marriage performed according to the rites and ceremony of a Christian wedding. Though she clings to the hope that her marriage will remain monogamous, some husbands take both inside and outside wives.

*Outside wife or co-wife* is defined as a woman with whom a man has a sexual relationship for several years without marriage rites or payment of a brideprice. He supports her financially during their relationship and her children are paternally acknowledged.

Sometimes a man marries a young woman before he becomes highly educated, then later acquires a newly educated woman with whom he may have more in common. The elite man, steeped in academia, also may make a public display by having an outside wife. These wives expect to have their own households and, as a result, the man has to provide separate residences for the *inside* and *outside* wives. The elite Nigerian woman, who desires monogamy, is the cause of some conflict, for Nigerian men wish to return to their traditional African culture of polygamy. Such men believe possessing *"outside"* wives and polygamy are simply an natural exhibition of their beliefs.

### ❤ Past vs present marriage tribal customs

In the past, young males traditionally fought each other to prove their fitness for taking on a wife. In eastern Nigeria, the bride was kept in a fattening room where she was fed well and her body oiled. There she was given instruction to prepare her for marriage and she learned certain dance styles. When she emerged, she had gained weight to display her "healthy" state for her wedding day. Now, fattening rooms are less prevalent; yet, starting at puberty, young women in the Nigerian Delta stay in fattening rooms for up to 18 months. The bride wears imported Indian fabric which covers her hips, a blouse, and a coral-beaded, gold decorated hat. Coral beads with bells and other ornaments, made into necklaces, are worn with ankle bracelets and a diagonal decoration over the chest. Some tribes have the bride hold a red parrot feather in her mouth to keep her quiet during the wedding proceedings.

Today, both girls and boys dance and flirt in the marketplace. Boys dance and sing songs expounding the charms of eligible girls and, in turn, the girls dance until they stop before young men they prefer. Couples, and their bridal parties, are usually adorned in blue and silver clothing at the marriage ceremony.

*Fullani.* Nomadic Muslim *Fullani* marriages are arranged at puberty. When a *Fullani* male becomes an adult, he is moved to a staffed location designated for unmarried men, where he is given cattle and some Koranic charms. His father's ambassador negotiates terms with the girl's representatives. Following their agreement, a bull is slaughtered at the girl's camp and the betrothal is celebrated by feasting at both camps. The bride moves to her husband's residence where she is sprinkled with milk, blessed with branches, and threatened with a grain pestle. The new wife spends her entire life with her mother-in-law while her husband tends to the cattle. Should her husband die, the wife often becomes his brother's wife.

*Hausa.* Even though polygamy is permitted by Muslim law, monogamy is more commonplace since the influence of Christianity. The Muslim bride and groom do not have to be present when their marriage contract is signed by family representatives. If the bride is married for the first time, a seven-day ritual takes place in which the bride is stained with henna and is secluded while taking marriage instructions.

*Ibo.* The *Ibo* believe delaying sexual relationships after puberty is against the law of nature. Before the marriage takes place, the girl's father hands his daughter a container of palm liquor. After she takes a sip, she gives the container of liquor to her groom. She indicates to all present that this man is now her husband so her father can accept the brideprice. The bride has high concentric circles created from hardened clay, charcoal, and palm oil high over her head on her wedding day. Her clothing, a cloth over her waist and another around her hips, is adorned by a waist belt of cowry shells and bells. On her legs are brass anklets.

*Yoruba.* Historically, the *Yoruba* considered virginity before marriage to be of great significance. If the girl was discovered not to be a virgin, the father could beat her and the mother was blamed for dereliction of her obligations.

A *Yoruban* man may take a wife from his own village. If his parents approve of his selection, they will assist in his efforts to attain a brideprice consisting of household equipment for the couple's home and gifts for her parents. When the groom's family takes gifts to the bride's home, a betrothal takes place. There, the groom vows to help his bride's parents in the fields.

The entire community is involved in the engagement ceremony which is held at night when all can come to watch. At that time the young man presents kola nuts to all present, along with beer. When marrying, the bridegroom gives gifts to the bride's kinsmen and elderly female relatives to display his worthy intentions towards their daughter. Harriet Cole says that during the *Yoruban* ceremony the couple *tastes honey for happiness, peppercorns for bitterness, and dried fish for nourishment.* If the man is polygamous and a good husband, he must guard his wife from nastiness of his other wives, carry on duties to his wives' relatives, give his wives gifts and provide each wife with gifts, and must visit each one in turn.

Today, the *Yoruban* wedding features colorful traditional music and dancing. If the parents are wealthy, disco dancing and a reception may be held at a hotel.

**References:** *Nuptiality in the Sub-Saharan, Cultures of the World, Nigeria,* **"Marriage and Family Systems in Nigeria" by Onigu Otite and Onigu Otite,** **Bankole Oni's References for Nigeria: "Contemporary Courtship and Marriage Practices among the Yoruba"** from the 1991 *International Journal of Sociology of the Family, Transformations of African Marriage (Wambi Wa Karanja's article), Jumping the Broom Wedding Workbook* **by Harriet Cole.**

# Rwanda

The Rwandan marriage is not only a marriage between a young man and woman, but it is the union of two families.

### ❤ Traditional customs

Families found the most suitable spouse for their adult child by consulting relatives, friends, and acquaintances.  During the period in which the investigations about a perspective spouse were made, either the girl or boy could refuse to marry; therefore, matchmakers searched for spouses in a very discrete, quiet manner.  The girl's parents considered where the boy resided, his education, his appearance, and how he composed himself while the boy's parents looked for a pretty girl who had good humor and was polite— one who was healthy and raised with good character.

Because marriage involved the uniting of both families, parents also chose spouses from families with whom they could be congenial.  Qualities both families considered were the other family's material resources, the way a future daughter or son-in-law was accustomed to living, tenderness, education, and the kinds of relationships within the family. Impotence and hatred, crimes, dishonesty, illegal acts, imprisonment and fighting within the family were negative things families wished to avoid.  They wished to discover if anyone in the family had married without family approval, if the boy or girl was lazy, and if anyone in the family had committed suicide, was selfish or unclean, and  if the candidate was polygamous, or divorced.

The boy and girl did not spend time together unless they were in the presence of others. Either the girl or boy, with adult supervision, could spend time with the other family to see if either wanted to be part of the family.  If the girl refused to marry the boy, she informed her aunts and mother. If the boy decided he did not wish to marry the girl, he informed his friends, brothers, and father.

### ❤ Present marriage customs.

Because of Western influences, some young men choose their spouses, and the girls are permitted to refuse.  Once a selection is made, the father and his family go  to the girl's home where the boy's father asks the girl to marry his son.  On that occasion, the prospective bride's family offers him beer, place mats, and sticks to show reciprocity.  The boy's family drink the beer first, then the girl's family.  If the girl accepts the proposal, her parents indicate that they expect to receive a brideprice in exchange for their daughter.  When her answer is positive, the boy's father brings beer, cows or goats as payment and makes plans for the wedding.   All applaud when the gifts are given and prenuptial traditions are met.

❤ 59

## Traditional Rwandan Wedding

❤ **Pre-wedding customs.** The girl receives gifts at her parent's home three days before the wedding.  The night prior to the wedding, the boy must have  his finger and toe nails trimmed.  During that time, his friends accompany him in order to give him the courage to marry and not dishonor his family.

The day of the wedding he wears all new clothing.  The colors vary according to the area of the country.  The bride, her Matron of Honor, her older sister, or another female family member gather together.  The Matron of Honor teaches the bride what to expect on the night of her marriage.  The bride has a light diet of milk and easily digested food, but no alcohol.  She regularly rubs butter on her body.

❤ **Wedding procession.** One woman, an aunt, is chosen to accompany the young girl to the home of the boy, but the girl's parents are not allowed to attend their daughter's wedding. A procession of relatives and friends of both sexes follows the bride and her aunt to the boy's house.

# Traditional Rwandan Wedding

❤ **Beer greeting.** When they arrive at the boy's house, his family gives them beer to drink. Later, the rest of his family arrives and all enjoy the beer.

❤ **Declaration of marriage.** The boy's father officiates at the wedding ceremony by marrying his son to the bride. He simply says to his son, *I marry you to this woman.* During the ceremony, the girl is crowned with flowers, and the groom sips *l'imbazi* from a jug and spits it on her hair.

❤ **Celebration.** When the ceremony is over, the older sister or aunt shouts with joy. Then all the young women in the room join in by screaming with happiness.

❤ **Wedding night.** The bride wears a silk tunic on her wedding night. That night a servant takes care of the young couple's needs by giving them food, tobacco, and beer. An older aunt, brother or sister is with the couple. The person in charge sees whether or not there is female blood after intercourse. If the new wife is not a virgin, the marriage can become null and void. If the female refuses to have sexual relations, the husband has the right to force her until she succumbs.

**Reference: *Rituel du Mariage Coutumier au Rwanda* by Sylvestre Ndekezi.**

# Senegal

60

About 92 percent of Senegal's population is Muslim and the rest either hold tribal beliefs or are Christian. Some Muslim men practice polygamy, which is permissible by Islamic law. Traditional Islamic families still arrange marriages, especially in rural regions. In the small villages, young couples simply reside together as long as the young men provide marriage compensation. In the country villages, civil marriages are infrequent.

In urban areas today, single people tend to choose their marriage partners, and civil or religious marriages are performed. Though young people meet spontaneously in groups or individually prior to marriage, they inform their families once they find their mate. The educated usually marry after they have completed their studies.

*Mlomp.* In the past, parents arranged marriages for their children when they were young. After a girl was selected, the boy offered a chicken to the girl's family. When he was ready for marriage, he gave the girl's parents palm wine or a pig as a marriage payment. Thereafter, the couple had a compulsory year after their harvest festival to become acquainted; then, they could wed at a church before residing together.

Presently, seasonal urban migrations to obtain employment affect Mlomp's traditional rural customs and have caused a rise in the price of marriage. Now the young people choose their spouses, but the amount of goods the couple must acquire before marriage takes several years of migrations; therefore, the time is lengthy between the marriage promise and the final marriage payment. As a result, the marriage usually does not take place until the woman is about 24 years old and the man, at least 30.

*Joola.* The Joola are monogamous.

**References: "Migration and Marriage Change: A Case Study of Mlomp, A Joola Village in Southern Senegal" by Catherine Enel, Giles Pison and Monique Lefevre and *Nuptiality in Sub-Saharan Africa*.**

# Sierra Leone

Sierra Leone is a farming country with a majority of families having indigenous beliefs. Twenty-five percent are Muslim. Sierra Leone's traditional family unit consisted of a husband, his wives, and their children. A tribal man had a right to his children only if he had made his marriage payments to his wife's family; otherwise, the children resulting from his marriage belonged to his wife's father.

*Mende.* A woman married between the ages of 14 and 16, but she could be chosen by the boy's parents when she was a baby or a young girl. If the latter was the case, her betrothal required immediate obligation for her educational training and a payment from the boy's parents. At puberty the girl had the opportunity to refuse to accept her parent's selection. If she accepted the boy, a brideprice, the *mboya,* given to the girl's parents finalized the contract. Such marriages were limited to the wealthy, mostly tribal chiefs. Chiefs could have up to 100 wives with their spouses living in separate dwellings. Polygamous marriages provided prestige for the man and symbolized affluence thereby increasing the girl's status.

Men with less assets initiated a friendship with a girl, then later lived with her. During their friendship, the man would present small gifts to the girl's parents or else he would work on their farm. However, if the *mboya* was not eventually paid, their children would be the property of the woman's family. Before the 1930's, a young man had to prove he could work, even to his own family so his father would provide the *mboya.* The amount and how it was to be paid depended on the status and wealth of the man. Once the man paid the negotiated *mboya,* a public declaration of their agreement legitimized the marriage. Their marriages were usually monogamous.

*Temine.* Marriage customs were similar to the *Mende.* The *Temine's* marriage payments to the girl's father consisted of rice, palm oil, locally made fabrics, and canes of salt. The marriage was complete when the suitor sent his sister with gifts for the girl and the girl's family, in turn, sent presents for his parents.

*Koranko.* Girls were engaged before 10 years of age. The man made gifts which he presented to the girl's parents. If her parents accepted them, this meant they agreed to the couple's betrothal. The brideprice, set by the chief, was sheep, goats, fabrics, and salt. During the several years it took to complete the payment, the groom's relatives trained the girl in their home. Should the girl refuse to marry the man at any time before the final payment, the girl's father refunded the entire accrued price.

**Reference:** *Peoples of Sierra Leone* by M. McCulloch.

61

# South Africa

**My thanks to Bhapahkamile Gongo**
**South African Embassy in the United States**

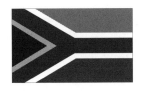

Since British settlers had a great influence on South African life, the main religion for both native Africans and Caucasians in South Africa is Christian. Only a minority of Black African people retain tribal traditional beliefs. There also are small numbers of Hindu, Muslim and Jewish minorities. Black Africans are 70 percent of the population; 20 percent of the people are white. The white community has Western dating and Christian marriage practices that are similar to those in North America and Great Britain. Men and women freely choose their marriage partners.

❤ **Black premarital customs: selecting a spouse**
Bhapahkamile Gongo explains the three types:
*1. Traditional.* The first custom demands that the girl should be a virgin before marriage. In fact, older women are customarily sent to inspect her. If the girl is a virgin, she is then qualified to wear a white dress as a sign of purity; otherwise, she must wear a colored dress. Widows must wear colored dresses as well.

When a mother and father believe their son is ready

for a wife, they recommend to their young man a daughter from another family. His parents do not look for physical beauty in this young woman. Physical attractiveness is only considered a bonus. Instead, over a period of time they look for the girl's favorable qualities. At the same time they observe and take into consideration the patterns of her mother and father. Once the boy's parents choose a young woman to be his wife, the son respects his parents' choice and does not refuse.

After the young man's parents select a girl of high character, they send an ambassador on their behalf to make a proposal to the girl's family. When the response of the girl's family is positive, long negotiations are held. The families agree on the amount of *labola*, the brideprice contribution in the form of heads of cattle, that will be paid by the boy's father to the young girl's family. The couple stays together after marriage until one dies. Almost without exception, until 1960 these traditional customs prevailed throughout South Africa. They are still carried on within rural areas and in some urban villages. Today, in certain cases, standards are relaxed, and sometimes couples marry when the woman is obviously pregnant with a child.

*2. Friend's recommendation.* The second form of selecting a wife occurred after 1960. If a friend knows a man is looking for a wife, that friend recommends someone whom he feels would be compatible. The man goes to the town where the girl resides, tells her parents the name of the friend who recommended their meeting, then asks to meet the daughter. If the young man likes the daughter, his father sends an ambassador to negotiate *labola* with the girl's parents.

*3. Freedom of choice.* The third type of mate selection, the most extreme deviation from custom, occurs when a boy and girl like and freely choose each other. They then seek parental approval. If the man's father and mother accept his choice of mate, ambassadors are sent to negotiate the *labola,* for in all cases *labola* must be paid.

## ❤ Weddings

Most of the black population in South Africa have a Christian church wedding, although couples may marry at a magistrate's office. A civil marriage is rare since it is not considered to be a true marriage unless a Minister of Religion officiated. Weddings take place on Sundays. The bride's family initiates the process by planning the date of the wedding. Then the minister makes three consecutive announcements at church on the three weeks prior to the wedding. If the groom comes from another town, he arrives in the bride's village one day before the wedding. The bride's family welcomes him by slaughtering a goat, in fact, it is considered an insult not to do so.

62

# Black South African Wedding

❤ Before the wedding ceremony, the bridegroom's family, sitting on one side of the church, is the first to sing a traditional insulting hymn to the bride's family seated on the other side of the church. The groom's and bride's sides continue to take turns singing hymns which become increasingly insulting. They contain words like, "Your son is too poor to marry our daughter." or "You treat your daughter so badly, but now she will be treated like a queen!"

❤ The Christian wedding ceremony which follows includes preaching and scriptural readings by the officiating minister. There is an exchange of vows and the pronouncement that the couple is man and wife. After the wedding ceremony is over, the two families sing meaningful songs celebrating their families union. Thus, both families become brothers and sisters to each other and are one extended family.

❤ During the reception at the bride's home, there is singing and the wedding cake is cut.

❤ Two days later, the bride goes to the groom's home where they start their life together. The good wife is one who will, under any circumstances, keep her husband's dignity intact. The couple usually come to love each other over time.

*Batswana.* Sabit Kaule, who recently wrote about Batswana's two districts in the *South African Journal of Sociology,* indicates a tendency towards later marriage, particularly among urban males. The monogamous type of marriage is most prevalent, and most wedded couples have very stable marriages. In fact, 95 percent of women are still married to their first husbands, even where sexual activity prior to marriage is widespread.

*Zulu.* When a girl has an initial romantic attachment to a boy, she presents him with a string of one-colored beads while she wears a matching one. Thereafter, love messages are sent to each other by wearing necklaces and wrist bands coded with colored beads, each color having a special meaning. Sometimes beads are sewn into a special design.

No matter whether the man is monogamous or polygynous, traditionally the boy's family gives a gift of cattle to the girl's family so that he can claim her children. After marriage, the sexes are separate so that a man has little opportunity to be with anyone other than his wife or co-wives. If a man has more than one wife, the wives are graded from the chief wife, who produces the main heir, to subordinate wives who live in different quarters. *Zulus* approve of sister marriages. In that case, the first wife shares her husband with her sister who becomes subordinate to her. The first wife enjoys her position and appreciates her sister helping her with her children and vice versa. The sister marriages secure lineages which tend to make the family stronger. If a wife dies, marrying a sister is proper.

Divorce is rarely even discussed and marriages are stable throughout their history. Chastity is highly valued. In the past, adultery was punished by death, flogging with thorny sticks, and inserting them within the woman. On the other hand, an impotent man can ask a kinsmen to have intercourse with his wife so he could be the father of her children.

An unusual form of *Zulu* marriage occurs when a rich and prominent *Zulu* woman marries another woman by presenting her with cattle. The rich woman thereby becomes the "father" of her wife's children who were fathered by a male kinsman of the rich woman. The children could thereby inherit the wealth.

Whenever a *Zulu* leader married, the heads of all subordinate families contributed marriage payments in the form of cattle for their leader's wives. *See the marriage of the present Zulu King to the Princess of Swaziland in the final chapter covering Royalty.*

**References:** *South African Journal of Sociology, African Systems of Kinship and Marriage* **and the article "Zulu Love Beads" by Celia A. Daniels in** *Faces,* **and** *The Cambridge Factfinder.*

# Sudan

Seventy percent of Sudan's population is Sunni Muslim, one-fourth of the people maintain their native religion, and five percent are Christian. Most men and women live according to Muslim customs and women live relatively secluded from men, except for a minority of young girls from elite families. In that case, the girls still remain at home and eat after the men. Usually, men entertain in their quarters and dine with their extended families.

Girls can be observed as marriage possibilities at another's wedding festivities. Unmarried girls, dancing at wedding parties with cloth draped over their arms, are on display for prospective husbands. It is at such receptions that future marriages are initiated. A potential spouse is often chosen from relatives, except for siblings. Older affluent men sometimes marry spouses from other families. They exclude strangers whose backgrounds are unknown, even if the girl is from a wealthy, successful family, is of the same religion, and has a high level of education. A bride has to maintain her chastity until marriage, for a virgin bride is considered pure and fertile.

Sedentary Arabic families who live in cities received a higher education and enter the bureaucracy or established lucrative businesses. They socialize with older established families. Even when the newly affluent men marry into the high social circle, focus on "good family" persists. They are not likely to have a spouse from southern or western Sudanese families, particularly the darker *Baqqara,* who are not considered eligible.

A tradition among northern Sudanese that still has an enormous impact on social and sexual relationships is the *Zar Cult,* which practices female circumcision. One Arab *Zar Cult* resides in Northern Sudan near the capital of Khartoum.

*Zar Cults.* A *Zar* is a ceremonial event presided over by female practitioners. Its purpose is to quiet evil spirits and to cleanse women of sicknesses produced by demons. The ceremony of female circumcision includes cutting out the external genitalia and/or sewing the vagina shut. At the *Zar,* women free the young girl possessed by demons. It is also a grand social event when women can enjoy talking with each other.

Girls are circumcised between the ages of five and 10 to purify their bodies. Those who are not purified cannot be married, but those who do, not only advance their position, but are thought to give birth to sons. Though girls eagerly look forward to their wedding day, they do so with some trepidation since they are also fearful of having sexual relations with their husbands. Because their circumcision causes painful sexual relations, it can take a couple of years for the man to penetrate. Many married women find relations so painful that they avoid sex unless they wish to have children. Women had more freedom in the southern Sudanese culture than that of the north, for female circumcision was not practiced and no *Zar Cults* existed.

The Sudanese *Azande, Fur,* and *Otoro* have similar marital customs. Their marriages combine both families, and the girls and boys involved are usually consulted.

*Azande.* The *Azande* group live in widely scattered homesteads throughout Sudan. Historically, marriages were contracted when the bridegroom presented a gift of spears to the bride's family. This initiated by a series of events during which families transferred goods.

While commoners did not marry within their own families, nobles kept their lineage and wealth within their extended family by marrying their own kinswomen, especially their first cousins. To gain wealth, the nobility practiced polygamy. Girls married young, their marriages sometimes arranged by their parents after birth. The male received full status once he was married. Though divorce is now common, it was always frowned upon because of its destructive force on the entire family.

*Fur* and *Otoro.* Both groups were also polygamous and practiced cousin marriages. Widows customarily married the deceased husband's brother. The groom and his family gave bridewealth payments to the bride's parents and their kinsmen.

*Humr Baqqarah* contracted marriages that united cousins; however, if the first marriage ended with divorce, future spouses could be freely selected.

# *Northern Sudanese Nile Wedding*

*Years ago, the wedding took one week to complete, but now since many are employed outside their villages, there is less time to accomplish the nuptials. Present wedding festivities usually last for three days. The bride's and groom's preparations and numerous wedding festivities are still held separately.*

❤ **Selection of the bride.** When a young man wants to marry, he consults his mother who knows many female members of the family. She tries to seek a bride who is morally beyond reproach, a future spouse with whom she can have a good relationship. Once she makes the choice, the groom selects a spokesman to negotiate a contract with the bride's parents.

❤ **Marriage contract and gift exchanges.** The marriage agreement involves the groom's payment of the *mahr,* or brideprice, to the bride's parents. After both sides agree on the amount and they sign a marriage contract with or without the bride's permission, the wedding takes place within a month or less after the agreement. Prior to the wedding, the groom gives the bride's mother great quantities of food for the wed-

64

# Northern Sudanese Nile Wedding

ding supper. He also provides the *mahr*: clothing, gold jewelry, and perfume for the bride and her family. Giving *mahr* demonstrates that he is capable of supporting a family. Included with the *mahr* is a red and gold shawl for the bride to wear on her wedding day. Bridal virginity and fertility are considered as mutual exchanges for his gifts.

❤ **Wedding preparations of the groom.** The night before the wedding is henna night, a ceremony held with the groom and his kin to protect the groom from harm. After dinner, the groom sits while wedding incense fills the room and an elderly kinswoman stains his hands and feet with henna. He is adorned with a red tassel bracelet and beads he received at the time of his circumcision. Aromatic oils with powdered sandalwood and fenugreek are placed on his head. A gold crescent is tied around his head with a scarf. The groom is sprayed with cologne. The groom's father accepts monetary gifts from the male guests.

❤ **Wedding preparations for the bride.** At her household celebration, the bride is not permitted to dance with her parents and sisters. Instead, she hides in another home in a secret location until the next evening. Closer to the wedding, women artists apply henna into designs on her hands and feet. Women braid her hair and massage her skin with paste and oils. She wears a charm (first dipped in milk) which she had worn at her circumcision which is supposed to prevent her from excessive loss of blood when her marriage is consummated. (Charms worn by the couple are initially dipped in a mixture of sprouted grain to make their union pure and fruitful.)

❤ **Day 1.** The next evening at dusk, festivities start at the groom's home where friends, relatives, and unmarried girls, in their most elegant clothing, gather to form a procession. Accompanied by beating drums, they go to the bride's home. When they arrive, the bride's family pretends to keep the groom and his party from entering. After gaining admittance, males and females separate and enjoy a lamb dinner. After eating, the band plays while female relatives of all ages honor the groom by performing a special dance.

While they dance, the groom finds his hidden bride waiting in the bridal chamber on a wedding mat. There the groom pulls threads from one of her garments and tosses them later to friends so that they might be married soon. When the groom returns to the gathering, he is greeted by attendants and the marriage is complete. Dancing occurs until the wee hours of the morning. After all are exhausted, the bride makes an entrance in her beautiful Egyptian dress, red Saudi Arabian wedding dress, indigenous outfit, or rented Western-style wedding white gown and veil. Even though she wears Western makeup and nail polish, she wears traditional jewelry, including a gold chain from her nostril to her ear.

❤ **Bridal wedding dance and unveiling.** After their marriage, the bride must wear clothing her groom gives her and thus, has to give away her maiden clothing. Those who receive the clothes are considered the next to be married. The bride wears clothing given to her by the groom for the first time while performing the wedding dance. The girls sing as the barefoot bride, with her eyelids shut, does stylized movements to each song. Then the bride is unveiled by the groom as she continues dancing. The groom spends the wedding night at the bride's home, though the couple stay in separate quarters.

❤ **Day 2.** The next morning festivities begin at the bride's home where her family serves a late breakfast. The bride's friends sing and dance only in the presence of other women. The bride, in a white dress but no veil, can now join in the female activities. Later, she goes to the bridal chamber with two female relatives and sits on the bridal mat where she receives female well-wishers. Later, the men congratulate her. When-

# Northern Sudanese Nile Wedding

ever the guests request it, the bride must repeat the bridal dance. Before the sun sets, the village young people and the groom walk along the Nile River. After the young guests wash the groom's face and arms with water from the Nile, the other men do the same. The returning groom steps into the blood of a sacrificed ram as he enters the bride's house for a dinner and a final evening of dancing.

❤ **Consummation of the marriage.** That night he finds his bride waiting on the mat in the chamber, and gives money to her. The bride struggles to show that she cannot be taken easily, and then they consummate their marriage.

❤ **Finale.** Dancing may continue for several evenings. The groom soon slaughters a ram for the musicians and women who gave the bride dance instruction. Sometimes, the newlyweds go on a honeymoon trip. A newly married woman does not assume household duties for 40 days.

**References:** *Wombs and Alien Spirits: Women, Men and the Zar Cult in Northern Sudan, and the* 1994 *Encyclopaedia Britannica.*

# Swaziland

*Swazi.* Wives and children are always considered the greatest asset to Swazi men and, as a result, the traditional ambition of all tribesmen is to accumulate as much wealth as possible in order to take many wives. The Swazis believe that it is the man's nature to be polygamous and woman's temperament is to be contented with children.

Their wealthy king is in a position to take more spouses than others, and one was known to have more than 40 wives. *(See the royal wedding of the former Swazi king's daughter to the present King of the Zulu tribe in South Africa on page 247.)*

Traditionally, the woman was a man's legal wife when the groom gave cattle to the bride's parents. This payment, called the *ukulobola,* gave the husband rights over the children. If the man was not married to a woman in a recognized marriage ceremony, the children would belong to the mother's kin. Although the wife retained her own clan name, she left her family to live in her husband's homestead which included land and dwellings. If a man had many wives, the homestead was divided into smaller living quarters for the wives and their children. Each wife in her own dwelling had a storage area and kitchen encircled by a tall reed fence. If the man's parents were still living, they resided nearby.

Today, although civil marriages are on the increase, most marriages recognize tradition with the payment of a brideprice. Polygamy is still common. A recent study *Women, Children, and Marriage in Swaziland* by Marge Russell reveals that marriage rites have changed so that the bride is no longer anointed with red ochre and the payment of the brideprice is increasingly disregarded.

**References:** *Marriage and Conjugal Roles in Swaziland: Persistence and Change* by Gary P. Ferraro in the *International Journal of Sociology of the Family*, *"Women, Children, and Marriage in Swaziland"* by Marge Russell in the International Journal of Sociology of the Family, *African Systems of Kinship and Marriage* by R. Brown and D. Ford.

# Tanzania

Almost half of the Tanzanians are Christian, 30 percent are Muslim, and the remaining population maintain indigenous beliefs.

Presently, societal changes are occurring in Tanzania. Young people no longer rely on parents and relatives to select mates; now they marry partners of their own choosing. Because of the influence of Christianity, the country is heading towards monogamy, although polygamy is still part of the Tanzanian scene. Since polygamous and monogamous marriages exist, the Marriage Act (1971) entitles all people, no matter what their religion, to choose which type of marriage they desire. Even among the Muslims, who are traditionally accustomed to polygamy, the legislation requires that the husband, who desires another wife, obtain permission from his first wife. The impact of the 1971 law is limited because many women lack knowledge of their new rights and the law is not strictly enforced.

The minimum age for legal marriage in Tanzania is 15 for the girls and 18 for boys. The boy no longer has to provide bridewealth (a brideprice) in order to marry. If a woman cohabits with a man for two years, she acquires the same legal rights as a wife.

Today, traditional bridewealth, the price for the bride in money or heads of cattle still exists. In some cases, bridewealth is used by young women's families to obtain a fortune. On the other hand, women, especially from rural areas, believe that bridewealth is needed to show their own worth and to gain respect.

### ❤ Marriage of a wealthy woman to a young girl

Among the Northern *Mara,* an elderly rich woman can betroth and marry a young girl who comes to live with her. This woman arranges for a male relative to live with the young woman and they beget children for the elderly woman. The young woman is thereby legally considered married to the elderly woman and the children born are to be considered the elderly woman's heirs to her fortune.

### ❤ Other tribal customs

*Wazanki.* The *Wazanki* people, agriculturists who reside east of Lake Victoria, pay bridewealth in cattle after the young man's parents select the bride. Today, the younger generation is more interested in selecting their own spouses. Where polygamy occurs, ideally the husband arranges visitation to each wife in turn. The length of each visit depends on the level of communication and love that exists between him and a respective wife.

*Maasiai.* The *Maasiai* pastoralists are polygamous. Men erect homes for wives in a circle; the husband's home is built in the center. His wives' dwellings are arranged according to seniority. If the husband treats his wives equally, he stays with each one in turn. However, it is his wife's decision as to whether or not he is welcome and respected.

*Washambala* and *Wapare.* These are mountain peoples of Northeast Tanzania. Each wife lives with her own children and has her own home with enough land to cultivate food. In households where polygamy still occurs, the man ideally makes arrangements to visit each wife without partiality.

*Swahili.* The Islamic *Swahili* men, residing in coastal towns and urban centers, may have several wives. They and their adult married sons live in the same compound. They may have many homes built on different streets in various locations for different wives.

In Paje, the Islamic community holds marriage in such high esteem that those who are not married do not have the respect of the public at large. Although polygamy is permitted by standard Islamic practice, it is not common there. If a man has more than one wife, he must work for each father-in-law.

*Mwera.* The *Mwera* man, usually monogamous, leaves his village to live with his wife in a new home near his wife's clan. His bridewealth for the bride's father consists of chickens. He slowly takes over his father-in-law's work, but if several sisters also have monogamous marriages, frictions may arise among the husbands as to which will take over the father-in-law's position. If a husband does not perform his work duties, a divorce is easily obtained, and the woman is free to choose another man. The groom is expected to bring beer and flour for the wedding party.

67

*Ngoni.* Years ago, the *Ngonin* man of southwest Tanzania paid four cows and 30 goats to the bride's father as bridewealth. The newlyweds lived in a new house near the man's family. Polygamy, which included a married man marrying his brother's widow or the sister of his wife, was common.

*Sutus.* Among the *Sutus* of southwestern Tanzania, the groom presented bridewealth, consisting of several goats and chickens, to the bride's father before being allowed to build his house on the father's compound. After he built the house, a joint sacrifice to the ancestors of his wife's family took place.

*Hadza.* To marry a woman, the suitor visited his prospective wife while family members slept. The suitor spent the night, then departed while members of the household were awake. Thereafter, the couple was husband and wife.

*Chagga.* The *Chagga* people took initial steps towards an engagement by performing a clitoridectomy on girls between the ages of 9 to 20.

# *Chagga Pre-Wedding Customs*

❤ **Marital arrangements.** Families arranged betrothals while their progeny were still children and even made promises to each other before their babies were born. Marital arrangements between the boy and girl were provisional since their consent was necessary when they became of marriageable age.

❤ **Pre-marriage celebration and planning.** If the girl's reply was favorable, she and her companions went to the suitor's dwelling. His parents left the premises earlier so that a party, which included the boy's friends, could take place. The young people enjoyed singing and dancing all night. Afterward, the suitor's father brewed beer and invited the girl's father to his home to make marriage plans. After the boy's sister gave his fiancee a necklace so she could show admirers that she was engaged, the betrothal was celebrated with an all-night beer party.

❤ **Circumcision.** The day of the operation was a time of celebration. Relatives of the girl and boy and the Chief gathered at another beer party. The mother adorned her daughter with her own jewelry and tied bells to her legs. Unclothed girls danced all day until sunset. Guests and her future relatives gave small presents to the girl before and after her circumcision. Relatives provided her with a trousseau, the Chief gave her a goat or money, and the boy's mother brought her goat's milk and fat. That day the suitor placed his cap on her head and announced to all that she will be his wife. After, the couple addressed each other as "Tindi."

❤ **Fattening hut.** Before the girl could be with her fiance, she was taken by her relations to a fattening hut. She stayed there for three months and did not work. She was anointed and fattened with milk, bananas, sheep fat, butter, and cooked foods supplied by the suitor. Although fat from a bull was sent by the boy's family to court the bride, the family sent animal flesh to her mother.

❤ **Beer ceremonies.** The Chief, the girl's father, and her brothers discussed final arrangements at a beer party. An instructor or guardian, called *Makara* or *Mwisi*, was appointed to assist the couple throughout their married life. He also took care of the father-in-law's interests in the negotiation of the brideprice. Beer ceremonies continued until the fat and brideprice were paid.

# Traditional Chagga Wedding

*Chagga wedding customs varied greatly. Most marriage traditions involved a series of beer celebrations at which time the bride and groom did not live together. Thus, it was difficult to assess at what the point the couple was married.*

❤ **First celebration.** The first ceremonial event involved the paying of the brideprice and the consent of the bride. Afterward, the girl was taken on the back of the female *Mikara* to her in-law's home. At that time, the bride was to cry, to resist, and to act as though she was taken there against her will.

❤ **Second celebration.** The bridegroom threw a beer celebration party for all his relatives, villagers, and friends. Feasting and dancing at the groom's dwelling continued all night until the next morning. The bridegroom often lived in his own hut, and the bride resided with his mother until the proper ceremonies were performed. Formal words were exchanged by the bride and the groom concerning the readiness of the groom to take his wife's virginity after which cohabitation was permissible.

*Reference: **Kilimanjaro and its People***

**Other references:** *International Journal of Sociology of the Family, Marriage Family Relationships* by Qwen J Broude, *Gender, Family and Household in Tanzania* by Charles Dundas.

# Togo

Half of Togo's population hold animist beliefs, 35 percent are Christian, and 10 percent are Muslim.

In the city of Lome, a high proportion of married women live apart from their husbands because their husband migrate away from the area for employment. Their marriages are often polygamous, but some couples who are monogamous may live at times in separate residences as well. With more widely increasing transactions with Western countries and the technology of radio, television and the web communications, Western ideas of romance and monogamy are penetrating their culture. The traditional form of marriage is being abandoned in favor of the Western model, especially in the cities. Varied marriage systems are being formed by borrowing the best from each one. Today, the man must declare to his wife at the time he is wed whether or not he will marry another woman in the future and thereby practice polygamy. Circumcision of women still occurs in some regions of Togo.

*Ewe-Mina.* The *Ewe-Mina* are an indigenous people who live in southern Togo. Their marriages are the union between two families and are arranged by the young man's aunts and the bride's family. On their third visit, the aunts carry drinks, clothing, and money to the bride's home to finalize the marriage. In the past, no civil or religious ceremony took place, but currently, a couple's declaration of their marriage is recorded.

**References:** *Social Change and Marriage Arrangements: New Types of Union in Lome, Togo* by **Therese** and *Nuptiality in Sub-Saharan Africa* and *The Cambridge Factfinder.*

# Tunisia

Tunisia is 100 percent Muslim. Historically, young men and women were separated according to Islamic custom. Marriages among Tunisia's nomadic tribes were arranged to strengthen family ties and resources. Today, more young women are consulted about their family's selection when their marriages are arranged.

Most Tunisians now reside in urban areas where many men and women meet while attending schools and colleges. A man may even ask a family member to interview a girl whom he met at school. Once a girl is being considered, the adult females from the man's family visit the girl's mother's home. As the man's family enjoys tea and snacks at the girl's home, they observe the girl's personality. If they like the girl, the boy's mother returns to the girl's home to talk seriously with her mother, and both families make further inquiries about each other's reputations.

## Tunisian Wedding

70

♥ **Civil ceremony.** The couple, together with their friends, and relatives meet at a city hall where the couple pledge their lives to each other and sign a contract.

♥ **Islamic ceremony and transference of *mahr*.** This ceremony ends with an *imam* reading passages from the Koran. The man gives his bride a monetary gift, the *mahr*, to indicate his desire to support her.

♥ **Accumulation of household goods.** The man brings his bride jewelry and fabric while she accumulates household goods for their future home, but they see very little of each other.

♥ **Reception.** Once the man has enough money to construct or rent living quarters, a large reception follows. Some brides wear a white Western bridal gown and veil at the reception hall while others prefer a traditional gold-sequined robe. The groom wears a gold decorated robe.

**References:** Sylvia Whitman's *Faces* article, *Tunisia: Arranging for Marriage.*

# Uganda

About 65 percent of the Ugandan population is Christian, 16 percent is Muslim, and the remaining observe their native religion. Most Ugandan boys and girls marry during their teens. Even though marriages are based on their own personal choice, the parents on both sides must sanction the marriage. In the past, when the boy wanted to marry a young girl, he gave her parents goats, chickens, cattle, and other gifts. Today, the groom is likely to give Western-style shirts, dresses, furniture, and a television set.

The transference of the brideprice is more meaningful than a ceremony or festivities. If the parents do not approve of the marriage, they do not accept the gifts. The young couple sometimes elope anyway.

**Reference:** *Places and People of the World* **by Alexander Creed.**

# Zaire

Zaire's population is 70 percent Christian, more Roman Catholic than Protestant, and only 10 percent Muslim. Because of the Christian influence, monogamy is the only legal form of marriage. In 1967, an Article was printed in Zaire's constitution placing the family under State protection so its stability will be ensured.

*Bakongo.* If a young man wants to marry, his clan chief or father may help him make the first inquiries about a young woman. Once a suitable girl is found, the father lets the son know of his discovery; then, the son is free to accept or reject the girl. Should a man find a girl on his own, he must then seek the approval of the chief and learn if the future wife is acceptable to his parents. Both families investigate to see if the members of the other family are of good character. After the future spouse is approved, the two family clans form a family bond.

❤ **Bakongo engagement**

When the man gives gifts to the girl's family, they offer him a present in return to let the young man know that he has their approval. The man then takes chickens and palm wine bottles to her parent's home. Later, a time is planned for the young man and his family to take gifts to the girl's village. Upon their arrival the girl's clan warmly greets them with the clapping of hands. The young man's father announces his reason for coming; then the girl's father consults his wife and receives his daughter's approval. Should his daughter refuse to marry the boy, her father returns the chickens and palm wine bottles given to him by the boy's family. If the girl says yes, the girl's family prepares a chicken dinner for everyone and afterward, they clap with joy.

❤ **Formal engagement**

The families form a circle, and the girl's father tells his daughter to take the palm wine if she wants to marry the young man. The girl takes the gifts and wine, then greets her family and her fiancé's family. The fiancé shows his love for her thereafter by sending her more gifts. The young man's family continues enjoying their meals at the girl's home. During the final visit, many gifts are provided to the boy's family, especially to the maternal uncle. As the groom's family arrives, the village people welcome them by singing and dancing. After the girl's family prepares a meal and palm wine is served, the families agree on the amount the boy should pay the girl's family. The wedding announcement is made after an agreement is reached.

## Bakongo Wedding

❤ **Procession to the man's home.** The girl, dressed in her best clothing, goes with her brothers and sisters, to her fiancé's home. They carry palm wine and bread, and bring animals. An elder from the man's family thanks the girl's family warmly, then the girl's fiancé offers them food and palm wine. The bride's sister and the bride remain at the fiancé's home, but the groom is not permitted to have sexual relations with his bride until *ta mvila*, a ceremonial when the names of the clans are spoken.

### Ta M vila Ceremony

❤ **Kindling the fire.** The bride's sisters gather kindling wood and during the evening set a fire at the hearth of the home and lay a mat before it.

❤ **Entrance of the groom.** First, the fiancé walks into the room, escorted by his brothers and family. The bride's oldest sister invites the groom and the bride to sit together on the mat. The groom's brothers provide two goblets of malafu and a rifle to fire shots of celebration after the ceremony.

# Bakongo Wedding

❤ **Uniting the couple and honoring ancestors.** Sometimes the couple drinks the malafu from the same goblet, then pours the remainder on the ground to honor their ancestors.

❤ **Combining of the families.** When the bride shouts the groom's clan's name, her brothers-in-law joyfully shout. When she shouts her father's clan and maternal grandfather's name, the crowd shouts.

❤ **Rifle shots.** Then, they celebrate the uniting of the families with rifle shots, celebrating with great joy, singing and chanting until morning.

❤ **Feasting.** In the morning, family and guests feast on banana and chicken. The brother-in-law gives gifts to his sisters-in-law before they depart.

*Mongo.* If Mongo parents believe their son's choice warrants consideration, his father, a representative, or the suitor goes to the girl's parents' home. The representative visits the girl's family and chief on a prearranged day. There, the representative announces that the suitor loves the daughter and asks to reserve her for his future wife. He then offers the "arrow of fire" his father gave to him. The "arrow of fire" symbolizes the love from the young suitor which penetrates his beloved's heart

After the girl's parents question their daughter, the representative invites her to accept the arrow. When she takes the arrow and gives it to her father, she is accepting the boy's proposal. The young man and the girl remain apart during a time period to test their love.

Again, the young man with his representative presents a dowry of symbolic spears, a ceremonial knife, and a copper ring to represent his love for the girl. In return, the girl's relatives provide the boy's family with animals and utensils. After receiving final advice from her mother, the girl departs to live with her future husband and in-laws   At that time, her parents bless the couple and wish them well. However, the couple is still free to break their engagement without legal difficulties.

# Mongo Wedding

*The ceremony with both families attending is held at the bride's home. The beating of a drum is a signal for all to assemble for the wedding. The two families face each other in a seated position.*

❤ **Father's speech.** The groom's father stands and gives a speech depicting the ceremonial history of the couple's proposal and engagement. After he thanks her parents for the good upbringing of their daughter, he and his representative conduct the marriage ceremony.

❤ **Dowry exchange and reverence for ancestors**. The valuable dowry is exchanged with reverence paid to their ancestors.

❤ **Bride's acceptance of marriage.** The girl accepts her marital state before witnesses by taking the rings from the groom's family or by placing them before him. Otherwise, her father simply insists, "Just take the gifts," from her husband's family.

❤ **Words of advice.** The father makes invokes a blessing from the ancestors so they will live an easy life and always be happy. The finale of the wedding ceremonial stresses love and the seriousness of the

# Mongo Wedding

relationship. It warns the couple that if they lack love and fidelity, they will be fraught with shame.

❤ **Bride's father's gifts for prosperity and wishes for children.** The bride's father gives his son-in-law chickens and a goat and tells the newlyweds to have many children. Finally, the bride goes to sit with her spouse's family.

❤ **Unity of the families.** Now, the two families bond, a tie that strengthens with the birth of children. The bride's parents go with the bride to the groom's home where a reception is held. Before the newlyweds sleep together, the new husband gives his wife a gift.

*Ngoni.* The young man tells the eldest male in his family, other than his father, about his intentions to marry. The elder is then the go-between, a *nkhoswe*, who visits the girl's family and presents money between two plates to the girl's parents. If the parents accept the plates, a date is set for him to return. When he returns, the girl is asked to respond to the proposal. If she is accepts, the suitor gives his betrothal gifts to the girl and to the girl's mother to symbolize his gratitude for her giving birth to the daughter and for her fine upbringing. The suitor's father sends a beast to be killed for the engagement feast. Beer and other foods are served at the engagement ceremony which is followed by singing and dancing. Afterward, the man's family returns home with gifts given to him by the girl's family.

The young man sends the bride's family the *labola* of cattle. (A royal family sends a large herd.) Should the girl be made pregnant prior, the man must pay a fee. Afterward, an elderly woman gives the bride instruction.

# Ngoni wedding

❤ **Departure of the bride.** The bride, dressed in skins with her hair in a chignon, departs with her friends and family for the groom's village. A goat's and a cow's gall are attached to her elbow. When they arrive, villagers greet them and the bride's party sings and dances praises for the groom's family. The bride and her chief go into the kraal where older females from the groom's side give gifts to the bride. The bride's female representative presents snuff boxes and beads to the village councilor and tells him that he will have to be substitute for the bride's father. The court councilor indicates that the bride will be taken care of as long as she is respectful. Songs are then sung.

❤ **Welcome to the groom's village.** The next day the bridal party and villagers dance while the groom's family kills a beast for the party. After the chief touches the bride's shoulder with the husband's spear, she is then a member of his village and feasting takes place.

❤ **Wedding ceremony.** The next morning, the bride walks to her husband's house where he is waiting for her. The groom then enters the kraal and sits before the singing bridal party. The bride carries a gourd of water and pours the water to cleanse him. This act symbolizes the first service provided to her husband after their marriage is consummated.

❤ **Departure of bridal party.** The bridal party then leaves with clothing the bride wore prior to the

# Ngoni wedding

wedding. She now wears the clothing her husband purchased for her. Her new clothing is given to her at a later ceremony where she is anointed with oil.

❤ **Cooking the first meal.** The final important ceremony occurs at the wife's new house where she cooks food for her new husband.

# Zaire Catholic Wedding

❤ The priest welcomes the bride and groom, then blesses them with holy water; afterward, their parents mutually consent to give their daughter and son to each other in matrimony. The priest congratulates them.

❤ The priest, the parents, and the couple walk towards the altar while music is played. A moral sermon is given and a litany of the saints is sung. The priest blesses the couple and conducts the signing of the marriage contract. He also says a universal prayer reflecting life, fertility, happiness, and hospitality with the emphasis on God. The couple, with their parents and witnesses, take offerings to the altar. After Mass, the priest provides final advice to the married couple. All sign the church register and depart from the church while a thanksgiving hymn is sung.

❤ 74

**Reference:** *Traditional African Marriage and Christian Marriage* by **Prof. Mulago Gua Cikala Musharhamina.**

# Zambia

*Thanks to the Embassy of the Republic of Zambia*

Seventy-five percent of the Zambian population is Christian, though over 20 percent maintain some tribal beliefs.

❤ **Traditional marriage customs common to all Zambian tribal cultures**

In the past, Zambian parents or close relatives arranged marriages. They often searched their own and nearby villages for spouses for their children. Courting was a form of immoral taboo behavior. Their children could not reject a spouse who was chosen for them by parents and relatives; yet, parents could consider a girl that their son met by a stream where she collected water. When a man wished to marry, he always needed the approval of his parents or older relatives.

The boy or his family paid a negotiated brideprice to the bride's family. Without marriage payments and/or services to the girl's father, the marriage could not take place. Such payments to the girl's family in goods and services showed the suitor's sincere desire to wed the girl.

The boy's family sent an elderly person of great wisdom as go-between to assist in the negotiating of marriage payments and to deal with marriage issues. After the proposals by the male's family representative, there was an important meeting of the girl's elderly relatives whether to accept or reject the young man's proposal. If, during this period, the man was shown to be lazy, the girl's parent could reject him. If all went well, a wise person was assigned to prepare the bride and groom for married life.

When the couple were from different villages, the groom and his companions went to the girl's village to bring the bride with them. The bride's procession walked quickly only when presents were given to them by the groom's party. Without the birth of a child, the marriage could not continue; therefore, all marriages included a sexual ritual before the wedding day. If their first encounter was unsuccessful, the marriage could be canceled.

The marriage was the uniting of two families who got to know each other in the lengthy wedding process which involved feasting, dancing, and singing and a period of living together as a married couple.

The post-marital residence could be at the husband's or wife's village, depending on tribal patterns. The newlyweds became part of an extended family where brothers were considered fathers and sisters became mothers to children. The first few years of marriage were often a trial period which was complete once the brideprice or service was paid or children were born. Extramarital relations were culturally acceptable, but divorce was rare.

### ❤ Present marriage customs

Today's marriages are preceded by some dating initiated by the male. Because of Western influences and increasing urbanization, the basic customs and features of family life are in the process of changing. Modern marriages go from the traditional arrangements with the transferring of the brideprice to more informal arrangements.

The relationship between a man and woman is usually based on love, monogamy, and a strong nuclear family. Women rarely search for a man to wed, for taking the first step was always taboo both in modern, as well as in the Zambian traditional society. Children still consult their elders about their choice of spouse. As long as the man has the approval of the girl's family that he may live with the girl, the couple may reside together without the husband paying a brideprice.

Fidelity is increasing among the educated elite who reside in urban areas. In fact, Western weddings are so common in the Zambian society that new generations do not know traditional marriage practices.

*Tonga.* Girls usually marry at about 18 years of age, three years after their puberty ceremony. In the past, if a child was born to a woman outside of wedlock, the father of her child had to make a payment to her parents before he could claim his child. At present, young people can choose their spouses. Elopement is common with total approval of the bride's father who is still entitled to the brideprice, cattle or other, and elopement damages. Another alternative is that the hus-

band constructs a hut for his wife near her relatives and works for them and/or continues final payments to her family. Once the brideprice is paid, the couple is free to set up an independent dwelling and attain full martial status evidenced by ceremonies. Mother-in-law avoidance by the new husband, a widespread custom to control marital conflict, may be adhered to before children are born.

Polygamous marriages occur, but most women do not wish to share their husband. Should the husband truly desire a second wife, he must have the consent of the first one. If she refuses, the marriage may possibly be in jeopardy.

*Bemba.* Girls were betrothed to older boys by the time they were 11 years old, their marriages traditionally arranged between two kinship groups. The betrothed children were permitted to have limited sexual contact before the bride reached puberty and was initiated into womanhood. After that, formal consummation of the marriage took place at the girl's home where they generally lived until the boy paid his debt to his father-in-law so he could establish his own residence. Formerly, the man gave bark cloths or a hoe (farm implement) as bridewealth, but bridewealth today is a piece of jewelry and a small monetary payment. If the young man worked in the mines, he was to send funds periodically to his father-in-law instead of providing service. During the first years of their marriage, the wife's parents presented their son-in-law with gifts of food to show their acceptance of him. Later, the wife's family welcomed him into their family. After these formalities, he, his wife, and their children can move to another village. The *Bemba* are mostly monogamous.

*Ngoni.* Before 1989, girls had to be virgins prior to marriage. Should girls have children before marriage, they were often killed. The brideprice, called *labola,* was the transference of cattle. A *Ngoni* marriage involved a significant step-by-step process with singing praises, dancing, and feasting. Bridal rituals which tested her skills occurred after a ceremony .

In polygamous families, wives were subordinate to the great wife and all lived in huts that were a short distance from each other. Should the woman not be able to bear children, her clan had to provide another female capable of bearing children to her husband.

Today, young people are entitled to choose their spouses. Because most jobs are available in mining or urban regions, the *Ngoni* people discovered new ways to find suitable spouses. They often meet at inter village dances. Relationships between the sexes vary from cohabitation to monogamy to polygamy. Adultery is accepted as long as it is discreet. A brideprice may be paid for a durable marriage, for less secure alliances, none is paid.

*Lozi.* During the early 1900's, a law was passed that two beasts should be given as brideprice for a virgin, and only one for a female who was not.

Actually, today a *Lozi* can be married in the following ways:

- ❤ An engagement, formal proposal, and marriage.
- ❤ Elopement without parental consent.
- ❤ The traditional marriage which occurs in stages.

To have a legal marriage now, the bride and groom must have the consent of the bride's parents or guardians. Once a couple wishes to marry, the man presents gifts to her parents so that negotiations can begin. A marriage payment of cattle, delivered to the bride's parents by the groom, provides the man with exclusive sexual rights and the ability to control his wife.

Sometimes, the groom simply takes his bride home where they enjoy symbolic wedding porridge together without ceremony. If they are both pleased after sleeping together, they provide each other with small presents. Once the brideprice is completely paid, they are considered married. Otherwise, the groom's family takes the bride from her parents and both sides of the family prepare traditional beer and food: wedding porridge and beef.

# Lozi Wedding

❤ **Procession to the bride's home.** The wedding ceremony begins at sunset when men and women leave in a procession from the groom's village to collect the bride. When they arrive at the bride's home, her parents welcome the group warmly.

❤ **Loss of bride.** When the guests inquire about the bride, the parents pretend to show surprise and not to know where she is. As a result, all enjoy the charade, joke, and have a great deal of fun. After the bride is located, the bride traditionally protests and cries.

❤ **Giving of gifts.** In spite of such emotions, celebrations begin in the bride's village. First, the bride is taken outside and placed on a mat where she receives money and gifts from the groom's party. Her close relatives give her last minute advice to which she responds by clapping her hands to show them she understands. Afterward, they wish her well, say farewell, and send her with the groom's party and some escorts from their village. There is much fun and glee during their journey.

❤ **Village welcome.** When they arrive at the groom's village, they are greeted by villagers. Dancing, drinking and feasting take place.

❤ **Consummation of marriage.** The bride and groom spend their first night at the groom's home. If the young man is happy with her performance, he gives her a gift. Accepting the gift means that she is pleased with him as well. This ritual confirms their marital union.

❤ **Dressing the bride.** The following morning before sunrise, the bride is bathed by her female escorts before the groom's female relatives. They sing as they clothe her in the *Mikabo,* clothing provided by the groom for their wedding ceremony.

❤ **Rituals for the endurance of a healthy marriage.** By mid-morning, meat, symbolizing the endurance and permanence of marriage, is prepared for her and set on a stone. Elderly women from the village introduce her to the people of the village, give her advice, and explain how to use the household utensils.

She is shown the fields. After being introduced to her work, she returns to her village with her husband and relatives to display gratitude to her parents. After spending several days in their village, she is given many items to take back with her.

# Lozi Royal Wedding

❤ Members of the royal family often married people who were from distinguished families. They could freely choose spouses from the common people as long as the families were not poor. After a man or young woman was selected by a royal family member, the chosen person was required to stay in seclusion at the king's village for seven days or more. Only a few relatives were permitted to visit.

❤ A royal wedding ceremony commenced at sunset. A justice was in charge of ceremonies for the royal family. If the future male spouse was a commoner, he was bathed in a stream by the justice prior to the wedding. The common female bride was cleansed by an older female member of the royal family. The cleansing ceremony was used to take the common background away. After the cleansing ceremony, the former commoner was given new clothing, an honored name, and a title.

❤ The royal wedding began at the Queen Mother's home which had a room allocated for the bride and groom. The King, or chief, hosted the ceremony. There, the groom was presented to the royal court and given a seat for future use while the court was in session. When the bride was presented to the King, she wore a *misisi*. She was provided with everything she needed by members of the royal family.

**References:** *Area Handbook for Zambi, Traditional Marriages in Zambia* **by Yizenge A. Chondoka,** *African Systems of Kinship and Marriage.*

# Zimbabwe

*Thanks to Henry Mukonoweshuro, Zimbabwe Consulate, Washington, D.C.*

❤ **Selecting a spouse**

Men start dating from age 25 to 35 years of age and women, from the age of 23. They meet in public places such as movies, restaurants and parks. A couple do not break the news about their relationship to their parents until they are certain they are serious. Instead of telling their parents directly, they tell a trusted man who informs his uncle and a trusted woman who informs her aunt that they wish to be married. Arrangements are made for the uncle to meet the prospective bride and for the aunt to meet the prospective groom. The aunt and uncle, in turn, inform the parents and then arrangements are made for the young man and woman to meet each other's parents and relatives. Even in rural areas of the country, this method of meeting the future in-laws occurs.

The bridegroom pays a brideprice to the bride's family to show that he is committed to marriage. The negotiated payment, called the *roora*, consists of heads of cattle or money. To arrange the amount of payment, the man uses a go-between. *Mbo* is another cash payment permitting the man to have sexual rights to his future wife prior to marriage. Sometimes, the groom may not hand over all of the money until he feels fully satisfied that his wife will perform all her duties.

The aunt of the girl sets the date of the ceremony after payment is given to the bride's parents. The bride is then brought to the groom's residence, and the couple legally become man and wife after a brief ceremony. Usually, the uncles and aunts are present at the ceremony, but the parents are not.

If a poor man is unable to pay the brideprice, he may leave his village to work in the fields of his father-in-law for several years and the couple may continue to stay with the bride's clan. When the brideprice is paid, the bride will live in her husband's village and adopt their clan name. The woman can divorce a man if he avoids paying the brideprice. Other couples may try to avoid paying the brideprice by simply eloping.

❤ **Present marriage customs**

Lately, traditional marriages are fading and Western-style marriages are increasingly common. Yet, much of Zimbabwe's population has tribal beliefs mixed with Christianity. Although the government has legally banned polygamy, it is still practiced.

*Shona.* The man and woman give each other a piece of clothing to show their preference towards one other. The woman often gives the man an intimate piece of apparel, like a petticoat. Among the *Shona*, a man is permitted to sleep with his future wife before marrying her. Marriage is for procreation. If the woman is not fertile or proves to be unfaithful, the husband can return her to her family and they return the brideprice.

He may otherwise be provided with another daughter from the same family. Should the man be sterile, he is in a shameful position, but can arrange for another man to impregnate his wife. The child born as a result can be brought up as his own.

**References:** *Land and People of Zimbabwe* by **Patricia Cheney,** *Cultures of the World: Zimbabwe.*

# *Island of Anjouan*

The Sunni Muslim *Shirazi* people reside in the town of Domoni on Anjouan, one of the Comoro Islands between Africa and Asia. Traditionally, a *Shirazi* man could have more than one wife at a time. His wives were permitted to remain at the homes of their mothers and sisters. In the past, fathers built homes to provide residences for their daughters. The husband paid visits to each wife, but did not live with her.

As the result of foreign influences and access to television and movies, marriage customs have changed since the 1960's. Young women, who now attend school with boys, presently desire freedom to choose their spouses based on love. The home can now remain the man's property and a wife may live with him. Still, many old customs still exist.

## *Traditional Shirazi Wedding*

*The first wedding for a Muslim man, especially a wealthy one, is a highly celebrated, elaborate and lengthy process. It begins with a betrothal of first cousins or non-sibling relatives when they are young. Parents take the children's opinion into account and also consult an astrologer to determine if the proposed union will be successful. The lengthy wedding process, a series of rites and celebrations involving animals (roosters, cows, etc.) and weapons (swords, cannonballs), is a combination of Muslim and Asian marriage customs. Throughout the wedding, men perform ceremonial dances to music reflecting African, Arabian, and European styles. Women dance separately to Asian music.*

💜 **Mafungidzo.** After the diviners (astrologers) determine the day and time of the wedding, the bride and groom are legally joined in matrimony during the *Mafungidza,* the contractual wedding ceremony. First, drummers and other men, dancing in double file behind them, lead the groom from his mother's home to the house of the bride. There, the men chant a Muslim prayer. A *cadi* asks the groom if he will accept the bride in marriage. When the groom agrees, the groom's friends and relatives give bridewealth in cash to the bride's father. After refreshments are served, the groom attends the women's ceremony where he joins his bride, who is veiled beneath a red and white garment. Once blessings and rites are performed, the bride and groom exchange rings. The groom gives the bride gold and silver jewelry. Finally, the husband lowers the bride's veil and gazes at her face, possibly for the first time since her childhood.

💜 **Harusi.** The following are a few of the many wedding festivities that occur: ceremonial dancing, bathing the bride in a seaside hot spring, dancing of the bulls, a men's cleansing ceremony which prepares the groom for the deflowering of the bride, cleansing of the bride, presentation and display of gifts, and a prayer to celebrate the start of married life. During the *harusu*, musician play, meals are served and gifts are given to participants. These festivities can take as long as three weeks.

💜 **Matsamidzo.** An old woman stays with husband and wife during the first night of consummation to obtain a cloth with blood from the bride. The people can then celebrate the deflowering of the virgin. On another day, dancing men and women form a procession and men carry the husband while he sits in chair, called a *shiri sha yezi*. Used by past Sultans of Domoni, the chair is used to take the husband from his mother's home to the house of the bride. During that time, a man holds a colorful parasol over the husband's head. The newlyweds stay in their bedroom during the *kentsi fukari,* "sit seven," where they are fed, bathed, and cared for by friends and relatives. Men read passages from the Koran. The day before the *kentsi fukari* ends, women from the bride's home stain the finger and toe nails of the newlyweds with red henna dye. *(For a vivid, detailed description of the entire cycle of wedding activities, please read* ***Marriage in Domoni*** *by Dr. Martin Ottenheimer.)*

**Reference:** *Marriage in Domoni* **by Martin Ottenheimer, Ph.D.**

# North America

# Canada

Canada's population is from a variety of national, cultural, and religious backgrounds; however, almost half of the Canadian people are originally from the British Isles. Other peoples who immigrated to Canada are from France, Germany, Italy, Holland, Ukraine, China, and Arab countries. About one fourth of the Canadian French population is concentrated in Quebec. Less than two percent are Native American (Indians), some of whom are Eskimos. Religions having the largest memberships are the Roman Catholic Church which serves almost half the Canadian population, the Christian United Church with about 18 percent, and the Anglican church (deriving from the Church of England) with twelve percent.

### ❤ Selecting a spouse

Canada's dating, monogamous marriage customs, and laws are similar to those of the United States. They are based upon the Western-style ideal of romantic love and Judeo-Christian customs brought from Europe. Single people are free to choose their mates through the course of their everyday lives. Some may choose to use introduction bureaus, mostly located in urban areas. They are located in both French-speaking Quebec and in the English-speaking Canadian provinces. The Canadian magazine, the *Maclean,* features touch-tone telephone romance lines as one popular way for

meeting people Toronto's Interactive Media Corporation's voice personals take up 11 pages which translate into approximately 4,000 ads for this weekly publication. Voice personal advertisements of single people are recorded onto a network, and anyone who is 18 years or older can hear the personal ads and leave their responses in electronic mailboxes. If a couple are mutually compatible, they arrange a meeting, usually in a public place.

The book *The Canadian Family* by K. Iswaran indicates that Canadian marriages usually take place between partners of similar social and educational backgrounds. Personal attributes desired in a mate are dependability, honesty, and faithfulness. Studies show that less emphasis is placed on love, good looks, and chastity.

Though many singles wed within their faith, increasing numbers have interfaith marriages. Protestants are the most inclined to have mixed religious marriages, but are less likely to cross racial lines.

Marrying outside the same ethnic group occurs more after the first generation of immigrants settle in Canada. Immigrant children may feel a certain degree of sophistication if they acquire a French or British spouse. The following original migrant groups often continue their own customs without assimilating totally into the populations:

*French Canadians* in Quebec are mostly Catholic. In the past, a suitor in Quebec visited a young maiden's home during Sunday evenings while her family was present so he could socialize with them. If the visits went well, he and the daughter could take buggy rides or sit on the front porch swing to converse. When the young man was ready, he would ask the girl's father for her hand in marriage. Today, the couple is free to meet at other locations. Now, as in the past, banns announcing the couple's intention to marry are read over three consecutive Sundays at the Catholic church before the wedding. Friends and relatives give a bridal shower party where presents for their future household are given. Unlike the United State's shower which only females attend, both sexes may be present. An amusing stag party may be given to represent cessation of the groom's bachelor life. Sometimes during the bachelor party, friends might eulogize the groom the way the priest would at someone's funeral to tease the him about his bachelor days being over.

After the church bells are rung for the nuptial mass, the couple are married in Catholic tradition and a reception follows. The splendor of wedding attire, the elegance of the ceremony and the reception depend on the affluence of the families involved.

In the past, women wore conservative clothing after marriage, and men announced to the world that they were married by wearing a mustache or displaying a gold watch and chain.

*The Hutterites.* The *Hutterite* community originated from central Europe and arose as part of the Anabaptist reformation. They believe in the spiritual unity among men and the unity between man and God. Regarding marriage, three concepts ranging, from the highest to the lowest, are involved:

- ❤ Marriage between God and the soul.
- ❤ Marriage of the spirit and body.
- ❤ Marriage of the body to another body.

Until 1830, marriageable males and females were assembled once or twice a year. At that time, the minister would provide each male with three females, but if he declined all three, he had to wait for the next mating ritual. They did not force marriages between incompatible people. Now, informal dating is permitted between the ages of 16 to 18, and *Hutterite* young people marry only after they are baptized which occurs between ages 19 to 21. If a baptized female cannot find a partner, formal meetings may be arranged by parents or elders for her to meet an eligible partner from another community.

Most opportunities for young *Hutterites* to meet are social occasions, like weddings and funerals, where they become acquainted with peers from host commu-

nities. Such occasions last for several days. Relationships are maintained by exchanging letters and visits. When an exchange of photos occurs, positive intentions for romance are perceived by both.

When no serious objections from family exist, a date is set considering the convenience of the community. If the young man desires that the wedding be held at another time, the community will respect his wish. An engagement and wedding usually occur within one week. The engagement ceremony occurs in the bride's community, but the wedding is held in the groom's community. Weddings take place during the spring or the fall, after the harvest.

Their union must receive the formal blessing of the church as well as the consent of the parents. The Sunday morning ceremony takes place with the groom's relatives on one side of the church and the bride's family on the other. During the wedding, the minister concentrates on the duties of the husband and wife. After an initial prayer, the bride and groom move to the front where they respond to questions until the minister declares them man and wife.

That afternoon people from committees enjoy dining in a hall where the bride and groom hold hands with the minister at the head table. A minister then leads a *Hutterite* song.

*Dutch Canadians.* K. Ishwaran says that they are not likely to lose their identity, for they reside and interact in a cultural ghetto. Engagement is celebrated by the family. Selected friends and relatives attend the wedding since the occasion is no longer a community affair. *(See the Netherlands for more information.)*

*Italian Canadians.* The Italian Canadians who settled in Montreal were quick to marry outside their ethnic group because of the prestige in acquiring a wife of French or British Origin. More Italians wed French Canadians than English Canadians because the French are also Catholic.

*Arab.* The Egyptians, Moroccans, Syrians, Algerians, Lebanese, and other Arabs are part of an immigration which commenced near the beginning of the twentieth century. Most live in Montreal, but others reside in major metropolitan areas in Quebec, Nova Scotia, and Alberta. About 75 percent are Christian and only 25 percent are Muslims. Ontario and Alberta have the highest population of Muslims. *(Please refer to Muslim traditions in Chapter 1.)* Muslims find that some of their traditions, such as having as many as four wives, cannot be practiced in Canada. Canadian law prohibits polygamy. Canadian law also discourages cousin marriages, though some do occur. The Arab marriage is now less of a contract between families, but more of a contract between individuals. The relaxation on controls of mate selection, less training in Islamic traditions, and fewer *mahr* payments have caused more freedom of selection and a small increase in marriages to non-Muslims. Furthermore, some non-Muslim wives do not convert to Islam.

**References: The Canadian *Family* by K. Iswaran, *The Gale Encyclopedia of Muticultural America*, February 20, 1995 issue of *Maclean's* magazine and *The Canadian Family* article "The Hutterite Family" by Karl Peter.**

## Canadian Native Americans

❤ **Past marriage customs of Canadian Native American tribes (Indians)**

*Eskimo.* The population of Northern Canadian Eskimo Indian tribes extends west from the Alaskan border through Northern Canada to Labrador. Eskimo girls were married without ceremony by the time they were 15 or 16 years of age. The girl simply took her possessions and moved to the igloo of her new spouse.

*Kwakiutl.* The Kwakiutl and other Indians, such as *Tlingit* were located in the Northwest Coast in British Columbia. Among the *Kwakiutl*, marriages were arranged by the bride and groom's families, who were of the same class. Since consolidating clans of high rank was a way to achieve greater wealth, the bride and groom were united only after the wealth of each family was verified.

Upon their first menses, girls were sent to a special hut provided behind their homes where they were secluded from all others, except from their mothers, grandmothers, and aunts from the father's side of the family. There the girl had to sit without moving and rub her lips and face with a stone several times per day. She was permitted no food or water until she completed the fourth day of seclusion. Then, she had to fast again until the eighth day of her indoctrination was completed. Failing to rub her face with a stone signified she would become a gossiping trouble maker. Breaking the fast indicated she would be either a glutton, a thief, or even a promiscuous woman.

While being secluded in the hut, she became proficient at the art of sewing and basketry which were required to be considered a worthy wife and mother. Her return to the community was celebrated by a feast provided by the her father. Now considered a woman, she had a curved piece of wood or bone placed within a slit of her lower lip and her first tattoo applied to her body.

When the girl was in solitude, arrangements for her future marriage often transpired. The young man's mother or maternal uncle presented the girl's mother with as many valuable presents as they could afford. If the girl's mother accepted the gifts within a couple of days, the couple would be united in marriage. Then, the girl's father gave the groom's family as many generous gifts as possible so he could honor the high worth his family placed on his daughter.

## *Kwakiutl Wedding*

❤ The girl waited in her father's home until guests arrived for the wedding. The groom sat in the middle of the floor of the girl's home. While singing and dancing, the guests spread a fur bridal path for the bride. She walked down the path with her eyes looking downward, then shyly sat next to the groom. The couple quietly attended the festivities, but they were not permitted to partake of the wedding feast. The couple could live together; however, they were not yet considered married. After several weeks went by, the groom's family had a wedding feast that finalized their marriage.

*Sub-Arctic Native Americans* of Canada were the *Chipewyan, Beaver, Kaska, Joibwa, Swampy, Naskapi, Kyukon, Tanana, Kutchin, Cree, Montignai, Msitasin--* to name a few. Female virginity prior to marriage was stressed in many Sub-Arctic tribes. When a girl had her first menses, she was led to a small dwelling away from her family. She lived in seclusion 10 to 30 days while she made crafted items with older women caring for her. If she needed to leave the hut, she was not permitted to step on hunting paths for fear she might infect others. To avoid further contamination, she wore gloves so she would not touch her body with her bare hands. She drank from a special bowl or cup. Every menses after her first, she was likewise banished for the length of her period.

*Matonabbee.* A good provider could have his selection of eligible young girls and would choose his spouse to strengthen his status within the tribe. Sub-Arctic Canadian Native Americans had no special ceremonies. A marriage was announced to tribal members, and the couple began to live together. Gifts were exchanged by the couple. Their family and friends provided the newlyweds with utensils and necessities.

# Greenland

*Indians of Greenland.* Before 1950, in West Greenland a man usually married a girl who was about the same age. He married as soon he could provide for a spouse and symbolically captured his wife by force. Even if the girl wished to marry the man, she pretended to resist. They resided in the dwelling which belonged to the man's parents.

Reference: *Handbook of North American Indians.*

# United States

**❤ Immigrants and their customs**

United States immigration policies have introduced people of different races and religions from countries all over the world. Approximately 80 percent of the United State's population is of European decent. They are from such countries as Great Britain, Ireland, France, Armenia, Albania, Russia, Germany, Croatia, Denmark, France, Greece, Italy, Latvia, Norway, Poland, Portugal, Serbia, Czechoslovakia, Slovenia, Bulgaria, Armenia, Spain, Sweden, and Switzerland. African-Americans, many of whose ancestors originally came to the United States as slaves to work on plantations, are 11 percent of the population. Recently, the United States has accepted immigrants from Mexico, Cuba, Vietnam, Bosnia, Haiti, and Somalia, and refugees from Iraq.

According to *The Cambridge Factfinder*, Christians are 86 percent of the United States population; these are 60 percent Protestant and 25 percent Catholic. Only two percent are Jewish; other minority religious groups make up five percent of the population The estimated number of atheists is seven percent.

A typical United States city has the following religious denominations: Assemblies of God, Anglican, Apostolic, Baha'i, various Baptist churches, Bible Churches, Church of the Brethren, Buddhist, Catholic (Orthodox - Byzantine, Eastern, Roman, Ukrainian), and Greek Orthodox. There are Protestant Churches such as the Assemblies of God, Church of Christ, Disciples of Christ, Pentecostal Churches, Presbyterian, Lutheran, Methodist, Episcopal, Christian and Missionary Alliance, Christian Science, Church of God Pentecostal, Church of Jesus Christ of Latter-day Saints (Mormon), Mennonite, Eastern Orthodox, Episcopal, Methodist, Gospel, Friends (Quaker), United Brethren in Christ, and the United Church of Christ. Other denominations are Hindu, Jewish, Islam, New Age, Nondenominational, Science of Mind, Sikh, and Unitarian Universalist. *(See Chapter 1 for weddings of various religious denominations and the countries of origin throughout the book.)*

**❤ History of courting and marriage**

Dating and marriage customs of first generation immigrant families were retained according to their religion and the regions of the countries from which they came. If they settled into an ethnic or religious ghetto where everyone had the same customs and morality, their children were less likely to be influenced by the customs of the Christian majority. Peoples who tended to retain traditions were the Hindus, Jews, Muslims, Mennonites, and Quakers. Marriage customs of succeeding generations were increasingly influenced by the Christian majority for whom Western-style traditions were perpetuated by mass media. European Catholic and Protestant traditions, therefore, were the most emulated. When Christian missionaries were sent to Indian tribes and their children went to Americanized schools, many became Christians. Even certain Buddhist groups borrowed the Methodist wedding ceremony. Over the years, the number of interracial and interfaith marriages slowly increased. *(Important: See Chapter 1 for Western-style marriages.)*

When immigrants began arriving in the Eastern United States during the Seventeenth Century, arranged marriages or chaperoned dates were still in vogue in European countries. During the European Regency, Victorian and Edwardian Periods, romance consisted of making clever remarks and pretty compliments. Manners were important and public courtship was considered immoral behavior. Such strict dating and marriage practices were altered by young people in the United States, especially when the families were traveling West. Saintly ways of chaperoning disappeared when youths left home to seek adventure across the plains. Single men and women met on the frontier at frolics and festivities, like apple butter bees, berry picking, balls, and taffy pulls to the sound of a violin. Former stiff etiquette of Eastern cities gave way when rural couples met and gaily sang songs and danced to polkas, square dances, and the Scottish reel. The church proved a place for flirtation that could initiate relationships and was a place which sponsored fund raising fairs where young girls auctioned off homemade picnic baskets to desirable young men, then enjoyed picnics with them on the countryside.

Their urban counterparts met at busy tea rooms and glittering dance halls. Men could take their dates to vaudeville theaters that offered a variety of pleasant entertainment. For those of Christian origin, Christmas was always a time for enjoying romantic conversation near a cozy fireplace.

In eastern cities, high society of European descent held coming out parties for their daughters. The coming out party signified that a young woman was ready to join the social world and to be introduced to eligible young men of the same status. These parties, held at elegant clubs, halls, or homes could have many guests, depending on the wealth of the family.

All immigrants, except for African-American slaves, had the opportunity to continue the marriage customs from their native country.

**Reference: "I Do!" by Cathy Luchetti**

### ❤ Selecting a spouse

The United States places a very high value on personal freedom; therefore, eligible men and women are free to choose their own spouses. Except for some new immigrants from foreign countries who have minority religious backgrounds, marriages are usually not arranged through family or family mediators. The Western concept of marriage in which two people meet and

fall in love prevails. Most marriages in the United States are based ideally on romantic love which consists of mutual affection, understanding, and acceptance. *(See "Western Marriages," page 35, Chapter 1.)*

Romantic love, highly accepted, is portrayed in Hollywood movies, on television, and in romantic novels sold by the millions. The date of February 14th, St. Valentine's Day, is devoted to love. Lovers, husbands, wives and hopefuls send or give Valentine cards to prospective partners or lovers. Men often purchase boxes of candy and flowers to give to the women they love.

### ❤ Ways singles find mates

If an individual has not found a mate in high school, at work, or in college, the person often has more difficultly finding a spouse. Because of the hectic work schedules and the mobility of the American people, many do not have opportunities to become acquainted with enough potential mates.

Presently, 65 percent of United State's marriages end in divorce. Serial monogamy and cohabitation are prevalent because many divorced people still desire a partner. Because single, divorced, or widowed people make up such a high percentage of the United States population, many people are in the process of looking for a relationship.

Since marriages are not arranged by parents and only some introductions are made by friends, single adults sometimes join dating services or place personal ads in publications. They increase their opportunities to find mates regionally, nationally, or internationally. They may join special interest correspondence clubs: religious, music, art, overweight, tall, astrological, vegetarian, handicapped, or one that has no age barriers. Special interest organizations have their members fill out profile sheets so they can explain their interests and desires. Interested parties of the opposite sex then read the profiles and have an opportunity to respond by mail or phone. More singles are logging onto their computers to use on-line matchmaking services on the internet. They can place their personal ads according to age, specific interests, and geographical location.

If a couple believes they are mutually compatible, they arrange to meet at a public place. Single people also look for future spouses at various social events planned specifically for singles by churches or businesses. Businesses sponsor lunch dates, sporting events, social events, lectures, and travel.

A detailed resource book which covers the United States singles scene for people who wish to find a spouse is titled *How to Find Your True Love, Now! No-nonsense Ways for Busy and Selective Singles* by Diane

Mordecai. This book is published by Diamondworks Publishing, P.O. Box 758, New Bloomfield, Pennsylvania 17068.

Because of increased longevity in the United States, widows, widowers, and divorced individuals locate, court, and often marry former lovers from whom they were separated from years ago because of financial problems, personal reasons, or parental objections.

### ❤ Dating customs

Courting couples, particularly the suitor, usually give each other small gifts, such as candy, clothing, or household items. A thoughtful suitor will bring the girl's parents a gift when visiting for the first time. Young couples go to dances, travel, enjoy restaurants, picnics, or movies, and spend evenings together alone. The girl's virginity was of utmost importance until the 1960's, but now more boys and girls engage in premarital sex.

Though couples usually prefer to have the blessing of their parents before marriage, couples of marriageable age often wed without parental consent. They may cohabit without being married, even though researchers have consistently verified that couples who are involved in premarital cohabitation were significantly less likely to have successful marriages.

Interracial dating in the United States has increased in the past ten years. The November 3, 1997 edition of *USA Today* reported the following statistics: 57 percent of all dating teens from urban areas date interracially and another 30% would do so if the opportunity would arise.

### ❤ United States marriage laws

Monogamy is the law of the land. Mormon settlers in the western United States originally were polygamous; however, their practice of polygamy ended in the 1890's. Marriages in the United States are legally dictated by each state in which the marriage takes place. Each state has an age minimum. Most states require that the bride and groom be at least 18 before marriage. If either or both are younger than the age minimum, parental consent must be obtained. Thirty-two states prohibit first cousin marriages, and 19 states have various laws regulating such marriages. In Arizona, first cousins are permitted to wed if they do not have children together. In Maine, they may marry after receiving genetic counseling.

Most states also require a marriage license to be obtained before the wedding takes place. The marriage license can be obtained at the county seat, a city governing each regional county in the state. To receive

**WEDDING AT YOSEMITE NATIONAL PARK**
*"Classic Weddings in Yosemite"*
*is dedicated to making the Yosemite wedding an easy and exciting option for couples in California and all over the World. For more information, call (408) 378-9187.*

this license, blood tests for sexually transmitted diseases must be taken, and there is a waiting period of three to five days. In the United States, weddings must be witnessed according to the laws of each state in order to legalize the marriage. Only a few states permit common-law marriages which consider the couple legally married after cohabiting for a specific number of years, sometimes seven. Some couples who plan to be married have a prenuptial agreement to protect their prior earnings and holdings in case of divorce.

Most couples marry in a church, synagogue, hotel ball room, or the parent's home where the wedding is usually officiated by clergy. Weddings can take place just about anywhere— indoors or outdoors— and portray a specific common interest the couple enjoy together. A member of the clergy or a Justice of the Peace can officiate.

Couples may elope in Las Vegas, Nevada, a city also famous for its entertainment and casinos. No blood tests and waiting periods are required. Thirty-five wedding chapels, even a drive-through, are available for the performance of hasty marriages. Marriage license fees are presently $35.

*Reference: Forbidden Relatives by*
**Martin Ottenheimer, Ph.D.**

84

Most couples wed in a church, synagogue, hotel ball room, parents home or garden where the wedding is usually officiated by clergy. Weddings can take place just about anywhere and may portray a specific common interest the couple enjoy together. A member of the clergy or Justice of the Peace can officiate.

# U.S. Military Wedding

❤ **Eligibility.** A military wedding, a dramatic way for a bride and groom to honor military status, may be officiated by a Christian minister in a church or Jewish rabbi in a synagogue. The military wedding may also be held at a chapel on the base site. Those who marry at a military chapel are military academy graduates, a child of a graduate, or a staff member or faculty. When the groom's residence is at a military post, officers and their spouses, as well as civilians, are invited to the wedding and reception. The American flag is displayed at the wedding.

❤ **Wedding Fashions.** Grooms wear the uniform of the Army, Navy, Marines, or Coast Guard. A groom from the Army wears white gloves and carries a saber. If he is from the Navy and Coast Guard, he wears a sword. Military men are adorned with military decorations, rather than boutonnieres. If the bride is in the armed forces, she has the choice of marrying in a full uniform or a traditional wedding gown. Even when she wears a uniform, she holds a bridal bouquet in her hands as she walks down the aisle. The bride stands to the right side of the military groom during the wedding because the sword is worn on the left side. *(The ceremony is conducted according the Christian or Jewish tradition described in the first chapter.)*

❤ **Wedding ceremony & honor guard.** Members of the honor guard are often attendants at the wedding. Each couple uses the rites and customs of their particular religious faith. After the ceremony, the honor guard in military dress line up near the chapel's main door and form an arch of swords during the recessional. Friends and relatives leave the chapel prior to this so that they can watch. The senior officer commands that the guard lift their swords uniformly at an angle so the tips of the swords touch. The bride and groom kiss, then walk under the arched swords while viewers applaud. The arching of the swords symbolizes the safe passing of the bride and groom into married life. The newlyweds then rush into the limousine and are driven to the reception.

**References:** *Your Wedding* by Yetta Fisher Guren, *Bride's New Ways to Wed* by the editors of *Bride's*

## *Research findings about choosing a mate in the United States*

Martin King White, a sociological researcher, defines two viewpoints concerning mate selection based on freedom of choice: first, a rational approach - a marketplace outlook in which a person dates as many people as possible before deciding to wed, or secondly, a quick choice and romantic view that "love conquers all." He offers that dating does not necessarily work as a valuable experience for successful mate selection. Dating and marrying young, particularly when pregnancy is involved, tends to produce unsuccessful marriages. These often lead to a high number of unwed or divorced young woman who are single mothers. His research also shows that couples who marry after a brief acquaintance were just as likely to have a successful marriage as couples who knew each other for years. Even those who marry their childhood sweethearts, and had little dating experience with others, are more likely to have enduring relationships. White's research causes him to conclude that "if dating does not work, perhaps love does!"

***The American Way* by Martin King White from the periodical *Society*.**

# United States Native Americans

### ♥ Location of Native American tribes

Historically, over 250 Native American (Indian) tribes inhabited regions of the United States. Their traditional tribal marriage customs differed according to the areas of the country in which they lived. Their numbers have dwindled since colonization. Today, most tribes are located in the Western and Central United States: Arizona, Montana, Alaska, New Mexico, Oklahoma, Kansas, Utah, North and South Dakota, Nebraska, Nevada, Washington, and Wisconsin. Many Native Americans who live in cities have become part of the United States culture.

### ♥ Wooing the maiden

During and before the colonization of America, most Native American tribes practiced polygamy and the men paid brideprices for their spouses. Some marriages were arranged by parents, but mostly, courting was based on mutual adoration and free choice. Dancing and gift giving were courting practices. Their ideal characteristics for a mate were selflessness, generosity, and clan compatibility. No one married a blood relative, but all were required to marry within their clan. Marriage took place during the children's early teenage years.

The suitor was a highly respected wooer if he was a skillful hunter who killed animals in the forest and set daily meat before the door of his intended bride. If his presents were accepted by the girl, then he could continue his quest to make her his wife. If she refused his advances, he would receive gifts of equal quality from the girl. Sometimes, many suitors courted the same young woman. When the girl selected her spouse, a brideprice was given by the suitor to the girl's family. It was in the form of livestock, mostly horses, furs, and blankets. The brideprice represented compensation to the bride's family for losing their daughter's assistance. When a man had more than one spouse, who were usually sisters, honors were granted to his first wife.

### ♥ Caucasion western migration

A Caucasian trapper and trader, who took an Indian woman for his wife, would receive friendly treatment by Native Americans and could more easily exchange furs for guns and knives. Since an Indian girl's husband could be forewarned of upcoming Indian raids, he could be assured of more safety.

### ♥ Assimilation of Indians into Western culture

During the Nineteenth Century and the early part of the Twentieth Century, an effort was made to assimilate Indians into the United State's culture. Many Native American children were taken from their parents and placed in government boarding schools. Often, young Native Americans became servants to Caucasian people. As a result, their traditional marriage customs were thwarted and marital patterns were disrupted. Because of their absence from home, they did not have the opportunity to emulate their elders.

Many Native Americans lived on government reservations designated by the United States during the treaty period. There they received monetary annuities issued by the United States government. As they became dependent on the government, courtship and marriage practices differed in the way they were transacted. Traditional gifts, such as animals freshly killed by Native American warriors, could not be offered during courtship and marriage. Traditional Native American beliefs were influenced further by the white man's Christian church and the missionaries.

### ♥ Present marriage customs

Over 60 percent of Native Americans live in the cities where they went to find employment. When they came to the cities, people from different Native American tribes tended to live within close proximity, thereby making it easier for Native Americans to intermarry with those from other tribes. Today, interaction between reservation and urban Native Americans occurs at *powwows* held in large cities or in the country. There crafts are displayed, tribes sing and dance, and they eat Indian bread and other foods. Young people have an opportunity to meet future spouses at these *powwows*.

Polygamy is discouraged by law in the United States, so Native American marriages are now monogamous. At present, Native Americans usually do not wish to divulge their present marital customs to people of other races, not even to other tribes, because they feel that they have been exploited. Many are now Christians and their weddings are performed in church.

The following descriptions are the past marriage customs of the Native Americans:

References: *"I Do!"* by Cathy Luchetti and *Urban Indians* by Donald L. Fixico.

*Apache*. Oklahoma. Courtship began when a girl gave a young man a special glance, a few words, or a slap of the hand to let him know that his attentions were welcome. She could later choose to dance with him at a social event. If he responded favorably, he frequently showed up on the trail while she was carrying water. Hidden in the bushes or over a hillside, he waited until the girl arrived at a line of stones. If she walked around the stones on the trail, she refused to have a future relationship with him. If she walked in between the stones, she displayed to him that his advances were welcome.

More often, the girl would stay in his dwelling several nights. During the final night, she cooked him a morning breakfast and saddled his horse. If he ate her breakfast and accepted the horse she saddled, he indicated that he accepted her as his wife

The young man was then expected to pay a brideprice of blankets, ponies, and trinkets to the girl's parents. He left the gifts near the girl's dwelling at night. If the girl's family concluded that his gifts were adequate and accepted them, the girl went to the man's abode to be his wife. If the gifts were immediately returned to the man, he had to add to what he already presented to obtain his wife. Sometimes, he was forced to borrow from relatives. The possibility existed that a suitor could be rejected by the girl's family, even after repeating the same process several times.

**Reference: *The People Called Apache* by**
**Thomas E. Mails.**

*Blackfoot*. Dakota. The male suitor was the aggressor during a Blackfoot courtship. When he liked a girl, he stayed near the girl's tipi at night. He paid attention to her while she carried wood or water for her family during the day. The young man was encouraged to show his sexual prowess as a highly desirable characteristic. If the girl was interested in him, she gave him a pair of moccasins which she secretly made for him. When the girl and her family approved of his intentions, he was permitted to sit on the same blanket with the girl during the daytime hours. The chastity of the girl was highly regarded by the girl's family; therefore the girls were married immediately after puberty.

Sometimes, families arranged marriages without the knowledge of their children. Once an agreement was negotiated between the two families, horses and other property were sent to the bride's family. The bride's family also sent gifts to the groom's family. When the young man's family was rich, they proudly sent a band of horses with clothing and other gifts for the bride. In return, the bride's family provided a comparable procession. Such a process was intended to display the wealth and social prominence of both families. In the end, the groom paid the brideprice above the value of the gifts the bride's family presented.

Marriage was simply assumed by the couple without ceremony when each performed their responsibilities and lived together in a tipi. Afterwards, the young bride made pairs of moccasins for each of her spouse's male relatives to show her worth to his side of the family. If the bride was lazy or behaved badly, the man could send her back to her parents. The husband did not have to be faithful, but the wife was obligated not to commit adultery.

The Blackfoot husband was not permitted to speak to or look at his mother-in-law. This taboo could be removed when either were in danger or more permanently when he gave her captured guns or horses. After four such presentations, the mother-in-law could lift the taboo by simply holding his hand.

**Reference: *Social Organization and Ritualistic Ceremonies of The Blackfoot Indians*.**

*Cheyenne*. Montana, Oklahoma, and Colorado. Marriages between relatives, no matter how distant, could not take place.

During adolescence, boys and girls were not allowed to associate with each other so they could not develop a direct relationship. Upon puberty, young girls and single women wore a protective rope, between their legs. If any man violated the girl who was wearing this rope, he would probably be killed by her relatives. When the young girl first attracted a beau, a woman, usually her father's sister, provided instruction on proper behavior. Courting was a long and bashful procedure which could take as long as four to five years.

When the man wanted to court a girl, he simply touched her robe as she passed, whistled, or called to gain her attention. He hoped she would at least smile, but if she rebuffed him, he became very upset.

A girl who was born into a group stayed in the same matrilineal group for a lifetime; thus, her children became members of that group as well. Although a married man was known by his own tribal name, he would live with his wife's group. A man could stay with several groups within his lifetime, but the woman could only stay with her maternal group.

In more recent times, courting occurred when a man became fond of a girl. Wrapped with a blanket over his head to hide his face, he would wait at her lodge until she would appear to fetch wood or water. As she passed, he stepped near her and closed his arms around

*Indian youth
attracted a maiden*

her, then covered her body with his blanket. If she did not desire his advances, she would break away and he would be extremely disappointed. If she permitted him to do so, he could hold her steady and converse with her. When she enjoyed having a discussion with him, he knew she accepted him. Should the girl be unavailable or stay inside her lodge, he could wait for hours until she came out; otherwise, he was forced to try again another time. If a girl was lovely and had a pleasing personality, she could have many suitors.

A young man might play a sweet flute, empowered by a medicine man, to assist in the courting process. The sounds of the flute often conveyed various intimate messages, such as he is waiting to see her or he will return the next day.

After a young man had courted a girl one to five years and desired to marry her, he would often ask a friend, relative, or elderly man to consult with the girl and learn if she would marry him. If her message was positive, the young man's messenger would take horses and tie them in front of the girl's residence. Usually, the messenger did not receive an answer right away. In fact, the messenger could wait for 24 to 48 hours until he received parental consent, for the girl's brothers and other relatives were also consulted. If the response from the girl's family was not favorable, the horses could either be turned loose or returned to the male's father's lodge. When the proposal was accepted, the girl's father sent his daughter with a number of horses to the lodge of the young man's father. Sometimes parents would talk the girl into marrying the young man against her will, but if she refused, they did not abuse her. If she decided she preferred another, she could simply elope.

When a young man and woman became engaged, in earlier times they exchanged horn rings. (Now, they are betrothed with metal rings.) The girl's mother and mother-in-law made a wedding outfit for the bride The

girl's mother was also responsible for providing furniture and cooking utensils for the married couple.

The day of the wedding the girl was placed on her parent's best horse. A woman who was not related to her family led her and the horse to the man's house. The girl's mother and other women followed behind with roped and bridled horses. As they approached the young man's lodge, his relatives, one holding a fine blanket, came out of the residence and spread the blanket over the ground. Someone helped the girl from her horse. Then she was placed in the center of the blanket and carried by men, holding the blanket's edges, into the young man's father's lodge. Otherwise, women would lift the girl over the threshold.

Then, the girl, with her sisters and cousins, returned to the lodge where she dressed in fine clothing for her wedding. Her hair was combed and rebraided, her face painted, and adorned with gifts of ornaments. The couple then sat together and the groom's mother offered them food for the wedding.

Friends and relatives presented the couple with other household items which the girl's mother also placed inside the couple's lodge located near her home.

If the lodge was not yet pitched, the newly married couple stayed at the husband's lodge. There she still could use her protective robe for the prevention of marital relations for about two weeks. Her husband would respect the robe for a certain length of time, for this custom enabled his wife to get used to him while sleeping together. Some sensitive young men willingly stayed awake all night for the sole purpose of making their wives comfortable with them. The new husband never talked with his mother-in-law or even stood close to her until years later when he gave her a war trophy.

**References: George Bird Grinnell who wrote *The Cheyenne Indians: History and Society, The Cheyennes: Indians of the Great Plains* by E. Adamson Hoebel.**

*Cherokee.* North Carolina. Cherokee marriages were arranged by elderly women. After a spouse was chosen, the girl and boy were ultimately consulted for their approval. If a young man had a preference for a particular girl, he could not directly make advances to her. Instead, he spoke to his maternal aunt and requested her assistance. Then, his aunt would approach the girl's maternal aunt to learn if the prospect of matrimony appeared imminent. If so, negotiations between the mothers and other females of both clans took place. Fathers were not consulted, only kept informed about their progress. After an agreement was made between the parties, the girl's aunt requested her approval.

The girl offered her acceptance or rejection by placing a container filled with hominy outside her home for the boy to eat when he arrived. If she permitted him to partake, her response was affirmative.

After the boy ate the hominy, the boy's clan prepared presents for the bride. The couple was then allowed to have a sexual relationship even though they were not yet married. Before they could live together, the boy constructed a residence for his bride and himself. He also killed an animal to demonstrate that he could provide for her. After he gave the girl an animal which he butchered, the girl gave him corn or foods she cooked for the occasion. This exchange of gifts was considered a wedding ceremony for a trial marriage which lasted one year. After they had resided together in the dwelling the boy had erected, both had the privilege to leave if they were unhappy. In that case, the dwelling became the property of the woman. If they cohabited together successfully for one year, there was a ceremony, for their marriage was considered by tribal members to be a solid union.

**Reference: Reader's Digest's book *America's Fascinating Indian Heritage.***

*Comanche.* Oklahoma. Comanche men waited for marriage until they acquired tribal respect based on their courage, wisdom, hospitality, and tribal dedication. They postponed their marriage until they gained a respectable number of horses to pay the brideprice.

Methods of obtaining a wife varied. A man who wished to marry young may have persuaded his father to supply enough horses for the brideprice, although his prestige would be diminished as a result. Many girls whose marriages were arranged by parents often dreaded leaving their parental households for a man many years older, especially if he were already married to an older sister. Occasionally, a girl would elope with her lover, especially if he was poor and unable to please the girl's parents.

While young men were teenagers, the girls were allowed to make sexual advances to boys, many of whom were truly bashful. Most relationships were initiated when boys waited for girls to fetch water and wood. Young couples were not to be seen in public. If a girl was so inclined, she might permit him to court her outside of her tipi at night. She was usually less inclined to permit him to lie down inside.

If a shy youth was attracted to a girl, he could ask an elderly woman, a distant relative or friend to assist him by arranging a clandestine meeting with her. Otherwise, he could cultivate a friendly relationship with a close relative who would speak on his behalf to facilitate his courtship.

To be accepted, the suitor later presented the girl with gifts, even a horse, to gain her favor. Should he wish to further gain the girl's interest, he went to a medicine man who could supply him with a love potion. Sometimes the girl's father would recognize an industrious youth who displayed promise and would ask the youth to marry his daughter. Though a Comanche youth might consider it a disgrace to accept a proposal from the girl's family, he still might marry her.

On the other hand, when the suitor wanted a girl for his wife, he chose an uncle, elderly relative or friend, to present an offer of a brideprice to the girl's parents as compensation for their daughter's loss. The messenger for the suitor brought the brideprice, consisting of horses and presents for the bride, and left it at her home. A suitor would tie his horse before the girl's door, hide, and wait impatiently. The girl was sometimes consulted; however, she was expected to accept the decision of the father or brother who may have already consulted with other family members. A father or brother was legally permitted to kill the young woman should she refused to accept his decision. In other cases, the girl made the final decision to marry the boy. When the suitor was rejected by the bride or her parents, his gifts were simply returned or the horses let loose.

The girl could respond by leading the horse to his herd to show her desire to take charge of his herd. The suitor surely knew that his gifts were accepted when the bride, wearing beautiful clothes, was brought from her home and given over to the groom.

The couple lived in his tipi often without a religious ceremony, except for an occasional official sanction from the tribal chief or a public announcement. If there was a ceremony, the groom would ask the bride if she would be *faithful to the lodge, faithful to the father, and faithful to his children.* The bride would reply that she would *always be faithful in joy and sorrow, in life or death.* After that, feasting and dancing took place.

**Reference: *The Comanches* by Ernest Wallace and E. Adamson Hoebel.**

*Crow.* Montana. *Crow* men married at the age of 25 after they proved their strength, health, and the ability to endure strenuous physical activity. As a perfect man, he had the right to paint his girl's face every day. After the couple married, the girl rode her groom's best horse when she transferred to his camp. While riding his horse, she held his lance and shield to display her pride that they were one in all they did together.

❤❤❤

*Eskimo.* Northern Alaska (extending through Northern Canada, Labrador, and Greenland). Traditionally, Eskimo girls were married without ceremony by the time they were 15 or 16 years of age, sometimes before. Marriages were arranged by parents when their offspring were young, sometimes before birth. The only controls for selection of a mate were that the parties could not be close blood relations or have the same name.

The young man could take a wife after he lived with the girl's family for a year. If he was a skillful hunter and got along well with her family, her parents approved of their union, and he could take his wife home with him. If he provided her parents with a year's supply of food in exchange for labor, he could take his wife away sooner. The girl just took her possessions and moved to her husband's igloo.

Polygamy was prevalent among adept hunters, but rarely did the total number of spouses surpass two; also, a woman could have more than one husband. An Alaskan Eskimo male felt some obligation to care for his brother's wife when he was away on a journey. This responsibility included sexual privileges. Other swaps were acceptable under other circumstances.

**References: *Indians of the Arctic and Subarctic* by Paula Younkin and Dr. Kaj Birket-Smith**

❤❤❤

*Hopi.* Arizona. In the past, the Hopi male did not court until he could raise a crop and become a good hunter. The girl had a grinding corn ceremony where she had to grind at least four days straight until her legs would be partially paralyzed. After the girl passed this ceremony, the young men and girls went on a rabbit hunt. The girls made corn dough and cakes to take along. If a girl had some cakes remaining during the evening, she gave them to a youth who interested her that day. The girl would then continue to grind corn with the hope that the same young man would court her. If not, she would try to find another man at a dance or picnic. Young men and teenage girls could attend the annual Buffalo dance.

When the maiden remained interested in a young man, she prepared *piki*, rolled blue cornmeal stacked

*Hopi Bride*

and covered with a sweet cornmeal mush which she took to the boy's home. If the boy accepted it and had the first bite, he was entrapped by her charms. Then, his mother invited her male relatives, and the *piki* was enjoyed by all. The entire clan became involved, and a four-day festival began, at which time the clan councils were called for the betrothal.

The groom could then live at the bride's dwelling before the wedding ceremony. The groom's father often delayed the ceremony for a lengthy time because the family was busy weaving the white cotton wedding robes. If, in the meantime, a child was born to the couple, then a little white robe was made for a female child as well.

The bride's relatives ground corn feverishly for at least 10 days to pay for the husband and the marriage robes. The white cotton wedding robe had red dots symbolizing blood that nourished the future children while in the bride's womb. Feathers were attached to each corner of the robe, and tassels hung from the lower corners. The bride wore white buckskin moccasins and carried a wedding sash which hung from a reed case. *(See drawing.)* The case was decorated with cotton corn tassels to denote rain and growth of crops. Red lines woven within the case signified the uterus which supplied the unborn child with nourishment; eagle feathers signified a long and healthy life. Inside the reed case was a replica of the wedding robe. The smoking blessing of happiness was given over the robes while the bride put her *piki* in the ground oven to bake.

The day before a wedding the aunts of the bride and groom slung mud at each other from buckets to insult their in-laws. They would shout words like "the bride is ugly and fat," or "the groom can't hunt!" After the initial traditional mud fight, the in-laws went to the groom's house to cover his father with mud and cut his hair. If he was not there, they looked until they found him. Later, the in-laws stormed the groom's home at a time when the bride was visiting her future husband. They left his home with food-laden bags of potatoes, soft drinks, and *piki* bread made from blue corn.

# *Hopi Wedding*

❤ During the wedding ceremony, the bride's hair was washed with yucca root shampoo. The groom made speeches indicating that it was his wife's duty to be good until she died. Once a lock of hair from the groom's head was tied with the lock of the bride's hair, they were pronounced man and wife. Then everyone carrying food, walked through the village to the bride's mother's home where they feasted on lamb with other traditional delicacies. In-laws no longer spoke the bride's name, but they called her *moewe* which meant daughter-in-law. The husband usually lived in the wife's house after the wedding.

❤ Today, the state requires the Hopi to sign their American names on marriage licenses. Their Hopi names, a secret to outsiders, are revealed only on ceremonial occasions.

**References:** *Museum Notes* **printed by the Museum of Northern Arizona and** *Marie Claire* **magazine article by Jake Page.**

*Iroquois.* The Iroquois marriage was based on a contract negotiated by the mothers of the bride and groom. The mothers could consult the elders or relatives about their selections, but basically they selected partners without their marriageable children's knowledge or concern. Polygamy was always prohibited.

In ancient times, a young man was given his freedom to be a warrior until he was about 25 years of age. Then, he was provided an older companion, about 40 years old, who had already experienced life. If he became a widower at the age of 60, he could be married to a 20 year old maiden. More recently, partners much closer in age were permitted to marry. The young man and woman were expected to marry or else they could be disowned if they did not obey their mothers. Fathers did not interfere with the mothers' decisions.

After the announcement of marriage, the girl's mother and female friends took the bride to the home of her intended husband. The bride gave her mother-in-law unleavened cornbread, which she had made as a demonstration of her domestic skill. In turn, the young warrior's mother gave the bride's mother venison and fruit. The venison was a symbol that the young man was capable of providing for his household. These exchanges bound the couple in marriage, and the mothers thereafter were in charge of their marital compatibility.

**Reference:** *League of the Iroquois* **by Lewis Henry Morgan.**

*Navajo.* Arizona, New Mexico, Colorado, and Utah. Traditionally, marriages were arranged by parents or a paternal uncle. Once the boy was in his late teens, his father searched for a suitable spouse for his son by consulting with local families. More recently, his son would have a girl in mind for his father to consider. No matter how the girl was selected, the boy's opinion and that of his extended family were valued. If no one objected, the father or uncle went to visit the girl's family and request her hand in marriage. The boy's family provided several horses as a brideprice.

If the bride's family agreed to the marriage and to the brideprice, a wedding date was set for a day which was an odd number of days away. Relatives and friends brought food for the bridal feast. A separate dwelling, called a *hogan*, was created of earth and branches. The *hogan*, where the wedding took place, later became the residence where the bride and groom would live.

While the bride was bathed and adorned in fine clothing during the morning of her wedding, her mother prepared the feast. The groom's party arrived at the bride's house before sunset. They brought livestock to the corral and presented the brideprice to the bride's maternal uncle. After the bride's family accepted that the dowry was satisfactory, the wedding proceeded. Otherwise, the wedding would be called off. Most of the time, all that was agreed upon was delivered.

Today, the brideprice may consist of jewelry and other household items.

# Navajo Wedding

- **Groom's procession.** Carrying a saddle, the groom and his party enter the wedding *hogan* and proceed south around a fire. The groom sits down and his party sits in pre-selected places near the groom, from the position of sunrise northward.

- **Ceremonial foods taken to wedding.** The bride's mother make plain corn mush in a ceramic pot, then puts it into a ceremonial basket. Other women prepare the food, especially meat for the bride and groom's wedding feast. The bride's mother stays behind because it is taboo for the groom to glance at his mother-in-law. Her daughter's bridal party, carrying the food for the feast, goes to the ceremony at the *hogan*.

- **Bride's procession.** The bride, carrying the basket of corn mush, leads the party into the bridal *hogan* where the men are seated. As the bridal party take their places south of the fire, the bride rests her basket before the bridegroom and sits next to him.

- **Cleansing of hands.** The officiator, chosen for his wisdom, places a water jug before the couple and offers a gourd ladle. He directs the bride to pour the water over the groom's hands. The bride then presents the gourd to the groom so that she can wash her hands.

- **Scattering of corn pollen.** When the woven basket is placed east of the fire, the officiator takes a small amount of corn pollen and scatters it in a cross over the corn mush. Then, he encircles the basket with pollen in a clockwise manner.

- **Focusing of the bride and groom.** After asking if anyone disagrees with their union, the officiator twists the basket a half turn, an act which symbolically means the turning of the couple's minds towards each other.

- **Partaking of the corn mush.** The officiator directs the groom to take corn mush from the east edge of the container and to place it into the mouth of his bride, then into the his mouth. After the bride takes mush from the south, west, north and the center and eats the mush, the ceremony is over. The officiator finally announces that all can enjoy the wedding feast.

- **Instruction.** Later, the officiator tells the bride and groom how to treat each other and provides honest instruction concerning their conjugal duties. After the festivities, the couple stays in their wedding *hogan* for four nights and days.

**Reference:** *The Book of the Navajo* **by Raymond Friday Locke.**

*Oglala Sioux.* South Dakota. Young men and girls were very shy. When they saw each other, the girls often hid their faces. When a boy did not have enough courage to speak, the girl would not respond. If he tried to get close to her, she would often disappear. The boy could simply hope to encourage her interest by glancing at her while she was filling a container with water at a stream. Get-togethers in the summer and conclaves in the winter offered other chances for a romance to flourish. Since young people had few other opportunities to become acquainted, they learned facts about one another by consulting friends or family.

Because chastity was important, young men and women were closely supervised by older relatives. In fact, the legs of a young woman were tied together during the nighttime hours so that the girl's and her family's reputations would not be at risk. If the girl lost her virginity, she was socially ostracized and sometimes marred by physical disfigurement.

A girl was prepared for marriage by learning hygiene, home making, and crafts. When a daughter matured into a woman, a public announcement was made that she was ready for courtship. A coming-out party exemplified her family's social position. Because courtship could not be accomplished in privacy, a girl would stand outside her home in the evening with a large blanket. If her admirer would show up, she would enclose them both in the blanket. They could whisper as they stood close to one other. Those in attendance pretended that they did not see what was happening. A popular girl often had several suitors willing to stand in line, and she was free to accept or reject each one.

For the most part, marriages were arranged by parents with the aid of intermediaries, but romance was never ruled out. A young man could persuade his parents to try to arrange a marriage with a girl he desired.

Sometimes, a girl's parents insisted that she marry a renowned, rich elderly chief. In that case, the girl usually believed her role was to accept the match without protesting. If the girl resisted marrying a young man she did not love, she would then elope with the one she loved. To elope, the couple would slip into the grasslands for a few weeks, then reappear as husband and wife. A disappointed family usually accepted their marital union within a reasonable time after their return.

Reference: ***America's Fascinating Heritage*, and *The Sioux* by Royal B. Hassrick.**

*Omaha.* Nebraska. The young man and woman customarily remained sexually inactive prior to marriage, for those who abstained were held in higher esteem. If a person committed earlier indiscretions, but was subsequently celibate, the individual could regain tribal approval. To marry, no formal religious rites or rituals were involved. Cohabitation, either lengthy or short, constituted marriage. Marriage was acceptable as long as a couple was not related by blood through their mothers. They could not marry if the man was on the warpath, for war meant the destroying of life. Most marriages were monogamous. When a man attained prominence, he could have two wives, usually sisters or his niece.

A young suitor usually had a male best friend to act as a go-between and help secure a conversation with the girl of his choice. Early morning meetings between the girl and boy usually took place near a stream during the spring of the year when girls fetched water, accompanied by sisters, aunt, and friends. At that time, a young man would hide behind bushes in order to have a chance to talk with a maiden he desired. He often made the girl aware of his presence by playing a love song on a flute. Some songs were standard melodies that expressed emotion, but often a man would compose his own love song for the girl so she could identify him when he was nearby.

Since sometimes more than one man claimed the right to marry the same young woman, she often had to escape secretly with the man of her choice. The couple who intended to marry took the final step by secretly meeting one evening so that they could gallop on his horse to his relative's dwelling. Within a day or two of this elopement, the groom brought the girl to his father's home. If she was accepted as his wife, other men's claims to the girl were nullified. Their marriage was recognized when the boy's family presented gifts to the girl's parents and relatives during a feast given by the groom's father. Once the girl's parents attended the feast and accepted the gifts, the marriage was secured beyond dispute. Several months later, the bride's father gave gifts to the groom's family. The husband often worked for his father-in-law for a year or two.

A marriage could also be arranged by the girl's parents, often without consulting her. The arranged marriage was frequently with a mature prominent man who would give valuable presents to the girl's parents and members of the family. The day when the girl was to marry, she was dressed in her best clothing, was mounted on a pony, and taken to the lodge of her husband by four elderly men.

Reference: *The Omaha Tribe* by Alice C. Flethcer and Francis L Flesche

*Osage.* Oklahoma and Kansas. Before 1910, Osage parents arranged marriages for their children. The choice of a young man's spouse was often determined without the son's consent, sometimes without his knowledge. Once the wife was chosen, often from another village or different clan, lengthy negotiations took place between the parents. Past wedding attire resembled the military uniforms and hats used during Thomas Jefferson's presidency. When the *Osage* chiefs visited Washington, D.C. during the Jefferson administration, they were impressed by the military hats and uniforms which were worn in their presence. After the 1880's, brides, grooms, and their attendants wore military-style tunics trimmed with gold epaulettes and hats decorated with silver strips and colored feathers for the occasion. Brides wore long wool skirts and moccasins.

The chosen girl and the young warrior were considered married when her parents accepted presents from the man's family. Should the girl's parents oppose the marriage, the presents were returned. Occasionally, a man could have more than one wife. Usually he married the sisters of his spouse. A man was also permitted to marry the widow of his deceased brother in order to provide for her and her children. Most women readily accepted the polygamous relationships since the death of a husband could leave a woman stranded.

By the 1920's, the lengthy process of negotiations between the parents of the bride and groom decreased. The marriage festivity was limited to a four-day celebration. On the wedding day, the bride and many of the bridesmaids were transported in a caravan to the groom's residence. When they arrived, all were carried inside on blankets which were supported on the edges by members of the groom's family. After an elegant feast, the marriage was official.

During the history of the Native Americans, Christian missionaries arrived and spread their influence and customs. Some couples were married by a Catholic priest. During those times until World War II, the wedding ceremony was a combination of Osage traditions and Christian rites. Later, Osage who wished to take pride in their own heritage once again re-established their own marriage customs.

Now the bride and wedding party travel in cars instead of on horses. The bride is carried over the threshold.

**Reference: *The Osage* by Terry P. Wilson.**

*Seminole.* Florida. Polygamous marriages, usually with a man marrying sisters, occurred in the past and through much of the twentieth century. Though past marriages were within their own tribe, marriage now occurs both in out of their clan. Intermarriages with other cultures are common.

*Yuman.* Arizona. If a man wanted to attract a girl, he would play a flute at a distance during a nighttime dance. Though elders often preferred industrious girls with high virtues, their sons were mainly interested in fleshy girls with broad hips. Both sexes liked long, thick hair. A girl could marry from six months to several years after her puberty celebration. Before the girl married, she was to learn how to cook and grind wheat.

Since open courting occurred, a man could obtain a wife in several ways. First, the young man could ask permission of his and the girl's parents to marry. Secondly, his parents selected the girl. In that case, the young man would obey his parent's wishes, even though he might not agree. Thirdly, during the night, the youth crept next to the girl's bed and slept near her, but he did not touch her. He had to make sure his joints did not crack for if she awoke, she might send him away or lie between her parents. Equally as difficult, he might wake one of her parents and either her mother or father would decide to lie next to the girl. If she slept without waking, he could stay until morning. Even if he slept with her one time, her parents, upon finding out about his presence, persuaded their daughter to marry him. If she protested, her mother and father would remind her that death might take her parents, and she could be alone; therefore, the girl would marry the young man against her will.

After the young man informed his parents that he spent the evening with the girl, the man's parents gave shawls and other gifts to the girl. Then, his mother would fetch her, but sometimes a girl would refuse to go along. Men and women gathered at his parent's house to wait for the girl's arrival. There his mother prepared a meal. If the girl could not grind a large basket of wheat when she arrived, she might try to hide the grain or shamefully run home. His parents also had her fill and carry over her head a large pot of water from a distance. If the girl was unable to grind quickly or to keep water on hand, she was rejected by the young man's family. Should another wish to marry her at a later date, her shortcomings were considered a character defect.

Replacing a dead wife with her sister was common; therefore, some men could have up to three or four wives. The man could either keep all his spouses within the same house, or else wives remained in the home of their parents. If a woman could not bear children, she was often divorced.

**Reference: *Yuman Tribes of the Gila River* by Leslie Spier. Courtesy of Phyliss Towner.**

❤❤❤

*Zuni.* New Mexico. When a maiden showed an interest in a young man, her mother, father, or a relative would inform the man and encouraged him to visit the girl's home. If their meetings were successful, the girl became his fiancee and the two were often seen in public. Thereafter, the girl combed his hair outside in the summer and in the wintertime while he sat before a hearth sewing clothing for her. Once he accumulated presents, including deerskin moccasins, he gave them to her. If the gifts were approved by the girl and her family, he was accepted as a son by the girl's father. When he began living with her, they were considered to be married. Among the Zunis, a wife was so highly regarded, she could send her husband back to his family when he richly deserved that action.

**Reference: *Zuni* by Frank Hamilton Cushing.**

## Native Hawaiian - Polynesian

❤ **Pre-Christian**

In the 1800's prior to the influx of Christianity, a suitable partner for a chief of the highest rank was his own sister or half-sister. Purity of noble blood was of utmost significance. The second female in line to marry a chief would be a brother's daughter or sister's daughter. Virginity of their daughters was strictly enforced prior to marriage.

A distinguished family in pre-Christian Hawaii betrothed their children, even prior to birth. Young people were considered mature enough to marry by the age of 20. During the couple's engagement, gifts were exchanged between the two families. Polygamy and polyandry were accepted.

# *Hawaiian Wedding Customs*

❤ **Betrothal.** On the Island of Hawaii, the traditional betrothal was finalized by a prayer and gift to Ka-lua-o-Pele. Three methods of engagement predominated the scene: *out of the night,* genealogical, and common engagements.

❤ *Out of the night* **engagement and wedding ceremony.** The boy's close relative told of a dream showing where the boy should search to find a mate. Simultaneously, a dream by a girl's relative indicated whom to expect and why. Selections were made from those of the same family, though neither the girl nor the boy was forced to marry if either did not approve, except in rare instances. If the plan was carried out, the boy's relative visited the girl's house where he was treated with respect. When the betrothal was settled by both parties, a date for the wedding was set. Relatives then constructed a new home for the couple. The boy's family brought material for the home, and the girl's relatives built it. Both sides made sure that their son and daughter had everything needed for their new home prior to the wedding.

When the engagement period was prolonged, the groom sent gifts to his future spouse to show he would be an excellent provider. After the construction of the home was completed and it was furnished, the couple were led through the entrance. The *kahuna* prayed that the marriage would be fruitful and that they would share everything throughout their lives. Except for Puna-Ka-u, the couple was draped with a *kapa,* a barkcloth. All enjoyed an outdoor feast and festivities in the shade of trees.

# Hawaiian Marriages

♥ **Genealogical engagement.** This form of engagement was arranged by families of rank. It was accomplished by researching the genealogy of another family, then choosing a boy or girl of equal status.

♥ **Common engagement.** When a common young man desired a certain girl for his wife, he consulted her parents or grandparents. If they agreed to the match and the girl accepted him, he just moved into her home and became part of her parents' household. Though girls were too reticent to propose, they used their feminine wiles to attract their mates. Occasionally, a girl's family would be attracted by an industrious, good-looking young man and would take the initiative on their daughter's behalf.

♥ **Wedding.** During traditional Hawaiian weddings, the bride and groom wore *leis,* necklaces strung with flowers and other plant materials. The bride wore a *muumuu* wedding dress, sometimes white. During the ceremony, the couple were draped together with traditional *kapa* - bark cloth, or shared the same blanket. The Polynesian greeting was the *honi*, the touching of their noses. *Kuilima*, holding of hands, was part of their traditional ceremony. During the wedding, the braiding of the *aha* or coconut fiber cord symbolically indicated the binding during the vows of marriage. There was a *hula* dance for almost every meaningful event, including a wedding.

♥ **Present marriage customs**

Today, monogamous marriages and the Western-style weddings characteristic of the United States prevail. Traditional Hawaiian-style weddings continue along with civil or religious sanctions to make them legally acceptable. Today, traditional weddings mainly exist as show pieces in plays and demonstrations. Wedding businesses sponsor Hawaiian weddings with a traditional flavor for tourists. They contain historical Hawaiian themes and language.

**96**

**References:** *Love in the South Seas* by Bengt Danielsson, **Traditional Hawaiian Weddings at (808) 671-8420 (Outside the Hawaiian islands 1-800-884-9505)** and *The Polynesian Society* by Handy and Pukui.

## Immigrant Minority Religious Marriages

*Mormon Church of Latter-Day Saints.* Founded by Joseph Smith in 1830, Mormons are a growing religious organization with about two-thirds living in the state of Utah. Polygamy, formerly permitted by the church, essentially ended in the 1890's.

Standards for the youth of the church indicate that dating can start at the age of 16. Dating is considered a preparation for marriage. Young people are encouraged to double date so that they will avoid pairing off with one partner too soon. They are to get to know one another first, then date only those who maintain the standards and follow the gospel of Jesus Christ. Because sexual intimacy is sacred, self-control and purity before marriage are expected from both partners.

Specified Mormon temples are reserved only for performing special religious rites, not for regular church meetings. Only family and church members who are in good standing with a temple and who are recommended by the bishop are permitted at a wedding held at Mormon temples. In order to be married in the church, both the bride and groom must have been baptized in the church. Those who are not allowed to be married inside the temple can have a civil ceremony performed by a church or local official.

Being married in the Mormon temple guarantees that the Mormon couple will be married throughout their next life into eternity if they are faithful to their religion. They believe that marriage of a husband and wife continues after their death; therefore, their marriage in the highest form is called a Celestial Marriage.

The bride wears special undergarments and older woman attendants prepare her for the wedding. Her white dress is simple and modest with sleeves. The groom's apparel is also white. The bride does not wear a veil or carry flowers.

The marriage ceremony ends with the words of the priest: *I pronounce you legally and lawfully husband and wife for time and for all eternity. And I seal upon you the blessings of the holy resurrection with power to come forth in the morning of the first resurrection clothed with glory, immortality, and everlasting lives.* The blessings of Abraham, Isaac, and Jacob follow. After the ceremony, friends sign their names as witnesses during registration. The married couple usually attend a breakfast or luncheon after pictures are taken. Later in the evening, a reception is held.

**References: Jesus Christ of Latter-Day Saints booklet:** *For the Strength of Youth,* **James E. Smith's article** *"A Familistic Religion in a Modern Society"* **in the book** *Comparative Studies of Marital Change Wedding Ceremonies* **by Jo Packham.**

❤❤❤

*Mennonite or Amish.* The Amish belong to a Mennonite sectarian Christian society of German descent and are located primarily in Pennsylvania, Ohio, and Indiana. Mostly farmers, they stress simple dress and self-sufficiency. They still use horses and buggies, for the use of machines is prohibited. The median age for Amish women to marry is under 22 years; for men it is slightly over 23 years. Age difference between a husband and wife is very slight, usually only one and a half years.

Though young men and women are not limited to marital partners from their own community, they marry Amish individuals. Young people intermarry freely among Amish districts and settlements. The best opportunity for young people to become acquainted is at a Sunday evening song meeting at a home. Courtship often starts when a boy, about 16, selects a girl, between 14 and 16. When going steady with a girl, a young man dresses in his best clothing and is equipped with a flashlight so he may visit her on Saturday nights. Formerly, the boy had to walk a great distance to see a girlfriend. Today's young men are permitted to quickly span the distance to his girlfriend's home using in-line skates (Roller Blades), for these skates are not considered to be machines. Before entering her home, he makes certain the parents have retired for the evening.

When the girl sees the lighted flashlight from her window, she opens the door for him. They may play games or enjoy the company of another couple until early hours of the morning. Amish courtship is secretive. The customary mode of behavior among parents and relatives is to respect the young people's privacy or pretend not to know what is going on. Bundling was an old way of getting to know each other in the warmth of a covered bed with a board between them at night; however, bundling has disappeared with modern conveniences. Some Amish were against the practice because they thought it might encourage sexual activity.

A young man, who wishes to be married, approaches the deacon or minister and makes his desire known. The deacon or minister becomes a go-between who goes after dark to the home of the girl's parents. He verifies the young man's desire to be married to their daughter and obtains consent from her parents. The community is informed about the wedding when the couple's announcement is given during a preaching service in the girl's district. The bridegroom may stay at the bride's home afterward to help make preparations for marriage. A bride's family provides a dowry of homemade objects and crafts, like quilts and comforters. They invite all their relatives to the wedding.

Though a wedding for a widow or widower may occur at any time, young couples' weddings and dinners usually take place from October to December. Having the nuptials after the harvest permits community-wide participation. Weddings are usually held on Tuesdays and Thursdays. Larger communities might have as many as 150 weddings within a few months. The union of each couple is important because it means another new home in which to hold a preaching service and a new family committed to the Amish faith. Divorce is not an option.

Wedding customs and feasts vary among communities and individual families, especially food preparations, setup in home, and social activities. Before daylight on the day of the wedding the bride and groom, wearing traditional Sunday clothing, go to a preaching ceremony. Wedding guests attend this ceremony which may last for hours. Once the house is filled with people and singing begins, the minister privately counsels the bride and groom as to their marriage duties. Upon returning to the congregation, the couple, usually holding hands, take their seats in the minister's row. After the sermon is delivered, the marriage ceremony and vows are carried out in Protestant fashion. The bishop concludes with the words, the *God of Abraham, the God of Isaac, and the God of Jacob be with you and help you together and fulfill His blessing abundantly upon you, through Jesus Christ, Amen.*

Later, all go in their buggies to the bride's home for a feast. Tables are filled with fowl, stuffing, potatoes and gravy, fruits, pies, cookies, cakes, doughnuts, candies and nuts. The dinner is followed by hymn singing, and the children play games in the barn. As many as 350 or more guests may attend.

**Reference:** *Amish Society* **and** *Amish Society* **by John A. Hostetler.**

❤❤❤

*Society of Friends, the Quakers.* Most Quakers live in the United States, though some reside in Australia, Canada, Britain, Ireland, and Africa. They believe that God is in all people and act accordingly when they meet a Friend. When they worship, they feel that they are united with God and with each other in a living brotherhood. The innate goodness and love for man and womankind is practiced in the spirit of Christ or the Inner Light within every person. Dealing directly with God, they have no priest or minister or formal creed. Their goals are freedom of speech, religion, and equal educational opportunities for all. Many are pacifists since they think war is contrary to life.

The American Friends Service Committee has worked with the United Nations and the United States government to ensure that people throughout the world are not persecuted and have the right to food, clothing, and assistance. Quakers believe that peoples of the world are becoming closer, and they should treat each other well.

A Quaker meeting house is simple with no altar or organ. During past worship services, attendees sat in silence, left their problems aside, and listened to the voice of God. Today, some Quaker Meetings have a pastor conducting services, congregational singing, and the reading of scriptures.

Before a couple weds, their upcoming marriage is announced at a Monthly Meeting where both submit a paper stating their intention along with the written consent of their parents. Their future marriage is investigated and approved by a Clearness Committee which determines the couple's sincerity and dedication. Wedding invitations are sent. Two men and two women of the congregation are then selected to see that the marriage is accomplished with dignity. The Friends assume a responsibility for the bride and groom throughout their lives. The couple, in turn, are responsible for other Friends. A Friend is permitted to wed a non-Friend and their wedding can either be at home or the Friend's meeting house.

# Quaker Wedding

**❤ Seating of participants.** Ushers show the wedding guests to their seats in the Friend's Meeting House. Benches are arranged in circular fashion or in a square with an aisle for the bride and groom to enter alone or with their families. The parents are led to the front bench. The bride and groom are sometimes accompanied by their groomsmen and bridesmaids into the Meeting House. The bride and groom are seated together in the front of the room between their parents. Rings may or may not be exchanged before the couple is seated.

**❤ Wedding ceremony.** During the worship service, the couple join hands and typically say these words: *In the presence of God and these our friends, I take thee, (name), to be my wedded wife (or husband), promising with Divine assistance to be unto thee a loving and faithful wife (husband) as long as we both shall live.* There is no minister or officiator, no one to pronounce them man and wife. Quakers believe God, not man, joins a husband and wife.

**❤ Signing and reading of the marriage certificate.** After the marriage certificate is presented for the couple's signatures by two groomsmen, the document is read aloud. The worship continues with meditation and spoken words. Later, at the reception, each member of the congregation signs the wedding certificate. A musical celebration and a potluck dinner may follow or a reception may be catered at home.

**Reference:** *The Quakers* by Kathleen Elgin and *Your Wedding* by Yetta Fisher Gruen.

98

*African-American.* Originally, the African-American (Black) people were forcibly brought to the United States from African countries to work on plantations as slaves. Because present-day African-Americans often do not know from which African country their ancestors came, most are not totally familiar with the marriage customs of their native tribes. Slave owners did not permit them to retain their native customs. Because slaves had to take on their owners' surnames, ancestors are difficult to trace. Finding ancestors is possible if the slave owners kept good records.

Since the slaveholders thought of the slaves as prop-

*Display the broom, symbolic of*
*"Jumping the Broom.*
*Photo from the*
*Wedding of Butch and Lori Brunson.*

President Abraham Lincoln's administration, most African-American weddings were performed by Christian clergy. Today, the African-American population is mostly Christian, with an increasing number of Muslims. A minute number are Jewish. The largest African-American religious denomination is the National Baptist Convention. Others belong to the Christian Methodist and Episcopal churches, while some attend the Church of God in Christ. From the 1980's through 1990's, the number of African-American memberships increased in the Islamic faith and in the Catholic church.

Today, African-Americans basically adhere to the Western tradition of choosing mates based on romantic love, but a revival of some African wedding customs with Caribbean and African cultural links is occurring. During the wedding, Christian and African-American ethnic customs are combined; yet, the lengthy process for marrying in many African countries that occurs between the two families does not apply.

Popular African fashions are sometimes a toga for the groom or a long skirt and blouse and high headdress for the bride. African drumming and dancing, food preparations and rituals, are now a meaningful part of many African-American wedding ceremonies.

Intermarriage with those outside their race is increasing.

*(Refer to Melanet on the WWW.)*
**Reference: *Jumping the Broom* by Hariette Cole.**

erty to be sold, slaves were not permitted to marry formally. The slave couples, locked into plantation life by their owners, said their vows and jumped over a broom which symbolized the beginning of homemaking and married life. The couples who jumped forward over the broom sometimes followed it by jumping backward to seal their marriage.

When they had their master's permission to wed, couples were obliged to marry according to European Judeo-Christian marriage traditions. After celebrating with food and drink, the newly married couple were often not permitted to live together.

After the emancipation of the slaves in 1865 during

*Debra*
*Golden of*
*Maryland.*

*Drumming during African-American*
*wedding.*

*All photographs on this page*
*are the Courtesy of Stann Golden of Golden*

**The Afro-American wedding of Eric and Allison Kareem held at the Union Temple Baptist Church in November, 1995, with Reverend Willie F. Wilson, Pastor, officiating.**
*Courtesy of UJAMAA Fashions.*

**Courtesy of Min Eric Kareem and Allison Kareem.**
*Custom wedding attire by UJAMAA Fashions. 1-800-576-6464.*

*All photographs on this page are the Courtesy of Stann Golden of Golden Wedding Photography*

**Flower girls always add that special touch!**
*UJAMAA Fashions*

# Baptist National Convention USA

*Courtesy of Warren H. Stewart, Sr., D. Min., Senior Pastor*
*of the First Institutional Baptist Church in Phoenix, Arizona*

❤ **Musical prelude by choir or soloist.**

❤ **Introduction.** *Dearly beloved, we are gathered together here in the sight of God and in the presence of this company, to join together this man and this woman in holy matrimony. Marriage is an honorable estate instituted by God, blessed by our Lord Jesus Christ, and declared by Saint Paul to be honorable among all men. It is not, therefore, to be entered into inadvisedly or lightly, but reverently, soberly, advisedly, in the fear of God. Let us, therefore, under the seriousness of this act, invoke the Divine Presence upon this occasion.*

❤ **Prayer.** *Almighty and gracious God, our heavenly Father, who settles the solitary in families: Look in favor, we beseech Thee, upon these Thy servants, this Man and this Woman. Be Thou the honored guest at their wedding and help them to speak the vows which they are about to make in sincerity and truth. Grant that they have been brought together by Thy Providence so that they may be truly and eternally joined together by Thy Holy Spirit; we pray through Jesus Christ our Lord. Amen.*

❤ **Biblical reading. Psalm 128 from the Old Testament.** *Blessed is every one that feareth the Lord; that walketh in his ways. For thou shalt eat the labor of thine hands: happy shalt thou be, and it shall be well with thee. Thy wife shall be as a fruitful vine by the sides of thine house.. . .*

❤ **Ministerial charge.** The minister emphasizes that true love and faithfulness should be observed. He says, *Keep the solemn vows you are about to make. Live with tender consideration of each other. Conduct your lives in honesty and in truth. And your marriage will endure. . .*

❤ **Marriage vows.** The minister separately asks each one: *Do you take this (woman, man) to be your wedded (wife, husband)? And do you solemnly promise, before God and these witnesses, that you will love (her, him), comfort (her, him), honor and keep (her, him) in sickness and in health; and that, forsaking all others for (her, him) alone, you will perform unto (her, him) all the duties that a (wife, husband) owes to his (wife, husband) until God, by death, shall separate you?* They each respond, *I do.* The minister firsts asks, *Who giveth this woman to be married to this man?* (Her parent usually replies, *I do.*) Then, the minister has the couple join their right hands and separately repeat these words: *I, _____ (name) take thee,_____ (name) to be my wedded (wife, husband) to have and to hold from this day forward, for better or for worse, for richer or for poorer, in sickness and in health, to love and to cherish till death us do part, according to God's holy ordinance; and, thereto, I plight thee my faith.*

❤ **Ring service.** The minister holds up the wedding ring(s) and says, *The wedding ring is an outward and visible sign of an inward and spiritual bond which ties two loyal hearts in endless love.* The minister gives the woman's ring to the man to place on the fourth finger of her left hand. The groom then says, *This ring I give thee, in token and pledge of our constant faith and abiding love; with this ring I thee wed, and with all my earthly goods I thee endow.*

❤ **Pronouncement of marriage.** *. . . . I, declare, by the authority committed unto me as Minister of the Gospel, that they are husband and wife, according to the ordinance of God and the law of this State, in the name of the Father, and of the Son, and of the Holy Spirit. Amen.* As the couple kneel, the minister says, *Those whom God hath joined together, let not man put asunder.*

***Wedding of Anthony and Tania Wharten.***  ***Dancers at Anthony and Tania Wharten's reception.***

*Photographer (both photos) George Smith for Golden Wedding Photography*

❤❤❤

*Arab-American.* Arab Christian and Arab Muslim weddings differ according to their respective customs and religious traditions. Though rare, mixed marriages do exist.

❤❤❤

*Oriental Asian-Americans* immigrated from China, Japan, Korea, Philippines. Many were Buddhist. During the frontier days in the United States, the Japanese men who came to find work had their marriages prearranged with young women in Japan. The Japanese women arrived in the United States by boat to meet their husbands who were selected on the basis of correspondence, photographs, and parental urging. For a long time, Asian Americans were isolated from Caucasian Christianity. More recently, Asian Americans have increasingly intermarried with other ethnic groups, particularly Caucasians. Oriental Americans tend to have stable households with both a mother and father in the family. Today, Chinese and Japanese-American women often delay their first marriages longer than Caucasian women and a higher percentage never marry.
**Reference: "Marriage Timing of Chinese American and Japanese American Women" by Susan J. Ferguson in the *Journal of Family Issues* (1995).**

❤❤❤

*Hispanic Americans.* Hispanic Americans are those people with a Spanish-Indian background as the result of past Spanish colonization. Hispanic peoples from every Central and South American country are represented in the United States, including Mexico, Puerto Rico, Cuba, and other Spanish speaking countries. During the mid-twentieth century, the number of Puerto Ricans, Mexicans, and Cubans increased in the United States while the immigration of Dominicans, Central, and South Americans declined steadily.

In Mexico, courtship often started with the suitor's tender serenade near the home of the prospective bride. The boy's representatives visited the girl's family to receive permission for the boy to court their daughter. After the boy's male relatives received acceptance, a four-year engagement period ensued. When the couple was married, the man also took on his wife's last name which was linked before his. If the family was wealthy, the groom would give fine satins and jewelry to his bride. When they married in Mexico during a Catholic ceremony, they were bound together with a rope made with wax beads. Similar Mexican weddings are performed in the United States during Mass.

Historically, Hispanic families are bound by strong kinship ties, and even close friends or friendly neighbors are considered family. Hispanic peoples have always placed an extraordinary value on the family. In the United States, many households consist of more than one family living together so they can pool resources. Traditionally, the machismo male is considered responsible for his wife's and children's well-being. Some families still believe in chaperoning their daughters on dates; yet basically, succeeding generations take on the prevailing American customs.

Mexicans who marry outside their group in the United States tend to marry Latinos from other Hispanic groups. Cubans and Puerto Ricans tend to intermarry extensively; however, in California the Mexicans marry Caucasians at a rate of 50 percent. *(See Mexico and South American countries in this book for Hispanic wedding customs.) (See Cuba on page 106.)*
**Reference: *The Gale Encyclopedia of Multicultural America***

❤❤❤

*Cajun.* The Catholic Cajuns who live in Louisiana are descendants of the French. Historically, the young girl was chaperoned by a parent or male relative when dating a young man. She was married before 20 years of age after a prolonged courtship. Her suitor proposed marriage to the girl's parents, since her mother, father, and her extended family had to give their final approval.

Today, Cajun young people date without chaperones, as others do in the United States. Since young people tend to wed people within the Cajun community, a high percentage of the population is related. Godparents are present at the *Cajun* wedding, and their Roman Catholic service resembles those of other southern European countries. During the reception, unmarried siblings dance barefoot in a bathtub. This symbolic action is taken so that the couple will give birth to children and thereby, with their assistance, will not be poor during their old age. If a couple's wedding reception is held at a rural dance hall in the country, guests pay entrance fees which are given to the newlyweds afterward. During the receptions, guests pin money on the bride's veil in exchange for a dance with her or a kiss. The guests also pin dollar bills over the groom's suit jacket so that the newlyweds will have a good start.

❤❤❤

*Jewish.* Jewish immigrants in the United States were originally from European countries, especially Germany, Poland, and Russia. Some made a stop in England before their arrival. The main concentration of Jewish people live in large cities, such as New York City, Los Angeles, and Miami.

In the frontier days, Jewish men were always known to be good providers, so some women who were not Jewish wanted to marry them. In the past, however, the Jewish population tended to marry each other. During the first part of the Twentieth Century, Jewish synagogues in small towns held dances so that young Jewish people from towns nearby could meet. Sometimes, the parents would arrange to import a prospective spouse from the city to meet their son or daughter. Singles who lived in the Jewish ghettos of the large cities had an easier time finding a Jewish spouse.

The centuries-old Jewish wedding customs from Europe have survived from the frontier days in the United States to the present day. Traditional customs, such as *chuppah* (canopy), the vows, wedding ring and smashing of the glass goblet, and the signing of the Jewish marriage contract (ketubah), still remain intact.

As in the past, *challah* (a soft braided egg bread), roasted fowl, apple strudel, honey cakes and wine are still served. Today, the menu for the wedding banquet varies and the white tiered wedding cake is served. After the wedding feast, the guests often dance the *sherr* or the Russian *kazatsky,* especially at Orthodox and Conservative weddings. The bride and groom are lifted up on chairs by guests during the celebration. Wedding customs differ slightly among Orthodox, Conservative, and Reform Jews.

Today, Jewish people make up only two percent of the entire United States population. Because the percentage of Jewish people who marry non-Jews have increased from 6 percent in 1950 to 57 percent by the mid-1990's, a significant number of Jewish people have been assimilated outside their religious and ethnic groups. On the other hand, one third of non-Jewish partners convert to Judaism. Because conversion of the non-Jewish partner to the Jewish faith is encouraged whenever possible, most Rabbis will not marry a religiously mixed couple. Orthodox and Conservative rabbis will definitely not officiate at mixed marriages, but Reform rabbis remain divided concerning mixed marriages. *(See Jewish weddings in Chapter 1.)*

**Reference: *The Gale Encyclopedia of Multicultural America* and *I Do!* by Cathy Luchetti.**

# *Bermuda*

Bermuda, part of the United Kingdom, has many vacationers who marry on the island. A marriage can take place at a Registrar's office or a Christian church.

Local Bermudans believe if a bride and groom hold hands and walk through a moongate on their wedding day, they will have good luck. After their wedding, newlyweds often ride in a horse-drawn carriage to their reception. During the reception, traditional fruit cake soaked in Bermuda Black Seal rum is often served along with a potent Bermuda Rum Swizzle. The Bermudans customarily serve two wedding cakes: the bride's cake and the groom's cake. The bride's cake is three-tiered and coated with white icing to symbolize purity. The icing is decorated with silver leaf and has a tiny cedar tree over the top. The groom's cake is a pound cake or rich dark cake embellished with gold leaf. A circular ivy wreath surrounding both cakes displays the couple's love for each other.

**Reference: Bermuda Wedding Associates, 1995, wedding planners on the World Wide Web.**

# Introduction to Latin America

## Central and South America

Latin America consists of the Central American, South American, and Caribbean countries. After Columbus's four voyages to America between 1492 to 1504, the conquest and settlement of Spanish and Portuguese took place in Latin America. The Spanish settled Chile, Columbia, Ecuador, Peru, Bolivia, Mexico, and the large Caribbean islands. Countries of eastern South America, such as Brazil, were under Portuguese influence as the result of the Treaty of Tordesillas in 1494. African slaves were also brought the Latin American countries.

Even though the majority of Latinos are Catholic, each national group has its own beliefs and forms of worship. In some regions, Spanish European Catholicism became combined with Native American Indian herbal and faith healing practices and with African tribal beliefs of former slaves. The New World combination of the Yuruban religion from Western Africa and the Spanish Roman Catholic beliefs is called *Santeria*. It is practiced in Puerto Rico, Cuba, the Dominican Republic, and Brazil. The *Santerian* religion, called *macumba,* fuses African gods with Catholic Saints.

Since early colonial times in Latin America, marriage was the concern of the state and was sanctioned by the Catholic church. Catholic ecclesiastical courts dealt with marital abandonment, adultery, and the dispensation for consanguineous (same blood line) marriages. Though Canon law did not permit marriages of closely related people, ecclesiastical authorities were less concerned about consanguineous marriages than they were about unmarried consensual unions and illegitimate children. The Roman Catholic Church and civil codes of various countries tried to help secure strong family ties, regulate marriage, and hinder divorce.

From the colonial period to the present, many couples delayed marriage and formed consensual alliances because of an insufficient number of clergy, the high price of marriage, conflicts with parents over spousal choice, class and racial differences. Marriage was practiced mainly by the elite. Those men and women with university educations tend to marry later.

In Latin America, social, economic, political standing, and the ancestral line of families were always valued throughout people's lives. These families used marriage to consolidate property and to strengthen their political power.

### ❤ Mestizo lifestyle and marriage customs

The cultural blood mixture of the Spanish and native Indians caused the development of the *mestizo* population and a *mestizo* lifestyle. Hispanic *mestizo* cultures have always placed an extraordinarily high value on the family and close kinship ties. Even friends or amiable neighbors were sometimes considered family. Many households had more than one family living together to pool their resources. The *machismo* male was responsible for his family's well-being.

Historically, courtship often started with the suitor's tender serenade near the home of the prospective bride. The boy's representatives visited the girl's family to receive permission for the boy to court their daughter. The boy and girl were often chapperoned on dates. A lengthy engagement period ensued. When the couple was married, the man also took on his wife's last name which was linked before his.

In Hispanic cultures, godparents— known as *compadrazgo* or *compadres,* were selected at birth or at the time of marriage. They always held respected positions during the wedding and throughout marriage.

Most Latin American Christian couples who marry in church wear Western-style wedding apparel; however, the children who are flower girls and ring bearers wear clothing to look like miniature versions of the bride and groom. Coins are used at many marriage ceremonies. For example, the bride's father often holds a covered dish of coins which symbolizes his daughter's dowry. During the wedding ceremony, the groom often gives the bride coins, or *aras*, blessed by the priest, to show his willingness to support her. The *aras* are also a symbol of future good fortune and prosperity.

**References:** *The Encylcopedia of Latin American History and Culture, and Everything You Need to Know about Latino History* **by Himilce Novas and WWW: http://members.aol.com Mjkar/ehnic.htm**

# Central America

4

# Bahamas

Left photo: **A View of Nassau Harbor, 1955.**

Right photo: **Mr. and Mrs. Daxon Leaving the church after the wedding ceremony, September 1995.** *Courtesy of the Department of Archives, Nassau. David Wood.*

Twenty percent of the Bahaman population are Anglican, the state religion derived from the Church of England. Forty-six percent are Protestant and 25 percent, Roman Catholic. On the Family Islands and other Caribbean islands people mix their Christian ideals with African tribal religion from ancient times. *(For more about the African religion, see Chapter 2, pages 39 and 40, and the "Introduction to Latin America." on page 104.)*

The traditional manner of Bahaman courtship still prevails. When a young man becomes 18 years old, he searches for a wife. After he finds a young woman who suits his fancy, he asks her parents if he may visit their home. After courting and making the decision that he wants to marry the girl, the suitor presents her with a ring and his letter of intention. Should her mother not accept him for a son-in-law, she returns the letter to him. Once the marriage is planned, the young man furnishes a house for his bride. The couple marry only after the house is built. The nuclear-family household for the married couple is held as their ideal. Rarely does an unmarried couple reside together.

**Reference:** *Bahamas* by Patricia E. McCulla

# Bahamas
# Costa Rica

The institution of marriage is highly valued. Since 95 percent of the population is Catholic, divorce is rare. Young teenagers social-ize in groups until they become closer to courtship. Before a boy dates a girl, he must first ask her parents. Boys are seldom permitted to visit girls after 10 o'clock in the evening. Dating activities include movies, bull fights, dances, picnics, and carnivals. Before marriage, families of the prospective bride and groom visit one another to indicate their consent.

**References:  Encyclopedia of World Cultures and Culturgrams.**

# Cuba
*Thanks to Julio Gomez.*

Almost half of the Cuban population is Roman Catholic and the remaining people are nonreligious, except for the few Protestants and Afro-Cuban Santerists.

Since Cuba was taken over by Communism, Fidel Castro has discouraged religious practice. Weddings are performed by state employees in Palaces of Matrimony, elegant homes that are state buildings. Since food is rationed, the family serves finger foods and cake that can be eaten indoors or in a lovely courtyard outside. The state gives the couple a bouquet which they later place on a Cuban hero's statue.

Only devout Catholics still hold Catholic wedding ceremonies. Some couples have a state ceremony first, then a wedding at the church. A couple who lives far from a palace may have a Notary Public officiate. Others simply choose to live together. On January 22, 1998, Pope John Paul II visited Cuba, where he met with Castro, and gave speeches encouraging the Cuban people to preserve their cultural heritage of God and Christianity by returning to the Catholic church.

**Bahamas.** *"A Proper Bain Town Wedding" during the early 20th Century.*

❤ **Cuban traditions:** Music and dancing may take place at wedding receptions where each man, who dances with the bride attaches money to her gown. Cuban people observe *Loving Day* for romantic matters of the heart.

**Reference:  *Wall Street Journal*, December 1974, *The***

# Dominican Republic

In the Dominican Republic, most of the population is Roman Catholic. Among the Dominicans, church wed-dings, civil marriages, consensual cohabitation, and common-law unions are the norm.  Lower class couples usually prefer free unions at younger ages.  They tend to settle into marriage as they obtain more economic security. Though the Catholic church plays an important role, the religious wedding is limited to the upper classes. Marriage is most favored by the middle and upper classes who believe the ideal is an engagement, a religious ceremony, and an elaborate fiesta; therefore, church and civil marriages occur most frequently in upper classes of society.

**References: *Dominican Republic and Haiti:  Country Studies, Encyclopedia of World Cultures*.**

# El Salvador

El Salvador is a Hispanic country with a heightened Roman Catholic personality. Because of continuous poverty, religious or civil ceremonies are not as common as in other Latin American countries. Godparents who are involved in unions and births are less prevalent. Those whose families have enough money can have a Catholic church wedding. The remaining population usually cohabits in common-law marriages or simply lives together freely.

**Reference:** *El Salvador: A Country Study*

# Grenada

*Thanks to Beverly Renwick,*
*Grenada Board of Tourism*

Grenada is located in the Eastern Caribbean 100 miles north of Venezuela. Well over half of the population are Roman Catholic. The Baha'i and Muslim faiths exist in Grenada. Its Protestant Christian churches are Anglican, Episcopalian, Baptist, Mormon, Christian Scientist, Jehovah's Witnesses, Methodist, Mennonite, Pentecostal, Presbyterian, and Seventh Day Adventist. Many Catholic and Protestant wedding ceremonies are performed.

Those from other countries who marry in Grenada must have papers presented or translated in English and have proof attesting that they are not currently married. Passports, if any, and birth certificates also must be presented to the Registrar's Office and applicants must live in the country for three days prior to applying. If one party to marriage is under 21, a form from the Prime Minister's Office must be signed by parents and certified by a Notary Public. The marriage license is obtained at the Office of the Treasury and stamps are purchased. All documents and stamps are sent to the Cabinet Secretary at the Prime Minister's office. The entire procedure takes two days.

# Guatemala

Although Roman Catholicism is the predominant religion in this country, the Mayan Indians and some other groups have their own marriage customs. Catholic wedding ceremonies are similar to those in Mexico. During a Catholic wedding, an intricately woven circular silver rope may be tied around the couple. In Guatemala, parents are anxious to protect the interests of their children; therefore, social status and family background are important in mate selection. The young man is expected to ask the girl's father for the hand of his daughter.

*Mayan Awakateko Indians.* Traditionally, boys and girls filed their front teeth in different patterns to look beautiful. Some were decorated with inlaid jade. Young warriors painted their skin with black designs, and after marriage, men and women decorated themselves with tatoos from their waists up. Because slightly crossed eyes were a symbol of beauty, parents hung small beads over their children's noses to bring about this condition.

When young men begin to take an interest in girls, they begin to save money. Either the suitor or his intermediary first approaches the maiden. If the girl is willing to wed her suitor, negotiations take place between the families to decide on the brideprice. Should the price be too high, the couple has the option to elope.

In ancient times, the brideprice was the cacao bean instead of a monetary exchange. Often the girl had to convert to her husband's religion. Friends, family, and the shamans attended the marriage ceremony. Though monogamy was most prevalent, men who were rich could have more than one wife. Adultery was punishable by death. Later, Christian missions recommended church and civil ceremonies.

**Reference:** *Encyclopedia of World Cultures* **and The Maya by Michael D. Coe.**

107

# Haiti

Haiti's population is 80 percent Roman Catholic and 16 percent Protestant.

There are two predominant types of Haitian marriages: the *placage* and the Catholic church's permanent marriage which makes divorce difficult to obtain. The *placage* marriage is one in which a couple fulfills obligations and ceremonies at the girl's parent's home, after which the couple establish a new home. The *placage* is the usual marital relationship among peasants and urban lower class. The *placage* seems proper to those couples who themselves make initial agreements about the economic arrangements as husband and wife at the beginning of their relationships. In the economic *placage* agreement the young man, often 19 years of age, promises to cultivate at least one plot of land, have livestock for his spouse, and provide her a home with the necessary furnishings. In turn, his wife, between 15 and 17, performs the household tasks. Even though the government does not recognize such relationships, the lower class people do not wish to legitimize the marital relations unless they care about the prestige of having the expensive religious ceremony or civil marriage.

Presently, marriages without religious ceremony are not as common as those having religious ones. Christians encourage legal marriages and affordable weddings. Increasingly, the lower classes are marrying legally, but those relationships are not any more stable than the *placage* relationships. Some still enter into extramarital affairs. On the other hand, the elite traditionally have a long history of civil and religious marriages. Because higher class women with jobs meet people through work or migration, they have a larger choice of marriage partners.

*Mirebalais of the Haitian Valley.* Though virginity is not demanded before marriage, the Mirebalais girl must divulge whether or not she has had relations with other men. Actually, the number of girls who do not have premarital sex is very small. Virginity is more common among women who reside in the countryside. There, if an unmarried girl has a child, she can be beaten. If the boy still wants the girl, he must face her angry parents.

Young people have freedom to choose their mates, but custom demands that the young man meet the girl's parents to make a plea for their daughter. Sometimes the man is investigated by the parents, particularly if he is not well known because he is not from the same district. If the suitor's parents live nearby, they approach the girl's eldest living relative with a letter of demand wrapped in a green silk handkerchief hoping he or she will react favorably toward their son. The girl's family expects to receive the letter and is ready to provide refreshments. If all goes well, the Mirebalais girl, returns the acceptance wrapped in a red silk scarf.

The wedding is delayed for a few months to assure the girl's parents of the boy's worthiness. During that time, the young woman might be asked to help her future mother-in-law, so she, too, may be observed. As many as two to three years may go by before the groom can fulfill his obligation of supplying a home with furnishings and a plot of land. During that time, a trousseau of linens and utensils is accumulated for the bride. Her father provides her with a horse and all types of livestock from pigs to guinea hens.

## Mirebalais Wedding

❤ **Wedding customs.** The Mirebalais ceremony is held at the family house of worship. Elders must make certain to avoid trouble from the gods. The bride and groom each carry a candle, pour water on the ground, and kneel to pray. The ceremony involves notifying the gods and pacifying them. The deceased of both families are told about the marriage when the living relatives make a pilgrimage to the cemetery. An ox is slaughtered for the wedding feast and music is played.

*The following is an alternative to the above rituals.*

❤ **Setting wedding date.** Church marriages do not occur during November or December because

# Mirebalais Wedding

they would impinge upon customs involving "the month of the dead" and the end of the year.

The Catholic wedding is usually held on Saturday morning, the day of the Virgin. If the couple lived together for many years and finally accumulated the money to pay for a church wedding, their children and grandchildren become attendants at their parent's wedding. As the couple depart for the church, water is sprinkled onto the ground near the door of the house three times symbolizing the Father, Son, and Holy Ghost.

❤ **Procession to church**. Wearing their finest clothing, all walk in a wedding procession to the church where the priest is to officiate. People in the town can hear the church bell ringing to let all know that the marriage is taking place.

❤ **Catholic wedding ceremony.** *(See Catholic wedding ceremonies in Chapter 1 and under Mexico.)*

❤ **Post-wedding customs.** The wedding reception is given for immediate family and friends. After the procession leaves for the newlyweds' home, a bush-priest functionary reads prayers in French. He stays at the gate with one girl or boy holding a red flag, and another holding a white one. Then, the priest pours water on the ground three times while holding a lit candle. He recites the Pater Noster, Ave Maria, and the Credo. The services are concluded when all the participants sing hymns.

The procession to the house is led by the priest. Next in line are the flag-bearers, then the newly married couple, the godfather and godmother, the bride's and groom's parents, and close family. Water is thrown three times in front of the door of the home, and the process is repeated until the participants quietly go into the house. Coffee, alcoholic beverages, and wedding cakes are served.

**References:** *Dominican Republic and Haiti: Country Studies and Mirebalais Life in the Haitian Valley* **by Melville J. Herskovits**

# Jamaica

Most of the population on the island of Jamaica is Protestant; about 25 percent believe in African animism, or a combination of animism, Christianity, and Rastafarianism. *(For more about the African religion, see Chapter 2, pages 39 and 40, and the "Introduction to Latin America," on page 104.)* Legal marriages are relatively rare in Jamaica, though lasting unions occur. Since many Jamaican men are not financially able to be responsible for the expenses involved in a marriage, sex before marriage is considered acceptable. Visiting relationships, in which the man has a sexual relationship at the woman's dwelling or at the home of her parents, are practiced by all classes. A visiting relationship often precedes marriage. Their illegitimate children are protected by law and often become ushers and bridesmaids at their parents' weddings once they can afford the wedding.

When a Christian wedding does take place, there is generally a prior formal meeting of the parents. The bride's parents are responsible for purchasing or making the bridal gown and the cost of the reception, while the groom and his parents supply a wedding ring and the couple's home. Gifts arrive from friends and relatives before the wedding. Some send eggs to be combined with the ingredients for the wedding cake which is usually a black rum-soaked cake made with dried fruits, then embellished with icing.

Guests sing and party the night before the church ceremony. After the short wedding service is conducted, the wedding cake is cut and speeches are made. The event culminates with a large feast of goat tripe soup, curried goat and rice, lentils, fried chicken, a salad, and rum punch. The celebration continues past midnight.

Rural Jamaican weddings are community events; therefore, the public is invited to the ceremony.

**Reference:** *Cultures of the World: Jamaica.*

# Mexico

***Palmilla Hotel in Los Cabos. Baja, California.***
*Courtesy of the Mexican Government Tourist Office*

**Thanks to Father Antonio Sotelo of the Immaculate Heart Church in Phoenix, Arizona**

In the past, young people were chaperoned on dates. Now, the boy and girl can meet on an unchaperoned date at a prearranged spot after receiving approval from the girl's parents. Many urban areas have adapted dating customs that are very similar to those of the United States; however, the matter of having the parents' approval of the boyfriend is of greater importance than it is for its northern neighbor. In some regions, if a girl stays out after dusk, it is considered a sign of bad character. Family and kin loyalty continue to play an important role in the lives of most Mexicans.

Until the 1920's, and later in rural areas of Mexico, a *portador*, a go-between, would deliver a written marriage proposal to the girl's father. Then, the father would decide whether or not the young man could marry his daughter. Though the girl's father could consult with his spouse and daughter, the father could override the advice of either or both.

Mexico received Spanish Catholic marriage traditions as the result of Spanish colonization hundreds of years ago. More recently, the number of Protestants has increased and many are evangelistic Christians. Others who live in rural areas remain untouched and still hold beliefs of ancestral gods and customs that have been handed down for centuries. Marriages in Indian villages are still arranged with the bride's family providing a dowry. There, a marriage takes place when the boy is in his late teens and the girl is from 14 to 16 years of age. In some Indian villages, the women wear feathers in their hair to show that they are married. Indian beliefs are often simply incorporated into their religious practices, especially since 60 percent of the Mexican population are *Mestizos,* a mixture of Spanish and Indian blood. *(See the "Introduction to Latin America." on page 104.)*

Should a southwestern Mexican bride's family object to their daughter's choice of a spouse, marriage by capture in which the bride is taken by force by her boyfriend, may occur. Once the couple's first child is born, peace is usually achieved with the parents. Those couples who live together because they are unable to afford the marriage license fee are usually considered married.

***Bride on the Palmilla Hotel grounds.*** *Courtesy of the Mexican Government Tourist Office*

# Mexican Catholic Wedding

**Mexican Wedding.**
*Courtesy of the Mexican Government Tourist Office*

***The following ceremony from Father Sotelo describes the rites of marriage, which can be modified:***

❤ **Introduction.**   The priest includes a passage saying to the couple, *Christ abundantly blesses you with His love.*  The couple then say they have *come to wed freely, without reservation.*

❤ **Consent.**   The bride and groom give their consent for marriage before God and the church by repeating the priest's words: *I, (name of bride, husband) take you to be my husband (wife).  I promise to be true to you in good times and in bad, in sickness and in health.  I will love you and honor you all the days of my life.*

❤ **Blessing of rings and coins.**   The priest blesses the coins the groom is to give the bride.  The priest also blesses the wedding rings which are a symbol of true faith in each other, always reminding them of their love for each other.  The prayer is, *May these coins be a symbol of mutual help throughout your lives, through Christ our Lord.*

❤ **Exchange of rings.**   The bride and groom exchange rings as the sign of their love and fidelity *in the name of the Father, and of the Son, and of the Holy Spirit.*

❤ **Coins.**   Next, the husband gives his bride coins as a symbol of his dedication in caring for their home and providing for their family's worldly necessities.  She responds by saying, *I accept your symbolic gift of dedication and promise on my part that everything provided will be used with care for the benefit of our home and family.*

❤ **Lazo.**   During the symbolic union of the Rosary beads, a *lazo*, or rope, is tied around the couple while the priest says, *Let the union of binding together with this rosary of the Blessed Virgin Mary and be an inspiration to you both.  Remember the holiness necessary to preserve your new found family as a family of God can*

# Mexican Catholic Wedding

***Musicians playing music at the wedding reception. Baja, California***
*Courtesy of the Mexican Government Tourist Office*

*only be obtained by mutual sacrifice and love. May the Holy Family of Jesus, Mary, and Joseph be your example for life.*

❤ **Prayers.** General intercessions include several prayers by the priest. He also expresses desire for *peace of the world, the welfare of the Church, and for the unity of all men.* All pray for the couple who are joined in the Christian marriage that day.

❤ At the reception, their friends and relatives often create a heart-shaped ring around the couple while they enjoy their first dance. Paper money for the newlywed's future may be attached to the bride's gown.

❤ Since godparents are an important part of the couple's lives before, during, and after their marriage, they often present the couple with a prayer book, rosary beads, and a kneeling pillow for their wedding ceremony.

*Aztec Indians.* Historically, Aztec parents searched for a suitable spouse for their son who was in his late teens or early twenties. Parents announced to the youth's schoolmaster that their son's schooling was over. A council of kinsmen chose a woman whom they believed was most eligible, perhaps a girl the youth found attractive at a public festival. A matchmaker was sent to the girl's parents to ask for their daughter's hand in marriage. The boy's parents would visit one or more times until the girl's parents make a decision. The process could last about four days. Astrologers were also consulted to make certain the marriage would turn out well.

Before the marriage, cacao was purchased, smoking tubes were made ready, flowers were gathered, ceramic bowls, and cups were brought for the occasion. Two or three days before the marriage took place, corn husks were filled with meat and ground corn. Friends, relatives, and the groom's former schoolmasters carried presents to the bride's home where a banquet was held. Honeyed pulque, a liquor, was purchased for the senior family members. At the banquet people gave congratulatory speeches, and the couple would receive advice from older members of the family.

# Traditional Aztec Wedding

♥ **Pre-ceremony customs.** During the evening of the ceremony, the bride was bathed, her hair was washed, and red feathers were fastened to her arms and legs. Her face was painted with pyrites, a yellow cosmetic paste.

♥ **Greeting well-wishers.** Adorned in her best finery, the bride sat near a fire greeting visitors. Elders from the groom's family arrived, welcomed her into their family, and wished her well.

♥ **Counseling the bride.** After being counseled by a kinswoman, the bride and the kinswoman led a torchlit procession to the groom's home.

♥ **Carrying the bride to the groom's home.** The bride was carried on a matchmaker's back in a procession. Relatives and unmarried friends holding pine torches followed them. They sang and shouted as they walked through the streets to the bridegroom's home where the groom's parents met the bride and directed her to the groom.

♥ **Wedding ceremony.** After everyone entered the house, the wedding ceremony began with the bride and groom seated on a mat before a fire-lit hearth. There, the couple anointed each other with perfume and incense. They exchanged gifts. The girl's mother presented a loincloth to the groom, and the groom's mother provided a blouse and skirt for the bride. After matchmakers tied the groom's cape to the bride's blouse, they were considered married.

♥ **Tamale rites.** The ceremony ended when the groom's mother placed four mouthfuls of tamales and sauce in the bride's mouth, then four mouthfuls into the groom's mouth.

♥ **Post-wedding customs.** After more lectures on how the newly married couple should conduct themselves, a feast of turkey stew, roasted corn, and tamales was served, and singing and dancing took place. The two families entered into a kinship thereafter.

**113**

---

If the Aztec couple eloped, the father of the bride sometimes feigned anger, but he generally accepted the inevitable union thereafter. Today, Aztec weddings are influenced by Catholic or Protestant traditions.

*Chatino.* The *Chatino* of the state of Oaxaca are, monogamous. A marriage, at the groom's request, is arranged by his older relatives or a respected intermediary. If the girl's parents permit, formal visits by the prospective groom commence. The young man brings presents of food, chocolates, wine, and money to the bride's home many times to display his continued interest while he performs service for the girl's father in his fields. No matter whether the civil-religious wedding is to be performed by a priest at the Catholic church or a common-law marriage takes place, a period

of sexual abstinence is involved. After the wedding takes place, feasting, drinking, and dancing continue for three or four days.

*Guarijio Indians.* These Indians live in the mountains in the state of Sonora. Traditionally, women married between 14 and 16 years of age and men, between 16 and 20. When a girl moved in with a man or married him, her parents gave her a dowry of cattle or horses. If her parents were poor (which was very likely), and there was not enough money to provide a proper wedding, the practice of bridal theft was common.

*Tarascan Indians.* Public wells and fountains were places where many courtships began. Before a marriage was formalized, the Tarascan male often kidnapped his mate with her happy cooperation.

*Tepehuan.* Among the Durango *Tepehuan*, marriages were arranged by the parents. Most of these marriages occurred before the bride or groom reached their twentieth birthday. Prior to the wedding, the boy's parents visited the prospective bride's family for five consecutive evenings. During the last night, the girl's parents either accepted or rejected the groom's parents' offer of marriage.

One form of marriage involved the groom's appearance before a native official, called an *ixkai*. While the groom was there, his hands were tied. After the *ixkai* provided a brief invocation, the groom's hands were untied. The couple could reside at the groom's parents home and later construct their own dwelling near his family. Traditionally, the new husband worked for his wife's parents for several months.

**References:** *Culturgrams: The Nations of the World. Encyclopedia of World Cultures*, *The Aztecs* by Warick Bray, *The Aztecs* by Richard F.Townsend , and *Cultures of the World: Mexico* by Mary Jo Reilly.

# Nicaragua

Nicaraguan people have a traditionally close Hispanic family with extended family ties and godparents. Their social, financial, and political status often are reached through kinship bonds. Marriages to people who are unrelated therefore establish new family bonds; yet, a spouse is often considered less important than blood relatives.

Though the population is mainly Roman Catholic, the church had little presence in rural areas until recently. Upper and middle class couples marry in the church, but fewer lower class couples formalize their marriages. As a result, during the 1980's, common-law marriages became legal. Monogamous unions with the father as the head of the home are still held as the cultural ideal.

**Reference: Nicaragua: A Country Study**

114

# Panama

Panama's population is 85 percent Catholic and 15 percent Protestant. In Panama, urban girls experience more freedom to date at a younger age than girls who live in rural areas. On the other hand, boys both in the cities and in the country are totally free to make liaisons.

In central Panama, common law marriages are generally accepted. When weddings do occur, couples must first be married by the state before they can have a church wedding.

**♥ Upper and middle class customs**

In cities of Panama, a variety of patterns regulate the conduct prior to marriage, yet class barriers rarely are crossed. Overall, more freedom is granted to upper middle-class Panamanian girls than to those in other Latin-American countries, for elite in Panama place a greater emphasis on romantic love. In some small towns and with some of the elite, generations of marriages within their groups create an elevated frequency of blood kinship.

On an upper-middle class girl's 15th birthday, her parents hold a party and dance in their home or social club. This coming-out party signifies that the girl can now welcome suitors. Should she meet a nice boy at school, at work, on the beach, or at a dance, and truly likes him, she takes him to meet her parents. If he is accepted by her mother and father, he may take her on a date, which is often chaperoned. Girls may only date one man at a time, but the men are able discreetly to date many young women. In fact, men are expected to have affairs before they are married.

During the past and in the present, formal legal marriage was prevalent among the cattle ranchers, urban middle class, and the elite. Legal marriage was always considered important where racial purity and wealth are major considerations to maintain family status. A formal marriage ceremony can be the climax of a couple's economically successful life of cohabitation for the *mestizo* and Antillean peoples. Their grown children often encourage their parents to marry. In fact, the priest often uses marriage as an incentive to anoint the sick in their family.

When a couple decides to marry, a large announcement party is held. It is later followed either by a civil ceremony in the judge's parlor or by a religious wedding at the Catholic church. Weddings are a mixture of old Spanish Christian traditions and newer Western-style customs. For the rich, the weddings are a display of wealth held in a fashionable church during the early evening. The usual attendants during a Christian marriage include the trainbearers, godparents, the *padrinos,* and the bearer for the *arras. Arras* are coins which the groom gives the bride during the ceremony to show that he will always grant support to his wife and his future children. The traditional cake served at a reception is soaked in rum syrup and decorated with candied fruit. *(See Mexican wedding on page 111.)*

### ❤ Customs for the elite

Men of all classes are expected to have sexual relations outside of their marriages. If the man is elite, he even provides support for his mistress and their children. It is actually considered acceptable for his mistress to accompany him on the most significant of social occasions. More recently, educated women resent their husband's division of funds to support mistresses.

### ❤ Lower class customs

Panama has a low marriage rate since so many people live in consensual unions. Among the lower classes and Panamanian *mestizos* (combination of Spanish and Indian peoples), men resist marrying because of the economic burden and legal implications involved.

Among the *campesinos,* the customary offering to the priest is more than they can afford. The traditional lavish feast prevents more marriages than the cost of the priest; therefore, there is no disgrace connected with those residing in concubinages or promised unions. Living together is considered to be respectable and may be as permanent as those marriages officiated by the priest. In many communities cohabiting couples are completely monogamous.

Loyalty to one's kin provides protection and aid for most lower class Panamanians. Such family solidarity, including the extended kin, helps the family attain their major lifetime goals. Thus, a man often gives more priority to his parents and siblings than to his wife.

### ❤ Marriage customs in rural areas

Historically, Panamanian marriages were stable in farm communities and in the central provinces where the land owning cattle producers lived. Their marriages were always the most secure. Not only were morals closely controlled by villagers, but also a sense of self-respect and family pride encouraged high values. Men stayed married to one woman.

Rural courtships often started when the boy and girl met at wakes, fiestas, and festivals. Thereafter, they saw each other near a river or else she would bring lunch to him while he was working in the field. Whether or not the ceremony was legally sanctioned, he or his father asked for permission from the girl's father. If the boy's father was financially able, he would provide the couple with a good start.

If an elopement occurred, the young girl stayed secluded in a rented room with her young man for a few weeks. When the girl opened the door, even a crack, she was considered married. In some small towns such as El Cocal and Sbanagrde, the girl's chastity was closely guarded. After meeting at a fiesta, school, or at a dance, the couple could sometimes enjoy a nightly visit without a chaperone or parents on the premises. In larger towns, if the parents liked the boy, he could take the girl to the park or movies unchaperoned, but the young couple often went to dances with their parents.

# Rural Campesinos Wedding

❤ **Procession to the Catholic church.** *Campesinos* country weddings are accomplished in high style. All guests, the bride and groom, and their relatives leave at dawn for the church.

❤ **Invitations to guests.** On the way, the bride's father invites friends from the village to the feast.

❤ **Wedding customs.** During the Catholic wedding ceremony, 13 coins are bestowed on the bride by the groom. After the blessing of the womb, all walk or ride to the village where the couple will live.

❤ **Post-wedding celebration.** Fireworks and rifles shots by the villagers are a sign of welcome. The bride's parents hold a feast at their home where suckling pigs, meringues, and painted tortillas are served.

❤ **Post-wedding customs.** Toasts are given to the newlyweds, and guests present the bride a handful of rice on a stem, beans, and ears of corn for prosperity. After an evening dance, the couple leaves for their new home, which is a present from the groom's father.

*Guaymi Indians.* Because the choice of a spouse involved ownership of land and acquisition of wealth, fathers generally arranged marriages for their sons and daughters. After an agreement, based on equal exchanges, was made to unite the young couple, the groom and his parents visited the bride and her parents. Since all marriages resulted from visits between the families, no formal wedding ceremony occurred. The balance of equal exchanges involved family members acquiring spouses in upcoming marital relationships.

Often the married couple lived with the bride's parents for almost a year since the new husband worked for his spouse's parents. After he completed his duties toward his wife's mother and father, the couple could reside with the husband's family. It was his wife's obligation to join him; otherwise, her brother could not have a wife since the balance of exchange was not fulfilled.

Only a small number of polygamous marriages occurred. They could take place when men had enough wealth and prestige to support more than one wife. Such a man often married his spouse's younger sister once he established the household. Because younger wives of wealthy men were inclined to depart after their husbands aged, polygamous men usually ended their lives with a monogamous marriage.

**References:** *The People of Panama* by John and Mavis Biesanz and *Panama: A Country Study.*

# South America

*For background information on South American countries, see the "Introduction to Latin America." on page 104.*

## Argentina

Argentina's population is 90 percent Roman Catholic. Boys' and girls' group activities often begin with dancing at the age of 15. Society agrees that girls aged 15 are old enough to date. Most become serious and marry by their mid-twenties. When a couple becomes engaged, rings are exchanged.

Middle class shower parties, sometimes surprise parties, are given separately for the bride and for the groom. During these parties, each will receive gifts that will be of use after they are wed.

A civil ceremony, which establishes a legal matrimonial contract, takes place before a state officer on weekday mornings. Wearing formal clothing, the bride and groom usually arrive with friends who witness the ceremony. Afterward, all throw rice over the couple while they depart from the building.

Often, a Catholic church wedding ceremony takes place after the civil one. Prior to this wedding, the bride is not allowed to see the groom, for they believe that seeing each other would bring them bad luck.

During the wedding, the groom is accompanied by his mother at the altar, and the bride is with her father. Generally, no bridesmaids or ushers are present, and only the parents stand for the couple at the altar. The ring, given to the bride prior to the wedding, is then transferred from the bride's right hand to her left hand as a symbol of marriage. Upon leaving, the couple is again showered with rice so that they will be prosperous and fruitful. A large reception with dinner and dancing follows, along with the traditional cutting of the wedding cake. After the bride puts on some leg garters, the groom takes them off and places the garters on the single females attending the party. Wedding gifts are purchased from a shop where the couple previously registered to obtain gifts they desire. These presents are delivered to them at home.

*(See the Catholic wedding ceremony, Chapter 1.)*

**Reference:** *Cultures of the World: Argentina.*

## Bolivia

Bolivia's population is mainly Roman Catholic, but there is a Protestant minority, mostly Evangelical Methodist. Recently, church membership of Mormons,

Jehovah's Witnesses, Seventh Day Adventists, and Pentecostals has increased. The major ethnic groups are the Quechua and Aymara Indians, with about 30 percent each. Another 30 percent are mixed along ethnic and racial lines and the rest are Caucasian.

Godparents, known as *compadrazgo* or *compadres,* selected at birth or at marriage, are very important to the marriage. Since the quality of *compadres* is of utmost importance for the couple, they are often selected without regard to ethnic and racial lines. *Compadres* are held in high esteem in Hispanic and Indian cultures alike. Even after marriage, *compadres* are involved in the welfare of the ongoing relationship with the couple and their parents. Godparents exhibit the highest loyalty, participate in the marriage ceremony, give gifts to the bride and groom, and have a moral obligation to take a continued interest in the success of the married couple.

*Aymara* and *Quechua Indians.* Both tribes value marriage as the most significant occasion in a person's life. It is to last a lifetime. The couple usually live together prior to their engagement.

Elaborate rituals are associated with courtship, engagement, and their various types of wedding ceremonies, including the formal Catholic wedding ceremony. The Indian marriage customs involve godparents, marriage and inheritance feasts, the planting ritual, and house roofing. By the time the couple and the community complete these rituals, the bride and groom will have received enough supplies to function in their own home. Reciprocal obligations for a marriage can take several years to complete. These celebrations not only signify the unity of the couple, but also provide their meaningful passage to full adulthood.

*Afro-Bolivians.* The Afro-Bolivian couples usually cohabit for several years until they accumulate enough funds to wed. Afro-Bolivians of South Yungas often marry Aymara Indians and *mestizos.*

**Reference:** *Bolivia: A Country Study* **and** *Encyclopedia of World Cultures.*

*For background information on South American countries, see the "Introduction to Latin America." on page 104.*

# Brazil

Brazil is a country of both immigrants and indigenous peoples. Its early immigrant population included African, Italian and Portuguese peoples, then later German and Japanese, most living in nuclear families. Approximately 90 percent of the population is Catholic.

### ❤ Past marriage customs

During colonial times, Brazilian people lived in extended families, which included blood relatives, in-laws, and even god-children. A father would enhance his financial interests and prestige by marrying his daughters to a wealthy neighbor's sons.

### ❤ Present marriage customs

Brazilian marriages may be civil, religious, or common law, but only the civil marriage is considered legal by the state.

Though most marriage partners are chosen according to their social class and background, during the 1980's, higher education began to be a way to increase mobility for the middle class into upper class. In addition, Brazilian women, even from traditionally-oriented families, expect to make the decision as to whom they wish to marry.

### ❤ Rural marriage customs

In rural areas, the family tends to be powerful among the aristocracy. Parents still demand respect, so the young man usually asks the girl's father for permission to wed. Most Catholic couples have a large family engagement party. At this celebration the groom gives his bride a gold wedding band which she places on her right hand. During the wedding, the bride usually wears a white gown and the groom, a formal suit. The wedding ring is placed on the bride's left hand. The godmother and godfather of the bride and groom are in the bridal party, rather than bridesmaids and groom's attendants. The reception is an extended family affair to which friends are invited. The feast includes a large variety of foods and alcoholic beverages. Music and dancing accompanies this fiesta and an older relative quietly gathers monetary donations to be given to the newlyweds prior to their honeymoon.

**References:** *Brazil*, **a Time-Life book and** *Gale Encyclopedia of Multicultural America.*

*For background information on South American countries, see the "Introduction to Latin America." on page 104.*

# Chile

**Thanks to Ximena Prudant, Embassy of Chile**

Almost 90 percent of the Chilean population is Roman Catholic, a heritage from European countries such as Spain, Germany, and France. These countries provide the models for church wedding ceremonies.

## ❤ Past marriage customs

Historically, marriage was a union between families of the same class, for it was a way to increase numerical and economic power; therefore, marriage within the extended family was common. Courtship was restricted by chaperones who frequently hindered couples from getting to know each other.

Young men were expected to initiate their sex life at a young age and had the opportunity of selecting among the slaves prior to marriage; however, high class girls were limited as to the places they could go and were always watched by adults. Girls married shortly after puberty; otherwise, they were sent to convents. This pattern was a product of Portuguese influence during colonialism.

Traditionally, when a couple between the ages of 17 and 20 were seriously dating, the boy gave the girl a gold ring which she wore on the right hand. This period was called an *ilusion* stage since there was no major commitment between them; however, this custom is seldom practiced now.

## ❤ Present marriage customs

Before marriage, young people date and are given freedom to choose their partner. The boyfriend talks to the father, often with the mother present, and asks for his daughter's hand in marriage. When they set an engagement date, the Catholic priest goes to the bride's home and blesses the rings, including the bride's diamond ring. Both wear the rings on their right hand until they are married. After the wedding, they wear the rings on their left hands.

## ❤ Wedding

The couple must be married at a civil ceremony prior to their church wedding. During the civil ceremony, the marriage law is presented to the couple, they are married, and are given a license.

Weddings are usually held at the Catholic Church on Friday or Saturday evenings without a wedding rehearsal. Weddings never take place on Sunday after six p.m. There are no bridesmaids or large processions which approach the altar, perhaps just a flower girl and ring bearer. The father gives the bride away. Her position is to the left of the groom facing the altar. The bride may stand next to her parents and the groom next to his, or their parents may stand behind them. The Catholic wedding ceremony may last about 20 minutes or take place during a full mass.

Family and friends who attend the ceremony often enjoy a cocktail party afterward. The party may be given at 10 p.m. at a hotel, at the parents' home, or at a beautiful home specially rented for weddings. Sometimes the festivities are held at a church hall. Wine and champagne are served at a banquet with meat, rice, salad, and cake. The parties are often catered. Dancing occurs after dinner and then the newlyweds leave for their honeymoon.

**Reference:** *Area Handbook for Chile and Cultures of the World: Chile*

*For background information on South American countries, see the "Introduction to Latin America." on page 104.*

# Columbia

In Columbia, Catholic marriage is considered the preferred union between a man and a woman; yet, Catholic marriages are more common between men and women of superior social and financial status, rather than the poor because of the heavy cost involved. In rural areas, a formal marriage is considered an unnecessary economic burden. Lower or middle-low class women have always had fewer restrictions on dating than those in the upper class, for lower status women had to be employed. By contrast, chaperonage during courtship could be more easily maintained by the upper class. Those who are well-educated simply wait to be married in the Catholic church. Girls try to marry a man of status and affluence. Even though many in the middle class hope for marriages in the upper class to facilitate higher social and financial mobility, the upper class usually marries within its own social strata.

Before 1973, Catholic marriages were the only valid marriages for those of the Catholic denomination. There has been increasing acceptance of civil weddings since 1973; however, most families who can afford to have an elaborate church wedding will do so. The Catholic religious wedding denotes social status and being wed is considered a means of social mobility. Matchmaking is more common with the aristocracy, since a marriage cements families socially, politically, and economically. In the past, some upper class families used a matchmaker, often a cousin, who is chosen to help keep money, social standing, and prestige within the family. Now dating without chaperones is increasing among educated families in urban areas. However, the young people do not date many people indiscriminately. Most develop a one-to-one relationship quickly, then are married.

*Afro-Columbian.* Afro-American couples usually have free informal unions. Near the Pacific Ocean, serial polygamy occurs with the man having overlapping short-lived involvements with women. Near the Caribbean, the man is likely to have a head wife to whom he is legally married, plus a mistress.

*Awa Kwiaker Indians.* Because the standard of youthful beauty is considered so important, girls are married by the age of 15 or 16; otherwise they might not marry at all. When a young man wants to marry, he confers with his father about the amount of land the young man's parents own. Marriage is a method of increasing property, so the girl's father carefully monitors his daughter's future by learning about the property in his prospective son-in-law's family. The couple is permitted to cohabit for a year in a trial marriage. If their relationship is quite stable with the woman performing her household duties well, they marry; otherwise, the woman must return in shame to the home of her parents with a decreased chance of ever entering a trial marriage again.

**References: *Encyclopedia of World Cultures and Cultures of the World: Colombia.***

# Equador

The population of Equador is about 40 percent Native Indian and another 40 percent a mix of Indian and white peoples. The remaining are white or black. Roman Catholic, Protestant Evangelist, and Pentecostal churches have made inroads in Equador.

Godparents, known as *compadrazgo* or *compadres* selected at birth or at marriage, are important to the marriage. They are held in high esteem in Hispanic and Christian Indian cultures because they are involved in the ongoing relationship with the couple and their parents. To exhibit the highest loyalty, godparents are expected to participate to the marriage ceremony and give gifts. They have a moral obligation to take a continued interest in the success of the married couple after the wedding. The *compadre* is held in such high regard that arguing with a compadre is unthinkable.

The couple's families are united and enjoy a close relationship even when a couple lives in a nuclear family. Since most marriages over the generations have taken place within a small village, webs of people are related within the community.

**Reference: *Equador: A Country Study.***

For background information on South American countries, see the "Introduction to Latin America." on page 104.

# *Paraguay*

Paraguay is a Roman Catholic country in which most adults marry. In Paraguay three kinds of marriages exist: church, civil, and consensual unions. Even though stable marriages are highly prized, men's extramarital affairs receive little criticism if they do not interfere with their families' total well-being. On the other hand, married women are expected to remain faithful throughout their married life.

The highest ideal is to have a Catholic church wedding and a fiesta afterwards. Because the combined expenses of such a celebration are considerable to both families, only parents who can afford the cost are able to have an elaborate ceremony with festivities. Civil marriage can be a mark of status for peasants and farm families who often find the cost of a church wedding beyond their financial capabilities. When civil or consensual marriages occur in peasants and farm families, a small party or barbecue is held afterward.

**Reference: *Paraguay: A Country Study.***

# *Peru*

**Thanks to Teresa Quesada, Cultural Counselor, Embassy of Peru**

Young people today meet through friends or at the universities or by engaging in activities during their everyday lives. People are free to select their own marriage partners. After dating for a year or more, couples become engaged. Knowing in advance that he will be accepted, the groom asks the father of the bride for her hand. A party is then held to celebrate the couple's engagement.

Since Peru is a Catholic country, 99 percent of the couples have a religious ceremony in a church. In order for the marriage to be legal, however, the law requires that a civil ceremony take place in the City Hall a couple of days before the wedding ceremony.

*Inca Indians.* When the Inca Empire flourished centuries ago, rulers took so much pride in their sacred blood that they married their sisters. Marriage customs between ordinary people and those of privilege differed. Marriage was so valued and widespread that spinsters and bachelors were rare. A marriage, civil rather than religious, was performed after the village chief gathered all the young people of both sexes before him, one row of maidens and another of youths. He simply wed each couple in turn. A couple in love could jockey for a position in line so that they could finally stand together before the chief. After the couple was wed, the man took his new wife to his stone or adobe dwelling where ceremonial festivities were held by the newlywed's families. The more privileged tended to be polygamous while the less privileged were monogamous.

*Amuesha Indians.* The *Amuesha* Indians traditionally married cousins, non-relatives, people from neighboring tribes, or colonists. In order to obtain a bride, the young man provided service, such as helping in the fields, to the father-in-law. If the groom was young, a close relative from his parent's generation asked the prospective bride's father for her hand. Before the bride and groom could reside together, they knelt before the bride's father during the wedding ceremony.

Presently, couples have a religious or civil marriage ceremony, or some do not marry at all. Many Indians have as many as six serial marriages; yet, others live in a monogamous relationship for a lifetime.

**References: *Encyclopedia of World Cultures*, National Geographic's book *Indians of the America*.**

121

# Trinidad and Tobago

Thirty-two percent of the population of Trinidad and Tobago is Roman Catholic, 29 percent Protestant, 24 percent Hindu, and six percent Muslim. In Trinidad and Tobago, between 1930 and 1946, Muslim and Hindu weddings were not recognized because they were non-Christian. After 1946, their weddings became legal. The Muslim and Hindu peoples retain their wedding customs. *(See Catholic, Muslim, and Hindu religious customs in Chapter 1.)*

*Hindu.* The Hindu marriage involves a *chheka* ceremony during which the bride's father, accompanied by the priest, gives a dowry to the groom. When ac-cepted, the young man is obliged to marry the young woman. In turn, the groom must pay the father a bride-price to marry the bride. The wedding takes place at the bride's family home where relatives and friends construct a nuptial tent. The bride traditionally wears a red sari at the wedding ceremony to display her happi-ness. A large reception afterward is filled with merri-ment and chanting to the beat of the drums.

*Afro-Caribbean.* The majority of Afro-Caribbean weddings are Christian with a prior engagement or co-habitation period. If the couple are devout Christians, they usually do not reside together as a couple until the wedding ceremony takes place. The Christian bride wears a white gown symbolizing sexual purity. The entire community is usually invited to weddings and receptions consisting of large feasts and rum.

**Reference:** *Gale Encyclopedia of Multicultural America.*

*For background information on South American countries, see the "Introduction to Latin America." on page 104.*

# Venezuela

Ninety-five percent of Ven-ezuelans are Roman Catholic. Other religions represented in Venezuela include the growing Baha'i and Protestant faiths, some Sephardic Jews from Spain, followers of Buddhism, and a few Greek and Ukrainian Orthodox congrega-tions.

When a young girl reaches the age of 15, families of status hold a *quinceanera*. It is a coming out party which signifies she is a woman ready to join the social world. These parties, held at clubs, halls, or homes, may have a hundred to a thousand guests, depending on the wealth of the family. They were originally in-tended to bring the girl in contact with eligible men.

## ❤ Past marriage customs

In the past, a conservative family frowned upon un-supervised dating without a chaperone until the couple seriously considered marriage; therefore, strict super-vision of girls was enforced. Before marriage, boys always were allowed a period of sexual experimenta-tion while being educated at a university and spending time on political activities. Upon graduation from the university or entering his profession, the man engaged in serious courtship which often led to marriage. More recently, both men and young women enjoy consider-able freedom, especially in the large cities.

In 1963, among the lower classes and peasants, unsanctified common-law marriages were as frequent as formal church ceremonies since church marriages with a fiesta afterwards were quite expensive. Upper and middle class couples were married in the civil cer-emony and in the Catholic church where the values of stability and family solidarity were strengthened. The husbands, heads of the family, were expected to take care of the spouse and children, or otherwise risk sig-nificant social condemnation. Extramarital relation-ships of many husbands were not observed as having an effect on marriage, for the man's moral and finan-cial obligation was to care for his legal spouse and le-gitimate children.

## ❤ Present marriage customs

High and middle class weddings are held at the Catholic church. Wedding fiestas of the middle class and the elite are large, elaborate affairs in which no expense is spared. When the couple is among the elite, they may sneak away from the large reception without anyone noticing. Their unseen disappearance is con-sidered a sign of good luck.

**References:** *U.S. Army Handbook for Venezuela and Cultures of the World: Venezuela.*

# Asia 6

# Afghanistan

The population of Afghanistan is primarily Muslim, Hindu, and Sikh with a Jewish minority. Marriages are prearranged by parents and guardians who take into account the prospect's religion, family ties, relationships, status, financial benefits, and welfare. The uniting of close relatives, especially cousins, is common and advantageous. When a man marries a relative, he can avoid paying a huge brideprice to her family to compensate for the loss of their daughter. A revolutionary government in 1978 passed a decree allowing freedom to choose a marriage partner and prohibiting the payment of the brideprice, but people do not abide by the law.

Even though a Muslim man is allowed to have as many as four wives, usually the Afghan man can only afford to pay for one. Since the brideprice in terms of money or livestock is so high, some urban men work as long as 10 years before they have sufficient funds to marry. As a result, these men generally marry brides 10 to 15 years younger than they are. On the other hand, in rural Afghanistan the boy is usually between 18 and 20 and the girl is between 16 to 18 at the time of marriage.

Once the brideprice is settled, an engagement ceremony follows and a wedding date is set. The groom's mother presents clothing and jewelry to the bride. In turn, the bride brings a dowry from her family consisting of clothing, bedding, and household utensils. Three days of prenuptial ceremonies precede the wedding. During that time, relatives feast and enjoy music and enter-

tainment. After the wedding ceremony, the relatives follow the bride and groom to their new home.

## ❤ Selecting a spouse in westsern Afghanistan

In the western section of Afghanistan, *Durrani* children may be betrothed prior to puberty to give young men time to accumulate a brideprice. *Durrani* men usually marry about age 20 and the girls by 15. Older girls are considered undesirable because they might have already formed attachments to another man. The boy's father usually initiates the quest to marry off his son, but relatives on both sides visit each other to discuss the suitability of marriage before a formal proposal is made. If the proposal is acceptable to both sides, the boy's family gives an engagement party and a gift to the girl's father.

## ❤ Durrani betrothal

Men and women attend formal engagement ceremonies. During that time, the girl's guardian gives *handkerchiefs*, symbolizing solidarity, to the boy's representative. A *mullah* and other senior men invited by the guardians representing both sides, 30 families or more, witness the exchange. After the bride's father calls out the pre-arranged brideprice and the groom's father publicly agrees to it, a small down payment is handed to the girl's father. Trays of sweets, covered by handkerchiefs, are brought forward and a prayer is recited. The ceremonial is followed by gunfire. Then, the groom's parents give a feast at their house where the handkerchiefs are hung. At this party, well-wishers shower the handkerchiefs with sweets to symbolize a sweet life for the couple. After eating, all sing and dance until sundown. Then, the groom presents the bride with clothing, and the bride hands embroidered handkerchiefs to all. Those who accept the handkerchiefs give the bride a token.

The betrothal contract permits the man to have sexual relations with his bride, but he is not yet entitled to her labor or their children until he pays the entire brideprice to her father. She then resides at the groom's home and the Islamic marriage ceremony takes place.

# Afghan Durrani Wedding

♥ **Pre-wedding customs.** Each evening before the nuptial approaches, young females congregate at the groom's house to sing and dance. After the groom's mother prepares personal gifts for the bride, women carry them to the bride's house. Older women from the bride's family accept the presents of jewelry, clothes, and the bridal veil, and display the gifts, along with those from the bride's family. All are treated to sweets at a midday party.

The evening prior to the wedding, the groom's family sends a cook and their relatives to the bride's home, accompanied by camels carrying foods and fuel wrapped in colorful handkerchiefs. A party is given at the groom's house where all dance to music played by hired musicians. That night, the bride is bathed and her hands are decorated with henna. The groom's hands are hennaed as well.

♥ **Fetching of the bride.** As the sun rises, the musicians play and all who hear the drum beat are welcome to be present at the bride's home. The groom's party walks to the bride's home. If they live at a distance, the women ride decorated camels while the men ride on horses. As they approach the bride's home, the men fire guns to let the bride's family know of their arrival. A bride's relative greets them; then, the men and women divide into separate circles to dance and play games.

The bride wears her wedding apparel and jewels. A white veil totally covers her face. She waits behind a curtain. The groom is also hidden somewhere in the house. Luncheon of rice and meat is served to men and women who eat separately. After eating, men and wives examine the trousseau. Women sing songs of approval or ridicule, depending on the quality and amount of the trousseau. The trousseau is then placed on the camels for departure to the groom's house.

The *mullah* dresses the groom in new white clothes and blesses him. The bride's father and friends kiss the groom, slap him on his back, and shower him with sweets and coins. Finally, the bride appears with her mother and older women who help her onto the camel. Before she leaves on the camel, she sprinkles her head three times with water from a container. She, too, is showered with coins and sweets as she, with her mother or sister, and the groom depart for the groom's home. The groom's male relatives again shoot their guns.

♥ **Wedding Ceremony.** Once the bride and groom arrive at the groom's home, she will not enter until she receives a gift, then a dinner is held with other invited guests. The ceremonial container of sugar-water, covered by a handkerchief, is set in front of the *mullah*. The sugar-water symbolizes that the couple should be sweet to one another. When the *mullah* asks if they consent to this marriage, all witnessing await their replies. Their representatives bargain over the *mahr*, a sum the groom pledges for his bride. Once an agreement is attained, the *mullah* takes the handkerchief off the sugar-water and recites Islamic prayers. Then, the sugar-water is passed to the males so they can each have a sip. After the ceremony, the newlyweds spend three days alone in a chamber or a tent.

All female relatives and friends are invited to the lifting of the couple's marriage bed so that they can see the bride discover a present beneath. During the following days, she will receive invitations from many women to eat a meal with them. At each home she is provided with a present or monetary gift.

*Bartered Brides* **by Nancy Tapper,** *Afghanistan: A Country Study,* *The Land and People of Afghanistan.*

# Arctic Eskimos

Parents arranged marriages between unrelated Asian Arctic Eskimos, with some unions being arranged at birth. The marriage process began when the groom's family gave gifts for the bride's relatives. The young man then worked at the girl's parents' home and hunted with her father for about 12 months. While he worked, sexual relations were permitted between the bride and groom. After the groom's service was over, the couple was considered married without ceremony. They resided thereafter at the home of the husband's father. Asiatic Eskimo husbands allowed their wives to give sexual favors to men who helped them hunt. Levirate marriages occurred.

**Reference:** *Encyclopedia of World Cultures*

# Azerbaijan

Azerbaijan, formerly in the United Soviet Socialist Republics, has a large Muslim population with Islamic wedding customs. The Azerbaijan Turks who live in this country had parentally arranged marriages. Children were married to a relative or another person who was known to the family.

According to the *Encyclopedia of World Cultures*, freedom of choice is increasing in cities. Young people receiving a higher education tend to marry later and even marry those outside their group or people from Iran and Turkey.

# Bangladesh

Over 80 percent of the Bangladesh population is Muslim and the remaining inhabitants are Hindu.

Because the sexes were historically kept socially separated in the Muslim world, typically, the man and woman did not know each other before marriage. Because extended families held property jointly, marriages between cousins and kin often took place. Thus, the uniting of the bride and groom represented the interests of the families rather than the young people's personal preferences.

Marriages were civil contracts arranged by the parents, though men occasionally had some influence over their parents' selections.

At the present time, the financial standing of the family or the marriage prospect may outweigh a highly respected family background. When negotiations are being held between the bride's and groom's families, the groom's family usually pays a brideprice. Generally, it is a cash payment, part of which is to be returned if a divorce must be initiated later.

Today, in urban communities, men often negotiate their own marriage contracts with the girl's father. Women have power to participate in their own marital arrangements only when they are of the highest class. A woman may properly wed a man who is of higher status.

Young people are not pressured to marry young, but are given a chance to complete their education. Educated persons are rarely married before the age of 25. Now, both young men and women have the right to say "no" to their parents' choice of partners.

**References:** *Bangladesh, A Country Study, Enchantment of the World: Bangladesh*

# Cambodia

Cambodian Thervada Buddhist marriages were traditionally arranged by the parents. They still are in rural areas; however, in cities Cambodians follow the western tradition of marrying for love. The bride may even wear a white wedding gown. Men marry between the ages of 19 to 24 and women, from 16 years to 22. Since remaining single is considered an insult, both male and females try to marry before the age of 25.

The traditionally arranged marriage occurs after the family appoints a representative to investigate the other family. This person assesses the social acceptability and economic standing of a prospective spouse. If families agree to the marriage of their children, they exchange presents of food and plants. Then, they question an *achar* for the best wedding date.

*(See the Cambodian Buddhist wedding ceremony on the next page.)*

125

# Cambodian Buddhist Wedding Ceremonies

❤ The elegant bride wears a decorative *sampot* and is adorned with wrist bracelets, necklaces, and ankle bracelets. The groom's traditional clothing includes puffed pants and a jacket.

❤ The wedding begins when the procession of friends and family carry food and drinks to the bride's house. There, the bride and groom sit before a table laden with fruit, candles, and a sword to ward off evil. The presiding monk cuts locks of hair from the couple's heads and mixes the hair in a container. This act symbolizes the togetherness of their future life experience. Guests give the couple money in paper envelopes. As the finale to the wedding, a knot ceremony called a *ptem* takes place. Knots are tied on a string bracelet to display the elders' good wishes for the newlyweds.

*or*

❤ Another type of Cambodian Buddhist wedding also takes place at the bride's house with a Buddhist priest performing a ceremony. At this ceremony, the couple exchange presents and rings; then the bride and groom's wrists are fastened together with red thread which was dipped prior in holy water. Married guests pass a candle to bestow a blessing on the newlyweds; then they hold a magnificent feast of meat, fruits, and cakes. Musicians play songs on historical instruments.

**References:** *Gale Encyclopedia of Multicultural America, Enchantment of the World: Cambodia.*

# China

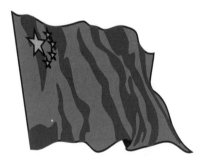

Historically, China's people were Buddhist and Taoist, but during Communist rule, the country officially became atheist. Buddhism had tolerance for all types of family structures, but recent laws made significant changes.

Throughout history, various types of marriages have existed among the Chinese, including multiple wives and concubines. Though marriage customs have changed more recently, the following marriage patterns still occur in the Chinese countryside:

❤ Marriages between cousins and close relatives still occur.

❤ Among the Zhuang, Dong, Bouyei, Miao, Yao, Yi, Va and Jingpo peoples, elders permit a "golden period of life" when boys and girls are allowed to have love affairs before marriage.

❤ Many regional groups encourage marriage be-

fore their young children become adults.

❤ Monogamous marriages are arranged by parents, matchmakers, or fortune tellers.

❤ Elements of polygamy exist among the upper strata of minority nationalities.

❤ Some polyandry exists among the Tibetan, Naxi, and Pumi nationalities.

Traditionally, marital arrangements of a prosperous man consisted of a wife and secondary wives. A woman was considered to have good marriage luck if she became his first wife because she was mistress of his household and of his secondary wives. Even when the husband strayed, he still took on the responsibility to provide for his first wife, and their children took precedence. Women often arranged their living quarters using the 4,000 year-old principles of *Feng Shui* to promote romance and improve their opportunities for happiness in a good marriage. (*See page 260.*)

❤ **Ancient customs**

## Chinese Legend

*When children are young, gods tie an invisible red string over the ankles of the couple who are*

*supposed to wed later. As the years go by,*
*the string becomes shorter and shorter*
*until the couple are united.*
*Nothing in this world can sever the string,*
*"not distance, changing circumstances, or love.*
*Marriage is their destiny."*

Confucius said that individuals having the same last name could not wed. His teachings involving betrothal included a betrothal letter from the groom's father to the bride's father, and an exchange of goods (gold chopsticks, foods, animals), and services.

The ancient engagement entailed the offering of incense, candies, wine, and fruit at altars. Engagement presents exchanged by the Chinese ancestors were symbolic gifts: deerhorn as an aphrodisiac and sweet osmanthus and pomegranate blooms indicating property and the birth of sons. The groom's family presented valuable teas to the bride's family. Marriage contracts were written in characters and verse.

Once gifts of food and money were exchanged, the couple were married. In ancient times, a promise of engagement was totally binding, even if couples were engaged as infants. Chinese courts of law decreed a broken engagement was punishable by 60 strokes.

### ❤ Traditional marriage customs

In the past, a young woman pinned up her hair at the age of 15 to show she was eligible for marriage, but dating was virtually nonexistent. The young woman stayed at home and was rarely in the company of those who were not family. Young people who wanted to make their own matches, jeopardizing family interests, were considered immoral. Marriages were arranged by families, a brideprice was paid, and a dowry was involved. Customs emphasized moral purity. Among the ruling classes, marriages were contracted by families to perpetuate the families' influence and to expand the families' social network. A rich man could have as many concubines as he could afford.

In Beijing, the marriage occurred before the Spring Festival. They believed that five days prior to the wedding, the Kitchen God oversaw domestic concerns abandoned affairs on earth so that nothing was forbidden. The marriage ceremony was then performed at an ancestral shrine. If the family was rich and politically prestigious, the bride and groom wore red and green silk and were transported to their new residences in wedding sedans embellished with birds and flowers.

### ❤ Historical changes in marriage customs

During the 1950's in the city of Chengdu and other urban areas, a shift occurred from the marriage arranged by the parents to the new trend in which young people selected their own marital partners. This increasing freedom occurred when the socialist transformation reduced the power of parents. Not only did the young people attain freedom of spousal choice, but the newlyweds became a nuclear family living apart from their parents. The Communist Party also enacted the Marriage Law of 1950 which changed traditional marriage practices and condemned traditional rituals and feasts. This law also outlawed concubines, child betrothal, multiple wives, and the sale of sons and daughters for marriage purposes. Monogamy was strictly enforced, and the right to marry one's personal choice was promoted along with marriage based on mutual affection. Because China's population was the highest of all countries in the world, Chinese people were encouraged to delay marriage so they would not overpopulate their country. In cities, couples who married before their mid-twenties were not eligible for certain jobs, benefits, or promotions. Those who attended college had to wait until they graduated in order to marry.

### ❤ Difficulty finding mates

In the early 1950s, over half of urban married couples met through relatives, neighbors, or colleagues, so young people were increasingly having difficulty finding mates. By 1957, eligible singles met through governmental matchmaking agencies, their associates, singles parties, and personal advertising in magazines, like *Chinese Women* and *Economic Life*.

During the late 1970's when the rule of only one child per family was imposed, the focus was upon having male heirs, so many Chinese girls did not survive to become adults. Today, the policy against raising daughters in China has thus created a surplus of desperate bachelors. Chinese government statistics show that of the eight million people over 30 who were single, men outnumbered women by nearly 10 to 1.

Young men now are resorting to unconventional means of finding mates so that they will not have to become lifelong bachelors. In 1980, the government, with the aid of women's federations, trade unions, and other entities, established matchmaking services in cities and in rural regions of China. Every other day, women are permitted to check through the files of male profiles. Men take their turn on the days in between. Males are only permitted to review applications chosen for them and decide which women they wish to meet. An introduction is made only when both parties think they are compatible. The first computer dating surfaced in Beijing in 1989.

### ❤ Further changes in marriage laws and customs

During the 1980's, the dowry and brideprice for marriages increased. Women relatives provided purses for the bride filled with gold jewelry to add to the bride's value because families wished to advance the status and prestige of a daughter. In order to keep up, both young men and women had to save their wages and bonuses for their future. The groom's family was expected to provide a new house for the couple.

When the Marriage Law of the People's Republic of China was put into effect in 1981, it emphasized free choice, monogamy, and equal rights for the sexes. It stipulated that money for girls in connection with marriages was prohibited. There must be a complete willingness to marry on the part of both parties and no third party is permitted to interfere. A man was not permitted to marry before the age of 22, and the woman, at 20 years of age, in order to encourage late childbirth. Marriages were not allowed between linear blood relatives or collateral blood relatives to the third degree. Individuals having leprosy or other incurable disease were considered unfit for marriage. Couples had to register at a marriage registration office where a marriage certificate is granted. The results of the law were mixed, for such changes worked better in the cities than in rural areas of the vast country of China.

### ❤ Present courtship and weddings

By the 1990's, the population was given more freedom to practice their religions, and there was a resurgence of Buddhism. Though demonstrations of affection were still not permitted in public, changes were occurring. Young Chinese were being influenced by Western culture after viewing satellite-television musical broadcasts from Hong Kong. By 1995, young people enjoyed meeting and taking their dates to the three major world-class discos with multiple-level dance floors and laser lights in the Chinese capital of Beijing.

Although traditional parentally arranged marriage customs have become almost passé, children still consult their parents and desire their approval, especially if they are financially dependent. A couple must also receive permission to wed from a local board. After they are given authorization, a legal certificate is recorded, and the couple is thereby considered married. Females keep their maiden names after marriage. Weddings, simpler during the Mao era, are now more elaborate. Affluent families have lavish weddings, especially in the town of Nanxi Zhen located in southern China. Because China is so large, not all changes in marriage customs occurred uniformly.

### ❤ Chinese premarital practices

When a marriage is traditionally arranged by a professional matchmaker, the matchmaker hosts a betrothal tea where the excited young couple meet for the first time. During this gathering, the young lady serves tea to the young man and his relatives. If the young man likes her, he offers an embroidered red bag on the plate which held the teacup. If she wants to be engaged to the young man, she will accept the saucer.

## *Chinese Wedding*

*Chinese believe that marriages are directed by the god of mirth and the god of harmony.*

❤ **Present wedding attire and weddings**. Today, an affluent urban Chinese couple may rent a Western suit and white wedding gown from a photographic studio. The bride may also hold a customarily open red umbrella and carry a bouquet of red roses to match. Though the couple do not usually exchange vows in the Western sense, they go to a government office to sign marriage papers. There, they are lectured by an authority and pronounced married. They enjoy a lavish banquet later at a restaurant. Their dinner can have as many as 12 courses. They usuallly enjoy spicy chicken, succulent pig, seafood, and long noodles for a lengthy life.

❤ **Tea ceremony.** The tea ceremony is thought to be witnessed by their ancestors and gods. It formally introduces the couples as husband and wife and establishes their place in the family as a couple. The bride serves tea to each guest, thereby obtaining monetary awards from each one in a red envelope; otherwise, the new husband offers (perhaps dragon's eye fruit) tea as he makes short humble bows to each parent. While a sip is taken by each relative, a red envelope filled with money or jewelry is given to him in return.

# *Chinese Wedding*

### *in Hong Kong*

❤ **Pre-wedding customs.**    If the family's fortune teller finds that the bride's and groom's birthdates indicate no bad luck for the future, the families will exchange their family records and family tree. *(optional)*  The groom's family send gifts to the bride's home. The groom pays a monetary gift to the bride's family that may cover the wedding cost and pay for a certain number of tables at the wedding reception. Whenever possible, a bridal bed is purchased and is traditionally covered with new red linen. Sometimes, the bride provides a monetary gift to offset the expenses for the banquet. On the evening prior to the wedding, a good luck person combs the bride's hair while she sits near a moonlit window. Her hair is combed four times so that her marriage will attain the following:

- ❤ Lasting qualities from the beginning to the end
- ❤ Harmonious relationship through old age
- ❤ Children and grandchildren
- ❤ Prosperity and a lengthy marriage

❤ **Departure of the bride.** Years ago, the groom sent a carriage with red decorations to the bride's house to pick up the bride. She wore a red gown with jewelry given to her by her parents. Her family stayed home. As the bride left, she carried a protective red umbrella, which when opened, would bring her descendants to the groom's family. If the bride's family were rich, servants would accompany her. As servants carried her into the carriage, the musicians played wedding music. Sometimes, the bride would be carried on the back of a female representative of the groom. The bride was forbidden to set her foot on the earth until she entered the groom's residence.

Today, the groom and his groomsmen decorate several cars and then drive to the bride's house. When they arrive, the bridesmaids answer the door, ask the groom tricky questions, and make amusing requests. The groomsmen help the groom so that he passes the tests; then, the groom gives the bridesmaids gifts wrapped in red paper. The bride and groom serve tea to the bride's parents and then to her relatives. In turn, each relative will present red packages, possibly with gold jewelry inside for the bride.

Their wedding customs include the signing of the marriage license at the government's Marriage Registrar or possibly a wedding at a church.

❤ **Arrival of the bride.** When the bride arrives at the groom's house, the bride and groom serve tea to the groom's parents and then to his relatives. Each will give the bride and groom red packages of jewelry.

❤ **Wedding feast.** The parents hold a banquet for friends and relatives out of respect for their kindness and at which they make the announcement of their children's marriage. The banquet itself has up to twelve courses: lobster, roast pig, fish soup, fried rice, noodles, and more, plus dessert and fresh fruit. While the food is served, wedding music is played. A Master of Ceremonies may conduct the proceedings, such as toasts, etc. Guests may trick the groom into publicly displaying his love for his bride.

129

**References:** *Under the Ancestors' Shadow: Kinship, Personality, and Social Mobility of China* by Francis L.K. Hsu, *Family and Kinship in Chinese Society* by Maurice Freedman, *Chinese Religions: A Cultural Perspective, Local Traditional Chinese Wedding* by Robert Lam Ping-fai, Rutledge@dnai.com., *The Complete Illustrated Guide to Feng Shui* by Lillian Too, *New Trends in Chinese Marriage and the Family published by the Women of China, Chinese Women and Economic Life, March 1995 News and World Report, Marriage and Family among China's Minority Nationalities as Viewed from Beijing, Chinese Families in the Post-Mao Era by Davis and Harrell, Encyclopedia of World Cultures, New York Time* article *Chinese Bias Against Girls Creates a Surplus of Bachelors* by Philip Shenon, Ruxian's 1991 article *Marriage and Family among China's Minority Nationalities as Viewed from Beijing* by Yan Ruxian in Mankind-Quarterly, July 1991 National Geographic, *Wild Geese and Tea* by Shu Shu Cosata.

# Hong Kong

*China*

Since real estate costs are so high, the bride and groom may work for many years to provide the cost of the wedding, aside from the amount their parents may provide. *(See the Hong Kong Chinese wedding on the previous page.)*

After the wedding, the newlyweds often spend their first night of wedded bliss at the same hotel where the banquet takes place. The close proximity to the festivities encourages friends to break into their room and play tricks on them.

*China*

### ❤ Selecting a spouse

Throughout Tibet's Buddhist history, monogamy, polyandry, and polygyny prevailed. Tantric masters and their consorts normally lived together without being united by a marriage ceremony. Buddhist marriage was primarily a secular affair and, although people married, there was no definite attempt to define a proper kind of marriage for lay Buddhists.

Buddhist people had the tradition of practicing polyandry with one woman possessing two or more husbands. A young man's parents looked for a suitable spouse by making inquiries to find a bride of the same social position. The woman had no choice but to accept the husbands selected by her parents. When a wife shared many brothers, the eldest was considered the father of a child. Virginity of the woman was not a priority.

Among nobility, however, virginity of a women was expected and blood lines were important. Once the girl of high rank was located, the parents communicated with the prospective bride's parents through a middleman. Before replying, the girl's parents privately would consult a priest or fortune teller. After the parents agreed, negotiations took place, often without the couple's knowledge.

### ❤ Tibetan wedding customs

The morning of the wedding, the bride's parents informed the bride that they all will be going to the temple for a *lingka* feast. Her engagement and marriage could occur that same day; otherwise, wedding feasts or prenuptial banquets were given two or three days before the wedding. Visiting relatives and friends brought such gifts as tea and spirits, then later wheat cakes and boiled rice combined with butter, sugar, raisins and persimmons. Dinner was served; afterward, guests enjoyed singing and dancing. At the end of the evening, the groom's representatives and attendees took breast money to the bride's home. Breast money was compensation to the mother for bringing up the bride. The representatives also provided the bride with necessary clothing for the wedding ceremony and a jewel to be worn in the center of her forehead. Her parents also adorned the bride with valuable jewels for her wedding day.

The parents of the bride gave her a farewell feast on her wedding day. At that time, the priest held a service in honor of the village and family gods. During the banquet afterward, a priest arrived and told the bride how she was to behave after her marriage to her spouse.

When the bride left her parent's home, her face was covered with cloth and remained so until she arrived at her husband's house. The entrance to the house was barred by a man who wielded a sword to rid her symbolically of evil spirits. After the bride was welcomed into the home, the groom's mother provided biscuits and a second feast was held. Another priest was brought from that village to inform gods of the village and the groom's house that a new person had arrived and for all to welcome her. All prayed, then presents of silk were given to the couple and to all the guests. The couple was now considered husband and wife.

*Before 1895, a suitor could plant an arrow in the girl's back, an action considered a survival of "marriage by capture."*

**References: *Tibetan Buddhism* by L. Austine Waddell, *The World of Weddings* by Bryan Murphy.**

*The Taj Mahal in Agra, India*

**The Taj Mahal**, *one of the Wonders of the Ancient World, was a mausoleum built by the griefstricken Moghul Emperor Shah Jahan in memory of his wife who died in 1631 during the birth of their 14th child. The emperor's wife, Arjumand Banu Begam, was called Mumtaz Mahal ("Chosen One of the Palace"); thus, the edifice known as the Taj Mahal.*

**Reference:** *Encyclopedia Americana, #26.*
**Photograph:  Nova Development Corp.**

# India

**Special thanks and credit to Sumitra Singh, of the Librarian Indian Embassy, Washington, D.C.**

India's population is 83 percent Hindu, 11 percent Shia Muslim, two percent Christian, and two percent Sikh which is a combination of the Muslim and Hindu religions. India is the birthplace of two major religions:  Buddhism and Hinduism, plus other religious groups, such as Jains and Sikhs.  The country has various religious ceremonies, marriage rites, and regional differences.

No dating or courtship occurs before marriage, though the cultures usually allow for the consent of the prospective marriage partners.  A recent *Life* magazine article indicates 20 percent of all marriages in India are uncle-niece unions.  In many cases, the bride and groom meet for the first time at their wedding ceremony arranged by their parents.  Their psychology is that love will gradually blossom after marriage.

## ❤ Bridal fashion

No matter whether their religion is Hindu, Muslim, or Sikh, bridal attire usually consists of *the sari*, *salwar kurta*, and *lahenga..*  This attire is traditionally worn with the added splendor of gold embroidery and bangles. The costumes and adornments are rich in symbolism and tradition.  Usually, *saris*, made of gold embroidered silk, are embellished with bright red, yellow, green and magenta drapes.  The predominate color of the bridal *sari* in Northern Indian weddings, both Hindu and Muslim, is red, while the North-Eastern Indian bride wears white with a red border.  The Southern bride wears yellow, green, and white Kanjeevaram silk. Brides in the Rajasthan and Gujarat states of Western India wear a large embroidered skirt with small pieces of glass decoration and a blouse which extends to the waist.

In some parts of the country, the bride's head is covered with a *pallav* to protect the most beautiful part of the body from evil eyes.  The *pallav* also identifies caste in Maharashtra.  In other regions, the *ghungat*, drawn over the bride's head and face, can only be removed by the bridegroom.

## ❤ Adornment

Gold jewelry from the bride's trousseau is worn profusely.  She is adorned with heavy necklaces, bangles set with colored glass, large earrings, and nose rings. In the north, a pearl or a gold ring is attached from the nose to the ear with a delicate gold chain , and rings are on the bride's fingers.  In the south, diamond studs, pieced on both sides of the nose, symbolize the deflowerment of the young woman. Each state has different jewelry designs; however, the *mangalsutra*, a gold chain with black beads, is accepted throughout India. Often, a yellow string necklace with a jewel set in gold is worn around the bride's neck to signify a good future.  When worn after the wedding, the necklace reminds the bride of her duties towards her family.

Silver anklets, or *payals*, are also worn by the majority of brides.  They make a tinkling sound while walking so that the newlywed's steps are audible and her whereabouts are no secret.   From the northern Muslims come the intricate *mehendi* designs painted on the palms of the hands and on the feet before the wedding. Historically, the application of artistic *mehendi* designs was adopted throughout India.

To add beauty and fragrance, the bride wears flowers in her hair. The floral garlanding of the groom also symbolizes the act of final selection by the bride.

### ❤ Hindu philosophy of marriage

For most Hindus, marriage is a religious duty since progeny are needed to continue the family line and perform Hindu rites for members who have died. Hindu marriage is considered a sacrament. Children are raised not to seek marriage partners in their schools or elsewhere while growing up because the marriage partners will be agreed upon mutually by their parents. The Gurus, or teachers, do not teach sex education, for they believe that sex comes naturally.

### ❤ Selecting a spouse

Parents arrange marriages with the belief that their children should have much in common; therefore, they must be the same caste. Parents also take into consideration the personal qualities of a future spouse, including the girl's virginity, which is considered to be the highest attribute an unmarried woman can possess.

A parent will ask a relative or friend if he or she has a person in mind for their marriageable-age child. After a selection is made, the parents of the son and daughter meet, exchange photographs, and talk on the phone. Though couples see each other for the first time on their wedding day, some parents make arrangements for the young people to meet to be sure they are satisfied with their selection. On the other hand, if a young man takes an interest in a girl, he may even bring a friend to intercede with her parents. After the families meet, like each other, and make plans for their childrens' marriage, an engagement ceremony takes place where gifts are given and sweets are served.

### ❤ The dowry

The dowry depended on the prestige and financial assets of the bride's family. Originally, parents gave the bride a dowry of land, clothing, or a maidservant so the bride would never miss the things that made her comfortable while she was living with her family. A substantial dowry, given by the bride's father, was a home for the newlyweds. Attracting a prestigious man in more recent years involved a large dowry, depending on the education and social standing of the groom.

*Mr. Saumitra Singh, wearing a sword signifying the bravery of a warrior, is going to get his bride. Courtesy of Mr. Saumitra Singh.*

If the young woman and her family wanted a highly paid professional, such as a doctor, a dowry could be worth as much as $20,000. The larger the dowry, the greater was the prestige attributed to the bride's family. Because of the abuses concerning dowries, there is now a law against the giving or taking of dowries.

### ❤ Hindu wedding customs

After an engagement, invitations are sent. The wedding generally takes place at home, usually in a beautiful tent filled with interior decor, flowers, colorful personal adornment, and jewelry. The wedding also may be held in a garden, a courtyard of a bride's house, or on a blocked-off street or square. Weddings are elaborate celebrations when 100 or more relatives gather and enjoy dining for three days or more. Customs vary according to the families' wishes and from region to region.

The bride spends many hours of preparation with her family and friends. Several days before the wedding, the bride's hands and feet are decorated with *mehendi* paste. The design may last for several weeks. Before the wedding ceremony, special makeup is applied and spectacular jewelry is worn, especially the gold chain which encompasses the bride's hairline over the face. Bracelets are placed around her wrists. If the groom is from northern India, he wears a *churidar kameez*, a silk decorated robe with tight leggings. A Hindu man in traditional dress wears a long white silk jacket with an erect collar and white trousers; otherwise, he may wear a western suit.

# Hindu Wedding Ceremony

133

*Mrs. Anupama Singh and Mr. Saumitra Singh during the performance of their marriage rites.*
Courtesy of Mr. Saumitra Singh, Mrs. Anupama Singh, and Sumitra Singh.

❤ **Groom arrives.** The wedding is usually held at eleven o'clock at night, although the priest may select another time after he has studied the stars and planets. Preceded by a brass band, the groom, carrying a sword, arrives on horseback. His parents are with him. The bride and groom often meet for the first time at the traditional Hindu wedding before assembled Brahmins or priests.

❤ **Readings, offerings, and exchange of garlands.** The Brahmin priest generally sits under a tent-like roof decorated with various flowers while the crowd gathers around him. The wedding ceremony is held before a fire-lit metal vessel, representing the *Radiant One*. There, the priest recites from sacred Sanskrit texts while the bride and groom pour offerings of rice and clarified butter. Later, the bride and groom exchange garlands and affirmations and walk around the fire seven times.

❤ **Five essentials.** The ceremony is characterized by such essentials as betrothal, virginity, acceptance, and the seven steps (*septa-padi*) signifying eternal friendship. Because virginity is considered a gift to the groom, the girl's father says, *I give you, for your son, my beautiful virgin daughter...* In return, the groom's father accepts the daughter for his son and receives her among his kindred.

❤ **Giving away the bride.** The bride's father declares his tribe and gives grains of red-tinged rice and betel plant leaves to the groom. He gives away his daughter and promises to pay all marriage expenses. The

# Hindu Wedding Ceremony

groom's father takes the hand of the bride and puts it into the groom's hand, then pours water over them. This water was previously blessed by a priest. A *tali*, a jewel set in gold, is fastened around the neck of the bride as a symbol of her married state. The guests are offered sandalwood paste, perfumes, and flowers, and blessings are given.

*(Please see additional details about the Hindu wedding in Chapter 1 on page 21.)*

**Shia (Shiite) Muslim customs**

Association between single young men and women is rare in India. Among the Shia Muslims, cross-cousin marriages are given preference in order to maintain the purity of lineage and family solidarity. Elderly ladies and other members of the family look for eligible prospective spouses for single members of their family. Caring friends and relatives make a special effort to find a partner if a cousin cannot be found. In the past, the Shias desired that their daughters be married immediately after puberty because they wanted to keep them chaste before marriage. Knowledgeable Shias now feel that a girl should be educated so she can support herself should a misfortune occur.

Shia Muslim criteria for selecting a mate include the same family status, personable attributes, and mainly, the girl's chastity and high morality. Usually, the guardian of the young man initiates the proposal to the girl's guardian. A proposal from the girl's side is considered humiliating and disgraceful. If both sides are inclined towards agreement and pre-negotiation occurs, a date for a settlement is set. The marriage ceremony is complete after the *Istikhara,* the settlement of the marriage contract.

The groom's mother, her female friends, and relatives then bring sweets to the bride. The bride's guardians accept the sweets, then entertain the groom's party with refreshments. The following ceremony may also take place: The bride, whose face is adorned with a veil, exposes her face to the boy's family and the groom. Then, the mother ties a *Imam Zamin*, a coin wrapped in silk, around the bride's right arm.

High caste Hindu and Shia Muslim widows are expected to honor their marriage contract even after the spouse has departed.

**Reference:** *Marriage Customs Among Muslims in India by Sheikh Abrar Husain.*

❤ **Sikh marriage customs**

Though northern Sikh Indian marriage is also a religious sacrament, it is different from that of the Hindu religion because the Sikh do not attach importance to rebirth after death. After the proposal is made, the entire marriage process takes several days. The groom's family gives a thread with five knots to the parents of the bride. According to custom, five days before the wedding one knot is started and knots are subsequently tied each day so as not to forget the wedding day in all the confusion and excitement. This custom began years ago when people had no calendars.

# Indian Sikh Wedding

❤ **Pre-wedding traditions.** When relatives and guests arrive at the bride's home for the wedding, they bring gifts of coconuts, sugar, and money. The day before the wedding the bridesmaids stay with the bride and paint five hand prints on the wall to bring her luck and fortune. The bride's relatives also draw a circle and place a piece of wood from a fruit tree in the center so that the marriage is fruitful. Leaves are placed above the front door to signify that a wedding is to be held in the house. After the guests arrive, all sing songs and take turns brushing oil and herbal powder into the bride's hair to make her beautiful. Relatives help make sweet pancakes which are shared with all guests. Sikh folk songs are sung to the sounds from Kiar's drum while women dance around the room and people clap. That night, the bride's relatives apply brown henna leaves with oil on the bride's hands and feet.

# Sikh Wedding

♥ The next morning the bride washes the oil and herbs from her hair, rinses off the henna, and waits for the groom's family to arrive at her home. The men from the groom's family and guests now wear yellow turbans and the groom is adorned with flowers. Gifts of jewelry are given to the bride and the bride's family. Guests are offered food and drink. A wedding ceremony takes place during the day, except on days connected with the death of Gurus. In the kitchen *chappatis*, a flat bread, is prepared. When the *granthi*, dressed in white arrives, he says a few prayers.

♥ The bride is adorned with wedding jewelry and a decorative shawl with gold decoration is placed over her face. The *granthi* officiates at the temple and reads from the Sikh holy book. The bride's father provides a long scarf which is held between the bride and groom as a symbol of their unity. After the couple walk four times around a holy book, the *Granth Sahib*, they are considered married.

♥ People sing hymns as temple musicians play. Friends make positive speeches about the bride and groom, all sign a register, and the final prayers are given. Then everyone enjoys foods made of flour and sugar. The men may go to a hall where they are served a banquet of meat and curried vegetables, salad, yogurt, rice, and chappatis which have been prepared by the bride's family. They may also be entertained by music and dancing.

♥ When the father arrives home with the other men to say good-bye to his daughter, she is adorned with marriage clothes and beautiful gold jewelry. Finally, the bride leaves with her husband and his family. Her relatives and guests say good-bye. Well-wishers surround the couple in the getaway wedding car which is covered with decoration. *(Please see details about the Sikh wedding ceremony in Chapter 1 on page 34.)*

**References: "Brides of India" from the *New India Digest, Culturgrams: The Nations of the World* edited by Grant P. Skabelunt, *Life, Welcome to the Indian Wedding, Encyclopaedia Britannica, A Sikh Wedding* by Olivia Bennett, "Marriage Customs Among Muslims in India by Sheikh Abrar Husain and *Culturgrams: The Nations of the World, Marriage Customs of the World, Welcome to the Hindu Wedding, A Sikh Wedding* by Olivia Bennett**

# Indonesia

*Information Division of the Embassy of Indonesia*

Approximately 88 percent of the Indonesian population is Muslim, 10 percent is Christian, and two percent are Hindu and Buddhist.

Indonesian Muslims in rural areas do not date because their marriages are arranged; however, individual choice of marital partners is more common in urban areas. An Indonesian marriage is considered legitimate if it is performed according to the religious beliefs of the parties concerned; therefore, couples who marry in Indonesia must declare a religion. Because Indonesian law requires that both the registrar and a religious officiator preside at the religious ceremony, it is arranged by a representative of the couple's own religion. The Civil Registry Office records marriages of persons of Islamic, Hindu, Buddhist, Protestant and Catholic faiths, but agnosticism and atheism are not recognized. Every non-Islamic marriage must be recorded with the Civil Registry. Marriages between couples of the same faith are preferred; otherwise, one partner must make a written declaration of change of religion.

Legal marriage of the Islamic faith is performed by a member of Office of Religious Affairs at a ceremony in a mosque, the home, a restaurant, or any other place. Recording by Civil Registry officials can be performed directly at the Muslim marriage ceremony. Christian, Hindu or Buddhist marriage ceremonies are usually performed at a church or a temple.

*Bugis.* The Bugis live east of Borneo, Indonesia. Wedding customs include a preliminary inquiry, a formal proposal, the acceptance, engagement, a *Beforehand Meeting*, a marriage, and wedding *pesta* (party). The meetings are usually held at the bride's home.

The boy's parents usually suggest a young woman they prefer. Then, they consult their son or the young man may inform his parents of his choice. The young woman is then asked if she has a strong feeling against the match. In most cases, children respect their parents' desires since they believe marriages arranged by parents or go-betweens are less likely to end in divorce. The go-between, if used, researches the prospective bride's social standing, her character, appearance, accomplishments, and the wealth of her family. A go-between learns if the prospective bride's parents are receptive to a proposal. Since rejection can lead to embarrassment, the groom's family considers their chance of being successful carefully before sending a go-between with a formal proposal.

❤ **Formal proposal and *Engagement Meeting***

If the wedding is large, a delegation from the groom's family visits the girl's sponsors at her home to present the proposal on the groom's behalf. There, cookies and tea are served and the groom's representatives may be asked to return for an *Acceptance of the Proposal* meeting. The *Acceptance Meeting* is sometimes combined with an *Engagement Meeting* at which time the date of the wedding is set and the brideprice is determined. If the bride's family is of higher rank, the groom's representatives ask the bride's representatives what type of personal engagement gifts are desired. If

the two sides are of equal rank, the groom's family can give whatever kind of engagement and personal presents they choose. Occasionally, the bride's sponsors ask for a *sompa*, a collection of traditional symbolic items set in a ceramic or brass pot. The items include gifts, sewn into muslin cloth. The pot, placed into a white sarong and trimmed with ribbon, is worn like a sling around the neck. An elderly man later takes the *sompa* to the bride's home at the time of the marriage.

The first public announcement takes place at the *Engagement Meeting* before family members and associates. As many as 100 invited people are invited to a high status meeting. White rice and side dishes of banana plant tips, beans, tofu, fish, and coconut cookies are served along with dishes of rich beef curries, spicy beef, eggs, salads, and relishes.

Those who attend the *Engagement Meeting* bring gifts. The women, dressed in silk tops and sarongs, place engagement gifts, such as cosmetics and clothing, on trays decorated with lace. Symbolic items, such as chicken, plum sugar, and sprouted coconut may be brought to the bride's home as well. After the formal acceptance in metaphorical dialog, representatives discuss when to hold a *Kawissoro*, a *Marriage Beforehand* meeting. At this time, bride and groom traditionally are secluded, not engaging in work, so they are not susceptible to witchcraft.

❤ **Marriage *Beforehand Meeting*.** The *Marriage Beforehand Meeting* occurs when the Islamic marriage ritual is performed, a ritual involving the partaking of traditional rice and palm sauce. The brideprice and spending money are given by the groom's family. During the ceremony, the bride, wearing a sarong-blouse and silk sarong, sits in a secluded area where she appears to be concentrating. Then, the guests, the *imam*, and the officials from the Local Office of Religion enjoy a *pesta* meal while awaiting the arrival of the groom and his escorts.

## *Bugis Wedding*

❤ **Kitchen gathering.** The *Kitchen Gathering* of women takes place a couple of days before the groom arrives. Cows are slaughtered, prepared, and served for a *Public Sitting* which may last a day.

❤ **Public sittings.** Guests arrive to observe the bride and groom and enjoy the *pesta* meal and presentation of gifts. (The couple do not consummate their marriage until all the spending money is received and the *Public Sittings* have taken place.)

# Bugis Wedding

**Cleansing ceremony.** During *Reception Eve*, the readings from the Life of the Prophet Muhammad and the *Cleansing Ceremony* and *Night's Vigil* take place. Cookies and tea are served on a long mat over the floor around which men are assembled. For the *Cleansing Ceremony*, the bride and groom sit before a pillow where henna leaves and a bowl of water are placed. An official selects a few leaves from the bowl, dips them in water, and places them on the bride and groom's hands. For good luck, men stay up all night, talk and play cards or dominoes; meanwhile, the women from the groom's family prepare presents to be given during the arrival of the groom the following day.

When the groom arrives the next morning, the bride is dressed by a costume specialist, the reception space is decorated, and a large gathering of women in the kitchen prepare to serve the groom's delegation and guests. A receiving line greets the formally dressed delegation.

The band and the groom's relations are given cookies, rice, and palm sugar sauce. The groom's relatives then escort him to the bride's home. From 50 to 1,000 people may be present at the time of a marriage ceremony. If a *Marriage Beforehand* marriage has already been performed, the groom sits in state on a throne-like chair next to the bride.

❤ **The *nika*** is the marriage ceremony. The groom's parents do not attend the *nika*. Women from the groom's house bring cookies which they deliver in pedestalled plates covered with woven cane lids. Personal gifts, set on trays for the bride, are carried inside by the groom's entourage. The marriage ritual, conducted by the *imam*, is witnessed by the bride's legal guardian, two witnesses, and an Office of Religion official. As the groom holds hands with the *imam*, the groom takes his marriage vows in the bride's absence, then signs the marriage contract. The groom's kinsmen present the brideprice which is spending money, rice, and palm sugar sauce in a container. Traditional rice and palm sugar sauce are served.

After the marriage ceremony, the groom goes into the next room where the bride is seated. Giggles and teasing occur as he first touches on her hand and head, and places the ring on her finger as he sits beside her. The marriage meal is served.

❤ **Public sitting.** Guests can number up to 1,000 people. They give the couple, flanked by sponsors and ceremonial people, gifts and money wrapped in packages. A band plays and singers perform. When music stops, someone chants passages from the *Koran*. The newlyweds rarely sleep together until all the meetings and receptions are over.

❤ **Visit to the groom's family and bride's family.** The bride and groom usually visit the in-laws and the graves of the bride's ancestors. Later, the groom's relatives, except for his parents, come for the bride and groom at the bride's house.

❤ **Balinese tradition.** On the island of Bali, the groom carries a sword during the wedding. The bride and groom lie on a table, with their heads hanging over its edge, while the priest files their teeth.

❤ **Javanese Muslim custom.** On one Indonesian island the father sits on the couch and the bride and groom sit on the father's lap. When the bride's mother inquires which one weighs more, the father replies that they both weigh the same. His response indicates that the couple will both be treated equally by the bride's parents. After they are blessed, the bride is secluded for six days. The newlyweds then eat yellow rice from each other's bowl to display lifetime unity.

*Muslims of Northern Sumatra.* Young people decide whom they wish to marry, but do not make formal proposals themselves. Instead, the groom's parents send a representative to ask the bride's parents for her hand in marriage. After her parents agree to the match, the representative hands them a *kong narit*, a gold ornament, and a cash payment for the betrothal.

Before the wedding, the bride's home is decorated with exquisitely embroidered wall hangings, mats, and other objects. The bridal chamber is also adorned with silver and gold fabric, silver trays, bowls, and dishes. A wedding throne is built on the verandah. The bride wears silk trousers and a skirt, silver belt, and a black or red blouse. She is adorned with scarves, necklaces, and hair combs, and wears bangles around her wrists

and ankles. The groom's attire is silk pants covered with a sarong, a white silk shirt, a black coat, and a turban. Around his waist is a silver belt with a dagger, gold and silver chains, and hanging gold keys.

The groom and his entourage are welcomed by the bride's party who recite poetry. The bride and groom go to the verandah where the Muslim leader waits. The leader recites the Islamic creed and verses from the *Koran*, then asks the couple for their consent to marry. After signing the contract, the newly-married couple sit on their wedding throne. Those present congratulate them and enjoy a feast.

**References: *Bugis Weddings* by Susan Bolyard Millar and Harold Stephens Wolfenden who wrote *At Home in Asia, The Last Voyage,* and *Three Decades of Asian Adventure and Travel.***

# *Japan*

*Thanks to the Japan Information and Culture Center, the Embassy of Japan, and to Reiko Minatoya*

**138**

Weddings in Japan are expensive, elaborate affairs. They combine traditional Shinto rites with ideas lifted from the West. Basically, about 63% of all wedding ceremonies are modeled after the 1900 Shinto-style wedding ceremony of Japan's Crown Prince, who later became Emperor Taisho. Today, both Western-style and traditional Japanese fashions are incorporated into the Shinto wedding. Other weddings presently performed in Japan are 30 percent Christian, two percent Buddhist, and the remaining are secular. Wedding ceremonies are held at a shrine, wedding hall, hotel, or church, followed by a reception with a wedding cake and often, live entertainment.

## ❤ Selecting a spouse

The traditional custom that remains throughout time is Japan's strong emphasis on marriage between people of equal social standing. What differs since World War II is an increasing number of love marriages. According to an article in *Sumitomo Corporate News*, July, 1993, only 13 percent of Japanese now find their mates through the use of a *nakodo*, a go-betweens. Those who still follow traditional customs have chaperones on dates. Today, engagement rings are given to the intended bride, just as in Western cultures.

Mid-1990's statistics from the Japanese Ministry

of Health and Welfare revealed that the average age for first marriages for Japanese men was 28.4 and 26.1 for women. Japanese men usually marry women three years younger than themselves.

*Miai kekkon,* the arranged traditional marriage, in which marriage is seen as a link between two families, still exists. The family selects a matchmaker, a *nakodo,* whom they know has a good reputation. Then, the family asks for the *nakodo's* help in finding a marriage partner for their child. After researching the family background of potential candidates, the *nakodo* identifies a person who would make an ideal match and arranges the first meeting. Young people who plan to marry for the first time are introduced to each other. They are not introduced to those who have been married before. After selecting a prospective candidate, a formal written request is made to obtain a brief personal history and photograph of the eligible young person, who usually lives in the same area. If the response is favorable, the *nakodo* arranges a formal meeting between the families; otherwise, the young man and woman and their parents may meet at a scenic place, a restaurant, or a theater. The *nakodo* is always present at the *miai*. After both parties gather and assess each other and the couple talk privately, both families must decide whether or not to continue negotiations. If the young man and woman like each other, they usually date until their engagement when betrothal gifts are formally exchanged.

Should either party feel that the match is not right and the *nakodo* cannot overcome their objections, negotiations may end. Many young people go through several *miai* before finding a suitable partner. A lengthy history of refusals may make future meetings more difficult. Meeting more than three times without having serious marriage intentions is considered poor taste.

Today, go-betweens are sometimes part of a computer-based marriage information agency which compiles data on prospective marriage partners. Confidential computerized profiles are displayed and matched. Agencies use another high-tech method of meeting, a digital imaging telephone where the client can see the person while talking. As in many parts of the world, magazines with advertisements appealing to spouse-seekers are now prevalent.

The Japanese people celebrate St. Valentines Day on February 14th. It is a time when women purchase chocolates and other gifts for their beaus and husbands. On the other hand, March 14th is "Wives Day" when the men purchase expensive gifts for women they love.

### ❤ Historical Japanese marriage customs

Reiko Minatoya says that if there are no men or boys in the girl's family to carry on the family name, the groom takes on the name of the bride.

Historically, a man was permitted to have a mistress if the wife was unable to have children, but the original marriage remained of utmost importance. The child from the mistress would be brought to the first wife and the man would reside with his first wife and his child.

Formerly, Japanese law required no religious wedding ceremony, and the marriage simply was registered with civil authorities. Influenced by Western culture, the Shintos and Buddhists now have marriage ceremonies held at shrines. When a matchmaker is used, the newlyweds receive a paper with the matchmaker's signatures and dates.

# Traditional Japanese Wedding

❤ **Fashion.** When a Japanese bride follows the traditional Shinto customs, she wears several kimonos, often changing them during the wedding. The Japanese bride may wear as many as five different robes the day of her wedding: a going to the temple robe, the ceremonial robe, a robe to greet people, one for dinner, and another for going away. Brides wearing kimonos may wear wooden clogs or low leather sandals with socks that have a slit between the big toe and the second toe. A white silk kimono with red lining, costing up to several thousand dollars, is rented for the wedding. This gown is often replaced later by a white Western-style wedding gown worn at the reception. The bride will often have an elaborate hair style or black wig and the groom wears morning dress or a business suit.

❤ **Wedding ceremony.** The brief, dignified Shinto ceremony takes place as the couple sit before the priest in the presence of their family and friends. The *nakodo* often leads the bride to the seat next to the groom, then takes a specially assigned seat. The families may sit on opposite sides with the go-between behind them. The priest offers prayers that the couple may be blessed and be free of ill fortune. Then, he waves his *haraigushi*, a sacred tree having white linen or paper streamers attached, as a symbol of purification. The bride and groom exchange presents displaying the status of each. Sipping rice wine, called *sake*, means that protective *kami* has been requested. The couple drinks wine, while exchanging their cups nine times to symbolize their bonding. A variety of foods is offered to the *kami*. *(For more details about Shinto wedding ceremony, see Chapter I on page 33.)*

❤ **Reception.** The reception begins later as bride, groom, the *nakodo* and spouse walk down an aisle between tables where guests are seated. At that time Mendlessohn's *Wedding March* fills the room. While the newlyweds sit at a table elevated several inches above the floor, they are applauded by their guests.

The Master of Ceremonies, often from the groom's party, gives the opening speech and introduces the *nakodo* who takes the microphone. The Master of Ceremonies discusses the backgrounds of the couple, announces their accomplishments, then reinforces marital ideals. Other speakers add embellishment. Some warn of pitfalls, give advice, and express their congratulations or read poetry.

# Japanese Wedding

♥ The wedding cake is cut with the bride's hand resting over the groom's to signify their first act together as husband and wife. After music is played, all give a toast to the couple's happiness. Next, the bride changes clothing to show her newly married status. A banquet and alcoholic beverages are served. The bride and groom stand together with a paper umbrella over their heads showing they are lovers.

♥ A series of congratulatory speeches continues. The bride changes from the traditional robe to a Western-style white wedding gown, and the groom into western clothing. Music is played and the guests applaud while the new husband and wife hold an unlighted candle. As they face the guests, the newlyweds light a single high candle on the center table to signify they are united in marriage. After traditional dances, the musical instruments are played and the recitation of classical literature are performed by older guests. The young people sing and dance. At the end of the evening, the bride and groom give the mother a floral bouquet and the father a carnation for his lapel as thanks. The groom's father will thank all for attending. Then, the newylweds go on a honeymoon.

**References:** *Modern Japan Through Its Weddings* by Walter Edwards, *Pacific Friend* magazine's article "Country with the Highest Rate of Late Marriages," January 1995, *Shinto: Japan's Spiritual Roots* by Picken, *The World of Weddings* by Bryan Murphy.

# Korea

*Thanks to the Korean Information Center
Embassy of the Republic of Korea*

***Korean bride and groom
Nova Corporation***

Korea has mainly Buddhist and Christian populations. One quarter of the people adhere to Shamanism, a folk religion involving predictions, avoiding bad luck by warding off evil spirits, and honoring the dead. On the other hand, Confucious influences emphasize such behavior as family piety, righteousness, and worshipping at shrines and ancestral tombs.

## ♥ Selecting a spouse

*Traditionally arranged Korean marriage.* In the past Confucian marriages were arranged by parents. Marriage arrangements were made in order from the oldest child to the youngest. Connections between families were more important than the wishes of the two people involved. Parents selected matchmakers, typically female, who had knowledge of the Oriental zodiac. A matchmaker could be an aunt, a neighbor, friend, or teacher. Parents who had children of marriageable age brought information about their family background, education, and social status to the matchmaker. After the matchmaker selected a person of the opposite sex whom she thought would be compatible, she arranged a meeting at a hotel or coffee house for the couple and their families. There, the families assessed the character, health, and personalities of the young man and woman as the couple remained self-consciously in the background. If the couple liked each other, their parents often permitted them to date.

*Western-style dating.* During the past couple of decades, marriage customs have changed. Families now choose whether or not they will follow traditional ways or Western influences. About half still observe the traditional matchmaking rituals which include a matchmaker and fortune teller. Other families freely permit young people to make Western-style love matches on their own. Young people first meet in groups while they are teenagers. They enjoy movies, hiking, conversing at bakeries, tea houses, and parties. As they get older, couples dine at fine restaurants where the meals consist of many courses, providing them a lengthy opportunity to become acquainted. Serious dating takes place for individuals with a higher education after they attend the university or begin to work.

Because working people are often too busy to look for a mate, modern people who intend to marry often resort to computerized matchmaking or professional marriage bureaus licensed by the government. Government regulations were established for marriage bureaus in 1988. Counselors at such bureaus have to be morally acceptable, at least 35 years or older, and have a college degree in psychology, social welfare, or education. Otherwise, they need five years or more experience of counseling with a religious organization and must be at least 40 years old. Personnel at marriage bureaus in Seoul use the computer to determine a single person's color preference. They believe a compatible color selection leads to harmony in other ways. They also request information about hobbies and interests and ask opinions on certain subjects.

### ❤ Fortune teller

Whether the couple use the traditional matchmaker or choose their own mate, a fortune teller is then consulted. Mothers provide the fortune teller with the birth information about their children. If the fortune teller indicates that the young couple is well matched, the teller proposes the best time for the couple's marriage to take place. If a compatible match is not predicted, the mothers may oppose their union. In any case, marriageable singles are always asked if they will be *eating noodles*, since noodles are standard fare at wedding receptions.

### ❤ Inducement for marriage

When the prospective husband is highly educated,

the bride's parents may offer a new car, an apartment, or a professional office as an inducement for a man to marry their daughter. If the bride's family cannot afford a house for the newlyweds, then the groom's family is responsible for providing a home. The bride is also expected to purchase Western or Korean clothing for the groom's entire entourage and relatives, and even provide quilted blankets for some. The bride's family also buys expensive jewelry for her future mother-in-law. Actually, the bride's family, if not well endowed with money, may have to sell their house to pay their dowry, for they are also expected to pay for half the costs of the wedding ceremony, reception, and furnishings for the couple's new home. Financial arrangements may vary according to the financial and educational circumstances of the families.

### ❤ Weddings

Christian weddings were originally brought to Korea by Christian missionaries. These weddings are now performed at a public hall, Christian church, or wedding hall. The wedding hall has pastel painted chambers, crystal chandeliers with soft colored lighting, and large spaces for parking cars. Presently, most weddings are held in the spring or autumn. In August, 1995, 35,000 young men and women were married in a mass wedding of the Unification Church which was held at a stadium.

The bride may wear a traditional kimono with expanded sleeves, but today's bride usually wears a Western-style white bridal gown, often rented from the wedding hall. There everything, including music and videotapes, is paid for by the hour. The wedding hall supplies floral arrangements, plenty of parking, and a beauty shop to provide makeup and fashionable hair styles for the bride and her bridal party. Hall tables are set up for the collection of money and other gifts wrapped in red.

When old rituals are adhered to, the couple may change into traditional Korean formal attire. Then, a photograph of the couple is taken in front of a traditional acrylic painting. Dots are applied over the bride's cheekbones to ward off evil spirits. She wears a crown on her head and a decorative silk kimono-like garb, with the collar of a shirt and tie peering through the neckline. The groom wears a robe.

During the wedding, the bride and groom offer fruit and wine to the groom's parents and bow to them with respect. A toast is then given by the newlyweds in honor of their marriage and to the new husband's family. Women keep their maiden names after marriage.

**❤ Korean wedding traditions**

The goose and gander historically symbols of fidelity, are included in the wedding because fowl mat for life. After the wedding is over, the groom's mother throws dates and chestnuts toward the bride. The number of dates and chestnuts that the bride catches in her hands corresponds to the number of children to whom she will give birth in the future.

# Korean Wedding

❤ The manager of the wedding hall asks guests to sit down; then, the moderator announces the names of the bride and groom. He also announces the name of the elderly man or woman who presides from behind a podium and acts as their Master of Ceremonies. The groom's family selects the male or female Master of Ceremonies, called a *churye*, because that person has flourished economically and socially. Not only does the *churye* conduct the ceremony with dignity, but also the *churye* ideally becomes the groom's advisor and mentor. The *churye* is believed to give good luck to the bride, groom, and their families.

❤ As the groom enters the hall and walks down the aisle, the pianist plays a rousing processional. The groom stops near the dais, bows, and then turns to wait for his bride. When the pianist plays the *Wedding March*, the bride with her head turned downward, comes down the aisle on her father's arm. She is given by her father to the waiting arm of her groom. Cups of wine are poured and the couple bows before them to pay their respects to their ancestors.

❤ The bride and groom then turn and greet one another with a slight bow from their waists, the bride bowing deeper according to Confucian ritual. The bride bows again. The bride and groom then say their vows: *to love and have each other always, whatever the circumstances, and to revere their elders, and to fulfill their duties as a faithful husband and wife.* They affirm their vows by a nodding of their heads. The Master of Ceremonies reaffirms that the couple have taken their vows before their family and friends and that the marriage is satisfactorily accomplished. He or she will then give the congratulatory speech and thank the guests.

❤ Upon the lighting of the wedding candles, the Master of Ceremonies gives a brief history of the bride and groom as the children of their families and then provides advice for a successful marriage. To insure fertility, dates and nuts are symbolically scattered over the bride's dress.

❤ The bride's mother brings packages of meats and wine covered with red cloth. The bride then presents these gifts to her in-laws at the finale of the ceremony. Middle class Seoul weddings include a congratulatory song, applause by well-wishers, and greetings from the bride and groom.

❤ Receptions may be held at the parents' homes, especially in the country. In the cities receptions are often given at restaurants where noodles, stew, a main course with soup, rice and rice cakes are served.

**References:** *Korea* **by Simon Winchester and "The Matchmaker was a Computer" by Laurel Kendall in** *Faces.*

142

# Kyrgyzstan

Kyrgyzstan in Central Asia, formerly under Communist rule, has a mostly Muslim population. Traditionally, girls and boys did not date, and the girl was expected to remain a virgin until marriage. For that reason, the girls married young. Kyrgyzstan women usually did not wear a veil and they could pray with their men.

Marriages were arranged according to their parents' desires and a brideprice was paid. Marriage was solemnized at a betrothal ceremony, a *nikka,* in the presence of a *mullah.* Mixed marriages were rare. Women who wed Russians or non-Muslims were often forced to depart from their region to avoid social stigma.

Under Communism, marriages were recorded at a regional Communist party office. During the years of Communist domination prior to 1990, a marriage feast, given by the boy's parents, was held at sunrise to hide it from Communist officials. Parents also hid their slaughter of sheep and the cost incurred for the marriage feast. Pilaf and other foods were served at the feast. Guests danced and sang songs accompanied by musicians. Brideprices, which were legally banned under the Communists, were now given in the form of livestock or consumer goods, rarely in money. Islamic traditions were always a challenge to the Communist system before its collapse and are stronger today as a result.

**Reference: *The Resurgence of Central Asia* by Ahmed Rashid.**

# Laos

**Thanks to the Embassy of the Lao People's Democratic Republic**

Laos is 85 percent Buddhist, although the highland ethnic minorities practice Animism, a religion which emphasizes a reverence for all living things. Young men and women have the freedom to choose mates and have ample opportunity to become acquainted before marriage. Eligible singles meet and talk privately at dances held during special festivals. Rarely do men and women show affection in public. Marriage occurs when the couple elopes or lives together, although families who can afford the expense may have an elaborate wedding ritual.

❤ **Traditional pre-wedding customs**

The custom was for the boy's parents to visit the girl's home where they talked with her parents about village matters and the readiness of the girl to become their son's wife. If a positive decision about marriage was made, a payment was usually made to the girl's village by both families according to their wealth. Although not legally required, a brideprice was also paid to the girl and her parents.

A horoscope was (and still is) consulted to find the most suitable wedding date. On that day, the groom's parents and their entourage went to the bride's home in a procession with people carrying plates of food as offerings to the gods. Bedding was carried while people sang to the accompaniment of drums.

**143**

# Buddhist Wedding in Laos

❤ As soon as the groom's party arrives at the bride's home, a wise person from the bride's family quizzes the groom's party. In order to receive an invitation to enter, the groom's representatives respond to the questions with wisdom. A bride's representative accepts a sum of money or a token bottle of a drink from the groom's family; the groom's party is then invited into the home.

❤ So that he may enter the house pure of heart and body, the bride's brother or cousin washes the groom who is then adorned with banana leaves .

# Buddhist Wedding in Laos

❤ Before the ceremony, the bride and groom stand in front of two floral displays in the largest room of the home. Friends, relatives, local officials, and Buddhist priests surround them. While the bride and groom sit on a beautifully decorated mat or rug, the wedding ceremony commences with the lighting of candles.

❤ White cotton threads, which are good luck blessings, are passed to those who attend. All tie the strands around their wrists while priests recite sacred passages. As a priest places strands of cotton around the newlywed's wrists, the couple hold an egg, symbolizing fertility, and rice wrapped with a banana leaf, symbolizing prosperity.

❤ The Buddhist priest says a blessing. Then, the bride and groom bow and provide each guest with a flower embellished candle. For good luck, the couple will wear the cotton strands the following week or until they simply fall off. Attendants congratulate the couple.

❤ **Traditional post-wedding customs.** In the past, a highly respected woman led the couple to their bedchamber where floral displays divided the marriage bed into two parts. The newlyweds slept for the first three nights with the flowers between them. They did not cross the barrier in order to show strength of character. Three days later, they visited the husband's parents' home. There the new wife gave presents of clothing to his parents and their relatives. The couple often reside with the bride's family, usually until their first child was born.

References: **Brian Murphy's book** *The World of Weddings,* **Embassy of the Lao People's Democratic Republic's** *Newsbulletin.*

# Malaysia

*Thanks to the Embassy of Malaysia's First Secretary of Information*

Malaysia's population is comprised of Muslim, Hindu, Buddhist, Tao, Confucian, and other local traditional religions. Customs and marriage practices also vary according to ethnic groups which occupy this country.

### ❤ Selecting a spouse

Malays usually select marriage partners based on the man's or girl's preference. When the young man chooses a girl according to his own heart, he will tell his parents, usually his mother, and on occasion, someone else in the family. When the young man's parents are pleased with a selected girl and accept her as their daughter-in-law, their son will be told.

Once the young man and mother agree on the chosen girl, secret inquires are made to find out whether or not the girl is free. To accomplish this task, the young man's parents will ask close relatives to obtain more information from the girl's parents. When the son and mother find out that the *flower* has no owner and the girl's parents have accepted the idea of an upcoming marriage, an engagement ceremony will be prepared. Asking for the girl's hand in marriage and the acceptance of the proposal is accomplished by representatives, a *syarak,* from both families.

### ❤ Engagement ceremony

News of the engagement is publicized by a headman who announces it at a mosque to villagers during Friday prayers. During the engagement ceremony, the date is set for sending the token. Gifts of money and clothing from the young man's family and the duration of engagement are discussed. The token is delivered to the girl's home, along with the ring for her finger. The value of the ring is announced at the ring ceremony. Some of the brideprice may be sent during that time, but mainly the young man's representatives will be sent at a mutually convenient date to deliver the brideprice.

They are welcomed by the girl's family. Headed by the Ketua Syarak, both families convey good wishes and the gifts are received in accordance with former agreements.

Close relatives on the bride's side inform people in the village about the wedding date. A set of clothing and money, arranged in pieces of folded cloth, are given to the girl by the boy's family. Other gifts include flowers, a betel box, a brass pedestal with floral-decorated eggs and yellow rice, cosmetics, fruit, and more. In Kelantan these items are delivered on the wedding day, except for some things, agreed by both parties, to be sent earlier. While carrying a betel box, relatives invite other relatives and friends to the house to organize the wedding celebration.

# Malaysian Wedding

❤ **Henna ceremony.** The first part of the marriage ceremony is a formal henna staining ritual during which the bride wears her wedding dress. The bride then "sits in state," called *besangin*, before the *berinai besar*.

❤ *Berinai* **ceremony and sitting in state.** Accompanied by men playing tambourines, the groom in his wedding attire arrives at the bride's home. First, the groom begins the *berinai* ceremony, then members of the family take turns to perform the ceremony. (In some regions of the country, the *suap-suap*, feeding of the newly weds, is held while the groom and the bride are sitting in state. During the *suap-suap*, close relatives who enjoy the honor of performing the ceremony take a lump of *adab-adab* (rice) and place it on the palms of the couple's hands for symbolic feeding of each other...first the groom, then the bride.)

❤ **Announcement of payment.** The *imam*, a religious leader representing a close male relative of the bride performs the marriage. Matters pertaining to the gifts and other affairs are formalized. The payment, in cash or on credit, is given to the bride. At this time, the couple are formally pronounced husband and wife.

❤ **Wedding feast.** On the wedding day, the feast is held at the bride's home. As prayers are said, the bridegroom and his party move in a procession from his house to the bride's home and arrive at night. If the brideprice hasn't already been delivered, it is taken now.

As the groom's party reaches the front yard of the bride's home, they are sprinkled with rosewater, yellow rice, and flowers. A middle-aged lady representing the bride's family invites the groom to sit on the dais. The bride in her wedding dress waits on the dais while the groom sits to her right. Gifts brought by the groom's party are received by the bride's representatives and placed before the dais.

145

# Mongolia

*Thanks to the Embassy of Mongolia Fhuulchin, National Tourist Organization*

The Mongolian population is primarily Tibetan Buddhist. Mongolian traditions date back to the Hunnu state which occupied their territory in the Third Century, B.C. Even though the parents may not know whether or not the young couple are in love before the marriage, messengers from the groom's family make an elegant proposal to the bride. Conversations between the messengers and the bride's parents are conducted in folkloric verse. During the ceremonial proposal to the bride, the head of the groom's messengers addresses the bride's parents with the following verse:

*Our son and your daughter have come of marriage age. We have chosen this day to visit you to obtain your consent to the joining of the lives of our two children.*

The consent of the bride's parents follows, along with all good wishes for happiness and a life of conjugal harmony. After the messengers express their gratitude for the joining of the lives of the young couple, they recite a traditional laudatory poem.

# Mongolian Buddhist Wedding

❤ The ceremony takes place in the bridegroom's *ger*, a traditional Mongolian abode covered by layers of felt and surrounded by wall-frame sections. Before guests arrive, the groom's relatives bar the door with wood. Barring of the door is a sign that they honor their guests. When the wedding procession comes, the host greets them and asks about their trip. Then, the guests ask the host why the door is closed, and the groom's people explain the ancient custom of Saga Geser Khaan. The groom's people then unbar the door and invite the guests inside the *ger*.

❤ A white felt carpet is placed at the entrance of the *ger* to signify that the young couple's life will be as pure and sacred as white milk. After the guests enter, the bride lights a stove while all take a seat. Guests are seated according to their age. They elect the Lord of the Feast, the eldest and most experienced with traditional weddings, to announce the order of the feast. During the beginning of the ceremony, honored guests, a wedding lord, and elders are presented with a cup of airag and milk.

❤ The person who is reciting receives a *hadag*, a blue silk scarf, which is draped over the silver cupful of airag. The *hadag* symbolizes well-being and peaceful coexistence, and a silver cup of milk symbolizes honor, purity, and deep respect. The recitor narrates a laudatory poem which covers joy of life, labor, friendship, and the necessity of continuing the best traditions. Afterward, the recitor wishes the young couple well-being and happiness.

❤ All take part in feasting and sing songs which are accompanied by music and dancing. At the end of the ceremony, a speech is given praising the mother's success in bringing up the bride according to tradition. The speech also acknowledges that the mother is now leaving her daughter by permitting her daughter's marriage. White food, baked goods, and whole roasted mutton are customarily served at wedding banquets. All are welcome to enjoy the food and join in song and dance. Later, farewell songs and a poem, which expresses the host's gladness in sharing the occasion with guests, are presented. Guests are urged to remember that they have their spouse and children and their responsibilities at home.

# Myanmar (Burma)

*Thanks to the Embassy of the Union of Myanmar*

Myanmar has an 89 percent Buddhist population. The rest are animists or Christian.

### ❤ Past customs

Years ago, marriages were arranged by parents with the help of an intermediary. Spouses were usually from a similar ethnic background, financial level, and education.

The wedding was only registered as a precaution against future quarrels concerning property rights and there was no such event as a Buddhist wedding. In fact, a union of husband and wife had no true connection with religion or the state. Often, a couple would simply live together and announce to relatives and friends that they were married. To formalize their union, they could announce their plan to someone who was highly respected in their village.

### ❤ Present marriage customs

At one time, the boy conducted courtship by sending love letters to his sweetheart; now, groups of boys and girls interact by telephone, enjoy tea shops, and go to the movies. Girls and boys, considered equal under existing laws, are free to choose their spouses; yet, dating occurs only when the girl believes that the boy is a prospect for marriage. Even though today's marriages are based on romantic love, parental acceptance of a child's preference is desired and pursued.

Today, marriage is considered valid as long as the two parties consent to live together and their neighbors recognize their cohabitation as a marriage. Some couples marry by signing a marriage contract at court before witnesses and an attorney or judge. In 1991 the mean marital age of a woman in Myanmar was 21.5.

Most weddings are marked by some ceremony, feasting, and enjoyment. If a ceremony does take place, the house is decorated. The bride's hair is drawn into a coil, and she wears her best silks with a long-sleeved jacket and scarf. She is also adorned with all the valuable jewelry she possesses and a ring decorates each finger. Men feast first. Women await their turn in the room where the ceremony is to take place. The money that the groom brings towards the union is displayed in urns between which are offerings of fruit.

**147**

## Myanmar Buddhist Wedding

❤ A simple wedding may be held at a bride's home. An older man reads the Buddhist scriptures, and then asks the groom to enter. After the groom sits down on a cushion or mat, the bride is summoned and sits on another cushion to the left of her future spouse. Sitting before their elders and monks, they show reverence to the Triple Gems and to their parents. The couple leans prayerfully forward toward the ground or floor and clasps flowers in their hands as Buddhist scriptures are recited. The attending monks are offered alms. The ceremony ends when the couple places their right hands together in a container of water.

The newlyweds' bedroom is decorated with silk, lace, tinsel and paper flowers. The guests file through the chamber to admire the scene.

*Or else*

❤ Exquisite weddings with hundreds of guests are given at Rangoon's hotels where music troupes and singers entertain the guests. At hotels the marriage ceremony is officiated by a Master of Ceremonies. The couple's hands are tied together with a silk scarf and then placed into a silver container filled with water. Conch shells are blown and silver coins and confetti are tossed over those attending the ceremony. During the reception, tea with cakes, sandwiches, and ice cream are served.

*The Rights Vested in Myanmar Women*, lecture by Dr. May Yi's lecture in 1995, *Cultures of the World: Burma*, *The World of Weddings* by Brian Murphy.

# Nepal

Since Nepal is close to India, the population of Nepal is about 90 percent Hindu. Most of the remaining populace is Buddhist and Moslem. Because Hindus characteristically have marriages within the same caste, intercaste marriages or marriages between people of other ethnic groups and other religions are relatively rare. Nepalese marriages are customarily arranged by the parents with a relative acting as a go-between to relay information, photographs, and negotiations. The couple may not meet until their marriage, although some couples are permitted time to become acquainted. *(See "India" on pages 131-134 and the Hindu religion on page 18 for more detailed information about Hindu marriage customs and weddings.)*

Three types of marriage customs prevail in Nepal's hill country: the arranged marriages, couples' freedom to choose their life's partners, or a boy kidnapping the girl from her family. Although it is illegal, polygamy still exists, especially if a wife is unable to bear a son. Also, polyandry, in which a woman may be wed to several men at a time, is practiced.

Newar girls are first married to a wood apple, a *bel,* symbolizing the god *subarana* Kuma. Her marriage to her husband later is of less importance.

**Reference:** *The Cultures of the World: Nepal.*

# Pakistan

Pakistanis are 97 percent Muslim, about three-fourths Sunni Muslim, and one forth Shi'a Muslim.

Many educated urbanites have adopted Western customs. In cities, the couple may be permitted to date with a chaperone after the couple's engagement; nevertheless, according to a 1993 *Life* magazine article, 50 percent of marriages in Pakistan are still arranged, and young people are trained to respect and obey their fathers and elders.

### ❤ Marriage customs in rural Pakistan

In the countryside where traditions have been slow to change, women observe *purdah* by publicly wearing unrevealing clothing and a veil, a long dupatta or scarf draped around the head and shoulders. Although some wear the more revealing Indian sari, they also tend to be secluded from men according to custom. Because marriages are still arranged, some couples may meet each other for the first time on their wedding day. Since Pakistanis believe in selecting the most prestigious partners for their sons and daughters, marriage becomes a union of their families. When they begin to find suitable partners for their children, the two families exchange photographs of their children. Investigations are made into the backgrounds of family members. If the parents believe a match is appropriate, they arrange for the couple to meet. The girl and boy are permitted to talk at a small tea party while their parents are present. If the couple does not wish to marry, many parents will respect their children's wishes.

### ❤ The wedding

The legal part of the wedding ceremony is accomplished by the signing of the marriage contract, the *nikah.* It is usually signed by the parents a few days before the elaborate wedding party. There are many days of feasting and exchanging of presents which are lavishly displayed. The more financially able and higher the family is on the social scale, the more valuable are the dowry purchases the bride's family is expected to provide. The dowry is a status symbol consisting of jewels, clothing, and modern electronic household equipment. In certain tribes, however, the groom's family present such gifts as well.

During the wedding, the bride, wearing a decorative red scarf and dress, and the groom with a ring of flowers around his neck, remain seated separately from their guests. Pakistani music is played prior to and after the ceremony.

The bride's parents host the wedding party, a very elaborate occasion which may be held in a hotel or on a blocked off road under a massive tent near the bride's or groom's home. Offerings of food trays are garnished by a circle of colorful flowers. Men and women dine in separate sections beneath the tent. The wedding festivities can last up to five days.

# The Pakistani Wedding

♥ The bride's father is responsible for the cost of the wedding entertainment and gifts. Several days before the wedding, a *mehndi* ceremony, signifying the coming together of both families, takes place. The traditional wedding feast occurs under a striped canvas tent which is constructed near the bride's home. Spiced rice and mutton are cooked in large pots and the dowry is shown. Sometimes, guards are hired to protect the valuables and a town crier is present to announce them. The bride stays at home while henna dye is applied to her hands by the female members of the groom's family. Nearer to the wedding the henna is removed. After the groom's parents visit the bride's home, another *mehndi* ceremony takes place. The dye is again applied, this time by an artist who creates beautiful floral designs on her hands and feet. This ceremony occurs while the groom's family visits the bride's home. At that time, prized jewelry from the mothers of the bride and groom is passed down to the bride. The jewelry is often worn at the wedding.

# Traditional Punjab Wedding

♥ Many years ago in Muslim Punjab villages, the groom's relatives came to the groom's home and watched while the barber gave the groom a ritual bath. The groom wore a white turban, with gold and floral decorations which hid his face, and a white satin wedding costume. He traveled by horse to the bride's home. Today, the groom, accompanied by relatives, usually goes by car. When he arrives, firecrackers are exploded and musicians play. While the bride remains hidden in the women's quarters, the groom signs the *nikah*, the marriage contract, in the presence of a religious scholar. At that time, he is asked if he is willing to marry the bride. Then, the bride's father, scholar, or priest hurries to the bride's room to obtain her consent. After the groom recites the wedding vows and signs the contract without the bride being present, passages are read from the Koran.

♥ The next day, the bride, wears a red dress adorned with jewels. She and the groom kneel and face each other with a mirror between them, their eyes looking downward. Then, a cloth is thrown over their heads and he asks his wife to open her eyes.

♥ As the band plays and the people celebrate, the bride and groom depart with the groom's wedding party in a decorated car to the groom's house where another feast is given by his father. Sometimes the couple visit both in-laws several times before they settle into married life in the groom's home.

**References:** *The Cultures of the World: Pakistan,* also *Ethnic Family Values in Australia* by **Hafina Dean-Oswald,** *The Land and People of Pakistan* by **Robert Lang,** *Pakistan: An Islamic Treasure* by **Jabeen Yusufali.**

# Philippines

*Thanks to Jorge G. Argarin*

The Philippines is the only Asian nation with a large Roman Catholic population. The remaining Philippine people are of the Aligpayan, Protestant, and Muslim faiths. Since the Philippines is a Christian Catholic nation, monogamy prevails.

♥ **History**

Many of their customs, like the serenading, singing, or recitation of poems, show a Hispanic influence, for Catholicism was the result of the Spanish influence in the Philippines after 1570.

Historically, a 1953 civil code made the family a basic social institution to be cherished and protected. During the seventies, marriage was considered the best way to become an adult and every Filipino was encouraged to wed as soon as possible. In 1973, the Philippine Constitution reaffirmed that the state should strengthen the family.

### ❤ Present marriage customs

Even though there are now nuclear families, family ties and kinship remain supportive of the family. Non-relatives are accepted into kinship as god-parents. They become godfathers, *padrinos,* and godmothers, *madrinas*, who are sponsors present at all important occasions, including marriage. Personal ties cemented by marriage is a way to advance politically, so all conditions favor the formation of strong marriage bonds.

Philippine marriages are usually performed in town at the Roman Catholic church or the barrio chapel. Only in rare instances when the couple elopes or lives in the large city do couples have civil marriages.

### ❤ Selecting a spouse.

Group dating occurs when young people are in their teens. In most areas they make their own decisions as to whom they should marry. Parents on both sides expect that the couple are in love prior to marriage. Even though young people choose their marriage partners, their parents have a great influence over their choice. When a young man wants to marry a girl, he (or his parents) go to the girl's parents house and offer a gift. They even offer to build a home. Often, a college diploma is believed more important than real estate as a guarantee of financial security for the future. After the initial visit of the suitor to the girl's home, their parents meet.

Dating and marriage traditions vary in urban and rural areas. Dating and dancing are popular in the cities, but in rural areas the young men may serenade ladies in the moonlight by singing love songs beneath the girl's bedroom window. In the countryside, pre-marital relations are less tolerated, except with a few ethnic communities where chastity is not believed to be virtuous. In rural areas with traditional customs, the bride's family still pays a large dowry to the groom.

The bride's or groom's parents may give the couple land, a home, or money which will be useful during their marriage. The man's family is usually responsible for gifts, the wedding apparel, and the wedding.

# *Philippine Wedding*

150

❤ **Pre-wedding customs.** Both in rural and urban areas, the bridegroom's parents, their friends, and kin take part in preparations for the wedding by preparing food and entertaining relatives. After the couple receive their wedding license at the town hall and consult with the parish priest, the wedding takes place at the Catholic church. On the wedding day, the bridal party and parents lead the bride in a procession to the church.

❤ **Wedding ceremony during mass.** The bride's father gives her away to the groom during a wedding ceremony before the mass. The bride and groom are sponsored by their godfather and godmother, who become allied with the natural parents of the bride and groom in a co-parenting situation.

❤ **Post-wedding customs.** After mass, photographs are taken of all participants, the priest, and all who attend the reception at the bride's home. The newlyweds depart later for a less elaborate feast at the house of the groom's parents.

❤ **Coin contributions.** At the reception a competition takes place between the two families and the guests as to who gives the most money. The bride gathers money from the groom's side while offering them drinks, and the groom gathers from the bride's side. The total amount collected is then announced. In rural Cebu Quisumbing, the marriage banquet consists of white rice, pork, beef, goat's meat dishes, tuba, mallorca, and an alcoholic drink made from sugar cane. The newlyweds start the celebration by eating from the same plate as a sign of perfect sharing. The godmother and godfather present gifts to the couple and are the last to leave the celebration.

# Philippine Wedding

*Or otherwise*

❤ **Showering or pinning of money.** In Laguna, Batangas, and Ilocos provinces relatives and friends pin money on the bride's gown and the groom's shirt and pants while dancing to the accompaniment of a guitar. Sometimes, money is placed onto plates, or the offerings are showered over the bride and groom while they are standing on a mat. The mat is then rolled so that the money can be easily gathered. Some families compete to give the most and the one who gives the most enjoys prestige.

❤ **Releasing of the doves.** Another custom in some communities is for the bride's mother to give both the bride and groom lighted candles as they approach their house. At that time, rice and money, as symbols of prosperity, are showered on the newlyweds by the guests. Inside a bell-shaped cage of flowers are white doves, signifying peace and the lasting love that the bride and groom have for each other. During the wedding festivities, the bride and groom open the cage to permit the birds to fly away. This act signifies that both newlyweds are sent off to a new life.

❤ **Wedding reception.** The groom's family pays for both the wedding and reception and often, a dowry is given to the groom by the bride's family. A simple inexpensive breakfast with native foods may follow; otherwise, the wedding feast is held at the bride or groom's home or at a restaurant in the evening. The most popular traditional folk dances at weddings are the Spanish *kuratsa* and the *balitaw*.

❤ **Wedding night.** On the newlywed's wedding night in their own place or at the bridegroom's house, they find an envelope on their bed filled with money from the bridegroom's parents.

**151**

*Tagalogs.* Among the *Tagalog*s, the boy and his parents, or sometimes the young man and his respected elders, visited the bride's parents to discuss marriage plans. The process is called a *pamanhikan*. During that time, the wedding date was set, taking into consideration astrological signs and other circumstances which make the day lucky or unlucky. They believed that the couple's economic future depended on selecting the right day. It was considered bad luck for the bride and groom to try on their wedding apparel or rings before their wedding ceremony.

Brothers and sisters did not marry during the same time of year. Children also married in order of age: from the oldest to the youngest. The wedding was held on a day when the moon was waxing, rather than waning, for the moon's waning meant lack of luck and prosperity.

During the evening before the wedding, the bride's parents, especially those of the upper class, gave a party for friends and relatives. Great effort was taken so that nothing unpleasant occurred. They made certain that all the visitors were well fed and happy, for a pleasant, bountiful feast was believed to bring luck and happiness on the nuptial day. The bridegroom and his family were invited so that they could become acquainted with the bride's family.

The Catholic wedding ceremony also included customs of nonreligious nature. Newlyweds raced to the door of the church after the ceremony, for the person who arrived there first was determined to be the dominant spouse. Sometimes, the couple tramped on each other's toes during the wedding and who ever did so first was considered the governing spouse. Other practices, like the throwing of rice and coins after the wedding, were to ensure prosperity.

*Bulacan.* In Bulacan, the wedding eve is celebrated by the bridegroom and his entourage going to the bride's house where everyone dances throughout the night. The bridegroom's family pays for this celebration.

# Bulacan Wedding

❤ **Cantata.** If the bridegroom's family is wealthy, they may hold a *cantata* (music) at the church where the aisles are decorated with fresh flowers and candles. There, the church choir sings during the ceremony and the bells ring. If a modest wedding is planned, the aisle is not decorated and the choir does not sing. The bride, wearing a white satin and lace gown, carries a bouquet of white flowers, usually butterfly orchids. The groom may wear a white *barong-tagalog camisa*, a long-sleeved shirt of Ramie fiber with embroidered silk floral designs or native motifs.

❤ **Betrothal and Arras ceremonies.** Rings are exchanged during the ceremony. As is the Spanish custom, there is a coin ceremony. The groom gives *arras*, silver or gold coins, to the bride whose hands are cupped to receive them.

❤ **Laso ceremony.** The priest offers nuptial mass for the couple. After the bell of the Sanctus rings, a veil is placed over the groom's shoulders and the bride's head and a silk cord or one of white flowers is entwined around their necks.

❤ **Post wedding activities.** The newlyweds then hurry back up the aisle with the noise of the church bells and well-wishers to congratulate them. Where transportation is available, the newlyweds ride in a decorated car as spectators witnessing the event.

❤ **Reception.** In Bulacan, the traditional transferring of the bride to the bridegroom's house is accompanied by dancing in colorful costumes with music from a live band or a string accompaniment. As they step out of the church, in some areas they are greeted with white banners, arches of coconut palms made into designs, and stately white pillars made from banana plants.

152

*Hiligaynons.* Being a spinster was not considered particularly shameful, but a man with no wife was thought to have something ridiculously wrong with him. A woman who flirted was to be avoided as a marriage prospect because she could not be trusted as a wife. Marriages were monogamous.

Historically, marriages were arranged by the parents. Looks rarely were important in the choice of the spouse. The following characteristics were taken into consideration before marriage could take place:
- ❤ If the man could make enough money to support a family.
- ❤ If the girl was industrious, of good character (subservient and modest), could get along well with the boy's parents.
- ❤ If the economic status of both families was satisfactory.

Several meetings involving negotiations occurred before the wedding. The young man had to do household chores at the girl's home to prove his sincerity and worth.

If all went well, the boy and his relatives went to the girl's parents home to ask for their daughter's hand in marriage. Only after the boy and girl became officially engaged were they permitted to meet alone. Before the wedding, the couple went to the town hall where a license was issued and a notice posted. If no one disagreed, a wedding date was fixed.

This courtship pattern has changed. *Hiligaynon* courtship begins at adolescence for both young men and women. While the boy works in the community, he has a chance to learn about girls in the neighborhood. If he takes an interest in a girl, he visits her with his *barkada* or tries to become acquainted with her himself. This is called an act of *serenading*, which is sometimes initiated by friendly letters prior to courtship. Often *serenading* is done during harvest time when girls assisted with the harvest. After serenading, the boy is invited to the girl's home to sing and exchange pleasantries. These preliminaries pave the way for future Sunday visitations with their *barkadas* attending.

Proper girls are not supposed to submit to friendship immediately so that they cannot determine the sincerity of the boy. Aggressive girls who desire the man right away are not considered to be acting in good taste and thus, not taken seriously.

After the boy pays several visits and is accepted warmly by the girl's family, he may see the girl without his *barkada*. However, the mother or another sibling is present during some subsequent visits to make certain that they do not engage in a sexual relationship. In fact, dried huya-hugya leaves and snail shells are used as charms to make the young man move slowly "like a snail," weakening his genitalia to render him incapable of accomplishing the sexual act. On the other hand, there were also charms to make the person of the opposite sex fall in love!

Today, boys and girls may meet secretly at the market place, movie, or on a river bank, and may enter a relationship which is not sanctioned by their parents.

# Hiligaynon Wedding

❤ Marriages are usually held at a Christian church where the wedding ceremony is performed by a priest or minister. Parents encourage their children to have church weddings. Although a marriage performed by a judge is permissible, it is not considered sacred.

❤ When the wedding is about to take place, an older man takes charge of the ceremonial festivities, and an older woman is responsible for the care of the bride and groom. The bride receives assistance from her mother and close relatives, and the groom from his male relatives. When the Christian ceremony is performed, traditionally the groom tramps on the bride's feet. This act is to assure that the bride will be subservient to him; otherwise, she will be the boss.

❤ The couple symbolically close their eyes when rings are placed on their fingers so that they can overlook and overcome hardships during married life. A veil is placed over the bride and groom while the groom presses his bride's left hand so that she will abide by his desires and thus, family harmony will be achieved. Traditionally, a *bolo* dance took place as the couple left the church.

❤ **Post-wedding Hiligaynon customs.** The newlyweds are showered with rice before entering the girl's house so their life will be prosperous. A couple who have given birth to many children greet them at the bride's home before the wedding feast takes place. Their greeting is to insure that the newlyweds will have many healthy progeny. Traditionally, the newlywed's hair was combed to indicate that they would have a smooth marriage.

Once the newlyweds are inside the house, they kneel to pray at the family altar where candles are burning brightly. An older person from the groom's family then gives the couple a monetary gift.

The couple kiss the bride's mother and the relatives, and the groom shakes hands with guests who attend. After the bride changes into her ordinary clothing, feasting and drinking takes place. They usually serve a Spanish meat stew, bananas, and sweet potatoes, rice dish, fruits, and vegetables. Care is taken so that no china be broken thereby avoiding ill luck.

Traditionally, the couple were not to stay with each other the first night after their wedding because it was believed they would become sickly. The marriage was consummated at the man's home the following night.

The next day, the newlyweds returned to the home of the bride's parents where they lived for a year until they resided at their own location. Not sleeping together the first night is no longer popular.

**References:** *The Hiligaynons: Philippines of Western Bisayas Regions during the '80s* by F. Linda Jocano, *The Filipino Family in Transition, Area Book for the Philippines, Marriage Customs in Rural Cebu.*

# Singapore

Singapore has a religious population of Buddhists, Christians, Muslims, Hindus and Taoists.

Marriage, according to Singapore law is monogamous, except for Muslims who are permitted to have up to four wives.

The couple must be eligible for public housing in Singapore and may wait several years before they obtain a flat. Many couples, therefore, live apart until they accumulate enough funds for a marriage celebration and a flat.

### ❤ Government matchmaking

The Singapore government takes on the responsibility of matchmaking. The country has one matchmaking agency for college graduates and another for those people who are less educated.

Government matchmaking was initiated during Prime Minister Lee Kuan Yew's administration in the 1980's because he had a single college-educated daughter. At that time, he began efforts to help single college graduates marry others who were professionally educated, especially women who had difficulty finding mates. His method was to promote moonlight boat trips where the educated young people could meet. Government personnel in Social Development Units were set up across the nation in order to organize non-graduate socials, such as singles tea dances and dinner parties.

### ❤ Arranged marriages

Arranged marriages still take place among Singapore's Hindu and Malay Muslim populations. The matchmaker helps parents obtain knowledge about the bride's or groom's background. The matchmaker then reports this information to the parent and plans meetings between both families.

### ❤ Hindu marriage customs

A Hindu wedding is usually held at a temple. The height of the wedding ceremony is when the groom places a gold pendant around his bride's neck as a sign of their marriage. *(See Hindu wedding in Chapter 1 on page 18.)*

### ❤ Malay Muslim marriage customs

The Muslim couple signs a wedding register before an *imam* at a ceremony. Their marriage is then announced to the public by the construction of *bunga manggarm* which symbolizes a mango tree. It is composed of two poles decorated with bands of colored paper attached to the tops.

While the couple sit on a platform like a king and queen, guests greet them. All enjoy a celebrating with a feast and the couple reside together thereafter.

### ❤ Chinese marriage customs

The Chinese often have a traditional tea ceremony. To show respect to their parents and grandparents, the newlyweds serve tea to them. The ceremony also establishes the newlywed's place in the family. A lavish feast may follow for family and friends. Although rituals may differ according to family, the bride usually wears a white wedding gown. The couple may go on Sundays and holidays to a park where wedding photographs are taken.

### ❤ Intermarriage

Intermarriages between religions occur often. More people are becoming secular, and there is an increasing number of Christians among the educated Chinese. These couples may marry at the Registry of Marriages.

### ❤ Mass wedding ceremonies

Because getting married is extremely costly, many couples opt to wed during a mass wedding ceremony. The wedding package includes a banquet and an overseas honeymoon.

**References:** *Something Old, Something New* by Vera Lee, "The Government as a Matchmaker," an article in the *World Press Review, Cultures of the World: Singapore.*

# Sri Lanka

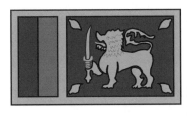

Sri Lanka has about a 70 percent Sinhalese Buddhist, 15 percent Hindu, and 7 percent Muslim population. A small percentage are Christian. Sri Lanka has a variety of marriage customs based on locations and regions of their country. Because of the close proximity of different groups, traditions are often borrowed from various cultures and religions. Most cultures celebrate the wedding festivities for several days. In urban areas, the rich have large receptions at lavish hotels.

### ❤ Finding a spouse

Marriage is considered the ideal state for Sri Lankan women. Both arranged marriages and love marriages, in which people are free to choose their spouses, exist side by side. Certain traditions still remain such as marrying within the family caste, marrying within their own ethnic group, and retaining the woman's sexual purity. These customs are decreasing.

Historically young people did not date and depended on parents to arrange their marriages through professional brokers or a friend. Friends and relatives were the go-betweens who investigated potential candidates and proposed marriages. After the young people became educated, economic factors, and status of family lines were taken into consideration. If all went well, an agreement was reached which would unite two families or clans. At present, 60 percent of marriages are still arranged.

Horoscopes, based on birth dates, were also used to match young people according to psychological and personal compatibility. If the horoscopes were incompatible, it was believed that an early separation might occur by death or other means. Many still rely on horoscopes to predict the future as well.

The bride was usually younger than the groom. There was also a strong preference for a young woman whose age was under 25. The girl was transferred from her father's authority to her husband's because the young girl was perceived as unable to look after herself.

Today, advertisements for a marriage partners are placed in the newspapers, making the traditional matchmaker unnecessary. The ads usually specify the person's age and indicate views on caste. Sometimes, the advertisers will request a prospective mate's horoscope.

### ❤ Christian

A small percentage are Christian Burghers or Christian Sinhalese, who marry in a church and have a reception after the ceremony.

### ❤ Hindu

*Tamil.* The Tamils, descendants from southern India, marry in the Hindu temple. The featured event during the wedding ceremony is the tying of a gold necklace on the bride. Having a medallion inscribed with conch figures on it, this necklace, plus a trident, and a ring represent Hindu trinity. While wearing these objects, the bride becomes the symbolic goddess of the home, and the groom, her god.

### ❤ Muslim

Sri Lankan Muslims have separate family laws concerning marriage, inheritance, and registration of marriages. *(See the Muslim religion in Chapter 1.)* Muslims hold an evening reception at the bride's home or at a hotel.

### ❤ Sinhalese

Sinhalese are descendents from the Indo-Aryans of northern India in the low country. Sometimes, the daughter's inheritance was transferred to her husband through marriage. Often, sacrifices were made by the bride's parents to accumulate a dowry which would increase their daughter's chances for enticing a prestigious partner. Past requirements, such as transference of a dowry, money, clothing and jewelry once considered essential components of marriage, are presently waning. *(See Sinhalese wedding on the next page.)*

Marriages between the Sinhalese people and those of other ethnic backgrounds are becoming more acceptable.

# Sinhalese Buddhist Wedding

❤ Sinhalese Buddhist wedding ceremonies are held in a decorated edifice called a *poruwa* where the bride's maternal uncle performs the rituals. The bride usually wears embroidered silk garments and heirloom jewelry from her family. If she is a Kandyan, she may wear seven pendants or necklaces which increase in length from her neck to her knees.

❤ During the ceremony, the fifth fingers of the bride and groom are tied together with a gold cord, then water is poured from a silver urn over the knotted cord to signify sharing of their lives. Girls will sing songs of good-wishes and celebration.

**References:** *Culturgrams: The Nations of the World, Family Ethnic Values in Australia* by **Hanifa Dean-Oswald,** *Sri Lanka.* **a manuscript by Herbert Keuneman.**

# Taiwan

Taiwan is an island near mainland China. The religions of Taiwan are Taoist, Buddhist, Protestant and Catholic.

## ❤ Traditional marriage customs

Traditionally, all were expected to marry. Children married young. Parents-in-law sometimes raised the young child as a future spouse for their own child. A horoscope of the prospective bride and groom had to show good luck. Their marriages were arranged by parents, often with the assistance of relatives or matchmakers. These go-betweens learned about a future spouse's background and made initial contacts for their parents. Because marriages were usually contracted when both children were teenagers, the children had little input in the marital decision. Once the agreement between both families was made, both sides exchanged gifts and the wedding date was set.

## ❤ Present marriage customs

Taiwan's marriage customs have changed since 1950. Industrialization and an increased standard of living created a population of well-educated young people who tended to marry later. Their more autonomous lifestyle permits freedom to choose partners based on personal attraction and love.

Today, only a small percentage of marriages are arranged by parents. Instead of the parents, their friends, or matchmakers being involved in uniting a couple, people increasingly meet their prospective spouses in the workplace or school. Still, most do not wish to marry unless they have parental consent; therefore, parents are still somewhat involved in their choices.

A rise in cohabitation before marriage and a tendency for more to remain single is now occurring.

**Reference: Thornton and Lin's book** *Social Change & the Family in Taiwan*

# Thailand

Thailand has a mostly Theravada Buddhist population with only a small percentage who are Muslim. Except for these Muslim inhabitants, young men and women are free to choose their mates. Today in Bangkok, Western-style dating is in vogue.

## ❤ Folk marriage in rural regions

Marriage customs continue to be more traditional among the hill tribes and in country villages than in the cities. In those places, the couples dress in costumes. Because unmarried women have different costumes than the married ones, it is easy to determine which ones are eligible for courting. When the bride is about to marry, she usually takes on the role of a shy maiden.

The tribes, like the *Akhas* or *Meos*, who live in the hills and country villages, have elaborate weddings. Although tribal people tend to marry relatives in other countries, the *Akhas* do not marry any member of the same clan for several generations. *Yaos* tribal marriages involve the brideprice, the giving of gifts from the groom to the bride's family.

A typical folk marriage in northeast rural Thailand starts with a courtship lasting a few weeks to several years. Young people meet in freedom at village festivals, at mobile theaters, or at work. During the courtship, parents have an opportunity to learn more about their child's selection. Once the children have consulted their parents, the senior relatives from the suitor's side formally approach the girl's parents to ask for her hand in marriage. If the girl's family agrees, the brideprice and a wedding date are set. When the expenses incurred for a formal marriage ceremony are too much, the couple secretly sleep together at the girl's home. Their parents are thereby forced to accept their marriage to avoid losing face.

## ❤ Past marriage customs

When the young Buddhist man found a girl of his choice, he moved into his future father-in-law's dwelling. There, parental wishes were highly respected. He would labor on the land for two years before he was permitted to marry the daughter. While he was working, the bride's family provided him with sustenance and often a separate home. Not only did he have to provide service for the bride's family, but he also had to attend a monastery where he received instruction as a monk for several months. Only after this, was he considered eligible to marry their daughter. The suitor was also expected to construct a home near the girl's parents, and after it was completed, the girl's father furnished the home and gave them household supplies.

The traditional concept of *bunkhun* in the Thai social system influences the timing of marriages. *Bunkhun*, a debt of gratitude, involves the payment from offspring to their parents. The son can easily repay this debt by entering the monkhood temporally, whereas the daughter must work to support her parents prior to marriage or solicit a brideprice. The *bunkhun,* although flexible, is the cause of delay in marriages.

The time for the wedding was planned by consulting with an astrologer. The wedding was held during the even lunar months of the year, with the exception of the tenth and twelfth months. The uneven ninth month is often selected because it is identified with wealth and progress.

The evening before the wedding, an even number of monks, a half dozen or more, recited Buddhist scriptures. To purify the couple before their wedding ceremony, holy water from an alms bowl was sprinkled on them while the text was recited.

The Thai Buddhist marriage was a union of two families into one extended family. Relatives from both sides offered companionship, business association, and thoughtful assistance. The ideal of family unity remains.

Only the wealthier members of the Thai communities have a wedding. Other couples simply reside together until they are accepted as married.

*(See the Thai wedding on the next page.)*

# Thai Buddhist Weddings

## Wedding I

❤ The wedding, performed by Buddhist monks, begins in the morning at which time the couple receives blessings. The couple wear narrow circular crowns joined by a white strand of yarn, called a *mongkol*. The yarn connection symbolizes unity as husband and wife. The monks then circle another white cord, called a *sai sin*, around the holy area where the couple are standing.

❤ An astrologer or monk chooses the time when the couple's heads are joined by the *mongkol*. Then, an elder joins the white strand of yarn to both crowns. The couple kneels in the sacred area while a respected monk sprinkles holy water over their foreheads with a sprig of Chinese gooseberry. Later that evening, the monk pours purified water onto the joined hands of the couple, allowing the rest to drip onto bowls of flowers. The guests also bless the couple by pouring water over the couple's hands.

❤ No vows or promises are made.

❤ A reception takes place at which time gifts from the groom are presented to the bride's family.

## Wedding II

❤ A typical city wedding is scheduled for the afternoon. Main guests invite the others to the wedding. Guests congregate and wait for the wedding to take place. Then, they enter the room for the ceremony. Traditionally, the elderly and most prestigious men go first.

❤ During the wedding, the bride and groom, dressed in beautiful silk costumes or Western-wear, kneel prayfully from their low bench, their heads bowed towards the floor with arms forward and their hands folded. Wreaths, created with threads, rest on their heads. The wreaths are joined to each other by thin thread.

❤ The monk gives each guest coming in the door a decorated conch shell with holy water and leaves placed inside. Each guests pours this water onto the prayerful hands of the bride and groom, blesses them, and offers them best wishes. In return, the couple make a respectful gesture of bowing their heads to thank each guest before each leaves the room. As the couple depart, a young maiden standing near the doorway gives each guest a garland, a little bouquet, or a perfumed handkerchief to remind them of their wedding. Finally, guests are asked to sign the wedding book.

**References: Chai Podhisita who wrote "Marriage in Rural Northeast Thailand: A Household Perspective" in the book *Perspectives on the Thai Marriage*: an article by Akin Rabibhadana, *Gale Encyclopedia of Multi-cultural America, Living Faiths: Marriage and the Family, Cultures of the World: Thailand.***

***Turkmenistan Brides. Double Wedding in Bagir.*** *They cover their mouths with handkerchiefs because they are not to talk during marriage proceedings.   James Hill, ©New York Times Picture.*

# Turkmenistan and Uzbekistan

*Turkmenistan*

Turkmenistan's and Uzbekistan's history is similar. Under Communist domination, marriages were recorded at the regional Communist party office.  Muslim marriages were still arranged according to parental desires. Girls and boys did not date, and the girl was expected to remain a virgin until marriage. When marriage occurred, the brideprice was paid.  Marriages were solemnized at a betrothal ceremony, a *nikka*, in presence of a *mullah*.

A marriage feast, given by the boy's parents, was held at sunrise before work to hide it from Communist officials. They also concealed  from officials the slaughter of sheep for that feast and the cost incurred.  Pilaf and other foods were served at the feast to the those on the farm.  Guests danced and sang songs accompanied by musicians.  Because brideprices were legally banned under the Communists, livestock or consumer goods were given instead of money.

Both countries separated from the Soviet Union after the 1990 fall of Communism.  Islamic traditions, which were always a challenge to the Communist system before its collapse, are stronger now.

***The Resurgence of Central Asia* by Ahmed Rashid.**

# Vietnam

Vietnam has a Buddhist, Taoist, Indigenous, Muslim and Protestant population. About two thirds of the people are Mahayana Buddhists.

Vietnamese Buddhists regard marriage as being permanent. Brides are expected to be virgins before marriage. Although concubines were permitted at one time, contemporary Vietnamese legal norms are based on monogamy. Marriage with cousins or within the extended family is not permitted.

## ❤ Pre-engagement customs

Traditionally, marriages were parentally arranged, taking into consideration social class, region, and religion. After the girl was selected by the boy's parents, a go-between was sent to talk to the girl's family. If all appeared positive, the girl's mother sent an intermediary to the boy's family to learn more about his family's social and financial status. Expectation was that a boy should be more affluent and of a higher social scale than the girl. If mother let her daughter go too easily, she would dishonor her; therefore, the mother considered all negative possibilities before agreeing to the marriage. Usually, the final decision for the couple to wed was based on the horoscope; in fact, if the horoscope did not show a long, happy life for the couple, the marriage was called off. A couple who ran away together could be disowned by their parents.

## ❤ Engagement party

After a mate was selected, a date was set for the engagement party where the boy asked for the girl's hand. Wearing dark lengthy tunics, pants, and black scarves on their heads, the groom, his friends, and relations went to the bride's house. There, the groom's father or friend, on behalf of the groom, made a speech asking for her hand in marriage. The girl's parents responded by extolling their daughter's virtues and glorifying her faults as well. They ended by stating that she would be well-behaved in the presence of her in-laws. A sum was paid by the groom to a fund in the community where the girl's family resided. Tea and edibles were provided to relatives and guests.

# Vietnamese Wedding

❤ **Procession to bride's home and departure of the bride.** The groom and his family usually provided the bride's wedding clothes and paid for the wedding reception. On the wedding day, set according to the horoscope, the boy's mother brought pink chalk, symbolizing a rosy future, to the bride to take to her new house. The groom and his entourage in a procession went to the bride's home with gifts: clothing, jewelry, money to help pay for the wedding, and lacquered leather trunks holding bedding. Before entering, an orator, representing the groom's family gave a speech and presented an entrance gift in a red envelope. The bride's family welcomed them, then they laid out more wedding presents which were covered by an embroidered cloth. They set the gifts before the altar dedicated to the bride's ancestors. Lamps, candles, and incense burned while the couple knelt. They later knelt before the bride's parents and grandparents who, in turn, presented them with red envelopes filled with money.

❤ **Wedding ceremonial at the groom's home.** After saying farewell to the bride's parents, the groom's procession led the bride to her husband's house. First, she stepped over a small stove with burning coals to rid herself of evil spirits and to purify her for married life. After tea was given to guests, the ancestors were introduced to the bride. The groom's parents sat before an altar and said prayers, and a professional officiator invoked heaven and prayed for the two gods of marriage to bless the couple. Bound together by a thread of cotton leading from the altar to their shoulders, the couple knelt. After their wedding, rice and chicken were taken to the bed chamber where the newlyweds could enjoy their first dinner together as husband and wife. Once the guests started feasting, the men called the groom and encouraged him to get drunk so that he would not have sexual relations that night.

**References:** *World Press Review* and *The World of Weddings* by Brian Murphy

# Europe

The southern countries of Europe have a highly Catholic population; northern European countries, on the other hand, have a higher Protestant population. Social customs pertaining to marriage are therefore more liberal in northern Europe than in southern Europe. Although the institution of marriage prevails in all European countries, cohabitation of couples occurs more in the northern countries.

Through past colonization, Christian marriage customs have extensively spread from Europe countries to Africa, North, Central and South America, and to Australia. Colonization accounts for the similarity of marriage customs in many countries throughout the world and for the development of Western culture. *(See the "Western-style Weddings" on page 35 and Catholic and Protestant weddings in Chapter 1.).*

Recently, varied cultural European marriage customs have become more standardized as the result of—

- Increased ability for people to travel.
- Industrialization which caused changes in the family structure, urbanization, and education.

- Political takeovers, such as Communism in countries during the mid-twentieth century.
- The close proximity of European countries. People who live close together interchange ideas and take on others' marriage customs which tend to appeal to them.
- Influence from intercultural mass media: television programs, regional movies, Hollywood films, and television shows from the United States, all depicting Western culture.
- Availability of wedding magazines in various countries. They play a part in the standardization of wedding customs and costumes.
- The world's vision of Europe's remaining royal families in magazines and on television.

In Europe, people of industrialized cities are more inclined to move away from traditional customs than those who live in remote villages where colorful traditions of folklore and customs are kept alive. Some folk customs are so remote from the present, they are only kept alive in theatrical productions.

# Gypsies

Yugoslavia, Romania, Spain, Hungary, Turkey, Russia, Bulgaria, Czechoslovakia, and France have the highest population of Gypsies. The Gypsy population also has scattered throughout other European counties and some have emigrated to the United States. The European *Rom* (Gypsies) are usually thought of nomadic people, although some are not.

### ❤ Selecting a spouse

Among many *Rom*, arranged marriages by two consenting families are considered normal because marriage is a social compact uniting two kinship groups. Some families desire to strengthen existing bonds and

cooperation, so they arrange marriages between relatives to form an extended kinship group. The groom's father has the honor and responsibility of finding a bride for his son, and he is often willing to travel miles to find the right girl.

Although marriage is taken seriously, it does not always imply legality. A couple will sometimes live together without legal sanction from the country in which they live. Elopements may occur with or without the permission from the couple's parents. If the couple falls in love and does not receive parental consent, they often elope and return to request their families' forgiveness with the hope both families will unite.

Sometimes an elopement is planned by both families because of the high cost of wedding festivities.

The ideal marriage is arranged by the bride's and groom's fathers after consulting with other male kin. Since virginity prior to marriage is so important, first marriages are arranged between boys and girls whose ages range from 16 to 18. The young man's father sends a go-between who offers the brideprice, a *daro*, and obtains the consent of the bride's father. The process may take several days to a year before an agreement and a formal betrothal are reached. Unrelated families who live far away usually desire to make an early formal engagement in case they lose communication. Traditionally young couples married without seeing each other, but now the couple usually has the right to become acquainted and refuse to marry. The son or daughter does not take part, but they may influence their parents' selection.

♥ **Pre-marriage customs**

The brideprice amount is affected by family status and financial condition. After settling on the brideprice which is the number of gold coins that the bride's father demands, a public formal engagement ceremony takes place. This ceremony is considered as binding as a legal contract and occurs without the presence of the bride and groom or female relatives.

During the engagement ceremony, the groom's father presents the coins to the bride's father, and the amount is verified by all men present. When the bride's father accepts the coins, he displays his approval of the union. The groom's father also gives the girl's father a bottle of whisky, a scarf holding an engagement present, and a piece of jewelry for the bride. After the engagement, the groom's family holds a lavish betrothal feast where a pig is roasted and other traditional foods are eaten.

# Traditional Gypsy Wedding

♥ The bride wears a dress, made by her relatives, from material purchased by the parents of the groom. A man and wife are chosen to sponsor the bride and groom *(kirvo/kirvi)* throughout the ceremony. This selected couple cannot have been married more than once. The *kirvi* dresses the bride and adds the veil at the right time. After the bride is dressed, she is blessed.

♥ The bride's veil *(diklo),* either red or has red in it, is put on a stick with a red rose. The *diklo* is a symbol of married status, and the rose symbolizes the bride's virginal blood which will be spilt. Red also symbolizes happiness and good luck. The *diklo* stick is carried by unmarried girls *(sheybari)* who dance in a circle with it, holding hands. The men do not dance. The embarrassed groom stands to one side. The bride is then brought onto the floor with no headdress and must dance in a circle with the young girls, one of whom holds the *diklo*. They all hold hands and move in a circle with the bride in the middle. They are weeping.

♥ The bride is taken away. Then, the *diklo* is removed from the stick and put on her head by the *kirvi*. This is placed on her head with great care as the women gather around her as she continues to weep. The women say that once it is on her head she is married.

♥ Next is a ceremony called the *Zeita*, which is translated as "bringing the bride home." When the *Zeita* is performed, the bride's married state is finalized. The *zeita* is accomplished by the relatives. The groom never enters in any of these ceremonies, for he must be modest and keep to one side. Above all, he must not look at his bride or be near her. After everyone gets together at the end of the hall, the sponsors bring out the bride. She is given a blessing from her immediate family, then they kiss her and say good-bye with good will. Shouting and confusion occur when a group of boys and girls traditionally try to stop the *zeita*.

♥ After this ceremony, everyone sits at the table and partakes of the feast. As soon as food has been consumed, the male sponsor hollows out a loaf of bread. With the bride and groom behind him, in that order, each holding the end of the *diklo*, the sponsor goes to each older head of family at the table. Money contributed by each man is placed in the bread for the bride. The man is given some beer by the boy who follows

162

# Traditional Gypsy Wedding

behind, and the sponsor makes a speech, each time exaggerating the amount given. Then, a *diklo* is taken and put around the neck of the man, and everyone cheers and claps. To add interest to the ceremony, someone might refuse to give money. A huge argument will ensue, everyone yelling and shouting, until he finally concedes. The bride's father is also supposed to give back a *plutchka* to the groom's father to help cover expenses of the wedding.

❤ After the feasting, the groom's family goes home and gives a further party for some of the wedding guests. The bride is expected to entertain the group, dance, and serve food. Her parents are not allowed to come as this will embarrass the bride in front of her in-laws and her husband. Her parents give a party at their house for other wedding guests. This emphasizes that she now belongs to her in-laws.

❤ The partying lasts three days. On the second night, the bride and groom may sleep with each other. Before, however, she must sleep with her mother-in-law or sister-in-law. On the morning of the third day they "put up the flag" to show to the people.

❤ The "flag" is the bride's nightgown. If there is blood on it, it indicates respect to the parents of the bride. On this third day, a party is given by the bride's family to celebrate her virginity. If the bride is not a virgin, it does not change the validity of the wedding, but it does make for more gossip. . .

❤ The mothers of parties comb the girl's hair into braids and plait it with a *diklo*. They both give her salt and bread to eat and a blessing. The girl wears the *diklo* from then on to show she is married.

*This wedding is reprinted with the permission of The Free Press, a division of Simon & Schuster from GYP-SIES: The Hidden Americans by Anne Sutherland. Copyright © 1975 by Anne Sutherland.*

**163**

Photographs in Jean Pierre Liegeois's book *Gypsies* show the creation of an earthenware pot for the wedding, the bride dressed in white, and the breaking of a pot over the groom's head during the wedding ceremony. A headscarf worn over a bride's head after the wedding is a symbol of wedlock.

**References:** *Gypsies: The Hidden Americans* by Anne Sutherland, *Roma: Europe's Gypsies* by Gratton Puxon, *Gypsies* by Jean Pierre Liegeois and *Gypsy* by Angus Fraser.

# Albania

Albania's population is primarily Albanian Orthodox Christian, Roman Catholic, and Sunni Muslim. Since Albania was one of the first countries that was proclaimed as atheist, church marriages were suspended during the Communist takeover. After the country was democratized in 1990, Christian and Muslim Albanians were freer to resume religious marriage customs.

❤ **Selecting a spouse**

In the past, Albanian weddings were arranged by parents or a matchmaker. Children could be betrothed by their parents at or before birth to promote mutual regard or peace with another clan. A partial brideprice was paid by the son's parents when the girl was born. The remaining amount was paid at the time of marriage. Girls and boys were wed while they were still teenagers.

❤ **Pre-wedding customs**

Albanian Christian or Catholic marriage festivities traditionally began with an engagement party given at the girl's family home. It was sponsored by both the bride's and groom's families. Instead of an engagement ring, the bride was presented with a gold coin during this party. A series of parties, where relatives congregated, was given by both sides. Those attending gave gifts and rejoiced by singing and dancing. The bride's dowry and her trousseau were also on display. During the final party at midnight, the bride and groom and their families went in different directions and filled containers with water from a lake or stream. While at each place, participants threw coins and anyone was permitted to grab them.

### ❤ The wedding

The day of the wedding, a *vellum* brought the bride

candy and rice-filled shoes bound in a silk scarf. He placed the shoes on the bride's feet while the women sang. The *vellum* then threw coins for those present to catch in their hands. Once the bride was dressed, she was given a cup of wine by her parents with their blessings. The groom's family accompanied her to the Albanian Christian or Catholic church. After the wedding ceremony, a reception was given. The next week family and friends visited the newlyweds and the bride gave gifts to the groom's family.

**References:** *Gale Encyclopedia of Multicultural America, Encyclopedia of World Cultures.*

# *Armenia*

**Thanks to Victoria M. Manoogian of the Armenian Apostolic Church in Scottsdale, Arizona**

Formerly, Armenia was part of the Soviet Socialist Republic until the 1990's. The population traditionally followed the Armenian Christian or Armenian Orthodox religions. They were only permitted to marry those who were "seven navels" away; that is, the blood relationships could not be close. Weddings celebrated the unity of both families. Girls were to marry at a young age, from 15-20, and if they did not, they were only considered good enough to marry widowers who lived in another village with their children.

### ❤ Selecting a spouse

Some marriages were arranged by amicable fathers when their children were young, or else, go-betweens or matchmakers were used when their children became of age to marry. Both families negotiated while the girl's family served coffee. When the girl's family served bitter coffee to the boy's representatives, her family indicated they were refusing the representative's offer. If the girl's family accepted the proposal, the boy's representatives told the boy that the *word was tied.* Both families exchanged visits, then after, the "viewing of the groom" took place at the future in-law's home. The process of becoming acquainted could last a year.

### ❤ The betrothal

After the girl's complete family had visited their future in-laws, they held a formal engagement party. There, the boy's mother gave a ring or gold coins to her future daughter-in-law as an initial welcome into her household.

The bride's head was covered with a veil. She and the groom, holding lit candles, stood before the priest and touched each other's foreheads. Then the groom's mother placed the ring on the bride's finger. While the entire ceremony took place, the boy's godfather held a cross with a long handle over the couple's heads to bless them. All celebrated with food, drinks, songs and dance for up to two days. Should the engagement be broken after the betrothal, the family would have to pay the other family reparations to maintain a good reputation. While engaged (possibly up to two years), the boy and girl were not permitted to speak to each other or marry until her older eligible sisters married.

### ❤ Pre-wedding customs

Prior to the wedding, the barber shaved and bathed the groom at a public bathhouse while his god-father and comrades cheered him on. The parish priest visited the girl's house on her wedding day so that he could bless her wedding apparel. Sometimes, a "half-wedding" occurred before the wedding to make certain the girl's parents did not try to marry their older daughter instead. Afterward, the bride's grandmother helped her dress. The bridal attendants, a talented local balladeer, or the bride sang lamentations to her parents before she left with the groom.

Then the groom and his procession arrived at his future in-laws house. Once the godfather gave his future brother-in-law a coin, they were permitted to go inside.

### ❤ The wedding

The wedding celebration, called the *harsanik,* was commonly held in autumn. It would begin on a Friday and continue from one to seven days. On the wedding day, the groom and his party would go to the bride's home where she was dressed by his godmother. If the bride was clothed by her female relatives, she would then be veiled by the godmother. An outer veil was removed after the wedding ceremony; an inner veil was not taken off her head until after the consummation of the marriage. After the bride was dressed for the wedding, the groom and his relatives escorted her to the church. Godparents of the groom usually presided over the ceremony as well as over the subsequent festivities. Two white doves, representing love and pleasure, were released at the church.

# Armenian Apolistic Wedding

*A traditional Armenian bridal costume*

165

❤ **Procession.** The wedding procession, with the bride partially veiled, proceeded to the groom's parish church.

❤ **Ring ceremony.** The marriage ceremony at the church was held during the Divine Liturgy. The priest blessed the rings. The couple vowed to support each other, compensate for each other's weaknesses, and satisfy each other's desires.

❤ **Crowning of the bride and groom.** As the priest walked to the altar and the wedding party entered, the *Urakh ler* was sung. The couple held candles while the godfather held a cross high over their heads. To crown their marriage with grace, wisdom, and integrity, assistants tied and then blessed the ribbons (or threads) they placed around the bride's and groom's heads. The couple faced each other and held hands as a symbol of unity.

# Armenian Apolistic Wedding

❤ **Past wedding customs.** The bride and groom wore metal crowns over their heads during the ceremony, and a *narot* was worn for several days prior to the consummation of the marriage. While the couple were enthroned, they sang a hymn *Ov yeranelid,* calling for the Armenian royal family to intervene for the solidarity and holiness of their marriage.

❤ **Singing of The Lord's prayer.** After the wedding, her husband, possessing a sword, took the bride to their new home. On the way, the wedding party enjoyed appetizers set on tables in front of relatives' and neighbors' houses.

❤ **Post-wedding festivities.** As the couple entered their home, the bride's mother, while dancing, placed two breads, called *lavish*, on the bride's head. The bride then went into each corner of every room with the bread over her head to denote her role as breadmaker and to insure that the couple would never be without sustenance.

Many other customs occurred which were too numerous to mention. Mainly, the veiled bride, while seated at the open house, took dried fruits, nuts, and candies from a drawstring bag and gave them to guests whom she wished to have good fortune. Often, the godmother collected coins for the newlyweds from each of the groom's guests whom the bride kissed.

❤ **Post-wedding customs**

❤ **Warding off evil spirits.** Later festivities were conducted at the groom's home where all the guests gathered. Upon entering the house, the bride and groom would break dishes, jars, or sometimes eggs to symbolize good luck in their new home.

❤ **Insuring fertility.** While entering the house, the couple wore lavish drapes over their shoulders to ward off evil spirits. In some regions of Armenia, the wedding festivities incorporated the pre-Christian practice of jumping over a fire three times to ensure fertility. The couple would "fly" over the fire together while the guests held hands and danced around them. This custom is still prevalent.

❤ **Assuring good luck.** While the newlyweds danced together, guests attached a ribbon of dollar bills to their clothing to assure good luck.

❤ **Celebrating the bride's virginity.** On the following day, the groom's parents sent a red apple to the bride's parents to recognize the bride's virginity.

❤ **Head washing.** The bride was not permitted to see her family during the first week after marriage, but on the seventh day her parents would visit her at the home of her in-laws. They brought with them symbolic gifts or the trousseau, and everyone enjoyed looking at her possessions. This activity was known as *head washing.*

**Reference:** *The Armenian Wedding* by Sylva N. Manoogian, *Gale Encyclopedia of Multicultural America, Encyclopedia of World Cultures.*

# Austria

## ♥ Weddings

Only civil marriages are legal in Austria, but the civil service is often followed by a religious ceremony. Civil marriages are performed by officials from the Registrar's Office *(Standesamt)*. There is no residency requirement prior to the ceremony as long as the necessary papers are in order. Couples have the option of holding their wedding in a tiny chapel, beautiful cathedral, or a historical castle's state room. They may have their wedding feast at an old cellar restaurant, in a lavish ballroom, at a hotel, at an aristocratic mansion, or in the Hall of the Knights, a 700 year old castle. Before the wedding, the bride inserts myrtle, the flower of life, in her headpiece. The couple goes through the streets in a horse-drawn carriage to their church wedding ceremony.

Cohabitation is increasingly common in urban centers where many had previously established their careers. These couples decide to marry when they intend to have children.

*Tiroleans.* Traditionally, the *Tiroleans* of western Austria received full recognition upon marriage. In fact, a young person was not able to inherit property until he found a mate. A man waited to marry until he could support a wife. Consent from the bride's brothers and sisters was needed prior to the marriage. Often, the bride was responsible for acquiring money to pay for the dowry or furnishings. Villagers were invited to the wedding which was held in the Christian church. Usually, the bride would live with her husband on his farm

The Roman Catholic custom of chastity before marriage is still practiced by those living in the countryside. Since marriage makes the family ties close, the newlyweds tend to live in near proximity with at least one set of parents.

**Reference:** *The Encyclopedia of World Cultures*

Austria is about 78 percent Roman Catholic, and the remaining are Protestant, Eastern Orthodox, Muslim, Buddhist, and others. Because Austria is mostly Roman Catholic, marriages are monogamous.

## ♥ Selecting a spouse

Today, the legal age for marrying in Austria is 19 for both sexes. Males, at least 18, and females, at least 16 years old, may be married if they present a written, notarized consent from both parents.

*Belgian Folk Wedding*

# Belgium

Belgium, a country with close traditional family ties, has a high Catholic population. According to Christian religious beliefs, women are expected to be virgins before the wedding and their marriages are monogamous.

## ♥ Selecting a spouse

Although Belgium is a highly modern country with international businesses, cars are not used for dating as much as in most industrialized countries. Single people can walk down cobblestone streets to cafés or shops where they can easily become acquainted with members of the opposite sex. Being picked up at one of these spots is normal and is not considered in bad taste. Otherwise, families and close friends introduce couples.

Belgians believe a successful marriage is based on affection, respect, understanding, and tolerance. Marrying someone of similar educational, religious, geographical and social background is commonplace.

In general, future spouses meet with each other daily or at least several times per week, then quickly move towards an engagement. Though people do break off engagements, most engagements usually last one to three years before the wedding. When a couple decides to marry, the future husband first approaches the perspective bride's family, then his own.

### ❤ Weddings

Belgian couples usually have a civil ceremony. A church wedding is followed by a catered reception at the bride's home.

### ❤ Other customs

Some married couples live with their parents for a while., reside close to them and visit them on weekends after they are married. Even when the family is primarily a nuclear family, the extended family remains the social focus and source of happiness throughout life.

Men celebrate May 1 as a day of love by bringing their girlfriends or wives a bouquet of Lily of the Valley purchased from a vendor at a street corner.

Reference: *Belgium, A Country Study.*

# *Bulgaria*

*Thanks to Daphne Kartchev of Bulgaria, Mihail Mihaylov, Bulgarian Orthodox Priest and to the other generous U.S. Phoenix immigrants from Bulgaria.*

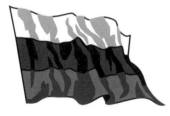

Bulgarian marriage customs and rituals vary from region to region and from sect to sect. In Bulgaria there are many dialects, and marriage customs are influenced by neighboring peoples and countries such as Rumania, Greece, Turkey, and Serbia. Bulgaria is 85 percent Bulgarian Orthodox (Eastern Orthodox) and 13 percent Muslim. When Bulgaria was under the Communist rule prior to 1991, religious church marriages were forbidden and couples were afraid to marry in the church. Though a generation grew up without a belief in God, many now prefer a church wedding.

### ❤ Selecting a spouse

As the children mature, those from small towns get to know each other from school or through relatives. Although single people can choose for themselves, they marry those who live in proximity because they are expected to live their entire life near where they were born. If a person marries someone from a distant town, he or she is permitted to move.

Young people go to bars, dances, and socialize in groups. The man may say how beautiful the woman is in a public place without being accused of sexual harassment. By complementing the woman, he creates an opening to ask for a date. Women in Bulgaria like

being told how beautiful they are and enjoy the attention. If the single couple goes to a restaurant, their main purpose is to converse intelligently about cultural subjects, new art, literature, and even the latest movies and their profits. If the suitor brings a bouquet of roses to his girlfriend, he must purchase an uneven number. His girlfriend represents the rose that is missing. After having a nice evening, the young man may serenade the young women at any time of night. Socially, their house doors are open and friends are invited inside for drinking, singing, and dancing.

### ❤ Pre-wedding customs

When a young man wants a girl for his wife, his parents go the girl's parents' house to ask for their daughter's hand. If the response is yes, arrangements for an engagement party are made and their closest relatives and friends are invited. Both families decide who will pay for the wedding and try to split the financial responsibility equally. Each side tries to pay for their own relatives and friends. The young man's parents are expected to purchase the wedding dress and rings. The girl brings a dowry of homemade bedspreads, rugs, embroidered towels, and blankets.

After the formal announcement of the couple's upcoming wedding, the girl stays at the house of the young man's parents until her marriage. She, thereby, becomes a helpmate to her prospective mother-in-law. After marriage, the couple usually resides in the house with his parents as well..

# Bulgarian
## Eastern Orthodox Wedding

❤ The bride wears a white gown and a veil which covers her face as she walks down the aisle. Prayers and songs are sung.

❤ The first part of the ceremony is the betrothal ring ceremony when the bride and groom take their vows by promising themselves to each other. The priest pronounces then that they are husband and wife.

❤ In between the vows and the pronouncement, jeweled gold crowns are placed on the bride's and groom's heads. The priest exchanges the crowns on their heads three times as they walk around the table. The veil is then taken from the bride's face and the newlyweds kiss.

*See Greece for more details about orthodox-style weddings.*

## Traditional Bulgarian Folk Customs

### ❤ Historical Bulgarian Folk Customs

Folk customs described here are historically based on nineteenth century and the early twentieth century. During this period, the Bulgarian majority were peasants who worked on small farms.

Couples met while they were line dancing at celebrations, when fetching water at village fairs, at the market, or while working. The girl, expected to remain otherwise passive, expressed her desires while singing and dancing. Her choice of clothing was intended to perform magic on men. Wearing festive fashions was a clear sign that young people were of marriageable age. The young men wore a fur headdress with a nosegay decoration inserted within. When the yearly feast arrived, the girl would cover her head with a scarf, wear coins and flowers over braids and a coin necklace.

Some folk wedding customs from the past are preserved today. Past customs include paying of the bride-price to the father, shaving the bridegroom, and braiding the bride's hair. The folk wedding was always festive in color and design. Its artistic quality, based on folk arts, included many beautifully woven hand-embroidered fabrics worn by the bride and groom, and eve the guests.

### ❤ Selecting a spouse

Young girls were considered of marriageable age at 16, after they developed bread-making skills. The boy was considered marriageable after he was capable of performing independent work.

In certain regions, a stick, symbolizing a wedding flag, would be attached to the roof of a home. It signaled that a girl was ripe for marriage. Songs linking the couple by name were sung by others.

Although the young man and his family were free to choose his bride, his choice was restricted by limitations on blood relationships, family name, and equal affluence. The qualities of the girl had to meet his family's standards. The bride had to be chaste, otherwise she would bring bad luck to a home and her extended family. Should the couple decide to elope, their social status was lowered and they were, at least temporarily degraded, into laborers.

### ❤ Former pre-wedding customs

If the young man was from a distant village, an uneven number of highly respected representatives were sent from the boy's family to take care of the business with the girl's family. The women of the young man's family often visited the girl's family earlier to create good will so that the family's male relatives could make a proposal during the evening. The girl's parents were usually cordial, thanked their visitors for the visit, but did not readily accept the first offer of marriage. They needed the girl's consent as well. The boy's representatives often had to return several times until an agreement was made and wine was served as a positive response. Finally, after all contracts were settled, the young man presented the girl with an engagement gift, a nosegay made of dried flowers with an engagement ring attached. The bride's parents provided a place of honor at a table where blessed gifts, nosegays, and kisses were exchanged between the girl's parents and their future in-laws.

### ❤ Historical engagement party

An engagement feast was financed by the young man's family. Neighbors, relatives, and friends were invited to the party where engagement songs, dancing, and gunfire were part of the celebration. Toasts and the betrothal ceremony were the high points of the party. The young man gave his future bride a more significant gift, a jewel. Pita bread was broken and a blessing performed. After salt was piled onto the pita, the pita was broken into smaller pieces so that each person could have a piece.

### ❤ Past pre-wedding rituals

Weddings were held after a productive harvest or during the early spring. Before the wedding, the girl's trousseau was prepared and gifts were created at work parties where all enjoyed singing. Bulgarians believed that a marriage should not occur without a *koum*, an honored godparent whose decision making was highly respected; therefore, a *koum* was selected. Second in importance was the appointment of a *staroiky* who held the wedding flag and could keep the wedding tree later.

The pre-wedding rituals began by making honeyed wedding breads which were kneaded and baked at the bride's and groom's homes. The bread was always kneaded in an odd number of kneading troughs while songs were sung. After the loaves were baked, honey was spread over them and floral stems were inserted into the top.

Before the bride was fetched, unmarried boys and girls danced special wedding dances accompanied by musicians playing folk music. Songs of lament were sung at the girl's party in the evening, for the bride was about to leave her friends and be separated from the unmarried.

The *koum's* dinner was given on the eve before the wedding day on a Saturday. During that evening, the *koum*, the first to be invited to the wedding, gave the groom a wedding tree made of plant materials with a loaf of bread as a base. It was then given to the bride prior to her departure from her father's house. The *koum's* dinner was often followed by a wild bachelor party.

Before the bride left for her groom's home, the wedding flag was prepared by each family. It was made from a headscarf and the man's waistband tied to a stick

bearing fruit. The flag had a nosegay tied to the top. Sometimes, an apple and threaded popcorn were attached to the scarf. The flag, secured to a high place, to a home or tree, showed that the wedding festivities had begun. The *koum* brought the bridal cover, wreaths for the church, and gifts to the bride's home.

The night before the wedding the bride was bathed and her hair braided by her friends who slept with her before the wedding. The groom was shaved outside beneath a tree while people sang amusing shaving songs.

The *staroik,* who carried a bridal flag, led the procession of wedding guests who brought money gifts, bread, and wine for the occasion to the bride's home. Her family made certain that all were welcomed. The bride later sat on a special stool while she and the guests enjoyed eating snacks.

### ❤ Fetching the bride

When the bridegroom, his parents, and the *koum* fetched the bride, wheat was thrown over the groom, shots were fired, or a circle of straw was set afire on the ground around him to ward off evil. The flag bearer, his deputies, singers, dancers, and the musicians playing music went to the bride's home with the bridegroom to fetch the bride.

In some regions when a bride was fetched, a ram was decorated with brightly colored fabric strips and taken along. The *koum* sent messengers to the bride's home to announce that the guests were about to arrive.

When guests entered the bride's home, they placed their gifts on the table. The bride and groom were hidden there separately. Lamentation songs were sung about the girl's dreadful departure to the home of strangers. The bride would weep, and her mother would sing verses of advice and well-wishes.

While the *koum* and other respected guests sat around a table in the courtyard, a blessing, long toasts to the couple, dancing by young men and women, and even bouts of wrestling took place. The wedding tree and wedding rooster, decorated with circles of popcorn and red peppers were presented to the *koum*. This presentation was accompanied by boisterous singing, shouting, and dancing.

Meanwhile, the bridegroom and the bride tried to have their first glimpses of each other. Whoever saw the other for the first time would be considered the boss of their family. The bride then performed several rituals with water, grains of wheat, and coins. Her friends helped her put on her wedding dress. They placed a wreath over her head and adorned her with flowers. The *dever* placed grains and a coin in the right shoe which he brought for her.

When the bridegroom approached, the bride kissed his hand and presented him a gift. In some regions, the groom would step on her foot or hit her to show he was the boss.

Merrymaking continued outside while the two flags from each family were joined together, showing the union of the young couple. As the bride kissed the hands of those present, she continued sobbing. The girl's father or brother handed the bride over to the *koum* who departed in the procession, but not before the bride's mother set a raw egg on the ground and the bride crushed it with her foot so she would have many children. The *koum* veiled the bride three times as the girls sang.

As the couple left, they passed though the hearth and grain was scattered over them. The bridegroom returned just long enough to open the neck of the bride's mother's dress and insert money to pay for the milk that his bride sucked from her bosom. The bride's trousseau was taken to the home of the groom's father by the groom's entourage. Although the group was just as merry with singing, dancing, and gun shots as when they came, they could not take the same route back. The bride was not permitted to look back. When they passed a stream, the bride would drink water three times before she could go with her mother-in-law.

### ❤ Historical wedding rituals

The wedding ceremony then took place at church, outdoors, or at home. In Eastern Bulgaria, the father placed a white cloth over the couple's heads and poured wine over the top. The *koum* blessed the couple and also poured wheat over them.

All the guests danced and sang until they were welcomed into the groom's home. The bridegroom's parents welcomed their son's new wife by giving her bread with wine or a jar of honey. All were served food and drink and gifts were exchanged. The bride's father-in-law gave the first present. Soon, the celebration spread to the village square.

Bridal virginity was of such importance that the closest relatives were present at the couple's first consummation to check the results while guests waited to be told. If she was a virgin, a huge bonfire was lit and men jumped over it as merrymaking took place.

**References:** *The Wedding: Bulgarian Folk Feasts and Customs* by Stoyan Genchev, Septemvir Publishing House, Sofia, 1988, *The Encyclopedia of World Cultures.*

# *Czechoslovakia*

171

The Czech Republic has a Roman Catholic and Protestant population.

### ❤ Traditional pre-wedding customs

In the past, a cash dowry was extremely important in Czechoslovakia. A young lady could not wed until women of her family made featherbeds for both the newlyweds and their first child.

After the suitor wooed her, he had to receive pardon from the girl's parents during a family celebration in order to start his life with their daughter. Once the couple received blessings for the engagement, a date was set for the church wedding, usually at the Catholic church.

The groom's friends and attendants would visit each house in the village to announce the upcoming wedding. They would ask villagers to help invite other guests to the wedding. The morning before the wedding, the bride, groom, and their parents would sit down to a wedding breakfast where much merrymaking took place. Thereafter, the bride and groom were not permitted to see each other until mid-afternoon, when the marriage ceremony was held.

Meanwhile, a sponsor advised the bride to be moral and the future husband to be kind. A rosemary wreath was created before the wedding so that the bride could wear it on her head during the ceremony to show her loyalty to the groom.

### ❤ Wedding and post-wedding activities

During this ceremony a bonnet, worn only by married women, was placed over the bride's plaited hair. At the reception, friends would tie ribbons to request donations of money for the newlyweds. Money for the couple's first child would also be collected at the feast. During the wedding feast, bridesmaids provided guests with sprigs of rosemary which symbolized fertility.

When the groom and his attendants went to the bride's house so she could collect her belongings, friends would try to prevent the bride from leaving. After saying good-bye to her parents, the bride and her belongings were taken in a wagon to the groom's home.

### ❤ Marriage customs under Communism

In 1982, 40 percent of the population became atheists and the other 40 percent remained Catholic. Because marriage customs were in a state of change, civil marriage became acceptable. A witnessed civil wedding ceremony at the national committee building was commonplace, although marriage could occur at church.

The couple still visited their parents prior to their wedding at which time a marriage agreement could be worked out. The couple then thanked their parents for their blessing and their betrothal. In cities, printed wedding invitations were sent to friends and relatives. In towns, guests for the wedding were invited by printed cards, letters, telegrams, and telephone conversations. Unlike the former custom where the entire village was invited, weddings were closed to the entire community. Guests were still entertained at a wedding breakfast. The parting from the parents was always symbolized by a celebration with much feasting and drinking; however, the wedding on a leisure Saturday was shortened and celebrations with merrymaking by the guests were tempered.

Before Communism, giving gifts to the bridal couple was a part of a traditional wedding customs. The number of gifts depended on a housewife calling village dwellers and asking them to donate to the household. Money for the couple was also collected during the wedding breakfast, and food necessary to prepare the wedding breakfast was given as gifts. Because of the gradual disappearance of the church ceremony, the traditional way of accumulating money for the couple changed. During the Communist era, money was collected in a shoe or container during an auction or at a midnight dance. Immigrants from the Ukraine or Romania continued collecting money in a tart or wreath. The custom of collecting money for the bride and groom was preserved, even in weddings held outside the home.

During the Communist era, national boards for civil affairs and folklore groups tried to keep alive the full use of wedding traditions, folk songs, and dances.

### ❤ Preserved and unpreserved wedding customs

More recently, many traditions reappeared, but sweets are now offered instead of tarts. Wedding cake has replaced the wedding bread. Instead of traditional wedding songs, modern music is played. The bride and groom kiss publicly at the wedding breakfast, and the bride is carried by the groom over the threshold into her new home. Splinters are still swept from the floor for good luck.

In the village of Ostrzka Nova Ves, other customs preserved from the past were locking the bridegroom out, ransoming the bride, and carrying the blankets. The blanket procession used to take place on the first Sunday after the wedding, and now it has changed to the day after the wedding. Merrymaking and the wedding supper still occur, but in more subdued fashion. Bonneting the bride, tossing money into a tart, and many wedding portrayals and songs were customs that faded..

Old folk wedding traditions of the Ukrainians of Eastern Slovakia still occur in some areas. These customs include the bridegroom traveling on horseback to fetch the bride, abducting the bride after a line dance, and stopping the wedding procession by using a bar. Guests even present the bride with gifts for remaining a virgin until marriage. Everyone in the family takes part in the wedding.

References: *Gale Encyclopedia of Multicultural America*, *Svatebni* by Libuse Strakova, *Encyclopedia of World Cultures and Svatebni Obrad* (the section by Vaclav Frolec).

## *Cyprus*

*Courtesy of the Embassy of Cyprus Press and Information Office*

Known as the legendary birthplace of Aphrodite, Greek goddess of love and beauty, Cyprus attracts hundreds of foreign couples who desire to marry and spend their honeymoons on this island. The majority of the Cypress population is Greek Orthodox and the other 18 percent of the population is Muslim. Presently, Cyprus follows contemporary European trends of free choice when it comes to dating and marriage. Town and city weddings are more Europeanized (Westernized) than in villages or in the countryside.

### ❤ Village wedding

The typical traditional village wedding occurs only after the parents have held favorable negotiations at the

***Coastline of Akamas Peninsula near the Baths of Aphrodite and the Fontana Amorosa, the Fountain of Love.***
*Spring, O'Brien and Company, Inc.., New York*
*Love, romance, and marriage are reflected for 9,000 years in the history of Cyprus. The legend is that Aphrodite, Goddess of Love and Beauty, was born in Cyprus.*

***Spreading of the Mattress Ceremony at a Traditional Cypriot wedding.***

***Folk Dances. Traditional Cypriot Wedding.***

*All of the above photos: Courtesy of the Embassy of Cypress Press and Information Office.*

bride's parents' house. While the bride prepares refreshments, families of the bride and groom discuss plans for the wedding and the agreement concerning property, animals, or household goods. After the agreement is finalized, the mothers of the bride and groom visit the homes of relatives and friends to invite them to the wedding. While visiting each house, a blessing for the couple is said over a glass of wine.

Rituals thereafter are celebrated by joyous singing and dancing. The festivities are accompanied by musicians who play the violin and the mandolin. One festivity is the "Spreading of the Mattress." The womenfolk take the bedding, which has been blessed by the priest, to the ceremony and dance with it. They lay the mattress cover onto a mat, stuff it, then sew the bed covering together while singing folk songs. People then give gifts to the couple. During the bachelor party, much singing and teasing occurs. Since the bridegroom receives his last shave, it is a time when he must be extremely congenial to his friends since he knows that the razor can cut his throat.

The wedding, usually held in a Byzantine-style church, is performed by a Greek Orthodox priest. Those included in the ceremony are the psalmists, plus the lineup of the best man and the bridesmaids. The priest blesses the bride and groom by placing a crown on their heads to make their union not only sacred, but royal. In his book *Romantic Cyprus*, Kreshishian says that when the priest expounds the words *to love and obey*, the bridegroom steps on the bride's toes as a future reminder. (*See the Greek Orthodox wedding ceremony.*)

After the ceremony, the newlyweds, their families, and guests walk to the bridegroom's house where sweetmeats and wine are served. A pig may be roasted and served to the entire village who were invited to the reception. At that time, the couple is given two white doves symbolic of a peaceful coexistence as husband and wife.

**Reference:** ***Romantic Cyprus*** **by Kevork K. Keshishian.**

173

# Denmark

Denmark is approximately 90 percent Evangelical Lutheran.

Dating begins at about 15 years of age. The young people attend dances, sporting events, and the movies. Often engaged for a lengthy period, couples may live together before making a decision to marry. Living together without a formal engagement or a wedding ceremony is common.

Historically, the Danes tolerated sexual relationships between betrothed couples. In fact, *handfasting,* clasping of hands as a marriage contract, was the ancient Dane custom that allowed for a trial marriage in which the couple lived together for one year and one day. Many who cohabit do not decide to marry until after their first baby is born. Weddings are held in the Evangelical Lutheran Church or the town hall. One fifth of all couples simply live together or have a common-law marriage without a formal ceremony.

A cornucopia cake decorated with marzipan medallions, symbolizing the bride and groom, or a cake with icing is served at the wedding reception. The cake is filled with candies, fruits, and miniature cakes.

**Reference:** *Culturgrams: The Nature of the World,* **1994** *Encyclopaedia Britannica.*

# Finland

*Courtesy of Embassy of Finland Press and Cultural Affairs Office*

Almost 90 percent of Finland's population is Evangelical Lutheran, but the Orthodox Church has many followers in western Finland.

### ♥ Pre-wedding customs

The Finns observe a popular traditional celebration called *polttarit.* The bride parties with her friends and the groom with his before entering into the fidelity of marriage. This celebration often is accompanied by laughing, teasing, singing, drinking, and by dressing in costumes. The *polttarit* may be a surprise party where the kidnapped bride or groom must change into a costume, or it may be simply a gathering of friends who enjoy going to a restaurant or an evening party at a home where small gifts are given and advice is offered.

During the most common *polttarit,* the future bride or groom is given a role to play while wearing a costume which has a certain meaning. The costume can be humorous, show the wearer's interest, or it may be grotesque or even sinful. Girls might be offered a sign to wear, such as *Take a Chance on Me!* The *polttarit* may start at a restaurant where the bride or groom is teased and given tasks to execute. Tasks for the bride could be singing opera in the public square or selling an unmentionable item to a passerby. The *polttarit* may continue at a public park. A female bath attendant or

striptease dance is sometimes arranged for the groom at a public sauna to test his ability to resist for one last time. The partying may continue until late at restaurants or someone's home.

### ♥ Historical wedding

The bride, who looked forward to her wedding, collected a trousseau throughout her childhood years. The Orthodox wedding ceremony was very colorful with gowned priests and the crowning of the bride and groom. After the wedding, the blindfolded bride handed her crown to a bridesmaid who is danced in a circle. People believed that this girl would be the next to wed.

Many colorful old Finnish wedding traditions have not survived. In western Finland, theatrical performances in the forest depict a typical old-fashioned wedding. Occasionally, young people wed at these performances with an audience of strangers observing. Brides wear a handmade dress and cone-shaped or crescent-shaped crown with trinkets hanging from each end.

### ♥ Present customs

Swedish-speaking Finns, usually bilingual, tend to marry those whose language is Finnish. Lutheran wedding ceremonies differ in various sections of the country. Before the wedding, laurel leaves symbolizing fertility are scattered onto the bride's path to the church or town hall. Since the late 1960's, open unions or cohabitation have increased, especially in urban areas.

**References: Stephanie Sinclair's,** *Polttarit: The Finnish Pre-Marriage Ritual,* **"L & EIF: Life and Education in Finland,"** *Finland: a Country Study,* *Bride's New Ways to Wed* **by the Editors of** *Bride's Magazine*

# France

***The Traditional Wedding of Ami Fritz, Alsace-Tlaslenheim,*** *Courtesy of the French Government Tourist Office, 444 Madison Avenue, New York, NY 10022-6903*
**Thanks to Celine Delasalle, Press Service-Documentation Center**
**Information from Quid magazine.**

Today, about 90 percent of the French population is Roman Catholic. In 1993, Catholic marriages were 159,097 of total of 254,000 marriages, and the rest were Jewish, Muslim, Protestant, or others. The Catholic wedding ceremony, described in the first chapter, is accompanied by grand festivities with families and friends.

### ❤ Past wedding customs

Historically, French marriages were not for pleasure or love, but they were mainly concerned with the experience of everyday living, working, and getting along together. Parents arranged marriages because they did not wish to leave the prosperity of their marriageable children to chance. Money was saved for the children from the time they were born. If the girl did not have a dowry by the time she was of marriageable age, she had a problem unless those who sympathized with her plight took up a collection. Thus, hard work and thriftiness were national habits in order to attract a suitable husband for a daughter.

On a couple's wedding day, the groom proceeded to the girl's home and took her, with a procession of relatives and friends, to the Catholic church. The couple took a pair of scissors, for they were often blocked by children holding white ribbons which they had to cut. When they arrived at church, the aroma of incense filled the sanctuary, flowers adorned the room, and they stood before the bishop under a silk canopy while he conducted the service. After departing from the church, the couple strolled along a path covered with laurel leaves. The newlyweds toasted their marriage by drinking from an engraved double-handled marriage goblet which was handed down from generation to generation.

Since October 14, 1791, the French Constitution recognized marriage only as a civil contract. In the 1800's in the rural countryside, if the husband was not satisfied with his wife, he would sell her at the marketplace or cafe where a crowd of people could watch the bargaining take place. Though wife-selling was illegal, it gained popularity and public acceptance.

### ❤ Present marriage customs

Marriages are not arranged and single people are free to choose their own spouses. Most couples meet at private events, through acquaintances, at work, or in public places. Although at least 2,000 dating services

*Restaurant Abbave. St. Michael in Tonnerre, Burgundy. Jacques Guillard, Photographer. The French Government Tourist Office*

After a French church wedding, laurel leaves are still spread outside the door of the church. The newlyweds still use a *coupe de marriage,* a two-handled marriage cup, passed down through generations, to make a toast during the reception. On the couple's wedding night, friends may bang pans and sing loud songs near the couple's bedroom window. Afterward, it is customary for the groom to invite his friends inside to have a small party.

Bernadette Bucher's article *France: A Country Wedding* in *Faces* magazine describes the following Vendean wedding: Family, friends, and neighbors follow the bride, clutching her father's arm, from the mayor's office down the street to the church. Because the groom pretends he does not want to give up his bachelorhood, he walks far behind with his mother. The bride's father gives away his daughter to the groom during the wedding ceremony at the Catholic church. Although everyone is invited to a reception where wine and a sweet bread, *brioche*, are served, only the closest friends and family come to the formal banquet. Between the many courses, people sing and play games. Some, dressed in costumes, marry the couple again. In Brittany, a toast is given, then the bride and groom drink from a glass of brandy which is poured over the *brioche*.

exist in France, only about four percent of the marriages are a result of meeting through such organizations. Presently, many couples live together before marriage, or they cohabit as a marriage alternative.

In central France among the Auvergne people, marriage involves two steps: both a civil marriage at the mayor's office and a religious wedding. In Western France, most couples have a civil ceremony performed at the town hall where the mayor officiates.

References: *France* by Eugene Weber. *Culturgrams: The Nations of the World,* Bernadette Bucher's article "France: A Country Wedding" in *Faces, Quid, and A Short History of Marriage* by Ethel L.Urlin.

# *Georgia*

Georgia's traditional customs were affected by the Communist revolution, but today Georgian young people of Orthodox descent are free to choose their marriage partners with the consent of their family.

Sometimes, a suitor's female relative may make arrangements for introductions to several potential spouses, preferably virgins. After negotiations between families, the fiancé or a representative from his family presents his fiancée with a ring or gold watch.

The bride, her bridesmaids, the groom, and his best man drive to the civil ceremony where the marriage is performed. The religious service may then be held in the Russian Orthodox Church. *(See the Russian Orthodox wedding on page 199.)*

When the newlyweds arrive at the groom's home, his mother hands them a plate to crunch underneath their feet. The first one to crack the plate is thought to be the one who will be the boss. The newlyweds are given a glass of wine and sweets. Later, they become king and queen at a extravagant feast which includes toasting, singing, and dancing. The festivities may last for three days.

*Abkhazians.* The *Abkhazians* of Georgia are 50 percent Russian Orthodox and 50 percent Sunni Muslim. The Abkhazian bride remains secluded throughout the feast, does not show happiness, or converse with members of the family out of respect for them. After the feast, the bride and groom retire to a special bridal dwelling where friends gleefully attempt to try to stop the couple from having sexual relations the first evening. Divorces are almost nonexistent.

Reference: *The Encyclopedia of World Cultures.*

# Germany

*At the "Fashion Wedding" in Hamburg, the German bridal couple, Stefan and Susanne, drive to the ceremony in the traditional white wedding coach, drawn by white horses. Before the church, they are met by three little girls in white and a little boy, ceremoniously dressed in black. The children strew the path to the bridal altar with flowers from their baskets. The bride, wearing white organza lace, carries a bouquet of orchids, calanchoes, and dracaena. On the evening before the wedding, Stefan invites his friends to a stag party. On the wedding eve, Susanne's friends and neighbors hold a Polterabend in front of her house, a very old custom during which cups and dishes are smashed so that the noise will drive evil spirits away. The bride must sweep up all the debris herself to bring good luck. Courtesy of the German Information Center*

**Courtesy Consulate General of the Federal Republic of Germany**
**Courtesy of Sharon D. Ringen**

Almost half of the German population is Protestant, and 37 percent of all Protestants are Lutheran.

### ♥ Past pre-wedding customs

Historically in Kostenbidder, a man designated to be the wedding inviter, adorned with flowers and ribbons, notified each guest at their homes. People were invited to the wedding by the inviter hitting a stick against their door. The inviter was also the emcee during the wedding reception and announced the name of all guests as they gave their gifts to the bride and groom. The bride or groom could also invite people and while doing so, could give each guest a little present.

### ♥ Present pre-wedding customs

Young men and girls meet, date, and choose a spouse as do others in Western cultures. *(See page 35.)* To meet other singles of the opposite sex, singles parties and personal ads are in vogue. Since many of the 12 million German people work and live alone, sold-out singles parties flourish. Usually each person pays for his or her own expenses while dating.

Sixty-two percent of all marriages are between those of the same religion. Marrying across religious denominational lines has become accepted, except for defined groups like the Catholics in which the majority still marry within their own faith. The increase in intermarriages seems to indicate growing social integration and societal openness. Couples often live together before marriage or instead of marriage.

Only half of all people wear an engagement ring

but, when they do, the man and his female partner both wear one. Traditionally, the engagement ring, a plain gold band, is worn on the left hand, and the wedding ring is worn on the right.

### ❤ Present pre-wedding customs

The *Polerabend*, held the night before the wedding, is a popular custom. Much happens on that occasion, including a wedding eve dinner served to relatives and friends of the betrothed couple. Next, a wedding rehearsal for the marriage ceremony takes place. A short play, operetta, or a charade pertaining to the future life of the young couple is then performed. The evening culminates in dancing and smashing of crockery and glass. Participants also bang saucepans and crack whips to drive evil spirits away. To attain future marital happiness, the bride sweeps away the broken pieces. All this excitement, accompanied by drinking and merriment, continues to the small hours of the morning;

*A wedding dance in traditional dress.* The Sorbs (or Wends), a West Slavic ethnic minority who live in the eastern German federal states of Brandenburg and Saxony. Courtesy of the German Information Center.

*The castle.* Burgen Und Schlosser. Scholb Neuschwanstein, Bundesbildstelle Bonn. Courtesy of the German Information Center.

nevertheless, the young couple and their guests are at the church the next morning for the wedding.

### ❤ Present German weddings

Today's weddings often involve three days of celebration:

*Day 1:* A civil ceremony with friends and family and dinner. Civil marriages, which are obligatory, are performed in city hall or at the registrar's office.

*Day 2.* A *Polterabend*, a party the evening prior to the church wedding.

*Day 3.* A religious wedding ceremony and a reception.

When a bride wears a gown handed down through generations, she usually wears a decorative wedding crown created with wire, tinsel, flowers, beads, and decorative jewelry. She must wear the crown until midnight for good luck. Then, it is removed and replaced by a bridal bonnet.

Upon leaving the church after the wedding, neighborhood children may hold a rope across the newlywed's path. The groom is therefore obliged to gain the couples freedom by supplying the children with sweets and coins which a person of his wedding party carries for the occasion. The wedding is followed by a reception at which friends place floral garlands and greens at the exit. While the new husband, his best man and the bridesmaids dance around the bride, the bride grabs a bridesmaid who is to be the next to wed. Married women then tie the bride's bonnet on this bridesmaid who must dance with male members of the groom's family. The bride's mother throws peas or rice, symbolizing fertility, on the bride. Before the couple can leave, the groom promises them a ransom of money or a party.

Optional religious ceremonies and receptions usually are held up to 10 days afterward. Married couples may choose the woman's last name for their family name, but few ever do, but they sometimes combine both last names.

**References:** *These Strange German Ways, May 1995 The World Press Review, The World of Weddings* **by Bryan Murphy,** *Kolner Zeitschrift fur Soziologie und Sozialpsychologie* **by Johen Hendricks, Osmund Schreuder, and Wouter Ultee,** *A Short History of Marriage* **by Ethel L. Urnlin,** *Bride's New Ways to Wed.*

# Great Britain

Most people in the United Kingdom are associated with the Church of England or the Roman Catholic Church, with approximately 2,000,000 belonging to each one. The English population connected with the Church of Scotland is 900,0000. The remaining religions are Methodists, Baptists, Muslims, Sikhs, Hindus and Jews. Minority communities, such as the West Indian, South Asian, Jewish, Quakers, Muslims and the Chinese, retain some of their own customs.

### ❤ Past marriage customs
During the Regency, Victorian and Edwardian Periods, romance consisted of clever remarks and pretty compliments. Manners were important and public courtship was considered immoral behavior.

Historically, marriage was a religious affair; however, a couple who were in a hurry to marry could elope in Gretna Green, located in Scotland close to the English border. No marriage license or waiting period was necessary until 1856, at which time a 21-day residence in Scotland was imposed.

After the mid-1800's, couples could obtain a license to have a simple civil ceremony at a registrar's office or nonreligious location.

### ❤ Present Marriage laws
In 1987, English marriage became a matter of the civil courts; their civil law stipulated that marriage had to be voluntary, monogamous, and should last a lifetime.

If a Muslim had more than one wife when he became a citizen of Britain, one of his wives is regarded as a wife and the other(s) are dependents over the age of 18.

In England, the Church of England can solemnize marriages. For those of other denominations, their law requires that a registrar be present at the ceremony or that the couple register to marry at the registry office prior to the religious ceremony.

### ❤ Selecting a spouse
Presently, Britain's dating patterns are similar to that of the Unites States, except that British young men and women date one woman or man at a time. *(See Western-style customs in Chapter 1.)*

### ❤ Weddings
A marriage ceremony may be performed at a town's registry office before two witnesses, but many couples have religious ceremonies at churches. The short 10-minute ceremony at the town registry provides the couple with a certificate of marriage. A new Marriage Act permits couples to devise their own vows and create their own format for a wedding service following the legal ceremony. Couples must choose from an authorized list of clergy who are willing to officiate.

Their Christian marriage ceremonies are like those of North America, for major denominations in United States and Canada have patterned their marriage ceremonies after the Church of England as the result of colonization years ago.

179

# England & Wales

### ❤ Past marriage customs
*Marriage by capture* was legal in England before the Thirteenth Century. Later, England's Christian morality and wedding customs prevailed.

Most weddings occurred in the church and banns were announced for three weeks prior. *(See appendix for more information about "banns.")* In the past, couples could apply for the "special" marriage license at Doctor's Common. The license was then granted by the archbishop of Canterbury. In that case, banns did not have to be read since couples with the "special" license could be married at anytime, anywhere.

The bridal tradition of wearing "something old, something new, something borrowed, something blue" came from English poetry, but this poem also has another line: *a lucky sixpence in her shoe.*

### ❤ Present marriage laws
Today, English and Welsh couples over 18 are free to marry anyone except for closely related family members. Those between the ages of 16 and 18 must have the written consent of parents or a guardian before their marriage. Under the Marriage Act of 1994, a marriage may occur at a place of religious worship, a

registrar's office, or a public place officially registered for marriage. During civil ceremonies, only nonreligious music and readings are permitted; however, a civil wedding may be blessed by an Anglican minister afterward. Some residence requirements are mandatory.

Since 1995, couples desiring a nonreligious wedding can wed at the registrar's office or any other approved edifice in England or Wales. Stately homes, castles and dignified hotels are often granted licenses, and marriages can be performed on the premises. One hour prior to or during the ceremony, no food or drink can be sold or consumed in the hotel or castle room where the wedding is to occur .

Because the Church of England permits a mixed marriage in the church only when either the bride or groom has been baptized (christened), special permission is required for an unbaptized couple to marry there. A Church of England marriage is solemnized after a publication of banns, which are announcements of marriage. An application for the publication of banns is made to a parish clergyman where each party resides. Should the couple wish to marry outside their area, they must apply to be placed on an electoral roll or reside at the parish for the duration of the banns. Banns are published on three consecutive Sundays and after publication, the parties are free to marry.

Jewish weddings require both religious and civil applications, and their ceremonies take place any time except on Saturdays. Although most wedding ceremonies occur in the synagogue, they can be performed anywhere. The bride and groom stand under a *chuppah,* a wedding canopy, during their wedding ceremony. The *ketubah,* the Jewish marriage contract containing the obligations of each party, is signed by the bride and groom. *(See the Jewish weddings in Chapter 1.)*

Catholic couples visit a priest before the wedding. They must come with their baptism and confirmation certificates in order to receive instruction several weeks prior to their wedding. When both are Catholic, the reading of the banns takes place.

# *Church of England's Wedding*

❤ **Wedding rehearsal.** A wedding rehearsal is held for those in the bridal party.

❤ **Pre-wedding protocol.** Young maidens scatter floral petals before the bride as she walks towards the church for the wedding ceremony. She carries a horseshoe embellished with ribbon to bring her good luck. As the couple enter the church for the wedding, church bells ring.

When the best man and groom arrive, fees are paid for the wedding. The bride's family and friends are seated by young male ushers on the left side of the sanctuary and the groom's on the right. The closest relatives sit in front pews near the altar. Before the start of the ceremony, the bride's mother walks down the aisle and takes her front right seat. *(In Wales, the churchyard gates are opened for the wedding only after youngsters are showered with coins.).*

❤ **Wedding procession.** Significant participants proceed to the altar in the following order: the priest, matron of honor and other attendants, and the bride, who walks down the aisle with her father. *(The order may be different depending on the family preferences.)* The bride hands her bouquet of flowers to the matron of honor who holds it until after the ceremony and the bride signs the register.

❤ **Introduction by the priest.** After the bride comes down the aisle, the minister gives an introduction while the bride and groom stand before him. Then, the priest announces the bride's and groom's presence under God who witnesses their marriage. He asks *God to bless them and to share their happiness* and informs the couple that *the Lord Jesus Christ's Spirit is with them now.* The priest emphasizes that *marriage is a gift from God.* He says that *the bride and groom will become of one flesh as they faithfully provide for each other's needs throughout their life under all circumstances . . . that they are now permitted to enjoy the love, joy, and tenderness of bodily union which will provide them with children and will strengthen their hearts and lives. . . .* also that *their new life within the community should embrace responsibility, be one of honor, and thereby blessed by God.*

# Church of England's Wedding

❤ **Inquiry.** The priest inquires, *If there is anyone present who knows any reason why these persons may not lawfully be wed, declare it now.*

❤ **Vows.** After the brief silence, the priest asks the bridegroom: *Will you take this bride as your wife, comfort her, honor and protect her, forsaking all others, be faithful to her as long as you both shall live?*

The groom responds, *I will.* Then, the priest asks the same question of the bride who then responds, *I will.* The bridegroom takes the bride's right hand as they face one another and each repeat the following words:

*I, (her name, his name), take you (her name, his), you as my (husband and wife), to have and to hold from this day forward; for better, for worse, for richer, for poorer, in sickness and in health, to love and to cherish, till death us do part, according to God's holy law; and this is my solemn vow.*

❤ **Exchange of rings.** The priest requests that the groom place the wedding ring on the bride's fourth finger. Then the groom repeats the priest's words that affirm that the ring is the sign of their marriage, that he will honor his wife and share all with her within the love of God, the Father, the Son and the Holy Spirit.

❤ **The pronouncement.** The priest pronounces the couple as husband and wife. Then, he joins their hands and says: *That which God has joined let no man put asunder.*

❤ **Blessings.** The couple then kneel while the priest and the congregation bless them and ask that they may be strong in their faith.. All pray that God will guide them to fulfill His purpose while they spend their earthly life as husband and wife.

❤ **Signing the church register.** Afterward, the church register is signed and photographs are taken.

❤ **The reception.** The bride, groom, parents, and attendants form a receiving line to greet their guests at the reception. During the banquet, the bridesmaids, the groom's father, the bride's mother, the groom and bride, the bride's father, the groom's mother and best man—in that order—sit at the main table. The bride's father toasts the couple. After the food is served, the groom thanks the bride's parents and proposes a toast to the bridesmaids. The best man responds for the bridesmaids, then reads telegrams, e-mail, and cards which relay congratulations from well-wishers. When the best man announces the cake cutting, the groom places his hand over the bride's hand as they slice the first piece. A member of the serving staff then finishes cutting the cake and serves the guests. Sometimes a fruitcake, made with raisins, cherries, and almonds, is served. The top layer, the christening cake decorated with marzipan, is kept for the baptism of the couple's first baby. *(The cake may be cut before the speeches are given.)*

❤ **181**

References: *Countries of the World: Great Britain*, *Wedding and Home* magazine; *Wedding World* magazine, and *Living Faiths: Marriage and the Family* by John Pricket; April and May, 1996, issue of *Wedding and Home*, London, England, Article "This & That" by Elisabeth Ashford in the Sept./Oct. 1997 *The Regency Plume* newsletter.

# Scotland

*Part of Great Britain*

In Scotland, young men and women who are sixteen and over do not need parental consent to wed and there is no residence requirement as there is in England and Wales. Four to six weeks in advance, both parties submit marriage notices to the registrar at the registration district where the marriage is to take place. This procedure applies to both religious and civil marriages performed before the registrar. It also applies to preplanned weddings held outside the registration district, even in Gretna Green, the traditional site of elopement.

Religious weddings are held mainly in the two churches: the Christian Presbyterian Church of Scotland and the Scottish Catholic Church. The Celtic call to worship and the playing of church bells often precedes a church wedding ceremony.

The number of intermarriages between the two churches has increased so much that a Joint Commission on Christian Marriage produced a leaflet *Inter-Church*.

## ❤ Traditional Scottish customs

In the past *reeling* was practiced in the Scottish Highlands. Friends filled a large basket with rocks and tied it to the groom's back. The only way the groom could escape the heavy weight was if his bride would kiss him.

A day prior to the wedding, the guests paid for a party with drinking, dancing, and toasts to good health. The bride's feet were washed in a tub of water with a ring placed inside. The first young woman to find the ring in the tub was considered to be the next to be married.

Floral petals were thrown over the bride while she left her home with the wedding procession for the church. The bride gave a coin to the first person she saw, and that individual had to join the procession before continuing his or her itinerary for the day.

The priest met the couple at the entrance of the church. The vows and the joining rites were spoken in vernacular Scottish. After the wedding ceremony a lengthy nuptial mass was spoken in Latin. When the mass ended, the priest gave a blessing over the food and beverages brought by guests and shared by all.

## ❤ Present pre-wedding customs

Today, in Scotland a *showing of presents* often takes place at the discretion of her mother at the bride's home.

At the open house, the wedding presents are on display with a card showing the name of the giver. Since the bride and her bridal party are present, guests have the opportunity to get to know the bridal party prior to the wedding. Tea, sandwiches, and cakes are served.

*Taking out the bride* follows the showing of the presents. At that time the bride may be dressed in a costume, perhaps with a veil made from old draperies. While the bride and her friends sing at the top of their lungs and bang pots and pans, they visit villagers. Carrying a baby doll and a plastic pot containing salt for luck and prosperity, the bride kisses villagers in exchange for money they place in the pot.

The groom also wears a costume for *stag night*, which is similar to friends taking out the bride. Sometimes, the groom is padded under his clothing so that he resembles a pregnant woman. More often than not, the groom and his companions go to a bar or party and drink alcoholic beverages and become drunk. The groom has to endure harmless tricks and joking. At the end of their partying the groom may be stripped of clothing and perhaps, tied up to a tree near his house.

As the wedding procession leaves for the church, often colorful confetti is thrown over the bride as she leaves her residence or after the church wedding.

After the nuptials, a celebration is held at the relatives' home where traditional waltzes, country dances, and contemporary music is played. A *ceilidh* band may be hired for Highland dancing.

*Reference: Continuum Internet Publishing Services at http://www.weddingcirlce.com/ethnic/scot/scoth.htm*

# Scottish Catholic & Presbyterian Weddings

❤ Before the wedding, the bride's and groom's announcement of intent is traditionally read in their respective churches. Shortly afterward, wedding parties are given to honor the couple. A *spree,* a shower, is held for guests to present household gifts. It is sometimes accompanied by dancing and games. Historically, the closest bridesmaid is expected to give a set of cups and saucers at the *spree.*

❤ Bagpipes are often played prior to the wedding ceremony and at the bride's and groom's reception where a Scottish sword dance is performed. Current marriage liturgy used at nuptial masses for the *Scottish Catholic Church* is published in two texts— one for the priest and another for the congregation. *The Church of Scotland's Presbyterian* wedding services vary, for the minister is allowed to create his own ceremony and thereby concentrate on what is meaningful to the bride, the groom, and their families. The minister simply must provide a statement which covers the meaning of a Christian marriage, include the vows, a ring ceremony, and the pronouncement of marriage, with a blessing, which follows. Hymns are standard before and after the ceremony. Their prayers of praise, thanks, request and exhortation are included within the order of service. Traditionally, the groom gives the bride a silver wedding spoon with the couple's initials engraved on it. After the ceremony when the couple comes out of the church, a special guard of men in kilts may honor the newlyweds. The groom may also wear a kilt.

❤ After most formal weddings, a reception line of bride and groom, their parents, and the bridal party greet their guests. In turn, guests congratulate the families and the newly married couple. Wedding presents can be lavish and are publicly displayed.

❤ A sit down luncheon or dinner is served with a rich dark wedding fruitcake for dessert. At a hotel, people gather for the banquet, the cutting of the cake by the bride and groom, speeches, dancing, and singing. The wedding cake is covered by a hard icing and decorated with silver bells and flowers. The decorations from the cake are handed out to elder relatives, but the top layer is saved for the christening of the first child. Those who are unable to attend are mailed pieces of cake. Feasting and dancing is done on an enormous scale. *(Those who marry at a registrar's office may have a reception at a restaurant.)*

❤ The parents of the bride and groom split the cost of the wedding. The bride pays for the reception and the groom covers the bills for flowers and alcoholic beverages which are usually champagne, whiskey, and sherry.

**References:** *Of Scottish Ways* by Eve Begley and *Rites of Marrying* by Simon R. Charsley.

# Northern Ireland
### Part of Great Britain

Northern Ireland is 28 percent Catholic, 23% Presbyterian, and 20 percent Church of Ireland.

Today, parental consent is required in Ireland for persons under 18 who wish to marry. For those marriages involving the registrar's office, prior residence is necessary before the notice of marriage can be served. A waiting period must take place after the notice has been provided so that the registrar can issue his authority for the marriage.

Family solidarity before and after the wedding is an integral part of everyday life. In western Ireland, people tend to marry those who live nearby and the couples always visit their parents' households. The couple may exchange claddagh wedding rings which have two hands grasping and a crowned heart to show their love. *(See page 187 for the Republic of Ireland.)*

**Reference:** *The Scotch-Irish Social History* by James G. Leyburn.

# Greece

***Jim and Christina Speros at the Greek Orthodox church.*** *See the dust cover which shows the connecting crowns they wore at their wedding ceremony.*
*Courtesy of Jim and Christina Speros.*

***My thanks to Reverend Theo Anastas***
*of The Holy Trinity Greek Orthodox Cathedral in Phoenix, Arizona, U.S.A. for providing the*
*Greek Orthodox wedding ceremony and traditional customs.*

The population of Greece is 97 percent Greek Orthodox.

### ❤ Past customs
Before the 1970's, the boy and girl were often chaperoned if they wanted to go to a movie. The chaperone could be an older brother or an uncle.

The traditional outdoor wedding was attended by more than 1,000 people from the village. Relatives of the bride and groom paid a huge sum for such a wedding and each guest brought a gift.

The evil eye, called the *vaskania*, was recognized by the church as initiated by the devil. A pair of scissors was (and still is) often inserted in a bridal floral bouquet to cut the evil eye. Single women would also sign their names under the hem of the bride's wedding dress to receive good luck in finding their own husbands.

After the wedding, young children were briefly placed on the marital bed so that the bride and groom would be fertile and give birth to many children.

The very important dowry of a young woman was unpacked and displayed at the reception. After the bride's procession entered into the groom's home, the mother provided the bride with honey which was used to make the sign of the cross upon the door. Honey signified a sweet, prosperous, abundant life.

### ❤ Present customs

Today chaperonage is no longer mandatory and young people are free to choose their own spouses. Dating begins when groups of boys and girls socialize. They go to pastry stores where waiters serve malts, ice cream and luscious Greek pastries. When a young Greek woman marries, her family may give her a plot of land. If her family is wealthy, they provide her a dowry of an apartment building, investments, or interest in an ocean freighter. Less affluent families might donate a small farm or enough financial assets for their son-in-law to receive a higher education on which he can build a solid future.

No wedding application is accepted by the bishop, unless the couple has premarital counseling to define the sacrament of marriage and to discuss psychological problems that might arise.

The wedding celebration lasts several days. In the small villages, an orchestra band plays at the bride's home and walks with her to church. Then the musicians repeat the same festive ritual for the groom. Prior to the honeymoon, women prepare the marriage bed with new sheets, blankets, and fresh flowers, and add coins.

On Psara Island near Greece, a woman is not permitted to marry a man from elsewhere unless he has a good reputation and promises to settle permanently on the island.

# Greek Orthodox Wedding

### Part I

❤ **Betrothal ceremony.** The first half of the wedding ritual is the engagement ceremony. The priest offers prayers invoking names of biblical characters from the Old Testament. During this betrothal service, the bride and groom exchange rings to seal the promise of love and fidelity to each other. Their pledge is a promise to God, not to any human being, and their rings symbolize God's circle of love in which there is no beginning and no end. The first half of the ceremony is over after this exchange.

### Part II

❤ **Crowning the bride and groom.** During the second half of the marriage ceremony, the couple holds lighted candles as a reminder that Christ's light is with them throughout the sacrament. After the priest joins their hands together, the bride and groom are crowned. The wreath-like crowns, floral and bead-decorated circles tied together by ribbon, unite the couple together and symbolize their physical and spiritual unity. Placing these crowns, often made of orange blossoms, on the heads of bride and groom signifies they are to be king and queen of their own home. An honored godparent of the bride, a close friend or family member, called the *Koumbari*, exchanges the wedding crowns three times on the heads of the bride and groom as part of the wedding ritual.

❤ **Sipping from a common cup.** The bride and groom each drink three sips from a common cup of sweet wine which symbolizes sharing their life together.

❤ **Dance of Isaiah**. Then, the priest leads the couple, all three joyfully holding hands, into *The Dance of Isaiah* three times around the small table in front of the sanctuary.

❤ **Post-wedding customs**
The attendees shower the newlyweds with rose petals and rice after their wedding or with sugared almonds. During the reception, the guests enjoy traditional lamb, wedding cake, sweets, *bouszouki* music, and folk line-dancing. At the wedding party, the bride and groom dance as they each hold the end of a white scarf.

**References:** *Enchantment of the World: Greece* by R. Conrad Stein, *A Guide to Greek Traditions and Customs in America* by Marilyn Rouvelas.

185

# Hungary

More than half of the Hungarian population is Roman Catholic, one quarter is Calvinist, and five percent is Lutheran.

After the spread of Communism, religious wedding traditions were affected and atheism was encouraged.

Before that time, the engagement party for the couple was organized by both sides of the family. People in villages went to the church in a wedding procession of horse-drawn wooden carriages decorated with freshly cut evergreen trees. To prepare for the wedding, snails were made into soup paste and a bouillon was made. A cow, sheep, or a pig was slaughtered for the wedding, especially in regional agricultural communities. Boiled meat, stuffed cabbage or a mutton dish were served and sweet semolina pudding and tarts were provided as desserts.

The marriage vow was symbolized by the giving of a table cloth filled with nuts, fruits, and beverages and an exchange of scarves. At the wedding, the couples' hands were bound to each other over ceremonial bread in which a twig had been inserted. The twig symbolized the groom and the bread symbolized the bride and together they formed a union. The symbolic twig was also inserted into the tarts and served to guests at dinners.

**References: *Enchantment of the World: Hungary, Svatebni Obrad*, the section by Erzsebet Bodi.**

# Iceland

Ancient Scandinavian influences on Iceland's marriage customs have continued to recent times. When Iceland was settled by the Catholic and Lutheran peoples, the betrothal ceremony was the Icelanders' only conception of marriage. They did not think of having a civil or religious service.

Historically, the non-Christian marriage was considered a union between two families. While both sides exalted the virtues of the future bride and groom, the two fathers bargained until a settlement was made. Although marriages were arranged, the wishes of the prospective marriage partners were respected. Marriage involved the formal negotiations and ceremonial betrothal. One year later, a wedding feast was held by the bride's people for both families. The pair could not reside together until after their wedding feast.

After Christianity was accepted, marriage evolved into a contract for the impending marriage. A man made his promise before witnesses at the ceremonial betrothal. The girl was not permitted to attend her engagement ceremony. Later, her partner said to her, *You are my legal wife*, and the bride responded before the witnesses that she was willing to be his wife. The Christians later required that a wedding ceremony take place at church.

From the beginning of Iceland's folk culture until today, premarital sexual freedom was condoned for both male and female. From 1960 to the 1970's, the number of marriages decreased, and many couples bore children out of wedlock; however, weddings are back in fashion. Couples most often marry after they can pay for their own home, and those who attend college wait until they are about 24. As a result, young couples often live together with one set of parents until they marry.

Today, weddings are similar to those of northern European countries and the United States. Most Icelanders have a church wedding after cohabiting for several years, even after their first child is born. If the bride and groom have children, they are included in the wedding ceremony as flower-girls or other helpers.

**References: *Iceland* by Richard F. Tomassion and *Cultures of the World: Iceland*.**

# Ireland *(Republic of)*

*Thanks to the Consulate General of Ireland, Ard-Chonsalacht Na Heireann.*

The Republic of Ireland occupies the south, west, eastern part of the island of Ireland. The Republic of Ireland is mostly Roman Catholic.

### ❤ Traditional marriage customs

During ancient times, the entire community was invited by spoken word to the wedding. Ireland has always had a tradition of robust partying and wedding celebrations. The wedding festivities started when the men competed in a race for a bottle of whisky. The one who was victorious was the first to kiss the bride.

The bride wore fine Irish lace at the hem line of her gown for good luck. The wedding celebration ended with the "bedding" of the newlyweds and obscene teasing. Family and friends heartily provided their best wishes for the couple to be blessed with a large family. The celebration peaked when the couple were serenaded by the sound of clanking pots and pans. Their traditional brandy-soaked wedding cake was a fruitcake recipe consisting of ground almonds, raisins, cherries, flour, and spices. One of the most exciting Irish wedding dances is the *janting char* at which time the groom is lifted on a chair.

### ❤ Present marriage customs

Before a person can marry legally, he or she must reside for 14 days within the district in which he or she is to marry. If both parties are under the age of 21, a consent form must be signed by parents. Should either party be under the age of sixteen, an application for permission to marry must be made to the president of the High Court. A couple can marry in the Registry Office, then after, have the option of marrying in the Catholic Church. *(Please see Catholic wedding ceremony in Chapter 1.)*

If neither partner attends a place of worship where a Notice of Marriage is given one month prior, a special notice must be inserted in a daily newspaper. Complete copies of the newspaper notice must be produced on the day of the wedding.

The wedding ceremony can take place not less than eight days and not more than three months after the Notice of Marriage is given. Two witnesses must be present at the ceremony which can take place any day, Monday through Friday, during specified morning and afternoon hours.

# Italy

*Thanks to Jerry Smallidge, Publisher of Wedding Day Magazine and to Vivian Jacobozzi*

Italy's population is 88 percent Roman Catholic.

### ❤ Ancient Traditions

The Western-style wedding originated in Rome centuries ago. Not only was there a ceremony with vows similar to today, but the bride also wore a veil and was given a wedding ring by the groom. The couple celebrated by eating wedding cake, and rice was thrown over them to insure that they would be fruitful and multiply. The new husband even carried his bride over the threshold of their home.

# Ancient Roman Wedding

❤ The bride wore a wool girdle fastened with the Knot of Hercules around her waist to hold up her hemless tunic. Over her tunic she wore a yellow cloak that matched her yellow sandals. She wore a metal necklace and a red or yellow veil with a crown of myrtle and orange blossoms. After she and her relatives welcomed her groom during a ceremony, a sheep or pig was sacrificed. The couple held hands and pledged their wedding vows before a Roman priestess.

**Reference:** *Wedding Vows* by Diane Warner.

### ❤ Past marriage customs

In the past, marriages were arranged by the parents who saved dowries for their daughter's marriage while she was growing up. Sex was not permitted outside of marriage, for sexual abstinence was encouraged by the Roman Catholic church; therefore, activities prior to the wedding were carried out under the observation of the couple's families and the community at large.

### ❤ Present marriage customs

Unlike the United States and Anglo-Saxon countries that place a premium on young men and women living independently from their parents, Italians have a history of having close-knit families in which their children generally stay at their homes until they are wed. Giovanni Istroni reported in the 1996 *New York Times* that single Italian men reside in their parent's home longer than men in United States and Anglo-Saxon countries. Approximately 50 percent of Italian men as old as 29 years remain in their childhood domicile. Because most college students commute from home to universities, prolongation of men living at home is reinforced. Young women, who have higher work and educational expectations, also delay marriage; thus, men marry at about age 29 and women at 26.

Though Roman Catholic values are still goals to be observed, Italian parents often must accept the fact that their children have sexual relations prior to marriage.

# *Italian Wedding*

❤ **Early Catholic communion.** The bride and groom begin their wedding day early in the morning by taking communion together at church. At the that time, the bride is not yet dressed in her bridal splendor. Later, they are married in traditional Western wedding attire at a church ceremony during a mass.

❤ **Wedding ceremony.** Much importance is placed on the blessing of the gold bands which are usually very plain and have no diamonds or jeweled adornments. The bride and groom do not kiss after the ceremony. *(See Catholic wedding in Chapter 1 for more details on rituals and the Order of Service.)*

❤ **Welcoming the bride.** After the wedding mass, the people of the entire small town come to wish the bride and groom *auguri* (good luck). The newlyweds often go to the groom's family house. There, the groom's mother welcomes the bride into the family by handing her a *palma* made out of confetti (Jordan almonds). The almonds are covered with colored cellophane and arranged in a leaf-like formation. People then toss confetti candy, rice, and grain over happy couple.

❤ **Wedding feast.** Later on, people attend a sit-down, multi-course wedding feast which lasts from four to six hours or more. A sample menu:

*Cocktails and Appetizers of Ham and Melon*
*Wedding Soup (made with little meatballs and spinach in chicken broth)*
*Lasagna, Cannelloni, and Ravioli*
*Veal, Pork, and Poultry, Fish, Cheese*
*Fruit, Dessert and Wedding Cake*
*Asti Spumante (for the wedding toast) and Coffee.*

Once the guests have finished the dinner, liqueur is offered. A *bomboniere*, a ceramic or silver plated gift with a *pranzo* attached, is given to each related family. Sometimes, the groom's tie is cut into sections and sold to those attending so that he will obtain honeymoon money.

**References:** *Thanks to Jerry Smallidge, Publisher of Wedding Day Magazine, and to Vivian Jacobozzi* **and** *Complete Book of Wedding Vows* **by Diane Warner.**

# Latvia

*Thanks to Liana Eglitis, Assistant to the Latvian Ambassador*

Latvia has a predominately Lutheran population with Orthodox and Catholic minorities.

### ❤ Past marriage customs

Historically, wives were obtained by stealing, bartering, contractual arrangement, or by betrothal and the wedding that followed. The man was the pursuer. Girls could improve their chances of marriage by guarding their reputations and displaying the highest qualities and appearance at all times. Young people met at celebrations, festivals, work or the marketplace. Sometimes, a matchmaker was employed by the parents.

### ❤ Present marriage customs

Single young people meet at school, in their neighborhoods, or through common friends or hobbies.

Once a couple is engaged, the wedding follows shortly afterward. Since Latvia has regained its independence from Communist control, church weddings are more popular than the civil wedding. If a couple has a civil wedding, the bride and groom bring their friends as official witnesses.

Latvian church weddings differ from many Christian weddings. Instead of having a best man and a maid or matron of honor, Latvians usually pick a married couple who are closest to them to act as role models. This selected couple becomes responsible for the organization of the wedding procedures and is charged with teaching the new couple about the expectations and responsibilities of married life. Another difference is that the wedding festivities such as the feasting, dancing, and speeches continue all night and often into the next day. The bride presents symbolic gifts to her new husband's parents who then accept her into their family.

## Historical Latvian Wedding

❤ **Engagement.** After the young man selected the girl he desired, intermediaries were sent to her house to deliver his proposal to the girl's mother and brothers. The father played only a minor role. Once the entire family, including the girl, agreed to his proposal, an engagement date was set.

❤ **Betrothal.** The betrothal party for the groom consisted of family members from both sides, the bride and groom, but did not include his parents. Instead of his parents representing the groom's interests, representatives were chosen by his parents to attend. During the betrothal celebration, which usually lasted until the next day, detailed agreements about the bride's dowry and a bride-stealing ritual took place.

❤ **Bride stealing and wedding.** Part of the wedding took place at the bride's home in the fall. It lasted from three days to a week. When the re-enactment of the bride-stealing ceremony took place, the wedding guests divided themselves into the groom's side and the bride's side, each retaining their allegiance to their side throughout the wedding.

❤ **Transference of dowry.** At the prearranged date, the groom's party, without the groom, arrived at the

# Historical Latvian Wedding

bride's home where an honorable married couple were to act as representatives to the transfer the dowry. Songs of rivalry again took place between the groups representing each family. The bride stayed hidden until the payment was presented to the bride's mother. This payment was given as compensation for raising her daughter.

❤ **Abduction of bride.** While the bride was dressing in clothing given to her by her family, they sang sad songs. After a coronet was placed on her head and she was bid farewell, the bride's mother led her through the door and through the honor guard of brothers holding raised swords. The bride, mounted on a horse, was then escorted to the groom's home by her brothers and sisters.

❤ **Wedding vows.** While the bride and groom sat at the table at the home of the groom's parents, vows and rings were exchanged before witnesses. After a *Diev's* blessing, the bread was broken and all enjoyed a meal. Later, all present took turns dancing with the bride.

❤ **Confirmation of marriage.** An artificial abduction could occur and the bride's relatives and friends hurried to catch up with the abducted bride. At that ceremony, the newlyweds were initiated as a married couple. After the bride, sisters, and girlfriends performed a farewell dance, the coronet on the bride's head was replaced by a scarf signifying she was now a married woman.

# Malta

*Thanks to C. Buttigieg of the Public Relations Office, Floriana, Malta*

The Maltese Islands are a small archipelago in the middle of the Mediterranean Sea. Malta is the largest of the islands. The Maltese population, just over 350,000, are almost all baptized in the Catholic church a few days after birth.

❤ **Selecting a spouse**

Young people often start dating between the ages of 14 and 18, and usually the young man introduces his girlfriend to his parents. Many young people come to know each other during their secondary education or while they are on the university campus. They also become acquainted in youth clubs and at entertainment spots, such as discos and cinemas. From that time on, the two young people pay frequent visits to each other's homes. The couple customarily do not leave their parents' homes before they marry.

❤ **Present marriage customs**

A going-steady period is expected to lead to an engagement ceremony, during which the engagement rings are blessed by the parish priest. While the couple are engaged, they take pre-marriage courses which give advice on the significance and importance of marriage. These courses are organized by the Catholic Church.

To give more extensive help to engaged couples in preparation for the Sacrament of Marriage, the church in 1995 inaugurated a pastoral project. The aim is to help engaged couples become conscious of their Christian beliefs and how to continue them throughout the marriage. The pastor, therefore, helps young people reach decisions and undertake initiatives so that the couple chooses a way of living in keeping with Christianity. The pastor is even involved in planning their vocations.

Thus, couples planning to marry are encouraged to make contact with the parish-priest as early as possible in order to make good use of expert advice offered to them by the church organizations at the national and parochial level. For those seeking a Christian marriage a preparatory course is provided as early as two years before their marriage.

Civil marriage was introduced in Malta in 1975, but the majority of Maltese couples celebrate a church marriage. There is an average of 2,000 church marriages per year. ( *See Catholic wedding in Chapter 1.*)

# Netherlands

*Holland*

**Thanks to Margriet Willems of the Royal Netherlands Embassy**

The population of Netherlands is 36 percent Roman Catholic and 26 percent Protestant.

## ❤ Historical wedding customs

Holland's ancient courting customs were colorful and romantic. Historically, the bride and groom would sit on thrones beneath overhanging evergreens at a party prior to the wedding to show their enduring love while guests would offer their best wishes. During the 1600's, a suitor showed a girl that he had meaningful intentions by attaching a flower or green wreath to her door. If the wreath was discarded, he would replace it in the following days with a bouquet tied with a bow accompanied by a card divulging his name. When the girl welcomed his advances, she would insert a love note in a small basket of candies or flowers and set it on her window sill. At a strategic moment, her suitor would then pin a white sprig on her dress and would carve his beloved's name on a tree trunk.

In some villages, the young man scratched on the girl's door two consecutive nights. When he tapped on the door the third night and heard a response, he knew that the girl accepted him. To entice the young maiden to speak with him, he would ask one or two musicians to serenade her while he stood near her window or at the door. Her parents, awaiting his visit, would then greet the young suitor and permit him to talk privately with their daughter. He could talk with her for hours, but he was especially on his good behavior even if he spent that evening or all night. Thereafter, he could return in the evenings.

In Texel, the suitor passed through the window of his girlfriend's home. Even if he had to lift or break the window to settle honorably in his girlfriend's bed, that is what he did. She supposedly lay beneath the sheet and the young man under the cover on top of the sheet. Needless to say, few windows were kept intact. Should the young man take too many liberties, the girl could strike a nearby iron cauldron with fire-tongs so that her parents could rescue their daughter and keep her honor.

Those who lived in Schermerhorn felt such intimacies should not be permitted. There, young men gathered together and employed a crier. The crier would announce to the entire town that these young men were in search of wives and that they would meet with the young women at an inn during an appointed time. While brandy and beer were served, these men had the opportunity to make their choices. Generally, North Holland's customs were more lenient than South Holland.

## ❤ Past engagements

In Broek, the engagement was celebrated when the couple, with their parents present, sat on the bed. There the couple kissed and exchanged engagement rings, sometimes decorated with engraved conjugal allegories. The young man also gave his fiancée a large amount of money covered with a linen cloth embroidered with the first letters of her name and the time of their betrothal. Because Dutch law made an engagement legally binding, shattering the engagement was a legal transgression for which love letters and the ring could be shown in court as evidence. Engagements were recorded at the municipal office, but the city officials publicized the upcoming marriage with banns. After the engagement, the marriage ensued quickly.

Wealthier people invited all their relatives and friends to a betrothal dinner where an engagement contract was signed in the presence of a notary. To show that the future bride was betrothed, the young man's father gave the bride a *chatelain*. It was a silver chain from which hung a pair of scissors, a small knife in a leather case, a needle box, a silver pincushion, a scented ball, and a mirror. The young man gave his future bride a pledge of love or a love poem.

After the couple set the date for their wedding, the bridesmaids and other girls were selected to decorate the house, to be in charge of entertaining, and to perform services for the bride and groom. One particular bridal servant assisted the bride after the engagement, before and throughout the entire wedding.

## ❤ Past pre-wedding customs

During the time between the formal engagement and their wedding, the houses of the bride's and groom's families were decorated for the many merry parties and

191

dinners that honored friends and relatives.

The bride's dress for these occasions was as expensive as the family could afford. If the bride's family was not affluent, she chose a Lyons silk gown or dress, sometimes in black instead of white so the same dress could be used for mourning. Brides who could afford the extras had a traditional fan and perfumed gloves. The groom's clothes were expensive, but in keeping with his social position. Those of average means wore a waistcoat and wool or serge trousers. Often, wedding attire was handed down from past generations.

### ❤ Wedding

The wedding, which had to be registered in the presence of a local magistrate, took place at the Reformed or Catholic church or at the town hall. Marriage ceremonies often began with readings from the Epistles of Saint Paul and by singing of Psalms between the readings. After the bridal party entered the sanctuary of the church, the bride and groom were escorted by their parents. Then, the pastor at the pulpit recited the formulas of marriage, the oath was taken, and a psalm was sung. A collection was taken for the poor. As the newlyweds and the bridal party left for the bride's house, they walked on a path covered with flowers.

The Reformed church wedding was held at night when the procession of lit torches would be most dazzling. The church was embellished with flowers and the young couple's chairs were decorated with green garlands. When the groom said *yes*, he gave the bride his ring, so thereafter, the bride wore two rings. As the couple left the church, flowers were thrown over them and they were taken to the wedding feast by a horse and carriage.

### ❤ Wedding feast

Guests were served sugar cake, marzipan, sugared almonds, sugared beans, Hippocras, and sweet cordials at the bride's home before dinner. Parents spent often beyond what they could realistically afford. Since oyster, crabs, lobster, game, fruit and pastries were in abundant supply, feasts were enjoyed by all.

Commoners often held a wedding feast at an inn while the more affluent nobility held their festivities at home in highly decorated rooms filled with garlands and gold leaf. Wreaths, wax cupids, and angels were hung from the ceilings. In the middle of the room two

thrones were decorated with colorful paper for the newly weds. The bride wore a heavy robe which attracted much attention. In some regions, the bride, while blindfolded, placed a crown on the head of a young girl who was thought to be the next to marry.

### ❤ Past post-wedding activities

As the bride and groom were about to leave, the bride was often seized by playful friends, and the husband had to resort to various means to get her back. Sometimes, the couple was so desperate to avoid such pranks they would secretly retire at a neighbor's house that night. If their secret was found out, all the guests, holding candles, crashed metal kitchen utensils and pans together noisily at a bonfire next to the home where the newlyweds took sanctuary. When the bride and groom finally joined them, all held hands and danced around the fire until they were exhausted.

### ❤ Present marriage customs

Because people living in the Netherlands come from different countries, their religious preferences range from Christian to Islam.

A majority of Roman Catholics still marry within their own faith, yet by 1986 crossing religious denominational lines became a normal pattern in the Netherlands. Sixty-two percent of all marriages were between those of the same religion. Only 50 percent of Evangelical Protestants and 20 percent of Jews married within their own religious faith. The increase of interdenominational marriages indicated the growth of social integration and societal openness.

Today, dating and weddings customs are like other Western countries, including the United States. (*See Western-style marriages on page 35 in Chapter 1.*)

Marriageable women and men may meet anywhere—at clubs and nightclubs, through dating services, or personal ads, but they rarely meet at church since only 10 percent of the total population attend. Because housing is in short supply, engagements can be lengthy. Couples marry at the town hall first, then many have a wedding ceremony in the church. When the wedding festivities are over, the newlyweds plant the perennial lily-of-the valley in their garden as a reminder to renew their love each spring when the flowers bloom.

Some young people live together before marriage.

Now, the Netherlands permits same sex marriages.

**References:** *Kolner Zeitschrift fur Soziologie und Sozialpsychologie* **includes the article "Religious Marriages in Germany and the Netherlands" by Johen Hendricks, Osmund Schreuder, Wouter,** *Life in Rembrandt's Holland* **by Ultee and Paul Zumthor, and** *Dutch New York* **by Esther Singleton..**

# Norway

*The Norwegian Information Service*
*The Royal Norwegian Consulate General*

Norway has a largely Evangelical Lutheran population and a small number of people from other Christian faiths. Except for rural and *Sameck* weddings, its Western-style weddings do not differ appreciably from marriage ceremonies in the United States.

### ❤ Types of weddings

An urban wedding in Norway takes on different forms, depending on whether it is a civil ceremony or a church wedding, and whether it is an early forenoon, afternoon, or late afternoon ceremony. The forenoon wedding is followed by a luncheon or reception. The late afternoon ceremony is followed by a more elaborate dinner for close family and friends. After the dinner, a large number of friends from the younger set is often invited to join the party for coffee and dancing.

### ❤ Wedding attire

At an early civil ceremony the groom may wear a dark suit and the bride, an afternoon dress. The groom wears a morning coat and striped trousers at an early church wedding. For a later church wedding, the groom wears a tuxedo and the bride, a wedding gown. A reception follows. A white tie is reserved for a gala dinner.

### ❤ Rural wedding

Festive traditional costumes of the district are often used at rural weddings. Traditionally, the bride, wearing a long dress and crown, walks to church for the wedding in a procession with her future husband, relatives and friends. They are accompanied by musicians playing old folk tunes. At dinner afterward, the guests are often served deer meat.

A festive and delicious confectionery cake called *kransekake* is the most common wedding cake, aside from the American-style white cake with decorative icing. The *kransekake* is made of almond paste, is baked in special rings, and is decorated with icing and bonbons. The newlyweds keep the top layer, then proceed to break, rather than cut the cake, for the other guests.

### ❤ *Lapp Sameck.*

The Lapp *Sameck* people live in the innermost northern Swedish-Norwegian region of Europe. The Lapps congregate to barter products in January and February. At that time, single young men and women have the opportunity to select a marriage partner from other clans.

The young man spends the first few days looking at, and becoming acquainted with, young maidens. He will try to impress the girl of his choice. The girl then waits for her suitor to call on her family so that he can be invited to her home. Once he is at their house, he asks to make coffee for her parents and the cups are then taken out. After he makes the coffee for her parents, he waits to see if they display pleasure. If they do, he presents a ring to his future bride. The bride will receive another ring at their wedding and add a third ring after the birth of their first child.

Their wedding, either at an Orthodox or Christian church, is followed by a feast. Guests deposit money on a plate and promise to provide the newlyweds with reindeer or a calf. Lapp couples have a tendency to be faithful throughout their marriage. *(See Laplanders on page 203 in this chapter for more information.)*

**Reference:** *The World of Weddings* **by Brian Murphy.**

# Poland

*Polish National Tourist Office, New York.*

Ninety-percent of Poland's population is Roman Catholic and the rest are Jews and Muslims.

Poland's many regions have different wedding customs and costumes. Girls accumulate their important trousseau from childhood to adulthood.

The Polish wedding is such a significant time of celebration that invited guests may take up to three days from work in order to attend. Brides wear a crown decorated with beads, ribbons, and family heirlooms.

Since Poles believe that a successful union depends on the lavishness, hospitality, and gaiety of the wedding feast, a family that cannot afford the cost of a wedding may sell their possessions to pay for it. During the reception after a wedding, men pin money on the bride's veil in return for a dance with her. She places the money in an embroidered white satin pocketbook.

***Men and women dancing in the mountains of Poland.*** *Women who are unmarried have their hair uncovered. Courtesy of Kinga Skorek, Polish Information Officer*

## Traditional Polish Wedding

194

❤ **Pre-wedding customs.** After parents inquire about a future spouse for their child and a selection is made, a proposal and engagement follow.

❤ **Unbraiding the bride's hair.** Young women who were not married braided hairdos. Prior to the marriage ceremony, a maiden party is held one evening for the unbraiding of the bride's hair to indicate her new status. Folk songs with words lecturing her on becoming a dutiful wife were sung to the bride.

❤ **Pre-wedding rituals..** Before departing for the Catholic ceremony, salted bread and sweet wine were given to the bride and groom to inform them of the bitterness and sweetness of living. Their parents also blessed them.

❤ **Post-wedding customs.** The wedding feast was a heavy vodka-drinking affair with a menu of borsht, roast pork, sausages, meat balls covered with cabbage leaves, and poppy seed cakes. The bride was bonneted to symbolize that she was a married woman. Young men played fiddles, usually wearing traditional garb of hats, light shirts, and colorfully designed pants. Traditional dances were performed, and guests paid money to dance with the bride.

The photographs of traditional costumed folk festivities in this book are not totally indicative of daily life in contemporary Poland; however, many folk traditions and costumes are still embraced during festivals and religious ceremonies as expressions of regional pride.

**Reference:** *Svatnbni Obrad* **by Krystyna Kwaisniewicz.**

# Traditional Polish Wedding

**Bonneting of the Bride.**

**"Oczepiny."** *After the folk wedding, the married women and the bride enter a room reserved for the custom called "oczepiny." The women cover the bride's hair with "czepiec," a white cloth tied into a bonnet. While they are performing this ritual, they sing traditional songs about the newlywedded wife entering a new life as a married woman and songs saying good-bye to her maidenhood. As a single maiden, her hair was uncovered. Now as a symbol of being a wife, she will always wear the "czepiec"*

*Photograph: Courtesy of Kinga Skorek, Polish Information Officer*

195

# Portugal

Portugal's population is Roman Catholic.

During Portuguese weddings, the priest covers both the bride and groom with his stole before the ring ceremony. After the wedding, bonbons are thrown over the newlyweds. Once the man and woman take their wedding vows, both families are united in a common bond; thus, the family groups expand and become very strongly knit.

*(See the Roman Catholic wedding in Chapter 1.)*

**References:** *A Short History of Marriage, Enchantment of the World: Portugal.*

# Romania

Seventy percent of Romania's population is Romanian Orthodox and less than 10 percent is Catholic.

Prior to the Soviet Socialist family legislation, the church was the center of community living and the marriage was a matter for religious authorities. During Communist domination before the 1990's, official marriages were held at the local mayor's office.

Since then, couples tend to marry later, for they no longer have to be concerned about being separated from each other because of the Communist government assigning them jobs elsewhere. Now, more weddings are held in churches and other places, and the wedding gown is now borrowed from the West. Religious rituals are combined with the former traditional customs of Romania.

## Romanian Country Wedding

❤ **Wedding announcement.** Past traditions are often celebrated at country weddings which are held on Sundays. A messenger on horseback announces the wedding date and time and summons the entire village of people. Standard bearers direct the parade of horsemen, fiddlers, and a variety of other musicians.

❤ **Preparations.** The wedding party includes the bride and groom, the parents, godparents, the matchmaker, the best men, maids of honor, speakers, cooks, cup-bearers who pour the wine, and tuica. Prior to the ceremony, the bridesmaids and best man help the bride and bridegroom to make preparations. By the time the wedding takes place, the director of ceremony, cooks, and musicians to play the pipes, dulcimers, and violins have been selected. An oversized loaf of bread is made. Before the wedding, guests and a horseman parade in traditional Romanian folk dress. Married women cover their heads with colorful silk or cotton scarves, called *naframa,* while unmarried women wear uncovered braided hairdos. The bride's hair is braided and covered with a coronet of colorful flowers, semiprecious stones, and colorful ribbons. The bridegroom, his beard shaved off by his best man, may wear a felt hat embellished with feathers, flowers and a fir tree. He also wears a white goat-skin vest decorated with colored leather strands.

❤ **Wedding customs.** During the wedding procession, the best man carries a colored pole adorned with handkerchiefs and bells. After the Catholic wedding ceremony, the band plays while people feast. The bride and groom take chunks from the loaf of bread, using the same spoon and plate. At the same time, the couple is showered with corn and drops of water signifying their joy and a future life filled with abundance.

When midnight approaches, a bridal dance and presentation of gifts to the newlyweds take place. While the dance is in progress, a hen, adorned with flowers and green leaves, is brought as a symbol of fertility. The bride and groom ask forgiveness of their parents and relatives for leaving them. The bride and groom retire until dawn at which time they are awakened by fiddlers and singers. The bride appears with her hair tied in a kerchief. Feasting begins that morning and lasts until noon.

# Traditional Romanian Orthodox Church Wedding

❤ **Procession.** The traditional church wedding begins when the bride and her father walk to the altar.

❤ **Giving the bride away.** The father gives the bride to the groom. The ceremony, conducted by a priest, proceeds with intermittent hymns sung by a choir or cantor.

❤ **Vows and ring ceremony.** Once the bride and groom say their vows, the priest blesses the wedding rings, then places a ring into each hand, one for the bride and another for the groom.

❤ **Placement of metal crowns.** After metal crowns symbolizing a peaceful rule over their family are set on the heads of the bride and groom, the couple sips wine from the same cup, or they take a few bites of a honey wafer.

❤ **Binding of hands.** Next, their hands are bound together with ribbon to represent the happiness and sadness they will share throughout their lives.

❤ **Circling the table.** The couple is led three times around a triangular table to display the recognition of, and duty toward, the Holy Trinity.

❤ **Final blessing.** The crowns are removed and the priest then offers the final blessing and words of wisdom to help the couple live a happy and fulfilling life together.

❤ **Reception and collection of money.** During the reception, given at home, hotel ball room, or restaurant, the *nasii* collects money as a gift from the guests for the couple and later announces the total amount. During the reception, popular or folk music is played for dancing.

197

**References:** *Romania* by Betty Carran, *Gale Encyclopedia of Multicultural America, Cultures of the World: Romania.*

# Russian Federation

Aside from the predominantly 65 percent nonreligious population, there is presently a high number of Russian Orthodox, plus a minority of other Christian groups, including the Adventists, Baptists, Lutherans, Mennonites, Pentecostals, and Roman Catholics, with some Muslims, Jews, and Buddhists. Russian Orthodoxy still remains, particularly in Eastern Russia. Since September 1997, it is considered the major official religion of Russia. The Muslim and Buddhist populations are mainly in the central Asian republics.

### ❤ Weddings under the Communists

Before the 1990's, the Soviet Union's Communist Regime officially discouraged religious worship and many churches were closed. Instead of having their weddings in church, couples held weddings at wedding palaces near their registration office. These palaces usually possessed a grand appearance, and a white statue of Lenin sat on a table at the Kiev Central Wedding Palace. Saturdays were the busiest days for weddings at the palaces which still exist today. The bride wore a wedding gown and white veil and the groom, a black suit. Couples took their vows at this state-witnessed ceremony with prescribed political statements. Until 1990, promises were made to love each other and to become good and loyal citizens of their country and the Communist government. After affirming they would perform the duties of a Soviet family, they became husband and wife. Later, the entire wedding party visited a monument. The bride left her bouquet at the grave of an Unknown Soldier, at the Lenin memorial in Moscow, or other historical place where photographs were taken of the couple. Then, they enjoyed feasting. Plenty of vodka was served.

### ❤ Weddings after Communist domination

Before 1987, single people married younger, but now young men wait until they are professionally secure and have a place to reside before they wed. Young people have sexual relationships prior to marriage, usually with just one person, so they cannot be considered promiscuous. A high number of marriages takes place on the frontiers of Siberia and Central Asia, since most of the newly settled people there are young. Marriages are registered at the local Citizens' Records and Licensing Bureau and no other ceremonial is required.

Churches have been returned to their believers. Although marriages still take place in wedding palaces originally established by the Communist government, many people in eastern Russia again hold the wedding ceremony in Russian Orthodox churches.

When urban couples marry, they may go from their wedding to visit a monument and for a mini-honeymoon in a specially decorated wedding taxi. It has wedding rings displayed on top, a bridal doll in front, and streamers.

## Russian Orthodox Wedding

❤ **Shower.** Prior to the wedding, the bride's close friends and relative hold a maiden's evening or *divych vechir*, during which gifts are showered over the bride. The groom and bride sit together. After a full course dinner, they open their presents.

❤ **Priest's blessing.** Before the church wedding, a blessing is given at the home of the bride's parents. After the priest blesses the impending marriage, all leave for the church where the wedding ceremony takes place during a full mass. The groom may carry a bouquet of colorful flowers with a burning candle set in the middle and other members of the family may carry such bouquets while accompanying the bride to church.

❤ **Carrying of lit candles.** After friends are seated in the church, the deacon goes down the aisle and meets the bride and groom at the door where he gives each a lighted candle.

# Russian Orthodox Wedding

❤ **Betrothal ceremony.** The deacon makes the sign of a cross sign three times on the couple's foreheads. As they are led toward a table at the altar, incense is emitted before them. First, the priest recites a litany, gives a prayer invocation, and blesses the couple; then, the priest gives each a ring from the table and proclaims they *are married now and forever.* He repeats this declaration three times as the bride and groom exchange rings three times. The couple's hands may be bound together with a long embroidered scarf, called a *rushnychok,* as the priest leads them around the table. The priest takes the rings and makes a cross on the foreheads of each. Afterward, he places each ring on the bride and groom's forefingers of their right hands. The priest then reads biblical passages sanctifying that *the ring is a symbol of union, honor, and power.*

❤ **Crowning the bride and groom.** Two laymen carry two high imperial metal crowns with a cross towering on top and give them to the priest. After the priest blesses the bride and groom, he places the crowns on them. A cup of wine is sipped by the priest and is then given to the bridegroom and the bride, who each take three sips.

❤ **Walking around the table.** After more prayers are recited, the priest takes the bride and groom by the hand and walks them around the table three times. The priest says, *Be thou magnified, O bridegroom, as Abraham! Be thou blessed as Isaac and multiplied as Jacob . . .* and another passage for the bride which indicates she should be *as joyful as Rebecca and multiply as Rachael* of the Old Testament.

❤ **Dissolving the crowns.** The "Dissolving the Crowns" ceremony begins and the lighted candles are extinguished. The bride and groom then receive congratulations from the guests. After this, the couple make hurried steps to stand on a white rug, for the first to stand on it is to be the boss, according to tradition.

❤ **Reception.** Dancing and feasting continue from three to eight days after the wedding. When the traditional dining and dancing starts, the bridal veil is taken off the bride's head, then replaced with a kerchief to show she is now a married woman. The veil is then placed on the heads of eligible women who dance with their boyfriends and other males in the bridal party. The bride's and groom's godparents give them bread and salt. Giving bread symbolizes that they should not know hunger, and the salt, that they should never know bitterness. Traditional bread, braided challah, and perogies are served at the banquet.

**Reference. Orthodox Wedding summarized from *Marriage Customs of the World*
by Dharam Vir.**

199

The *Greek Orthodox* people who live in Russia have a wedding ceremony which is similar to the Russian Orthodox ceremony. If there is no Greek Orthodox church in the area, the wedding takes place at the groom's home. After the nuptials, Greek families enjoy a banquet and dancing.

*Russian Jews (Southwest Mountains).* Traditionally, the bride, wearing a veil over her face, is taken by horse to the groom's home where guests are invited. Before entering their home, the groom's mother throw rice and wheat over the bride. Azerbaijanian songs and dances are performed to an accompaniment of clarinetists and a drum player. The customs of the bride avoiding members of the groom's family and the husband avoiding parents are observed over the first couple of years. *(See Chapter 1 for more information on the Jewish Culture in Europe and Asia.)*

*Muslim* The Muslim Tats live near the southwestern mountain Jews. (Because of religious persecution, mountain Jews also call themselves Tats.) Muslim Tat marriages are within their religious group, and marriage with a blood relative are considered the best match.

Girls can be abducted without their agreement and elopement with and without parental consent can occur. Mainly, marriage, even marriage at birth, is arranged by parents or else a matchmaker is chosen by the parents to find a spouse. Marriage occurs at 14 years of age for women, and at about 18 for young men. Before the wedding, the girl collects a dowry. During the betrothal party, where sweets are served, relatives of the bride and groom present gifts of clothing and jewelry to the couple. The marriage is accepted after the exchange of gifts and the brideprice is given by the groom to the bride's mother.

The marriage contract is signed in the presence of a mullah and witnesses. The groom gives the bride's father a horse, a dagger or rifle, and cattle in the amount negotiated previously. The wedding festivities last from two to seven days while food celebrations occur intermittently at the home of the groom and bride's parents.

*The Ukraine.* In Eastern Slovakia, folk weddings occurred before the acceptance of the civil marriage under socialism. Prior to the 1980's, elements of the very old traditions remained, such as the abduction of the bride when the bridegroom went on horseback to fetch the bride. The abduction of the bride could occur after a line dance. The wedding procession was sometimes stopped by using a bar. Magic powers were thought to be dispelled by clematis, wearing a fur coat, the shedding of grains over the wedding guest, the blessing of water, fire, use of candles, and more. The wedding guests washed in a brook, then presented the bride with gifts for remaining a virgin until marriage. Sacred breads baked for the occasion were decorated with motifs symbolizing eternity and the unity of both families. All people in the family took part in the wedding.

Taking the wedding wreath from the bride's head and replacing it with a bonnet still occurs.

In some parts of Russian, a bridal capture is depicted during the wedding reception to commemorate the many times their land was invaded by war.

**References:** *Gale Encyclopedia of Multicutural America, The Soviet Union Today, USSR Today: Facts and Interpretations* by Leo Hecht, *National Geographic* book published in 1990, *Marriage Customs of the World* by Dharam Virm, and *Svatebni Obrad Mikulas Musinka* by Svatebni Obrad.

# Spain

### ❤ Present marriage customs

Since Spain's population is Roman Catholic, weddings are usually held in the Catholic church. In fact, in August of 1953, a law was passed declaring that only marriages performed in the Catholic church marriages were valid. The Catholic church has always imparted strong pressure against premarital sex. In much of Spain, the couple's decision to marry is made freely after a courtship.

Today, civil ceremonies are allowed. Common-law marriages, usually among landless laborers, are recognized although they are not sanctioned religiously or formally recognized by the state.

### ❤ Wedding

During the Spanish Catholic marriage ceremony, the groom gives 13 coins to the bride to display his ability to take financial responsibility and care for her. She inserts them in a purse or a young girl carries the coins on a pillow. At the reception, a dance, the *seguidillas manchegas,* is performed during which time guests give the bride wedding presents.

### ❤ Country weddings

Young girls pray to the Catholic saints to grant them worthy spouses. Couples often meet at fiestas where the girls flirt with boys of their liking. While they are dating, the woman is expected to be modest and virtuous. Because the young men wait until they have finished the service or their education, and they are employed, a couple often waits until they are at least 25 to wed. Even though marriages are not arranged by the parents, the young man formally asks the girl's parents for her hand in marriage. Usually, couples who marry are of the same status. In the countryside, church weddings remain in vogue.

*Basques.* The *Basques* of northern Spain transfer title of the family farm to the newlyweds as part of the marriage settlement. This transfer thereby encourages cousin marriages so that the land will be kept in the family.

*Pasiego,* the herders of the north, court in cabin kitchen. Those who do herd not date publicly. Herder couples live together after banns are posted before the nuptials, but non-herders do not.

Girls usually have a trousseau of clothing and family embroidered heirlooms are added once they become engaged. The young man still may pay a token sum. The ceremony is held in the bride's church where godparents, aunts, or uncles stand with the couple while they are being wed. A white veil is held over the bride's hand and groom's shoulders, an act which displays the submissive position of a good wife.

Traditionally, the bride wears orange blossoms in her hair and a black silk wedding dress, a black lace veil, and gold, pearl, or emerald jewelry which are often given to her by the bridegroom or his family. Peasant brides wear black to show their devotion to their husband until they are parted by death. The groom wears a shirt artistically embroidered by the bride. To celebrate, the groom delivers food delicacies and wine to village males.

Reference: *Encyclopedia of World Cultures.*

# *Sweden*

Most of Sweden's population is considered Evangelical Lutheran, although the Swedes are a secular society with religious freedom guaranteed by the constitution.

❤ **Past marriage customs.**

Before industrialization, arranged marriages occurred among the rich southern farmers. Families exchanged gifts and made financial transactions as part of the marriage ritual. Customs involved the bride's dowry and a gift presented to the bride by the groom.

Bridesmaids, surrounding the bride, held potent scented herbs, and the groom attached them to his suit to scare away the trolls, imaginary dwarfs. The couple would skip around the maypole.

Prior to the wedding, the groom handed his bride a metal goblet piled with coins covered with white tissue paper. The shirt which the bride gave the groom for their wedding day was never worn again until he died, then he was buried in it.

Sometimes, after the ceremony, picnics were held outside where carpets were set over the grass, and plates of delicacies were placed on them. People enjoyed the picnic while children played around them. The bride took some of each type of food, saved it, and then gave it to people who live in poverty. Some of these practices still occur.

❤ **Present marriage customs.**

During the 1900's, young men and women were free to date at a young age, engage in premarital sex, and to cohabit rather than marry. According to *Cultures of the World: Sweden* copyrighted in 1992, one of every five couples were cohabiting. The Sambo law, passed in 1988, gave those who lived together more rights as partners.

Generally, couples live together several years before marriage, their weddings often motivated by the birth of their first child. Children often attend their parents' weddings; therefore, marriage is not out of fashion, just delayed for various reasons. Those who decide to marry may have either a civil ceremony or a religious wedding. If both belong to the Church of Sweden, they may be married there. Those of other religious faiths wed in their place of worship.

*Lapp Sameck.* Lapps, who live in Sweden and Norway, congregate in January or February and barter products, and at this time young men and women can select a marriage partner from other clans. Young men spend the first few days looking and becoming acquainted with prospective partners. After deciding, the young man will say impressive words to the girl of his choice. The girl then waits for the young man to call her family and be invited to their home. Once he is there, he asks to make coffee for her parents. The cups are then taken out. After he hands coffee to her parents, he waits to see if they display pleasure. If they do, he presents a ring to his future bride. The bride will later receive another ring when she is married, then add a third after the birth of their first child. The Orthodox or Christian Laestadism wedding is followed by a feast where guests deposit money on a plate and promise to provide the newlyweds with reindeer or a calf. The Lapps have a tendency to be faithful throughout their marriage. *(See Laplanders on page 203 in this chapter for more information.)*

References: *The World of Weddings* by Brian Murphy.

# Switzerland

**Thanks to the Embassy of Switzerland**

Because 50 percent of the population is Swiss Italian Roman Catholic and almost 50 percent Protestant, traditional Catholic and Protestant weddings are commonplace. Eighteen to twenty percent are foreigners, so interracial marriages do exist. Those from Germany tend to have Lutheran weddings and those from Spain have Catholic weddings.

The dating scene and customs in Switzerland are influenced by Western-style customs which are similar to those in the United States. Young men and women have the opportunity to meet each other at discos or sporting events; otherwise, single people meet at school, at work, in neighborhoods, and by traveling. Matchmaking institutions and personal ads provide other ways for singles to meet. Certain cities and remote parts of the country have their own dating customs.

In cities, many couples live together without being married. Young people often cohabit before they are wed, but usually marry once the girl becomes pregnant. In remote regions, boys and girls meet at church festivals. The young man presents his future bride with an engagement gift.

Presently, a couple has both civil and religious wedding services. After they are wed, rice is thrown over their heads as a symbol of fertility. As a bridesmaid leads the line of guests to the reception, she hands colored handkerchiefs to each guest for good luck. A guest accepting a handkerchief gives a coin toward the bride's and groom's nestegg. The festivities are held at a restaurant or community room where a banquet and wedding cake are served. Later, there are dancing and fireworks. The bridal wreath is set on fire. Should it burn quickly, the bride will have good fortune.

**References:** *Culturgrams: The Nations of the World, Encyclopedia of World Cultures.*

202

# Turkey

*Chapter 1.)*

Since the population of Turkey is almost entirely Muslim, the marriage customs in Turkey follow the religious customs of Islam. *(See Chapter 1.)*

### ❤ Past marriage customs

Marriages among those in the extended family were preferred to keep the lineage and financial interests in the same family. A newlywed girl lived with her husband's family in an extended household comprising about 10 people, including the groom's parents and their unmarred daughters and sons.

Prior to the Civil Code of 1926, the bride was hidden behind the door while the groom signed a contract in the presence of an *imam*. The brideprice was paid to the bride's family as compensation for the loss of work from their daughter. If the couple was under age, a religious ceremony was celebrated before the civil ceremony.

### ❤ Present marriage customs

Polygamy, permitted by the Islamic religion, has virtually disappeared. The levirate marriage of a widow to a husband's brother is still commonplace since such a marriage protects family interests; yet, widow remarriages remain unsanctioned. Marriages between Muslims and non-Muslims are discouraged. However, a Sunni Muslim man is permitted to wed a Christian or Jewish woman without his wife having to convert to his religion. Because their religion is passed through the male line, a Muslim woman is unable to marry a Jewish or Christian man. A conversion to Islam must take place before a marriage can occur.

Today, many Turkish men wed in western clothing before civil authorities. Women may now give their consent to these contractual negotiations in which the payment of the dower is awarded to the bride, property details are settled, and inheritance rights decided. Some modern families may even allow their children to select their own marriage partners. The trend among the educated is for parents to arrange a marriage in consultation with their children. A dowry is not considered important.

Turkish weddings in both cities and towns are short ceremonies at city halls followed by a private festive feast with a musical accompaniment. In the countryside, however, the marriage is preceded by the parents' discussion of the couple's suitability for marriage. In many cases, their agreement still includes a brideprice.

During a traditional country wedding, the bride, dressed in white and accompanied by musicians, is taken in a parade to the groom's home. Today, a procession of cars, mini-buses, and tractors converge on the groom's home. After the ceremony, the celebration comes alive with a nighttime of music and dancing. Folk dancing, with segregated men and women holding hands in a line dance, is performed in traditional costumes.

*Yoruk.* First-cousin marriages are encouraged; however, kidnapping and elopement are practiced among 20 percent of the Yoruk in southeastern Turkey. Bridal theft tends to adjust their marriage system to permit individual choice and eliminates the groom from paying a high cash brideprice. Otherwise, the marriage contract is negotiated by the heads of the two families. Inter-ethnic marriages have increased recently.

**References: *Ethnic Family Values in Australia* by Hafina Dean-Oswald, *Cultures of the World: Turkey* and *Life: World Library*.**

# *Laplanders*

Lapland lies above the Arctic Circle and appears to have no borders, but in actuality, Lapland runs across the northern countries of Norway, Sweden, Finland, and Russia. The Lapp people, called the *Sami* or *Sameck* of Sweden, Finland, and Norway can marry in the Orthodox or Christian Laestadism church. They wear colorful red and blue tunics, decorated profusely with bangles of silver and gold. The women wear bouffant-style hats with a circular band of rick-rack ribbon while men wear extended cylindrical headdresses at the wedding.

The bride is adorned with a lengthy shawl with a long fringe, an overlay of circular metallic decoration and the bouffant-style hat with a band of metallic decoration. The groom has a decorative silver-studded belt around his waist with fringe hanging from a large metallic ornament on his left side. A broad ribbon, hanging around his neck and crossing over his chest, is accented in the center with a metal medallion. All wear white reindeer-skin boots, with pointed toes which turn up.

Today it is very common for Laplanders to take pictures of their weddings with video cameras and for the newlyweds to leave in a taxi. *(See Norway for more details about Sami marriage customs.)*

**Reference: *The Reindeer People,* written and illustrated by Ted Lewin.**

# Middle East

8

The desert Persian Gulf states, such as Kuwait, Bahrain, Qatar, Jordan, Yemen, United Arab Emirates, Saudi Arabia, and Oman have large Muslim populations. In those countries Islam is their state religion. For centuries, Muslim families who lived in the desert have banded together into tribes composed of clans, which are further divided into households that include groups of families. Although marriage occasionally takes place outside tribal blood lines, people usually marry within the same tribe unless a plan is made to establish a mutually beneficial alliance with another tribe. Persian Gulf states usually have wealthy ruling families who intermarry to keep wealth and social standing within the family. However, marriage customs do differ in countries with large Muslim populations. Like the Europeans, traditional Muslim cultures are generally more strictly maintained in rural areas than in the cities, except for Saudi Arabia.

# Iran

Iran's population is about 95 percent Shi'a Muslim.

### ♥ Traditional marriage customs

The Islamic permanent marriage, called an *ahkam*, was arranged by the girl's parents and her father negotiated his daughter's marriage contract for her. Sometimes, marriage was arranged for a couple in infancy. Marriages were arranged particularly with cousins in order to strengthen the family economically and numerically. Prior to marriage, the girl was expected to be a virgin.

The traditional village marriage was initiated when the boy's parents visited a prospective bride's parents to learn if they displayed an interest. If so, a brideprice was negotiated. The wife received a *mahr*, or brideprice, in exchange for relinquishing her body to the man. After a period of time during which the young man performed duties for the bride's father, a marriage contract was signed. Once it had been signed at a notary's office before a government representative, called a *mullah*, the man was given exclusive rights over his wife's sexuality and assumed financial responsibility for her. An amount of wealth was guaranteed to the wife should her husband die or in the event of a divorce. The marriage contract's rights and obligations spelled out in the Koran were believed to be divine and enduring. After the contract was signed, friends and family would bring gifts and money for the bride. The women celebrated with the bride at her home, and the men met at the groom's residence. During public celebrations, the affluence and prestige of both families was emphasized.

Since 1979, adult Shi'a Muslim women were permitted to have a degree of choice, and sometimes the young woman could arrange her own marriage. On the other hand, the law was nullified if the father had already promised her in marriage as a child. Divorced and widowed women were free to negotiate the marriage contract on their own behalf.

### ❤ Present wedding customs

Presently, marriage customs differ in various villages. Marriage practices in the cities tend to follow those in Europe and the United States, particularly among the middle and upper classes. Young people are freer to choose a spouse and marry without parental consent. Some couples still marry within their kin group and their parents still voice their disapproval or consent. The brideprice may be given in installments or may be eliminated altogether.

The legal age for marriage is 16 for girls and 18 for young men, but girls commonly marry younger. Girls of the nomadic *Basser* tribe are usually younger than their legal ages before they marry. Urban men of higher economic status with a university education and military duty wait until they can provide for a wife. Many Muslim Iranian students who now attend European and American universities are meeting Christian spouses and the number of mixed marriages is increasing. Although daughters need their parents permission to marry, sons are not required to have parental consent.

The rate of marriages is much higher in rural areas than in the cities and for those who have economic security. The number of marriages rises after harvests and tends to drop in the springtime.

Presently, the number of marriages has decreased because of the high cost of the brideprice, which covers gifts for the bride and her parents, plus receptions. In Tehran, young girls and their families have reduced the marriage payment to attract eligible suitors.

### ❤ Temporary marriage

The *mut'a* is a temporary marriage for pleasure. It can be made between a woman and a man who is either married or unmarried. The temporary contract for a *mut'a* includes the duration of time they wish to be married and the amount of money to be provided to the woman. Unlike the permanent marriage, the temporary marriage is often negotiated secretly by the couple. Witnesses do not have to be present and, depending on the local requirements, their marriage need not be registered.

The temporary marriage primarily occurs in urban contemporary Iran and is mostly associated with travel and trade with other countries. In temporary marriages, men and women choose their own sexual partners. In spite of the rules of modesty and segregation in Iran, men and women find each other at shrines where they provide direct nonverbal and verbal signals.

The length of time which must pass after a temporary marriage before a woman can wed permanently depends on their initial temporary marriage agreement, Upon parting from a temporary marriage, the Shi'i Muslim woman must undergo a time of sexual abstinence in order to identify the father in case of a pregnancy. The father is required by law to support children resulting from the temporary marriage. If he denies his child's legitimacy, he is not responsible as he would be if he were in a permanent marriage.

The problem for women is that they must be virgins in order to be married permanently; therefore, the *mut'a* marriage has never gained popular support.

**References:** *Area Handbook for Iran, Law of Desire* by Shahla Haeri.

*Iraq*

Over half of the Muslim population of Iraq is Shi'a Muslim, about 35 percent are Sunni Muslim, and three percent are Christian.

### ❤ Past marriage customs

Devoutly religious Muslim girls avoided making eye contact with strange men, never dated, or kissed them. Parents arranged marriages and negotiated a marriage contract for their children while they were teenagers. Proof of virginity upon marriage was and still is immensely important for girls.

### ❤ Present marriage customs

A Muslim man by law was and still is allowed to have four wives. If he wants to marry a second wife, he is first required to obtain approval of the court.

Young people today delay marriage until they are in their 20s and early 30s. Educated young people may make their own choice of partners, but their parents must give couples permission to wed.

According to America Online news during the first week of February, 1998, the traditional Muslim society is straining after seven years of United Nations sanctions as the result of the Gulf War. Fewer couples are marrying, and sex outside of marriage is more prevalent. The reason is that dowry, paid by the groom to the bride's family, is about $325, too much for most men.

# Iraqi Marriage Contract and Wedding

❤ Shortly before the wedding banquet, the groom and the bride's father hold hands under a cloth. Then, they sign a marriage contract called an *aqd,* a legal civil contract between the two families, which defines how much the groom pays the bride upon their marriage and how much he will pay her should he decide to divorce her.

While a clergyman is present, the father gives his daughter, *an adult virgin*, in marriage to the groom *according to the law of God and of his prophet.* The groom, in turn, responds that he takes his wife in marriage, *the adult virgin, according to the law of God and of his prophet.* Then the father says, *God bless you with her.* To that, the bridegroom responds, *I hope in God she may prove a blessing.* All present then recite a brief passage from the first chapter of the Koran.

❤ To celebrate, the bride, dressed in a bridal gown, enters into the banquet room where guests await her arrival. She comes with a procession of musicians playing drums, cymbals and horns.

❤ Traditionally, the bride is taken by her family to her new husband on her wedding night. There, the groom removes her shoes and cleanses her feet with water. As he initially touches her, he says, *Oh Allah, bless me with her affection, love, and her acceptance of me and make me pleased with her and bring us together in the best form of union and in absolute harmony.* The groom places his hand on her forehead and they pray that God will spare from Satan any child born of their marriage.

*Reference for wedding:* **Geraldine Brooks'** *Cosmopolitan* article *"Nine Parts of Desire."*

**References:** "Nine Parts of Desire" for *Cosmopolitan* by Geraldine Brooks and *Iraq: A Country Study.*

# Israel

*Tel-Aviv. Courtesy of Israel Tourist Office and Dr. Barry Goldberg*

Jewish, Christian, Muslim, and Druze are the four major religious groups that constitute Israeli society. Eighty-two percent of Israel's five million people are Jewish. Over half native-born and the remaining Jewish people come from other countries. Sixteen percent of the Israelis are Sunni Muslim and the remaining two percent are Druze located in villages of northern Israel. The rest are Circassian Sunni Muslims, Christian Arabs, Greek Orthodox, and Roman Catholic.

❤ **Present marriage customs**

Since the Declaration of the Establishment of the State of Israel in 1948, freedom of religion is guaranteed to the entire population. Each religion is entitled to practice and exercise its faith freely and each has its own council and courts which have jurisdiction over personal status, such as marriage and divorce.

Rituals and content of Jewish wedding ceremonies vary from the religious liberal to strict Orthodox, according to the countries from which the immigrants come. Immigrants are divided into three broad categories: *Ashkenazi* Jews, *Sephardic* Jews, and *Eastern or Oriental* Jews. The *Ashkenazi* Jews are from Central and Eastern Europe. Their brides wear a European Western style white wedding gown. The *Sephardic* Jews were originally from Spain and Portugal. They migrated from Holland, Italy, Bulgaria, Greece, Turkey, and other Arabian countries to the Land of Israel. The *Sephardic* bridal apparel and customs are therefore similar to those of Arab countries. The *Eastern or Oriental* Jews originated in Islamic countries of Northern Africa and the Middle East.

About 20 percent of immigrants adhere to the strict Orthodox Jewish religion, about 60 percent vary between lenient and strict traditions, and the other 20 percent are non-observant. No matter what degree of Judaism is held or the place of origin, marriage, founded by God, is considered the ideal state for men and women.

# *Orthodox Jewish Wedding*

*Jewish Israeli bride and groom in front of the Knesset.*
*Courtesy of the Israel Govenment Tourist Office, USA*

❤ **Nissuin ceremony.** The Orthodox Israeli wedding may be held outdoors, at home, at a synagogue, or a hotel. During the *nissuin ceremony* where a *minyian* of 10 men and other guests are present, the bride's and groom's mothers accompany the bride to the *chuppah*, the canopy, symbolizing their home. The groom also walks forward with his father and the father of the bride. The couple then stands under the *chuppah*, its four poles often held by four men, while the wedding ceremony is conducted.

❤ **Ring ceremony.** Once blessings are given by the rabbi, the bride and groom sip wine from the same goblet and the groom places the object of value, the ring, on the bride's right index finger and says, *Behold, you are consecrated unto me with this ring, according to the law of Moses and Israel.*

❤ **Seven blessings.** The rabbi, with the second wine goblet in hand, recites the seven marriage blessings.

❤ **Crushing the glass.** Finally, the groom crushes a wine goblet beneath his right foot, an act which symbolizes the destruction of the Jewish Temple at Jerusalem in 73 A.D.

❤ **Quiet rendezvous.** After the ceremony, the couple is allowed to enter a private room where they can spend some private time together. When they come out of the room, they are considered married. *(See details of the Orthodox Jewish wedding ceremony on page 29 in Chapter 1.)*

❤ **Druze Muslims**

The Druze Muslims (about 80,000), many of whom live on the Golan Heights or in Haifa, have their own family law and Druze courts. Contrary to Muslim customs, the Druze religion prohibits polygamy and divorce against the wife's will. The women are permitted more freedom of expression in worship and their status is equal to their husbands. Among the Druze, a woman's chastity is honored and the virginity of the bride is a condition of integrity.

The selection of the spouse is usually accomplished by relatives, and care is taken that a prospective hus-

band will assure the girl's future. Their selection must be approved by the girl, for it is against the Druze law that a husband should be selected against her will. The legal age for marriage is 17 for the bride and 18 for the groom, so the engagement often lasts until the couple is old enough to marry. In reality, the girl is not always consulted about the selection of a spouse once she is old enough to assess characteristics of her future mate.

The contract of engagement is considered a family matter. The bride may be reserved at the time of engagement by a sum of money the groom provides in

# Druze Wedding

❤ **Engagement.** The couple becomes engaged one year before their wedding. A *fatichah*, an initial oral agreement, is made over a Druze religious book. Then the village *imam* ties a handkerchief that represents their union.

❤ **Akid ceremony.** The *akid*, the male religious ceremony, takes place.

❤ **Marriage contract.** The bride receives permission from a medical doctor before her marriage. The marriage contract is then signed by the groom, if he is 18 or older, and the bride, if she is 17 or older.

❤ **Shaving and wedding ceremonies.** The groom enjoys a shaving celebration with his friends, and the seated bride is decorated with henna at a special women's ceremony.

❤ **Wedding celebration.** The family prepares a feast for guests at the groom's father's house. (Sometimes, wedding celebrations are catered in a hall.) The couple must wait until the wedding occurs before they can consummate their marriage.

**Reference: Druze Wedding by Gaye Hilsenrath in the November 1997 issue of *The World and I.***

advance on the dower. It is property given to the future wife. Upon their engagement, the man gives his fiancée gifts: cash, personal items, household products, clothing, and jewelry. The Fatiha from the Koran is recited at that time.

Only a few marriages are polygamous or temporary. The Druze have tried to abolish polygamy legally, but evidence exists that polygamy still occurs. Although a Muslim man is permitted to marry a Christian or Jewess, the Druze law strictly forbids a Druze man or woman to marry a non-Druze. Intermarriages between Druze men and Jewish, Christian, Muslim and Baha'i women are fairly common, but Druze women are barred from social contacts within the Druze community if they marry outside their religion.

Marriages are performed by the *ma'dhun* after receiving permission form the local Druze court; therefore, an application for permission must be made a few days before the wedding. The bride's father usually provides a dowry for his daughter as well as contributing to the cost of the wedding and buying the *jihaz*. The dower, part of religious law and custom, is given to the bride in the form of fruit trees and is usually paid before the marriage or its consummation. On the other hand, a deferred dower is rather frequent with the Druzes. A voluntary agreement may be made by both

parties that the debt of the husband is only paid in the event of divorce or death. The advantage of the latter is that the husband is deterred from rash divorce thereby stabilizing family life and preventing divorce. However, a promissory note which matures upon dissolution of a marriage, when offered, provides complete security for a wife. The prompt or deferred dower conditions must be expressly stated in the marriage contract. Though the Druze lifestyle has religious elements, it also has characteristics of secular, nuclear, and extended families. Most wives want to live in a dwelling with their husband away from the husband's family.

❤ **Sunni Muslim**
*Palestinian* Arabs who are Sunni Muslims live on the West Bank and Gaza Strip. Only eight percent is Christians. Mixed marriages between the two groups are relatively rare. In traditional Muslim families dating is unacceptable. Because of emphasis on sustaining family ties, marriages between cousins are common. Girls marry at the age of 18 and boys at about 22. By the late 1960's, many marriages were not traditionally arranged. Now, young people have freedom of choice. Those who are permitted to date or meet at parties in private homes are not allowed to drink heavily, use drugs, or have sexual relationships. *(See Jordan for the Sunni Muslim wedding customs.)*

**References: *Marriage Divorce and Succession in the Druze Family* by Aharon Layish, *Facts About Israel: Society* from the Israel Information Center and *Cultures of the World: Israel.***

# Jordan

*My thanks to Ghada Abdullatif.*

*The following marriage customs also apply to Muslims living in Jerusalem.*

### ❤ Selection of a spouse

More than 90 percent of Jordan's population is Sunni Muslim; less than 10 percent is Christian. In Jordan a young man and woman may become acquainted through a friend, relative, or parental arrangement. They cannot meet in public while dating; in fact, other people must be present while they speak to each other. The couple can have no serious relationship with each other until introductions are made to their parents and their parents become acquainted. If the couple wish to marry, they must have parental approval. To obtain permission for marriage, the prospective groom invites the oldest man in his family to go to the future bride's house where the bride's father provides a special dessert. The oldest man in the groom's family asks the girl's father for permission. If the young girl's father says "yes," they worship by reading the following passage from the Koran:

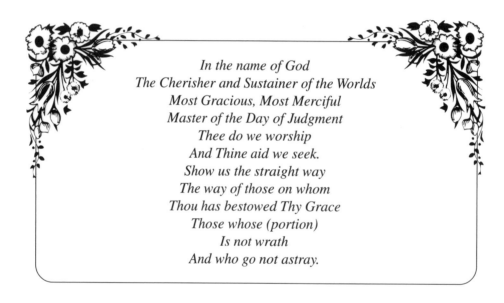

*In the name of God*
*The Cherisher and Sustainer of the Worlds*
*Most Gracious, Most Merciful*
*Master of the Day of Judgment*
*Thee do we worship*
*And Thine aid we seek.*
*Show us the straight way*
*The way of those on whom*
*Thou has bestowed Thy Grace*
*Those whose (portion)*
*Is not wrath*
*And who go not astray.*

### ❤ Marriage customs

Before the wedding reception takes place, the groom's father, the groom, the bride's father, (and perhaps the bride) meet in court to sign a wedding contract before a witness. If the bride is present, she may give her consent to marry the groom when she is asked. Usually, the bride gives her consent for marriage to her father (or older brother, if the father is not alive). She also gives her father the honor of signing the wedding contract. After the fathers from both families sign the contract and a monetary gift from the groom is presented to the bride, the couple is considered officially married.

The wedding reception takes place at a hotel or home, depending on the size of the reception. The bride wears a formal white bridal gown and her husband, a tuxedo or dark suit. A buffet with wedding cake is served to the guests who congratulate the couple and their families. At large weddings, musicians entertain the guests and a dinner is served. Gifts from close family are given to the couple the same day. Gifts from others are given later.

*(See King Hussein of Jordan's marriage to Queen Noor as described on page 235 in the final chapter of this book.)*

# Kazakhstan

Since Kazakhs are Sunni Muslims whose marriages traditionally adhere to Islamic law and customs. In the past a cradle-betrothal occurred in which marriages were arranged and negotiations between two families occurred at the birth of their children. Very young teenage marriages were also arranged by the parents. Unlike many Muslim countries, the young man sometimes abducted his spouse either by agreement or against her parents' will. After the abduction, the groom later asked her parents for forgiveness and generally her family forgave the couple. This still may occur in rural areas.

**♥ Traditional marriage customs**

Kazakh men can have up to four wives, but rarely take wives of other religions. Levirate marriage, a man marrying his brother's widow, and polygamous sororate marriages, with the man marrying sisters, still exist.

In Kazakhstan, the bride was expected to have a dowry and the man's family was to pay the brideprice called the *kalyn*, in the form of livestock to the bride's father. After partial payment of the brideprice was exchanged, the young man could see the bride secretly. Once the entire brideprice was paid, the bride, her face covered with a veil, was escorted by the groom and relatives to the groom's home. Upon entering the groom's home where a fire was set in the hearth, the groom's relatives sang songs of celebration expressing the obligations of the young wife. The man's young relatives used a small stick to raise the veil which lightly covered the bride's face. Guests inspected the display of gifts for the bride and inspected them.

During some ceremonies, the bride and groom were showered with sweets and the uniting of the couple was consummated simply by sipping water from one cup. Many of these customs are being resurrected today. In urban areas, friends, relatives, and the bride and groom simply gather for the wedding around a table where a lavish feast is provided. After the wedding, the bride's dowry is delivered.

**Reference: The Encyclopedia of World Cultures.**

**211**

# Kuwait

Kuwaitis have a high population of Sunni Muslims; only 20 percent are Shi'a Muslims. After the Gulf War, in March 1992, the government approved a resolution to provide young men with a sum of money to defray the coast of the brideprice. The purpose of this was to encourage marriage and population growth.

**Reference: *The Persian Gulf States: Country Studies.***

# Lebanon

Seventy percent of the Lebanese population are Muslims, mostly Shiite Muslims, called the *Metawli*. Some are Druze Muslims and the remaining people are Christians, many of the Maronite faith.

Separate courts handle marriages according to the customs of each religion. The family law of Lebanon states that the legal age for marriage is 18. A minor must receive consent from parents. Virginity for people of both the Muslim and Christian faiths is highly valued and obligatory. It is often part of the marriage agreement. Girls in villages marry during their late teens and boys in their early twenties. Urban youths tend to marry somewhat later, especially the educated who often postpone their marriage until their thirties and beyond.

### ♥ Shiite Muslim

Both in the country and the cities, the young Muslim men and women usually live with their parents before marriage. In rural areas of Lebanon, marriages are still arranged by parents, although the girl usually has a voice as to whether or not she wishes to accept their selection.

In the past, young men and women were obliged to marry a patrilineal first cousin for family security and to keep property within their lineage. Premarital sex was so dishonorable that the father and brothers would kill the couple or drive the man from his village. If a settlement was not obtained, fighting between the two lineages could transpire. The Shiite girl is free to come and go in her own village but, if she is permitted to visit another town, she must be accompanied by brothers. A boy's life is freer than that of his sisters.

Presently, the brideprice negotiated for Muslim marriage contracts is still influenced by the bride's virginity, prior marital status, social class, politics, relationship with her family, geographic proximity, and age. When the Muslim couples' engagement is announced, the formal contract is devised with the young man paying the brideprice, a token gift to his fiancée's family. This marital contract is signed with the consent of the couple; thus, their marriage is considered legal before the wedding celebration takes place.

The bride's and groom's families have separate parties at their homes where neighbors and relatives enjoy feasting on lamb and rice. The bride's family and friends then take her to the groom's family house where the party continues for both the bride and groom. Bread dough, symbolizing prosperity, is placed over the entrance to the groom's home. The bride and groom, stained with henna, sit on a platform while they are honored by guests who sing and dance before them. After the newlyweds return from their honeymoon, people bring them presents.

Most marriages are monogamous. Intermarriage is frowned on, although it does occur. Islam permits Muslim men to marry Jewish and Christian women.

### ♥ Druze Muslim

The Druze, residing in the agricultural Mount Lebanon area, are monogamous and do not permit polygamy. *(For more details, please refer to Israel).*

### ♥ Christian

Maronite Christians are permitted to choose their own spouses. Christians and other urbanites follow Western dating customs. Men wait until they are financially independent, in their late 20s or 30s, before marrying and then usually marry a younger woman. A dowry is provided by the bride's parents. Intermarriage between Muslims and Christians is rare, except for a few educated people in the cities who are not as bound by traditional ways.

References: *Lebanon, New Light in an Ancient Land* by Elsa Marston, *Lebanon, A Country Study* by Thomas Collelo, *Ethnic Family Values in Australia* by Des Storer, Cultures of America: Lebanese Americans by Sandra Whitehead.

# Oman

### ♥ Selecting a spouse

Traditionally, marriage between relatives, with a preference towards cousins, constitutes about one third of all marriages. The marriage was arranged by the parents and often the marriage contract was entered into before the bride and groom met. Presently, males and females are free to choose their own marriage partners. Often, the male suitor consults a close female relative as to whom to marry, for the sexual segregation keeps the man from observing unrelated girls. Another way of searching is to consult neighbors and store keepers about eligible girls from other places. Sometimes, the groom must choose knowing the bride only through hearsay. After finding a prospective partner, the suitor asks the girl's family for permission to see her. He may then observe her while she serves tea to his family members.

### ♥ Marriage customs

After he selects a bride, negotiations take place between the groom's father or the groom and the girl's guardian, who is usually her father. The brideprice, called *mahr,* takes into consideration the beauty of the bride, her ethnic status, the amount of property and mainly, if she is a highly prized virgin. A man pays less for a relative than for a stranger. Often, if a man marries a relative, he does not have to pay at all. Paradoxically, a man having a lesser position must pay more for the privilege of having a bride of higher status. During the signing of the marriage contract, the groom is present, but usually the bride is not.

# Oman Wedding

❤ **Signing the marriage contract.** A day or so before the wedding celebrations begin, the marriage contract is signed by the groom or his representative and the bride's father in the judge's office.

❤ **Separate wedding festivities.** Traditional Muslim wedding festivities in Oman take place over several days. Throughout the celebrations, there is a conspicuous segregation of the sexes. The bride's and the groom's families also celebrate separately. Generally, the groom's family celebrates for three days and the bride's, for one or two. Guests now use cars instead of camels, with women following the men to these parties. The bride actually waits in a room with children while wedding festivities take place at her home without her. The father of the bride purchases all the customary jewelry for his daughter.

In both male and female areas of the groom's home, a small band of male drummers accompanies singing and line dancing while many of the guests watch. Men wear white robes with turbans or head cloths. Women dress in brightly colored clothing and are adorned with gold and silver necklaces, earrings, and bracelets, plus rings on the nose, toes, and fingers. Gold decorations adorn their face masks and shawls.

❤ **Fetching the bride.** On the third day of the wedding celebration at the groom's home, people are dressed even more beautifully. The children are decorated with red henna paste and singing continues with more intensity. Later that day, the groom and his male friends, with the women following, leave in cars to get the bride. The head car, often decorated with banners, arrives at the bride's home where they find a large crowd of guests greeting them. Still in the company of children, the bride is bathed by her mother and dressed in her green wedding clothes, shawl, and jewelry. The bride, often frightened, wears a green shawl and black cloak, her hands and feet dyed with henna. Older girls shower sweets over her head. On the other hand, the mother often wears her ugliest clothing to display her unhappiness upon the loss of her daughter as the bride's relatives and friends are entertained and served spiced porridge and melted butter and sweet halvah. Later, the women form a tight ring around the bride and lead her to the waiting car. Many friends accompany the bride to the groom's home and stay for a meal. Early that morning, the bride's wardrobe is transported to the groom's home.

❤ **Party for the bride.** When the bride and her party arrive at the groom's home, singing and dancing continue while the bridal party is served food. The groom is then shaved by a group of men and boys who tease him. He also wears a green sash, for green is thought to bring good fortune. Men sing songs accompanied by men playing tambourines. A fire is started outside where the men pray. The groom is ceremonially stripped of clothing, except for a loincloth. He then puts on clean clothing. After dark, they enter the groom's house where spiced rice and meat are served. While all this is going on, the bride is being attended by other women in another place.

❤ **Honeymoon and virginity test.** The bride and groom spend their wedding night and their seven-day honeymoon free from duties in the nuptial hut, built at the groom's family home by the groom's male friends. There, several layers of reed floor mats are covered by an Oriental rug. Colored cotton sheets

# Oman Wedding

hang over the ceiling and colored pillows and mirrors decorate the room. Embroidered dresses and jewelry and pieces of colored materials are hung from the ceiling by the female kin.

That night, the groom is led by his closest relatives and companions to the bridal hut where the marriage is consummated. There the bride, often as young as 14 years of age, is attended by a female friend of the bride's mother who lends support during the bride's transition. The bridal attendant places an egg on the floor for the newlyweds to break with their feet to promote fertility. She cares for the couple's basic needs and tries to make the honeymoon as luxurious as possible. Since chastity of the woman is highly valued, it is important that after consummation a handkerchief show blood as proof of the bride's virginity.

The bride resides with her husband and his family thereafter.

**Reference:** *Behind the Veil in Arabia* **by Unni Wikan.**

# Saudi Arabia

214

Saudi Arabia is celebrated as the birth place of the Muslim prophet Mohammed. In Saudi Arabia, Islam is the official way of life, both legally and religiously. The Saudis live in large extended families and socializing is done generally within the kinship group.

### ❤ Traditional customs

During the 1980's, parents, their sons, daughter-in-laws and their children, were an autonomous social unit and economic entity owning herds and land. The extended household dissolved when the elderly husband or wife died or remarried. When a mother had been divorced or widowed and remarried, her older sons created their own households.

By segregating males and females, Saudis were able to ensure the women's reputations and their families' honor. Women were supposed to be virgins prior to marriage. The segregation of the sexes occurred mostly in urban areas where non-kinsmen lived in close proximity. In cities, unknown men were thought of as possible enemies and were looked upon with suspicion. On the other hand, women from small rural villages and Bedouin (nomadic pasturalist) women actually enjoyed more freedom than those in the cities.

Historically, it was not proper for a girl to display interest in a man before marriage. Islamic parents looked for a congenial, personable companion for their son or daughter, then arranged marriages for their children. They believed romantic love will grow after marriage. Most Saudis married since they were not respected as adults if they did not wed and have children. Arranging a marriage was the most important decision a family made. Linking sons of brothers kept their social and economic heritage secure; therefore, cousins of a young woman took first preference as prospects for marriage. The advantages of cousin marriages were–

- ❤ The closer the relative, the more certain the family was of a good reputation.
- ❤ Since the bride and groom had limited opportunities for mate selection, they were more likely to accept such an arrangement.
- ❤ Disagreements between cousins or brothers could be quickly mended through marriage, thus promoting family harmony.
- ❤ Monetary assets and land can be held within the same family generation after generation.

Women were in the better position in their households to evaluate the prospective bride first hand and provide information. Men depended on the women in the family to select a spouse that would serve the family's best interests.

The prospective bride and groom had to give their consent for marriage. A refusal to wed was gently expressed in such a way that the suitor's family was able to save face.

Marriage outside the extended family was rare, except for families uniting with a royal family or with another tribal family for political reasons. Sometimes the parents would arrange a marriage between another family of known good reputation. In almost every instance, families involved in the marriage were of equal status. To permit a daughter to marry beneath her status was virtually unthinkable.

The parents and older brothers of the couple negotiated the contractual agreement. The brideprice, stipulated in the agreement, was paid by the groom's family to the bride's family and her kin. If the bride and groom were first cousins, little money was given to the bride's parents. The contract also indicated terms and what recourse was to be taken if certain terms were broken. Their marriage was then registered by the groom and a male representing the bride.

### ❤ The present:  selecting a spouse

No dating takes place in Saudi Arabia. Because chastity before marriage is highly prized, women are discouraged from interacting with other men outside their families. Although many women are educated and are now employed, the Saudis have tried to structure society to leave sexual segregation intact by increasing separate female facilitates in education, social, and business settings.

Muslim men are permitted to have as many as four wives as long as they treat them equally, but most Saudi men have only one. Saudi Arabian girls marry at the age of 16 to 18 and boys, from 18 to 20. When the young woman is ready to meet a young man, the mother, aunt, or cousin finds a prospective mate who is suitable. The dowry is negotiated on the worth of the bloodline, financial, and social connections.

The ideal marriage is still one between first cousins. After a relative makes an introduction, the man and the woman decide whether or not they wish to be married. The girl can reject the choice of her family, but she rarely does. The woman considers her wedding the most important day of her life, for it allows her to fulfill her ultimate destiny of having children.

The male, needing to ensure the tribe's survival, desires a son for security in his old age and as proof of his virility.

### ❤ Present marriage customs

Contractual arrangements are made when the brideprice is settled. The groom gives her family the amount agreed upon in gold jewelry, money, and other gifts. These gifts become the bride's personal property and she is able to keep them in case of divorce. Wedding celebrations occur after the marriage contract is signed privately in the presence of a religious leader called an *imam*. During the signing ceremony, the *imam* asks the prospective bride if she will accept the man chosen by her parents. Before four witnesses who are unrelated to the family, the *imam* then asks the groom if he will accept the woman for his wife. The marriage contract is signed and officially recorded by the *iman* after he reads passages from the Koran.

Because the poor in Saudi Arabia do not have the finances to purchase a wife, Skeikh Abdul Aziz ibn Baz established a fund for less prosperous men who wish to marry for the first time. Grants worth several thousand dollars are donated by the wealthy. The only requirement is that the local *imam* testifies that the groom performs certain prayers.

The well-to-do enjoy large wedding parties. These wedding parties, attended separately by men and women who bring gifts, are held at the bride's home or hotel. The bride is not seen by Saudi men, except for her close male relatives, since she is traditionally veiled according to Muslim custom. A more recent innovation is that photographs may be taken by a male at the men's party and only by a female at the women's party. The new husband and wife make a formal appearance at the women's party where the couple accepts their congratulations. Dinner, singing, and dancing festivities last late into the night.

Nuclear families, one couple and their children, are a recent phenomena. These families, considered the new middle class, reside mostly in the cities. A son and his new wife is able to establish their household by receiving their rightful portion of their family assets.

**Reference:  *Saudi Arabia, A Country Study* by Richard F. Nyrop.**

*(See Saudi Royal Wedding Celebration on the next page.)*

# Royal Wedding Celebration

*The royal family of Saudi Arabia consists of more than 5,000 people.*

"Wedding celebrations, attended only by the female guests, are held in the evening in the bride's home, or, for the wealthy, in the posh new hotels. A wedding can consume the net worth of the bride's family, for her father, to retain his honor, must stage a ceremony as elaborate as he can muster. All guests arrive in their best attire and jewelry.

'The men celebrate elsewhere, casually sipping their own supply of tea and coffee and never seeing the bridal couple. The festivities start about 9 p.m. with the wedding party eventually arriving about 11:30. The bride and groom, accompanied by several of his closest relatives, slowly proceed through the guests... They then take their seats on a lower-decked platform to receive the congratulations of the guests. After greeting the last guest, they depart."

Ms. Sandra Mackey, who wrote the book *The Saudis*, describes a royal wedding held at King Faisal Hall, where elaborate royal weddings take place: "Veiled women stepped out of the luxury automobiles, climbed the steps, and entered the hall where female servants were singing and dancing. They then entered the main hall where a receiving line, adorned with jewels, greeted them.

"The hall itself was enormous. A peach-colored carpet, purchased especially for the wedding, ran down the length of the room, creating an aisle between the senior women of the family. To my left, at the front of the room, was a pole covered with dense bouquets of flowers, extending approximately 20 feet toward the ceiling. Thirty of these floral posts fanned out behind the platform where the bride and groom would sit to receive their wedding guests, and more flowers stood in great bunches on the stage... Behind me a group of professional women musicians played drums and a lone lute while they crooned Arabic traditional wedding songs. Sixty servant girls, many of them Oriental, dressed in matching costumes passed coffee and tea in hand-painted cups and glasses that matched the peach color scheme of the wedding.

"Between the time the wedding began and the bride made her appearance, approximately 2 1/2 hours later, the bride's sisters and myriad of cousins pranced up and down the aisle in chic dresses directly out of the designer salons of Europe. . . .

"I was absorbed watching all of these scenes around me, when I was startled upright in my chair by a series of high-pitched screams emanating from behind the tall doors to my right. . . . The doors flung open and four heavy-set women in tight white satin dresses slit to the hip entered the room, beating hand-held drums. They were followed by four belly dancers balancing tall candelabras, each containing 12 lighted candles, on their heads. . . . They in turn were followed by six flower girls, who preceded the bride. The bride herself wore a western-style dress with a great train, carried by two young girls. The procession of chanting drummers, shimmying belly dancers, flower girls, bride, and train bearers took 20 minutes to transverse the long room and reach the podium. As the dancers reached a frenzied climax, they were hurried away so the groom, escorted by four of his relatives, could enter the hall. It was approaching 1 a.m. when the bride and groom finished receiving the congratulations of the guests and the party moved into the adjacent Intercontinental Hotel for the wedding feast. There was a 20-layer cake, and a variety of food was served to the highest and to the lowest who all sat together."

216

### ❤ Rwala Bedouins.

In 1928, the northern Saudi Arabian Rwala Bedouins believed procreation was a duty because the more numerous they were, the more power and influence they would attain. The Bedouins were one of the cultures in the Arabian countries whose choice of mates was motivated by love. Even at the tender age of 12, a girl and boy were free to have romantic feelings towards one another. Sararat women, widowed or not, were predisposed to lend their tent to a young couple. The boy could visit a girl privately in her tent while her parents were working, and the more mature male was permitted to be with his beloved any time or any place. When the weather was cold, they could enjoy the night by a fire. During the hot season, the couple chatted on a sand drift.

When a youth wanted to marry, he confided in an older friend. The friend then asked the girl's father to permit the suitor to marry the daughter. If the suitor's father believed his son's destiny was Allah's will, he arranged for a prominent man to discuss the marital agreement with the girl's father. A brideprice, called a *sijak*, was agreed upon to compensate the girl's father, and the couple was betrothed.

Before the bride and groom could live together, a she-camel was killed as a sacrifice and the women pitched a marital tent. Toward sunset, the groom's female kin took the bride to the tent. After the bridegroom arrived, the relatives departed and the tent was closed. No wedding, presentation of gifts or reception took place and often no one nearby noticed the small newly-constructed tent until the next day.

The following morning, the men congratulated the groom and the women visited the bride. After her father-in-law presented a gift to the bride, she joined the females in the father-in-law's tent. She was not required to work for several days, but her husband was expected to continually labor so he could purchase a trousseau of carpets, quilts, and clothing for her. Should a man have another wife, he must devote time to her as well so she would not be jealous. A husband could have sexual relations with a widowed woman in the family as well, in order to console her.

**References:** *Cultures of the World: Saudi Arabia, The Manners and Customs of the Rwala Bedouins* by Alis Musil, and *Saudis: Inside the Desert Kingdom* by Sandra Mackey.

*(See Turkmenistan under Asia)*

# Yemen

### ❤ North Yemen

The Zaydi Shia and Shafii Sunni Muslim reside in North Yemen.

Males and females are separated and the practice of veiling is still part of their Islamic culture. Women tend to live in seclusion, except for the Akhdam women and educated urban women who usually no longer cover their faces.

The legal minimum age for a girl to marry is 16, but the law is difficult to enforce. Parents arrange marriages. Even though the bride is permitted to reject a prospective spouse, the bride is rarely consulted about her preference.

Though Muslim men are permitted to have as many as four wives at one time, polygamy is rarely practiced because of the high cost of the brideprice The brideprice, consisting of cash and other gifts, has increased. In North Yemen, the bride usually receives up to one half of the entire payment of the brideprice. It remains under her control even after the marriage takes place.

***Yemen bride.*** *The exotic Yemen wedding attire of gold fabric is adorned with gold jewelry to display high status. The entire community is invited to the celebration where musicians perform their sacred duty to please the newlyweds. During the party, everyone eats sweet fritters, predicting a sweet life for the couple.*

## ❤ South Yemen

The population of South Yemen is mostly Sunni Muslim. Veiling of Southern Yemeni women has declined, although female circumcision was widespread as late as 1985.

Since 1974, law requires that the bride must be 16 and the groom, at least 18 at the time of marriage. The groom cannot be more than 20 years older than his prospective wife. The brideprice is limited. Polygamy is permitted, especially if a man's original spouse is disabled or infertile. A woman now may marry a man whose social class differs from her own.

**Reference:** *The Yemens: Country Studies.*

# *Polynesia*

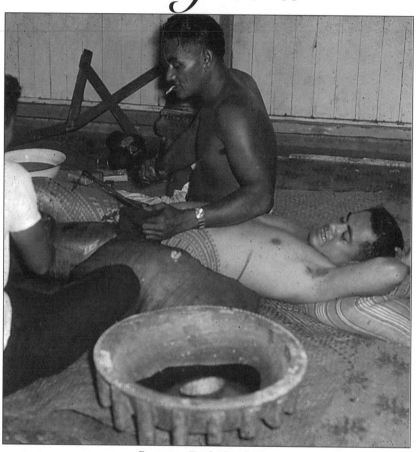

***Samoan Body Sculpting.***
Thanks to Harold Stephens Wolfenden, photographer
and author of *Three Decades of Asian Adventure* and *Travel and At Home in Asia*.

*The Polynesian bride and groom are adorned with feathers and seashells.*

218

# South Pacific

*Oceania*

*9*

# Polynesia

**Thanks to Harold Stephens Wolfenden, author of** *Three Decades of Asian Adventure and Travel.*

Polynesia encompasses the Pacific islands east of Micronesia. Historically, Polynesian societies have experienced openness and pleasure in love-making and have possessed a social tolerance towards short-term experimentation prior to marriage. Unmarried boys and girls gathered by moonlight for hula dancing, for their way of life was, and still is, expressed in music and dance.

Years ago, polygamy prevailed. Marriages were between people of the same culture and class, and purity of blood was of utmost importance. Although marriages were arranged between two families for political and social alliances, a person could never marry a close relative. Sometimes, parents arranged marriages for their progeny during childhood or prior to birth. If the young people did not want to marry later, they were severely punished. Their marriage took place as soon as they matured. Only the lower classes had freedom of choice, although the couple had to seek parental approval. Among the lower class, cohabitation was recognized, approved by elders, and understood by the community.

When a young man in some Polynesian regions wished to marry a woman, he or his respected representative (man, friend, or parents) would bring fish, a roasted pig, or mats to his prospective in-laws. The man's representative would plea his case by glorifying the social prestige and advantages of this marriage. Similar practices, as well as other unique tribal marriage customs described in this chapter, still exist in some areas.

In past Polynesian marriages, no promise of lifetime fidelity was made during the wedding ceremony; yet, a code of fidelity existed. Only certain types of extramarital relations were permitted; for example, the married man could be with his sisters-in-law. When a male guest visited, the husband would cordially offer him the pleasure of being with his wife. Other forms of unfaithfulness were punished. The chiefs were allowed more sexual freedoms. Newly married couples lived with the parents, usually the husband's, for a year.

Past customs, many which are very unique, exist at the same time as Western cultural influences in certain Polynesian countries. Harold Stephens Wolfenden saw several recent Polynesian societies in which the man could not marry until he proved his manhood. In Taumotuas, the man dives into a pool in the lagoon to wrestle with man-eating sharks. A young Pendercost man wins the hand of a girl by diving head first from a 90-foot towers toward the ground. Only vines which are knotted to his legs keep him from a hard landing, since they stop him in his flight a mere six inches above the earth. Newly married men in Gambiers paddle their brides to distant islands to show their worth.

As a result of European and United States influences, in many Polynesian countries Western-style marriages occur and their weddings take place in church. Because better educational and employment opportunities now exist in some Polynesian countries, urban men and women marry outside their tribal cultures. Despite differences, wedding feasts are a real banquet in all of Polynesia.

219

**References:** *Oceania: The Native Cultures of Australia and the Pacific Islands* by Douglas L. Oliver and *Love in the South Seas* by Gengt Danielsson and Harold Stephens Wolfenden who wrote *At Home in Asia, The Last Voyage,* and *Three Decades of Asian Adventure and Travel.*

# Australia

Australia was settled mainly by European colonists from Holland and the United Kingdom. Immigrants also came from Ireland, Italy, Germany, Greece, and Yugoslavia, and later the Americas. Approximately 90 percent of the Australian population is of European descent. Thirty percent are Anglican and 25 percent are Roman Catholic. (*See the Roman Catholic and English Anglican weddings.*)

People from Turkey, Pakistan, Vietnam, Sri Lanka, and African countries also settled there and brought their own marriage customs with them. Because the British monarchy was the head of the Australian state, Western culture has primarily influenced its lifestyles. Children of original settlers from various countries gradually tend to take on the morals and marriage customs of the host country. Immigrants from Muslim countries were surprised by the lack of modesty of the Western dress of their male and female counterparts.

*Native Australians, called Aboriginals.* Almost two percent of the Australian population is *Aboriginal*. Australian law, particularly the 1982 law, allowed the *Aboriginals* of Australia to retain their own identity and tribal marriage customs.

Traditionally, *Aboriginals* were permitted to marry outside their close kin group and men had multiple wives. A promised marriage was made for the young girl, often before she was born, even if the couple decided not to marry later. While the girl was maturing, the promised husband would provide gifts for the girl's family in order to establish a cordial relationship between both families. A teenage girl could be pledged by her parents to marry a man who was in mid-life. The man could take on a pre-teenage junior wife even though sexual relations did not occur until puberty. The first marriage for a young male generally occurred when he was in his late 20s.

To avoid a promised marriage, a couple who were in love simply could elope and hope that their marriage would be accepted by their families and community over time. After marriage, the wife usually moved into her husband's group. Her sexual services could be lent as a part of a communal ceremony or occasionally as a thoughtful consideration to a male visitor.

Younger generations increasingly resist promised marriages, polygamy, and marriages of young girls to old men, for *Aboriginals* could not remain completely untouched by prevailing Australian Western values. Many Native Australians now choose their own spouses based on the Western concept of romantic love. Presently, they closely follow the Western pattern of monogamous marriage between those of similar ages. The new pattern also resulted from the concern that men would have so many children from multiple wives that they would not be able to care for them. Aboriginal women are more likely to wed outsiders because Aboriginal men have inferior occupations..

## ♥ Greeks

Virginity prior to marriage has always been important to Greek Orthodox people, thereby making the rate of premarital pregnancy lower than in other segments of Australian population. If a pregnancy does occur, most single girls of the working class feel pressured to marry the father. In the past, unsupervised dating for girls before a formal engagement was an exception to the rule. If a girl wanted to date before her engagement, she would have to conceal arranged meetings with boyfriends. Keeping their activities a secret from their parents, instead of confronting them, was a way to deal with the problem. Today, freedom of spousal choice has increased over arranged marriages, but Greek daughters still prefer to unite with men of similar backgrounds. (*See Greek Orthodox wedding.*)

## ♥ Turks

The Turkish population is mostly Muslim. Their Islamic values and customs relating to sex and marriage are more resistant to change. Women still do not court openly, and marriages are arranged by the fathers with the aid of go-betweens. A cash brideprice is paid to the bride's parents by the groom. The bride's respectability is of the utmost importance, and most villagers expect that the new wife to reside in the father's household after marriage. Some customs have changed for urban nuclear families who are highly educated. More recently, inter-ethnic marriages have increased.

## ♥ Lebanese

The Lebanese people in Australia are mostly Sunni Muslim, but some are Druze Muslims. Thirty percent of the Lebanese population are Christian. Lebanese marriages in Australia are generally still arranged by parents. When a marriage between a couple appears to be likely, the parents still make the ultimate decision. (*See information under Lebanon for more details.*)

### ❤ Pakistanis

Muslim Pakistani women in Australia generally do not observe *purdah*, the wearing of the veil. They often wear the sari. It is considered their religious duty to insure procreation and legitimate sexual satisfaction. Marriage is contracted by the parents and a witness. This agreement, sometimes made with the groom's consent, stipulates the payment of the dowry awarded to the bride, property details, and inheritance rights. Some modern families may permit their children to select their own marriage partners.

The trend among the educated Pakistanis is for parents to arrange a marriage in consultation with their children, even though modern secular Australian law permits couples to marry without parental consent. A brideprice is not now considered important among the educated. Because Australia is Westernized, traditional customs are relaxed for Paskistani immigrant children.

**References: *Ethnic Family Values in Australia* edited by Des Storer and *The Cambridge Factfinder* edited by David Crystal.**

# *Cook Islands*

In the past, girls were protected from boys prior to marriage. In order for boys and girls to acquire spouses, the chief would periodically invite boys and girls to his abode. The boys and girls would then stand in lines opposite each other. Each boy, in turn, would take his wife in the order in which they stood. If a boy and girl wanted each other, they had to be certain they stood in the exact numerically opposite place in line.

**Reference: *Love in the South Seas* by Gengt Danielsson.**

# *Fiji Islands*

The Fiji Islands have a 70 percent Muslim and a 25 percent Hindu population formerly from India. Native Fijians are now mainly Christian and Roman Catholic. Although traditionally arranged marriages are the dominant form, arranged love marriages in which the children are consulted now occur. Bureau marriage and Western-style marriages, based on romantic love and courtship, are also taking place.

### ❤ Selecting a spouse: past and present

Parents notify the community that they want a marriage partner for their son or daughter. After a desirable candidate of the same race, religion, and class is found, parents take a closer look at the family history. The male's employment, family status, and his character are taken into consideration. The female has to be chaste and respect her elders. In the past, romantic love and courtship were omitted.

After a potential spouse is found, the man's family visits the female's family to view the bride's appearance and behavior while food and drink are served. Sometimes, she sits with her head bowed and says as few words as possible in order to appear demure. Conclusions as to whether or not the prospective bride is to be chosen are made in private after members of the man's family consult each other.

If the woman is not rejected by the groom's family, negotiations are begun. Sometimes, the woman's opinion is solicited. Since it is commonly understood that parents know best, there usually is little resistance from either the young man or woman. If the young woman has a secret romance and her parents find out about it, she often receives angry accusations from her parents. In some cases, when the male's religion, race and class are compatible, the parents agree to their union. The arranged marriage in that case becomes a combination of a Western-style love match and a traditionally arranged marriage.

Romantic love marriages, stressing individual choice and self-fulfillment while staying within cultural boundaries, are most prevalent among the urban educated. Love marriages occur among the Indo-Fijians since they are most influenced by Western education and the media. On the other hand, couples are restricted from staying out late at night and living away from home during courtship.

Some of the Indo-Fijian working class women or uneducated girls with no job prospects have overseas marriages with European, American, Australian, or Canadian males, regardless of their religious or ethnic associations. These marriages, for the purpose of improving their economic status, may be arranged through marriage bureaus, agencies, pen pal clubs, or newspaper advertisements. After the girl's family pays the agency a registration fee, the woman's name, address, and personal profile and photograph are sent overseas. Once the woman begins to receive letters from interested parties, she chooses the men with whom she will correspond. She sends her picture to the most desirable men. A man arranges to meet the woman in Fiji. If all goes well, the man returns to his native country, obtains a visa for the woman, and she joins him at a later date. A further amount of money is payable to the marriage bureau once a successful match is made.

**Reference:** *The Business of Marriage, Transformations in Oceanic Matrimony* by **Achsah Carrier.**

# Gambier Islands

*Harold Stephens Wolfenden, author of Three Decades of Asian Adventure & Travel and At Home in Asia.*

On the Gambier Islands, south of Tahiti, a wedding festival begins at night when fowl, pigs, breadfruit, and taro are cooked over hot stones in open pits. The festivities begin with the playing of wood blocks and shark-skin drums. Men and women, wearing grass skirts, dance near lighted fires. When the bride appears, everyone cheers and claps. She steps into the circle and dances with tempting body gyrations before selected men. Just as one is enticed, she goes to another until finally she stops before the groom. The drums do not play as she opens her arms before him. Suddenly, the bride and groom dance savagely, then hurry into the dark palm forest. When the bride and groom appear about a half hour later, they are married.

# Marquesas Islands

In the past, a sexual rite occurred at the finale of the traditional Marquesan wedding. All men who attended the ceremony formed a line headed by the elderly and chiefs. The bride, her head lying on the groom's knee, received the men for copulation. Her new husband was the last to have sexual relations with her. The new bride was expected to accept other men for a few days afterwards. The practice was not considered shameful or sinful, for the more men the bride comforted, the prouder she was. When the ceremony was finished, the bride's relatives laid face down on the ground next to each other and formed a human carpet for the bride and groom to walk over.

Marquesans now have European wedding customs and wear Western bridal attire; yet, they still maintain of the tradition of the living carpet for the newlyweds as they depart from the church.

**Reference:** *Love in the South Seas* by Gengt Danielsson.

# Micronesia

On the Island of Pohnpei secret courtship, called "night-crawling," is a highly popular activity among different clans. Both men and women take an active role in initiating such activities. Ideally, the male arranges a night time rendezvous through an intermediary who assists him in obtaining the girl he desires. The girl first must decline, for an initial acceptance is considered disgraceful. If the young man remains persistent, the choice is left with the female as to whether or not they meet. If she agrees, the man slips into her room or they have a clandestine meeting elsewhere. If their sexual and communicative relationship endures, they will exchange small gifts and bring simple tokens of respect to the other's family members. They give presents of sugarcane, coconut, and the kava plant.

These courtship activities are considered to be shameful only if the couple are seen together in public. The word quickly spreads and the details may become a titillating part of gossip should friends find out. Even though their courtship appears spontaneous and adventurous, much is at stake because the social status of a future spouse is a major consideration for a marriage. The man wants a spouse whose matrilineal group would give him status in the next generation. He also desires beauty, character, harmony, fertility, and competency to raise children. A woman wishes for a man with achievement potential, a man who has access to good land. She wants him to be good looking, kind, and generous.

❤ **Traditional marriage customs**

In the past, marriages were arranged to enhance the status of both families. Landholdings were a symbol of wealth and so important that some parents betrothed their unborn children. When royal polygamy existed, only the first wives were eligible for the highest title. Royal cross-cousin marriages were prevalent to maintain wealth and status.

Men and women who moved to a higher caste through marriage were revered, while those who married down in station were deplored. Most men married girls within their own villages. At the other extreme, civic leaders arranged unions with persons from other regions to cement political alliances.

Both individual choice and family sanction for the selection of the bride were traditional in Pohnpei, and many possibilities existed to insure a successful outcome. When the man's representative was sent to the prospective bride's family with gifts, he would plead for marriage on the young man's behalf. Should the girl's family agree, the couple could simply live together within the wife's or husband's family or in a compound nearby. They could then appear in public without condemnation. After the couple stayed together for a lengthy time and had children, the union was considered to be lasting and a divorce was less acceptable.

### ❤ Past and present marriage customs

During early days of contact with foreigners, the friendliness of the women and the beautiful, bountiful harbor gave Micronesia a sensational reputation. The willingness of Phonpei women to engage in sexual relations was within Phonpei rules and morality. *(See Polynesia.)* Phonpei's welcome to visitors began a period of intermarriages. As the Phonpei people converted to Protestantism and Catholic Christianity, chastity was encouraged prior to marriage, unions were increasingly based upon romantic love, and church marriages were considered ideal. Now, the church marriages are elaborate celebrations that include both Western and Pohnpei traditions.

Today, the traditional desire to marry individuals of high status remains constant, although less consideration is given to matrilineal group membership. The decision of marriage is still usually based on caste. Since college educated or cosmopolitan people who work and travel throughout the world tend to marry their equals, these men and women give less attention to social background and more to education and employment, things which influences future achievement as wage earners. A promised marriage is a consideration if one or both parties leave the island to obtain an advanced education and intend to return later. The ideal among the educated and elite is to wed an educated partner who holds the key to a good life.

*Yap islanders in the Federated States of Micronesia.* Because Yapese people were influenced by colonial domination and governed by the United States until 1983, male-female relationships reflect Western-style courtship and marriage.

**223**

## Traditional Marriage in Pohnpei

❤ Courtship is initiated by the couple meeting secretly after dark at a time in which the they can develop a loving relationship. Both coat their bodies with oil and decorate themselves with necklaces made of sweet-smelling flowers or leaves. The boy presents the girl such gifts as betel nuts, flower leis, and shell necklaces. The girl brings presents to the boy in case she decides not to have sexual relations with him.

❤ If they enjoy their secret rendezvous, they meet again, and the brings larger gifts to encourage the girl's commitment. In return, she offers him gifts to inform him she desires a continued relationship. If they return to the man's home during the daylight hours after spending a secret night together, this would be considered their declaration of marriage. Upon this recognition, the boy's father brings shell money to the girl's father to ask permission for the couple to remain married. Should the girl's father accept, the couple are considered officially married and reside at the husband's home. A public ceremony could occur a few years after this marriage.

**References:** *The Business of Marriage* by Suzanne Falgout and Sherwood G. Lingenfelter.

# New Zealand

Eighty-eight percent of New Zealanders are of European British and Dutch origin and nine percent are native *Maori* Polynesian. About 60 percent of the population is Christian, mostly Anglican, Presbyterian, and Roman Catholic. Therefore, weddings often takes place in a Christian church. *(See the Church of England for the Anglican wedding.)*

Traditionally, the New Zealanders had simple religious ceremonies with blessings and prayers. Then, hundreds of guests feasted for a week or two. Presently, among the general population, dating and marriage practices are Western-style and derived from European countries. *(See Chapter 1.)* Young people enjoy movies, dancing, and partying prior to marriage. They often have religious weddings in church.

*Maori.* Before the introduction of Christianity by the Europeans, love and matters of the heart were considered a normal part of living. Charming, beautiful young girls with excellent dancing skills were in demand. Youthful suitors sang love songs to their young girls or played the European Jew's harp. Suitors used verbal love charms to gain the affection of resistant girls. In return, the young maiden handed her suitor a floral bouquet with a sprig of bracken fern to show him that he was accepted.

Commoners often had many transient love affairs, yet certain rules of conduct did exist; for example, young men and women were not to marry if they were closely related by blood. Parents were lenient about the love relationships of their older children. A *Maori*

boy and girl often lived together in a trial marriage. Couples frequently cohabited long enough that the relationship was recognized as acceptable after a parental discussion. Their marriage later would be legalized by the church or state. The marriage norm for the masses of the Maori was serial monogamy while their distinguished, wealthy chiefs were polygamous.

Historically, parents of high social standing arranged marriages for their children. Betrothed while they were children, girls were protected by their parents from having other love relationships. Shattering the troth would bring them humiliation and possible retaliation. Marriages were made with others of high rank in order to continue the family lineage. Men married at 25 years of age.

Initially, parents sent an intermediary to the other family with a valuable present. The intermediary conducted long negotiations with the other family, especially when they lived far away. After an agreement was made, the bride with her attendants left in a procession for the groom's home.

Parents took much care when seeking a suitable husband from another tribe in order to advance their goals politically and financially. Entire families took part in the decision. Aristocratic families of the bride and groom gathered, exchanged speeches, and partied together. The groom's family laid away clothing and jewels for the bride, and the bride's family did the same for the groom. If a couple made their own choices, they often would elope.

The high chief's daughter was expected to remain a virgin until a union was made with a high ranking male. Furthermore, female attendants were provided to guard a girl from aspiring lovers to enable her to attract an eligible high class suitor.

**Reference:** *Coming of the Maori* **by Te Rangi Hiroa and** *The Cambridge Factfinder* **edited by David Crystal.**

# Ponam Island

*Ponams.* The *Ponams* converted to Catholicism during the decade of the 1920's, after which time couples were wed at a mass. Although in the past, the selection of a spouse was based partly on social class, the youth are now free to choose partners. Marriages

arranged by *Ponam* leaders or by families are now disappearing.

Unlike Western Catholic customs, however, the groom or bride exchange gifts that include raw or cooked food. A brideprice is paid by the groom.

# Papua New Guinea

Papua New Guinea's population is mostly Christian with 64 percent Protestant and 33 percent Roman Catholic. The remaining population retain a local religion.

## ❤ Traditional marriage customs

In the past, marriage was a way to create alliances between kin groups. A union between a man and woman involved a brideprice or, often child-wealth. Marriages were arranged by parents and the brideprice was given to the girl's family. Arranged marriages were of such importance that young adults' behavior was controlled by their adult relatives. If a couple preferred a love marriage based on freedom of choice, elopement or suicide was their only alternative.

## ❤ Present marriage customs

In more recent years, some marriages have been based on psychological and sexual attraction. Love-based selection of a spouse sometimes disturbs the older generations because love has never been widely accepted in Melanesian society as a reason for marriage. The elite are concerned with the brideprice which can be a major cause for disagreement. Many educated young women prefer that no brideprice should be paid since some men then feel they own their wives; therefore, the transference of the brideprice is no longer practiced.

Today, Port Moresby is a contemporary urban community with sprawling suburbs, large coastal villages, and a downtown port. It is inhabited by the educated elite. Most of the city is westernized and has department stores, supermarkets, luxury hotels, and a variety of entertainment, including city night life attractive to singles. Educated people living in the city seek spouses with similar education and common values. They desire partners whose goals are upwardly mobile and financially successful based on Western concepts. The educated elite's marriage customs are influenced by popular culture and Christianity. Because of their new roles, women who have moved to urban centers have flexibility and are able to provide for themselves, so they are selecting their own marriage partners. The concept of romance crosses over ethnic, national, and racial lines. Even the young men and women of the highlands of New Guinea have freedom to choose their spouses.

*Chimbu.* Historically, after the age of six, *Chimbu* boys and girls lived in separate residences. The girls resided with their mother. All males stayed in a dwelling built on a hilltop so they could protect their clan against enemies. Women were never permitted to enter the male dwelling.

"Carry-leg" courting parties, called *kwanande,* gave *Chimbu* youths opportunities to meet teenage girls from other friendly clans. About 30 young men and women at one time enjoyed talking, singing songs, and exchanging gifts at such a party. Young men wore feathered headdresses and their bodies were embellished with painted decorations. Couples sat with their legs crossed or together because sexual contact was to be avoided. Boys and girls were taught that if they had sexual contact, their skin would no longer possess the glowing health of youth, and would instead become loose and dry.

After singing a song, a young man could sit next to a girl. If a couple really liked each other, they could rub their faces together. Marriages could only be arranged by parents. In order for a marriage to take place, the boy's family had to pay the brideprice to the girl's family.

Today, marriage customs are changing rapidly. Traditional patterns appear to be breaking down partly because there is an increasing disregard for kinship bonds. The brideprice is now paid in cash, and traditional items once used in marriage exchanges and ceremonies are now outmoded. Islanders are encouraged to marry for wealth. A high brideprice is demanded by fathers because females are considered commodities, especially among the Ponam Islanders. Islanders regard marriage as a commercial transaction involving money, hence marriages are postponed so that the man can accumulate enough funds.

Since the price for Telephol women is so high, men tend to look for brides outside their region. The *Gende* are unable to meet the high prices of non-*Gende* women so they must marry their own kind. *Manga* couples simply choose to live together and have children.

225

**Reference:** *The Business of Marriage, Transformations in Oceanic Matrimony*, by Achsah Carrier and Paula Brown's article "New Guinea: 'Carry-Leg' Courtship" in *Faces.*, **Reference:** *Love in the South Seas* by Gengt Danielsson.

# Samoa

Today, Christianity is an integral part of Samoan life with the major denominations being the Congregational Christian Church, Catholic Church, Methodist Church, and Church of Latter Day Saints. Christian marriages are presently conducted according to Protestant and Catholic traditions; thus, Western-style marriage customs prevail. *(See Chapter 1 for Western-style customs.)*

### ❤ Past marriage customs

Historically, groups of young men would visit a nearby community where they knew a young beautiful woman with good qualities lived. Hoping this woman would pick one of them for her spouse, the young men would dance, sing, tell stories, show their athletic prowess, and even extol their accomplishments. The young men often got caught in amusing antics and schemes. In return for their struggle, villagers would sponsor festivities and entertainment; later, the young man who won the young maiden was congratulated by the villagers.

### ❤ The chief's marriage

When a chief took a wife, he and his representatives, the "talking chiefs," would bring gifts and make their proposal to the girl's "talking chiefs." Both sides had to agree on a lucrative and suitable match, based on rank and appearance. Since the union was seen as a social and economic arrangement, villagers provided land where a house could be built for the chief's bride and the future children.

The chief's ambassador and a "talking chief" would go to the future bride's home to work for the family. The "talking chief" then returned to the chief and informed him whether or not the girl had high character. The engagement period was a good time for a chief to acquire wealth for the upcoming event. Since the engagement would take place with little attention to the girl's desires, the girl might choose to go through the dangerous and possibly socially unacceptable process of eloping if she discovered that the chief was not acceptable to her.

Prior to her marriage to a chief, the girl would be guarded carefully by an elderly woman of her household to protect the girl's virginity. The girl could never go to the village alone. The chief's bride had to be a virgin, for her defloration would be later accomplished in public while she sat unclothed on a white mat. Sitting directly across from her, the chief would rupture his bride's hymen by inserting two fingers of his right hand. Onlookers cheered and applauded the deflowering as tears ran down the bride's face.

### ❤ Margaret Mead's research

In 1928, when anthropologist Margaret Mead wrote *Coming of Age in Samoa*, the established courtship ritual required a young man, accompanied by his ambassador, to go to the chosen girl's home with a basket of fish, octopus, or chicken. If his gifts were welcome, the girl's family permitted him to speak with her and he was welcomed into their home. The suitor sat with a bowed head during an evening prayer; then, her parents asked both to dinner. The suitor did not approach the girl at that time, but indicated his desire for her. She might signal to him in return. He had to watch closely or he would not observe her indications. The *soa*, an elaborate plea on the suitor's behalf was made. After dining, the young people might communicate pleasingly, play cards, or sing.

Although gifts were not required each time the suitor visited thereafter, a sincere courtship required several visitations. If the courtship resulted in a marriage proposal, the boy and girl sometimes consummated their union at her parent's home prior to their wedding. Both families received more status, however, if the bride remained a virgin until their marriage. A marriage ceremony could be delayed until the boy's relatives planted and gathered an acceptable amount of food and the girl's family acquired a decent dowry of tapa and mats.

### ❤ Present customs

Today, boys have sexual relations before they enter a single male organization, called the *aumaga*. Both sexes have had flirtations and sexual freedoms prior to marriage. Samoan men tend to be married by the time they are 25 years old.

Harold Stephens Wolfenden, author of *Three Decades of Asian Adventure and Travel*, describes preparations made by young men in Western Samoa when they intend to marry: *A dozen islanders, all wearing colorful lavalavas, or sarongs, and flowered wreaths for a head-dress came to escort us to their village. Before we reached the village we could hear the drums. The ceremony had begun. We rounded the last bend in the path and came to a compound of thatched houses. We were led to one which seemed to serve as the community center... Two young men, with their faces drawn in agony were being held fast by village elders, while two other men clutching crude, evil-looking instruments in their hands, bent over them. . . . The men doing the tattooing used jagged pig bones dipped into lampblack to do the work. Crude, but the results were no ordinary tatoos. They are almost solid designs which extend from the waist down to a few inches below the knees. (See the photograph on page 218.)*

*The ordeal, which everyone came to witness and to drink kava, lasted three days. Each young groom submitted to the tattooist's tapping for half an hour and then rested for two. The tattooist would then move onto someone else. . . . Assisting the tattooist was an elder whose job it was to inspect the wounds and wipe away the blood and excess ink with a soiled cloth. Most*

*of the young men we met had their lower bodies elaborately carved. It was the mark that distinguished the men from the boys.* Afterward, the boys, displaying their glistening oiled tatoos, have the right to marry.

Their wives are generally five years younger. Once an upcoming marriage is announced, both families visit and exchange presents. The girl's family provides, mats, cloth, and food while the boy's relatives give money, food, and clothing to the girl and her relatives. During the 14-day engagement period, wedding invitations are usually sent to guests and village chiefs. The girl's family prepares the wedding dress, and the groom's family gives the bride dresses to be worn afterward. The wedding takes place in the Christian church.

# Samoan Wedding

❤ **The wedding ceremony.** The bride and groom are accompanied by four to 40 of their wedding party mostly consisting of friends. They attend a civil wedding ceremony before the district judge. The bride and groom and their attendants then walk in couples to the Protestant church and proceed down the aisle of the sanctuary where the relatives are assembled.

❤ **Feasting.** Usually, the newlywed's families combine their resources and have a large feast with speeches made by "talking-chiefs" from both families. The feast is then followed by dancing, After all the festivities, both families exchange wedding gifts.

❤ **Elopement.** If a young girl is pregnant, the couple may elope or reside together only a day or as long as a week. Disapproving parents may cause this stiuation. Yet, after much ado, the parents may decide to prepare a wedding.

**References:** *Coming of Age in Samoa* by Margaret Mead, *Love in the South Seas* by Gengt Danielsson, and *Quest for the Real Samoa* by Lowell D. Homes, and quotes from Harold Stephens, author of *At Home in Asia, The Last Voyage,* and *Three Decades of Asian Adventure and Travel.*

227

# Tahiti

❤ **Past marriage customs**

Before the settlers arrived at Tahiti, girls were often betrothed in childhood. A girl was given to her fiancé's relatives to be trained and fattened until she matured. The simple Tahitian ceremony was of a religious nature with blessings and prayers after which hundreds of guests feasted for about a week or two. Those from the upper class were not permitted to marry lower class individuals. Those of upper class status had formal weddings, while lower class marriages usually were consummated without nuptial rites.

❤ **Present marriage customs**

Approximately 55 percent of the Tahitian population are Protestant, 30 percent Roman Catholic, and about 10 percent Mormon. The rest are Seventh-Day Adventist, Jewish, or Buddhist. Many marry in the Christian church.

Today, Tahitians enjoy group dancing, singing, conversation, and sports. They always have believed in love, even at first sight, and suitors have always made a grand effort to gain a maiden's affection.

# Historical Tahitian Wedding

### Part 1

♥ **Procession.** The groom's representatives, carrying gifts for the bride's relatives, arrive at the bride's home, then they escort her, her friends, and family to the groom's house. Pigs, fowl, foods, barkcloth, and feathers compose the gifts, called *welcome insurers.* The bridal party, in turn, bring gifts for the groom's parents.

♥ **Gift presentations.** Gifts are presented while the young bride and groom are seated on two overlapping barkcloth sheets supplied by the groom's parents.

♥ **Eliciting blood.** Relatives puncture their heads and faces with shark's teeth to promote bleeding as a way to express their feelings of joy.

♥ **Festivities.** A large feast is held by the groom's family to honor the bride.

### Part 2

♥ **The wedding.** Family and guests go to the groom's ancestral temple where the following three rites are performed before their ancestors' skulls and other symbolic objects:

*Rite 1.* The bride and a male of her family are permitted to consume food untouched by the groom.
*Rite 2.* The couple is covered with barkcloth.
*Rite 3.* Family members on both sides elicit more blood from themselves. They place the blood stains on a cloth mat on which the bride and groom sit. The bloodstained mat is later buried outside, close to the temple.

♥ **Post-wedding nuptials.** The three rites are repeated after all the people congregate at the bride's home. The newlyweds are given a marital name.

♥ **Festivities.** Feasting lasts for several days at which time the bride's and groom's relatives contribute a display of goods and foods.

228

**References:** *Oceania: The Native Cultures of Australia and the Pacific Islands* by Douglas L. Oliver and *Love in the South Seas* by Gengt Danielsson.

Until the Twentieth Century, princes, princesses, and their families could consider qualified persons for marriage by perusing the *Almanach de Gotha*, a vast reference which provided a list of other European royal families. Families assessed the prospect's rank and family history and then arranged marriages for their children. Using such a reference is relatively rare today for the following reasons:

- ❤ Young princes and princesses, particularly in European cultures, are less likely to accept arranged marriages. Although rank is still considered, marriage for love is now the prevalent norm in their countries.
- ❤ Today, marriages based on such a reference almanac would drastically reduce the choices of prospective royals. Crowned heads and royal families have diminished as the result of two Twentieth Century world wars and revolutions affecting certain countries.
- ❤ About half of the 10 European monarchies are Catholic and the other half are not. Laws concerning intermarriage between Catholic and Protestant are not favorable to future successors to the throne.

As the world approaches a new century, royal families still exist in the United Kingdom, Bahrain, Belgium, Britain, Cambodia, Denmark, Japan, Jordan, Liechtenstein, Luxembourg, Netherlands, Norway, Monaco, Morocco, Sweden, Spain, Saudi Arabia, Syria, Thailand, and Tonga. Other royal tribal families exist in Africa. The royal houses of such countries as Germany, Austria, Italy, Yugoslovia, Romania, Portugal, Russia, and Greece no longer officially exist. Even when royal families have been banished from their countries and deprived of their citizenship, they are often still recognized as royalty by existing royal families. Royal families from the former Communist block countries still appear at royal weddings, parties, and funerals. Their members may also be considered as potential spouses with the remaining royal families.

Some royal families are the ruling monarchs of their countries while others are not. Non-ruling monarchies usually represent their countries by performing public relations work for charities, the arts, and sporting events. They entertain influential people or celebrities from other countries.

Royal families continue to affect a nation's public relations and its politics, and to command media interest, particularly in European countries. Many people enjoy watching and discussing their ongoing generational family structures, their joys, and difficulties as they learn about these things on television. Some colorful publications, such as the French *Point de Vue* and *Paris Match*, and the English magazines, *Majesty* and *Royalty*, keep the public abreast of royal activities and large social occasions, especially weddings. They, and other European publications, include information about royalty from other countries throughout the world.

The weddings in the United Kingdom of Charles and Diana, Prince and Princess of Wales, and the marriage of the King of the Zulus to the Princess of Swaziland in Africa were two of the most spectacular ceremonies of the 20th Century.

**Reference: *Royalty* magazine, London, 1996.**

# Belgium

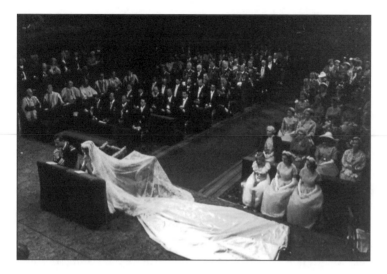

**The wedding of Italian Princess Paola and Belgium's Prince Akbert of Liege** at the Church of St. Gudule in Brussels. The Catholic wedding ceremony was conducted by Cardinal Joseph van Roey.

*ARCHIVE PHOTOS.*

# Brunei

**Brueni's Princess Hajjah Rashidah and Abdul Rahim, August 18, 1996.**

*Brunei Princess Hajjah Rashidah sits with her husband Abdul Rahim as they toured Bandar Sen Begawan in a colorful mile-long procession after the wedding ceremony at the Nural Iman palace. Twenty-seven year old Rashidah is the elder daughter of Sultan Hassanai Bolkiah, reputed to be one of the world's richest men. To celebrate this joyful occasion, she invited thousands of guests, including Philippines President Ramos and Singapore's Senior Minister Lee Kuan Yew.*

*REUTERS/DAVID LOH / ARCHIVE PHOTOS*

# Luxembourg

*Prince Jean leaves Luxembourg's cathedral with his bride, Belgium's Princess Josephine, following their wedding on April 9, 1953. Nobility from 11 European nations were present as the Prince, 32, and his 25-year old bride, sister of Belgium's King Baudouin, were married. The couple, who had known each other since childhood, participated in both civil and religious rites.*

AP/WIDE WORLD PHOTOS

## The Grand Ducal Family

**Princess Josephine Astrid married His Royal Highness Prince Jean of Luxembourg in the Cathedral of Our Lady in Luxembourg on April 9 1953.**

Her Royal Highness Josephine-Charlotte, Grand Duchess of Luxembourg, was the daughter of Prince Leopold of Belgium and Princess Astrid of Sweden. She was born in the Royal Palace in Brussels, Belgium. After their marriage, Grand Duke Jean of Luxembourg ascended to the throne, and the princess became the Grand Duchess of Luxembourg.

231

# *Luxembourg*

***Flowers for the Bride.*** *The former Maria Teresa Mestre, the Cuban born bride of Luxembourg's Prince Henri, hugged a little girl who presented her with a bouquet flowers as the couple left the Luxembourg cathedral after their wedding.*
AP/WIDE WORLD PHOTOS

**Grand Duke Henri of Luxembourg, heir to the Throne, and Maria Teresa Mestre were wed at the Luxembourg Cathedral on St. Valentine's Day in 1981.**

Maria Teresa Mestre was born of Latin Roman Catholic parents in Cuba in 1959. Because of Castro's revolution, she and her parents left their homeland and moved to New York, then to Spain and Switzerland. Maria Teresa had a conservative, protected upbringing with strict rules. She wanted to study political science because of her interest in performing humanitarian work.

While attending the University of Geneva, she met Henri, the Hereditary Grand Duke of Luxembourg. He was born in the castle of Betzdor. Duke Henri and Maria Teresa became friends while working together in the same study groups at the university.

Because Henri was interested in Maria Teresa, the Grand Duke and Duchess invited her to Luxembourg She then had the opportunity to tour Luxembourg and visit Henri's family, who were descended from the dynasties of Bourbon-Parma and Massau.

The Duke Henri and Maria were wed on St. Valentines Day in 1981 at the Luxembourg Cathedral. The Kings and Queens of Belgium and Norway, the Queen of Denmark, and the Duke of Edinburgh attended the wedding ceremony. The royal couple have five children and live in the lovely white French-style Chateau of Fischbach.

**Reference:** *Majesty,* **Vol. 17, No. 6, 1997, London.**

# Indonesia

*President Suharto (right), prepares to kiss the groom, his son Hutomo "Tommy" Madala Putra, as the bride, Ardhia "Tata" Pramesti Rigita Chayani, watches. Tata's lineage is traced from Java's ancient royal family of Solo. Tommy's mother, who is deceased, was a descendant of the same royal family.*
*AP/WIDE WORLD PHOTOS*

**Hutomo "Tommy" Madala Putra, 35, and his bride Ardhia "Tata" Pramesti Rigita Chayani, 22, were married on April 30, 1997, in Jakarta, Indonesia.**

Tommy, a multimillionaire businessman, was the last of President Suharto's six children to marry. Tata was a student who studied landscaping in Australia before her engagement to Tommy.

# The Wedding

❤ Three thousand five hundred guests were invited to the three-hour Muslim-Javanese ceremony held at the Jakarta cultural theme park. Cabinet ministers, generals, entrepreneurs, politicians, and their friends and relatives attended the wedding. Tata wore a golden sarong and was adorned with jewelry. Her hair was held in place by gold pins. Tommy's high silky hat is a symbol of royal ancestry. As the couple knelt before Tommy's 75-year old father to show their respect, his father told them to be grateful for God's blessing

❤ Indonesian Gamelan played classic Indonesian Gamelan music before the couple said their vows in presence of a Muslim cleric. Tommy took off his shoe, then crushed an egg with his foot. This symbolic act indicated, "I do," that he wished to marry the bride. Tommy's wedding presents to his bride were 3.5 ounces of gold and special Islamic prayer attire.

**Reference: *Associated Press* article "Indonesian leader's son marries in lavish ritual" in the *Arizona Republic*.**

# Iran

*The Shah of Iran and his wife, Empress Farah.* Formerly Miss Farah Diba, the Empress had been Shah's art student. This photograph was taken after their wedding in the Hall of Mirrors at the Imperial Palace of Teheran on December 22, 1959.

*ARCHIVE PHOTOS*

# Japan

**Wedding of Crown Prince Akihito and the commoner, Michiko.**
*ARCHIVE PHOTOS*

Emperor Akihito ascended to the throne on January 7, 1989. He met Miss Michiko Shoda, a commoner, on the tennis court at a resort ten years earlier. She was the daughter of a prominent industrialist who was active in academic circles. The Speaker of the House of Representatives, the House of Councillor's President, the Chief Supreme Court Judge, and the Grand Steward of the Imperial Household Agency were consulted and unanimously consented to the marriage.

The Prince married Miss Shoda on April 10, 1959. The public embraced her immediately because of her dignified way of life.

The Emperor and the Empress are both published authors and share an interest in music. The Empress plays the piano accompanied by the Emperor on the cello. Their son, Crown Prince Naruhito, who is married to the Crown Princess Masako, plays the violin with his parents during family concerts. All of the Emperor's children are now married.

**Reference:** *Their Majesties the Emperor and Empress of Japan*, **Ministry of Foreign Affairs.**

# Jordan

King Hussein, descendant of the Prophet Mohammed, ascended to the throne of Jordan at the age of 17 on May 2, 1953. Head of the Hashemites, the first family of Islam, King Hussein is known for expertly managing the economy of Jordan and for his international efforts to negotiate peace in the Middle East.

King Hussein was married to and divorced from Princess Dina, a distant cousin, and Princess Muna, and his third wife, Queen Alia, unfortunately died in the helicopter crash in 1977.

Happily, today he is married to Lisa Halaby, a former United States citizen whose father, Najeeb Halaby of Arab decent, served as advisor to President John F. Kennedy. Lisa attended schools in Los Angeles, Washington, D.C., New York, and Massachusetts before receiving her degree in Architecture and Urban Planning at Princeton University. After her graduation from Princeton, she was employed by an architectural firm in Australia. Her initial assignment took her to Iran, but later, she was sent to Amman, Jordan, where King Hussein was developing an Arab Air University. Lisa was introduced to the king during a ceremony celebrating the landing of the first Jordanian jumbo jet. The next day, the king invited her to the Royal Palace, where a series of work lunches progressively turned into tender one-on-one courtship luncheons. For a month and a half, King Hussein courted Lisa by taking her to the desert in his BMW and to Jordan beaches by helicopter. As the sun set over the Red Sea, he proposed to her during dinner at the Royal Palace Because the King was still affected by the accidental death of Queen Alia, Lisa hesitated to accept his proposal. After helping him with his sorrow and upon converting to the Muslim religion, Lisa, 27, finally took her vows before *Allah*. Wearing a Christian Dior white crepe dress and shimmering royal jewels, she held a bouquet of orchids as she became the queen. Lisa whispered to the king, *I give myself to you in marriage*. The religious Chief of Justice Kadi Alkoudat Ibrahim Kattan read verses from the Koran. King Jordan called her "Noor al Hussein," which translates as the *Light of Hussein*. The couple's reception took place in the park of the Sarhan Palace where the king cut the tall wedding cake with a sabre before 500 guests.

King Hussein and Queen Noor have four children: Hamzah, Hasem, Iman, and Rayah. The king is also the father of Alia, Abudllah, Feisal, Zein, Aisha, Prince Haya, and Ali, and an adopted daughter Abir from prior marriages.

235

**References: The article "Noor de Jordanie" from the magazine *POINT DE VUE.***
**My thanks to Brigitte Ballard for the French translation. *Jordan*, WWW, Current Biography Yearbook, 1826.**

# Morocco

***Moroccan Royal Family Wedding.***
*The wedding of Lamia Sohl, daughter of a Lebanese father, and Moulay*
*Aballah, brother of the King of Morocco, was held at the Royal Palace in*
*Rabat on Novermber, 18, 1961. Lamia was heavily veiled. The ceremony*
*and wedding feast were held at the women's quarter in the Hall of Festivities.*
*ARCHIVES PHOTOS.*

236

# *The Wedding of Lamia Sohl to*
# *Moulay Aballah*

❤ Lamia, who is Lebanese, arrives at the Royal Palace on the arm of King Moulay for the Muslim
ceremony. Shortly afterward, Lamia goes to private quarters to change from her western clothing to
traditional Moroccan Muslim attire.

❤ Servants carry her to the Hall of Festivities on a pallaquin. The unveiled young Princess Lalla
Hamina, the King's sister, is seated next to Lamia at the front of the hall. *(See photograph above.)*

❤ Lamia's mother lifts her daughter's veil and kisses her while the King watches.

❤ Henna paste is spread on Lamia's scarf, then dots of henna are painted to the bride's face. An egg is
broken.

❤ A wedding feast for the women is held in the women's quarters.

*Rainier II, Prince of Monaco, and his bride, Grace Patricia Kelly of Philadelphia, Pennsylvania, USA, pose in the throne room of Monaco Palace on April 18, 1956 following a brief civil marriage ceremony. Later, they were wed in a Roman Catholic ceremony at the Monaco Cathedral.*
AP/WIDE WORLD PHOTOS

**Grace Kelly's and Princess Rainier III's marriage took place at Monaco's Cathedral of St. Nicolas in April 19, 1956.**

Grace, age 25, had just won an Oscar, a highly prized Hollywood award, as best actress in the film *Country Girl,* which was to be shown at the film festival in France. Because of Grace Kelly's increasing world popularity as a Hollywood movie star, the French government invited her to attend the 1955 Cannes Film Festival. She was hesitant about going to this film festival, but the Motion Picture Association of America encouraged her to attend.

Since Grace was to be the festival's central attraction, the editor of *Paris Match,* a French magazine, desired to have a newsworthy photo. The managing editor urged his movie editor, Pierre Galant, to arrange a meeting between Grace Kelly and Prince Rainier.

Prince Rainier, head of the House of Grimaldi, was 32 years old and had just given up the idea of marrying a French actress, Gisele Pascal, because doctors had informed him that she was unable to bear children. According to a 1918 French treaty, Monaco would be returned to French control if the Prince and his wife could not produce an heir.

Galant told Grace that she would be relieved of attending so many receptions if she visited the handsome young bachelor, Prince Rainier at his palace in Monaco. Before her visit, Galant learned that Grace did not have a hat and she could not meet the prince without one. Grace's wardrobe mistress suggested adapting a headband which she had in her suitcase. They hurriedly arranged the artificial flowers on the band to contrive a suitable hat.

When Grace arrived at the palace, Prince Rainier was late so she was given a tour. After Rainier arrived, he was stirred by her refined, quiet, and dignified beauty. As they began to take pleasure in each other's company, the reporters and photographers appeared as if they were only bystanders. This initial meeting was all too brief, yet Grace left Monaco thinking that Prince Rainier was quite charming.

Rainier initially began wooing Grace by telephone. He also asked his spiritual adviser, Father Tucker, to take serious note. As communications became more intimate, the Prince seriously considered Grace for his bride. Excited about their closeness and the prospect of becoming a princess, Grace tried to keep the possibility of marriage private for fear of premature press publicity. At Christmas time in December of 1955, Rainier, accompanied by a physician, Dr. Robert Donat, and Father Tucker, traveled to the United States. Their purpose was to urge Grace marry Rainier.

When the party arrived at the Kelly home in Philadelphia, the Prince charmed Grace's mother and enjoyed private conversations with Grace. Grace was radiant and sensed that she had fallen in love with the Prince. Her feeling was verified after Rainier helped with the dishes and all present were enjoying themselves. When they became engaged, Grace and the Prince spent as much time together as they could.

Before they could marry, Grace was obliged to have a medical checkup at Johns Hopkins University with Dr. Donat present. Rainier had to learn if Grace could produce an heir to the throne. After Dr. Donat confirmed that Grace could have an heir, marital arrangements were made with her father in accord with Monaco's European tradition. Grace's father was shocked that he would be expected to pay a hefty dowry in order for his daughter to wed Prince Rainier. Grace's father transferred the dowry to Prince Rainier after being convinced by Father Tucker and shown proof that His Highness was not cash poor and possessed fabulous wealth.

News reporters in Europe announced the betrothal of Grace Kelly and Prince Rainier III. After Grace appeared in the movies *High Society* and *The Swan,* their engagement party was held at the Waldorf-Astoria in New York City. As Rainier left for Monaco from New York's Idlewild Airport, he indicated that Grace would no longer be a movie actress. MGM was powerless to keep Grace under contract thereafter.

While Grace crossed the Atlantic on a ship bound for Monaco for the wedding, she partied with family and friends. The Prince warmly greeted her and her parents and took them aboard his white yacht. Thousands of people greeted them when the yacht landed, and Monegasque officials boarded the yacht for a reception. After a windy drive through the country to the palace, they were saluted by Rainier's honor guard, wearing red feathered helmets. Grace and her parents stayed in an apartment on the palace grounds for several days until the wedding.

On April 18, 1956, in the presence of family members and dignitaries, Grace and Prince Rainier were first married at a civil service in the throne room of the palace. The wedding was followed by huge reception held in the palace courtyard.

The following day, the couple had a Catholic double-ring wedding ceremony at the Cathedral of St. Nicholas which was lavishly decorated with flowers. Famous movie stars, Aristotle Onassis, the King of Egypt, and about 600 other guests attended the wedding. Trumpets resounded in honor of His Serene Highess who wore his uniform with medals symbolizing French and Italian military history, a plumed helmet, and a red and white sash.

Grace, in a white wedding gown, was accompanied by her father. *(See Grace's photograph on the page facing Chapter 1.)* Her maid of honor and bridesmaids followed them down the aisle. They did not kiss after taking their vows. The wedding ceremony was followed by a mass at which time the newlyweds exchanged glances of affection. After their wedding, they passed through an honor guard formed by members of the Prince's guard.

The wedding reception took place in the palace courtyard. Champagne, caviar, fish, ham, cold lobster, and a five-tier wedding cake were served. The entire wedding party went to a soccer game at the National stadium, then Grace and Rainier left for their honeymoon. As they departed on a boat, rockets were shot into the sky and two flags, one representing Monaco and another representing the United States, were unfurled. They cruised the Riviera from France to Spain, then went ashore in Madrid.

Three children born of their marriage are Princess Caroline, Prince Albert, and Stephanie.

Princess Grace was unfortunately killed in 1982 in a car accident while driving on a mountain road approaching Monaco.

**References:** *Grace: The Secret Lives of a Princess* **by James Spada and** *Grace* **by Robert Lacey.**

# Netherlands

***Queen Beatrix and Prince Claus***
*Photo Archive of Netherlands Government Information Service (NIS)*

**Queen Beatrix and Prince Claus were married on March 20, 1966.**

When Princess Beatrix wanted to marry Claus von Amsberg, a German diplomat, the Parliament had to pass a Bill of Consent. The reason was because provision in the Netherlands Constitution indicated that "all members of the ruling dynasty and their descendants who marry without the consent of Parliament shall be excluded from succession." By November 10, 1965, the Lower House of Parliament consented to the marriage of Princess Beatrix to Claus von Ambsberg and the bill was passed by the Upper House on December 8, 1965. Queen Juliana and Prince Bernhard then announced their daughter's engagement during a television and radio broadcast to the people of the Netherlands, Suriname, and the Netherlands Antilles.

The couple were married by the Burgomaster of Amsterdam in a civil ceremony at the Amsterdam Town Hall. The union was solemnized later by Reverend H. J. Keter during a religious ceremony in the Westerkerk. The titles of Prince of the Netherlands and Jonkeer van Amsberg were bestowed on Claus by Royal Decree.

Princess Beatrix became Queen on April 30, 1980. Having studied law at Leiden University, she maintained an interest in social and cultural matters. Prince Claus is concerned with town and country planning and environmental protection. The royal couple have three sons.

239

---

**Reference: Royal Netherlands Embassy Press and Cultural Department government publications: "The Kingdom of the Netherlands: The Monarchy" and "Holland Information."**

# Norway

*The Crown Prince Harald of Norway and his bride, the former Sonja Haraldsen, pose for the photographers after their wedding at the Royal Castle in Oslo.*
AP/WIDE WORLD PHOTOS

**His Majesty King Harald was married to commoner Sonja Haroldson on August 29, 1968.**

King Harald, son of King Olav V and Crown Princess Martha, ascended to the throne in January 1991. In 1968, King Olav V had announced that his son Crown Prince Harald wished to marry a commoner, Sonja Haraldsen, a young lady he had known for nine years.

Sonja Haraldsen received a diploma in dressmaking and tailoring from the Oslo Vocational School and a diploma from the Ecole Professionelle des Jeunes Filles in Lausanne, Switzerland. She later completed her upper secondary education and received a Bachelor of Arts degree in English, French, and art history from the University of Oslo.

The couple had their first significant meeting at a private party. Two months later, the Crown Prince invited her to the ball given to celebrate the end of his studies at the Military Academy.

Because Crown Prince Harald's decision to marry a commoner sparked a heated political debate on the future of the monarchy, King Olav consulted the government, the President of the Storting, and the leaders of the various parliamentary groups in the Storting before giving approval to the match. The marriage of Crown Prince Harald and Miss Sonja Haraldson was celebrated with a formal banquet at the Royal Palace. Four kings, one queen, and two presidents from other countries attended.

From the very start the Norwegians accepted Crown Princess Sonja with enthusiasm and regarded her as a member of their beloved Royal Family. Their first child, Martha Louise, was born on September 22, 1971, and their second, Prince Haakon, on July 20, 1973. The people of the world saw King Harald and Queen Sonja play an active role in the 1994 Winter Olympic Games in Lillehammer.

**References: Royal Netherlands Embassy Press and Cultural Department government publications: *The Kingdom of the Netherlands: The Monarchy* and *Holland Information*.**

# Sweden

**The wedding of Carl Gustsaf XVI of Sweden and German commoner Silvia Sommerlath at Stockholm's Storkyrkan Church.** *They met during the 1972 Olympics in Munich.*
*AP/WIDE WORLD PHOTOS.*

# Thailand

**The Buddhist wedding of Prince Rabibongse and Sirima on March 29, 1965.**
*Prince Rabibongse is a cousin of the King of Thailand. Express Newspapers. ARCHIVES PHOTOS.*

# *Thailand*

**The King Bhumibol Adulyadej and Queen Sirikit of Thailand**
*ARCHIVE PHOTOS*

## The marriage of King Bhumibol Adulyadej and Queen Sirikit

King Bhmibol, born in the United States, ascended to the throne on June 1946 when he was 18. He has ruled the country of Thailand for over 50 years.

His father, a physician and Harvard graduate, died when King Bhmibol was young, leaving his mother, the Princess of Thailand, to return to her country with her children. Later, the family went to Switzerland where the King was educated. While attending the university, Bhumibol was in a car accident which caused him the loss of one eye. After an operation, he told his mother that his greatest wish in the world was to see again the lovely daughter of Thailand's ambassador to France. He had met her briefly once before. His mother then arranged a meeting with Princess Sirikit at Brumibol's bedside in the hospital. While he was recuperating, their romance began to blossom and they were later married.

King Monghut's great-great-grandfather was King Mongkut of Siam who was immortalized in the Broadway musical *The King and I,* and in the book, *Anna and the King of Siam.*

**Reference: Article "King Bhumibol of Thailand by Ingrid Seward," *Majesty*, December 1996.**

# *United Kingdom*

***Princess Elizabeth and Prince Philip, Duke of Edinburgh,*** *hold hands as they walk from Westminister Abbey on November 20, 1947 after their wedding .*
AP/WIDE WORLD PHOTOS

**Marriage of Princess Elizabeth to Prince Philip, Duke of Edinburgh.**

Queen Elizabeth was still a Princess when she married the former Philip Mountbatten.  Philip was a member of the Greek royal family exiled to Paris, and he was also a descendant of Queen Victoria.  The title of Duke of Edinburgh was created before their wedding.

**How they met:**

Elizabeth first became acquainted with Philip when she was 13 years old.  She met him during World War II while accompanying her parents to the Royal Naval College.  When 18 year-old Philip gave Elizabeth and her sister Margaret a tour of the college, Elizabeth was enticed by his dashing appearance, his blond hair, and broad smile.  While Philip served in the Royal Navy, she sent him friendly letters and saw

243

him a few times. Once, at Christmas-time, Philip was invited to a pantomime performance at Windsor castle where Elizabeth played a part in Aladdin. She tap danced, sang, and joked while Philip laughed at her amusing antics. As the war continued, Elizabeth harbored high hopes that he would return to her.

In 1944, King George II of Greece sent a letter to Elizabeth's father, King George VI, asking that he consider seriously the prospect of Elizabeth marrying Philip, since they obviously loved each other. King George VI was annoyed and replied that his daughter was too young. When Greece's King George repeated the proposal during a visit to Buckingham Palace, George still refused. He simply told his daughter to enjoy her horseback riding lessons. Her father really wanted to spend more time with his daughter, to fish, and shoot deer and birds in Scotland with her. Elizabeth was obedient to her father for many years; however, in 1945, when Elizabeth became nineteen, Philip returned with the Royal Navy from the Far East. They then had more opportunity to spend time talking, dining, and listening to music.

By 1946, Elizabeth and Philip planned a secret rendezvous at the home of the Duke and Duchess of Kent who were sympathetic to their plight. Not only were the Kents supportive of their union, but Lord Louis Mountbatten, Philip's uncle, also encouraged the match. In August of the same year Philip, now 25 years old, proposed to Elizabeth who was 20.

King George VI, Elizabeth's father, was concerned that Philip, though a member of the Greek royalty, had no family funds, not even a home. Not only that, King George was disappointed that the engagement was so secret that he did not have the opportunity to give his official permission. Philip ignored protocol. Even though King George VI thought his daughter was more important than association with Greek politics, he soon discovered his beloved daughter was truly in love with Philip. His characteristics were quite the opposite of Elizabeth. A few days later when Philip asked the King for permission to marry Elizabeth, he was told

that officials in the government must approve.

A tabloid poll indicated that 40 percent thought that, if Elizabeth married Philip, she should give up the throne. In response to public opinion, Philip renounced his Greek titles and became a member of the Church of England. After that, King George received permission from the Prime Minister and the British and Commonwealth governments for Elizabeth's engagement to Philip. Elizabeth's father publicly gave his sanction in April 1947 and alone, he held Elizabeth's head in his hands while he kissed her. Philip's friends gave him two stag parties not far from Buckingham Palace.

On Princess Elizabeth's wedding day, November 22, 1947, she rode in a glass coach. She removed the veil from her face so that the multitudes could see her as she waved. She wore a white satin gown decorated with Belgian lace and a double strand of pearls. The viewing crowds shouted their blessings and well-wishes. Decorative flags lined the streets as the Princess traveled toward the west door of Westminister Abbey.

The King, Queen, and Queen Mother sat on thrones near the altar of the church sanctuary. Princess Elizabeth walked slowly down the aisle on the arm of her father, George VI, carrying a bouquet of white orchids. The bridesmaids wore silver dresses and head veils. Princess Maud and Lady Mary Cambridge carried Elizabeth's 25 foot train. Philip wore his Naval uniform. The Princess wanted the word *obey* to be part of the wedding vows since she did not want to outrank her husband. She spoke all her words with conviction.

After the ceremony, 150 guests attended the wedding breakfast. They were soon interrupted by more than 1,000 people who rushed through the police lines to have a glimpse of the bride. The newlyweds were obliged to stand on the balcony of the palace and wave to the throngs of people. A few hours later, peoples' enthusiasm had peaked, and they had to repeat their performance. They honeymooned at Mountbatten's country home in South England where they were besieged by the press.

References: *Royalty in Vogue* by J, Ross, *Queen Elizabeth II* by Nicolas Davis.

# United Kingdom

***Prince Charles and Princess Diana*** *on the balcony of*
*Buckingham Palace on their wedding day.*
AP/WIDE WORLD PHOTOS

**The wedding of Charles, Prince of Wales, and The Lady Diana Spencer, age 20, took place on**
**The wedding of Charles, Prince of Wales, and Lady Diana Spencer took place on**
**July 29, 1981 at St. Paul's Cathedral.**

Prince Charles and Diana Spencer had met at a shooting party in 1977, but their first significant meeting was in 1980 during Cowes Week, a time when yachts from all over the world assembled to race in The Solent channel. Sarah Armstrong-Jones, Princess Margaret's daughter, invited Lady Diana Frances Spencer, 16 years of age, to spend a day on the Royal Yacht Britannia during the meet. Charles was windsurfing so Diana, an excellent surfer and swimmer with an ancestry of British aristocracy, decided to do the same. Before they knew it, Charles, age 29, and Diana were laughing gaily and weaving around each other. Later, they boarded a speedboat headed for the town of Cowes where they visited pubs and clubs together.

Charles, heir to the throne, and Diana enjoyed a warm conversation about their families. As they returned to the yacht, he noticed her fresh directness

and sparkle in her face. That evening, guests were invited to a formal dinner held in the yacht's candle-lit dining room where the Royal Marine Band played. As all gathered around the piano and sang, Charles kept his eyes on Di. That night, people watched while Charles held Diana close to him as they danced to the slow music.

While Diana worked as a preschool teacher, their relationship progressed. Diana was considered by the royal family as a future prospect to be queen and mother to an heir to the throne. Di met Charles for teas and early dinners. Sometimes, she would go to Buckingham Palace or stay privately with the Queen Mother at Birkhall while waiting for the Prince. Because Di was the granddaughter of one of Queen's close friends, her company delighted the Queen Mother. Di and Prince Charles also spent weekends at a friend's home to avoid the press. Diana, considered a virgin by all who knew her, realized that Charles was serious about their future when he purchased their future private home on 347 acres in Gloucestershire, close to London.

Charles proposed to Diana, then asked her to think about their future while he took a two-week vacation in Australia. The only people Di confided in about a possible engagement were her roommates who carefully guarded her secret. Once photographers realized Prince Charles, the world's most eligible bachelor, had taken a serious interest in Di, they photographed her at Young England Kindergarten where she taught. Diana continued to work at the school because she felt the children required her total involvement. Di confessed she loved Charles when she and Charles gave and interview to the press outside near the preschool. After that, photographers went after her relentlessly.

The Queen gave her formal consent to the union after Diana received a ring from Charles. On February 24, 1981, Queen Elizabeth and the Duke of Edinburgh announced the betrothal of their son Charles to Lady Diana Spencer. Within a day, Prime Minister Thatcher went to Buckingham Palace to express governmental support for the marriage.

Two nights before the wedding ceremony, the Queen gave a dinner party with family and friends attending. A stag dinner was held for Prince Charles the night before the ceremony. Di spent the July 28th night with her mother, grandmother, and the Queen Mother at Clarence house. The same night, a spectacular fireworks display took place in Hyde Park where the military band played. July 29th, the date of Charles and Di's wedding, was declared a national holiday.

The wedding of Charles, Prince of Wales, and Lady Diana Spencer, 20, was one of the most beautiful and elegant weddings of the Twentieth Century. The procession to St. Paul's Cathedral and the 70-minute wedding ceremony were televised in countries all over the world to millions of viewers. Spirited citizens, carrying with flowers and flags, lined up along the route to observe the pageantry. Crowds watched as the Royal Foot Guards in red and black uniforms with high black headdresses and the Royal Horse Brigades accompanied the royal family to the church.

The Queen and Prince Philip led the procession from Buckingham place to the mall in their horse-drawn carriage. Prince Charles and his brother, Prince Andrew, followed. Diana and her father rode to St. Paul's Cathedral in a glass coach. She wore an ivory silk gown

decorated with mother-of pearl and sequins, a lengthy train, and a ruffled neckline.

Prince Charles, wearing a Naval uniform with a blue sash, waited at the altar of the cathedral. He stood next to his brothers, Prince Andrew and Prince Edward. Prince Andrew was in possession of the wedding ring which was presented to Diana. Diana's bridesmaids, India Hicks and Lady Sarah Armstrong Jones (later to become Prince Andrew's wife), wore white. The royal family sat in the front of the sanctuary.

All of the family and guests stood when Diana's father accompanied her down the red-carpeted aisle to the altar. The Archbishop of Canterbury, wearing a long white robe and tall white headdress, performed the ceremony. After the first part of the ceremony was completed, the Prince and the Princess sat down to listen to the Archbishop's address. During the wedding, Diana did not promise to obey, nor did she walk behind Prince Charles. When the Archbishop pronounced them man and wife, crowds outside listening to radios and television, roared and cheered. The newlyweds did not kiss, but signed the register and returned to the west door of the Cathedral.

The long procession returned to Buckingham Palace while excited observers threw rice, confetti, and rose petals at the newlyweds. After arriving at the palace, the entire Royal Family waved to the crowd from the balcony. The royal wedding party dined at the palace. The main 16-layer wedding cake was a 168-pound fruitcake made with raisins, cherries, currants, preserved fruit, and marzipan. It was covered with white icing containing powdered sugar and lemon juice. It stood 4 1/2 feet high. The Prince cut the first piece with his sword.

Princess Di and Prince Charles later honeymooned at the Mountbatten estate where Princess Elizabeth and Prince Philip had spent their honeymoon. The two children from this marriage are Princes William and Harry. In July, 1996, Prince Charles and the highly-admired Princess Diana were officially divorced, and Princess Diana lost her royal title of Her Royal Highness.

On August 30, 1997, the internationally-admired Princess Diana, age 36, was killed in a car accident with photographers unrelentlessly pursuing her in France. She was known for her loving support of the sick and disadvantaged and for her ability to relate to the people. Even though Diana had lost her royal title, she was hailed by all the world as "The People's Princess."

**Reference:** *Invitation to a Royal Wedding* by Kathryn Spink.

# Kwazulu & Swaziland

***King of the Zulus with dancers who are performing the nuptial dance on his wedding day.***
*©Volkmar Kurt Wentzel/National Geographic Image Collection*

**The wedding of the Zulu King Goodwill Zwelithini to the Swazi Princess Manitfombi, daughter of King Sobhuz II of Swaziland, took place in June 1977 at Nongoma in KwaZulu, South Africa.**

The Zulu King Goodwill Zwelithini, 28, met Princess Manitfombi for the first time in 1971 at his coronation, at time when King, Goodwill Zwelithini was to preside over 280 clans in KwaZulu. During his coronation, Princess Manitfombi was present as royal guest from the independent nation of Swaziland to the north.

After forming a relationship with her, the King constructed their palace and they had become parents of two children. The Princess and the King Goodwill became formally betrothed two years later. The King already had two other wives from other clans in order to maintain goodwill among peoples; however, Princess Manitfombi became his main wife. Their children became heirs to the throne since Princess Manitfombi was of royal blood from the country of Swaziland.

Before their wedding, Princess Manitfombi, age 21, accepted presents from Swazi villagers while holding a lengthy knobkerrie stick in her hand.

Unclothed to the waist and wearing an ox's gallbladder in her hair for good luck, the Princess and her sisters danced before her father, King Sobhuz II in Swaziland. They danced before a calabash (gourd) which contained beer. In the Princess's right hand was a knife which she carried to enter her new land. That traditional custom symbolized that she would be moving to another household.

The next day in KwaZulu, the Princess was bathed at a stream and anointed with ox gall. Then, older Swazi women helped her dress for the wedding.

Prior to the wedding, the groom gave King Sobhuz II *labola,* a brideprice of 200 cattle, which legalized King Zwelithini's marriage to the Princess and made his children legitimate.

More than 25,000 people attended their wedding. Citizens of Swaziland, the Zulu people, and South African dignitaries, many wearing Western clothing, arrived for the ceremony to cement the friendship of the nations.

# The wedding of
## King Goodwill & Princess Manitfombi

❤ **Procession, singing, and dancing in KwaZulu, South Africa.** The bride wears a huge decorated headpiece of red wing feathers and carries a sword to symbolize that she is the daughter of the King of Swaziland. The smiling Princess leads a procession of Swazi women as they sing with joy while making their way between the Zulu dancers. All of her attendants and dancers wear in traditional, colorfully-patterned clothing as they encircle the premises two times.

❤ **Inserting the assegai spear into the ground.** The Princess forces the spear into the earth to show that she is willing to be under the King's protection.

❤ **Announcing the bride's arrival.** Twenty-five thousand people watch outdoors as the bride walks through the crowd. Praise singers sing and the band play *The Hills are Alive to the Sound of Music* from the Broadway musical *The Sound of Music*. Dressed as warriors, Swazi men launch a symbolic charge and open the way for the Princess.

❤ **Wedding dance.** Wearing a leopard skin cloak over his body, a leopard band around his head, and a necklace of lion claws around his neck, the King joins the Swazi Princesses for a wedding dance.

❤ **Wedding.** The wedding begins when the Swazis dance for the Zulu dignitaries and royalty. Then, the King Zwelithini finally sees his Princess who comes forth from a group of chanting women. She carries a long shining sword in her hand, then directs its point toward the king to choose him as her husband. Her feathered headdress is handed to the King to seal tribal bonds. A policeman presides over their civil marriage by asking the Princess and the King whether they love one another.

❤ **Post-wedding customs**. Friendship between the Swazi and Zulu continues while people dance. Wearing a string band around her head as a symbol of her marital status, the Princess transfers gifts of blankets, mats, and pans to her in-laws who are seated on the ground. The Princess, now the Queen, is unclothed to the waist to show respect for her in-laws as she hands over the presents. Later, she pours water from a pitcher to consecrate her presentation to her in-laws.

**Reference:** *Zulu King Weds a Swazi Princess,* **Text and Photographs by Volkmar Wentzel, Foreign Editorial Staff of** *National Geographic* **magazine in Washington, DC, United States of America,**

# United States

***John and Jackie Kennedy*** *step out of the Catholic church into a life of political ambition which was and is famed family tradition. Because of the political visibility of the Kennedys generation after generation, they are considered to be United States royalty by the news media and many citizens.*
***Photograph: Courtesy of John F. Kennedy Library.***

**President John (Jack) Fitzgerald Kennedy and Jacqueline (Jackie) Lee Bouvier were wed at St. Mary's Church in Newport on September 12, 1953.**

Jackie Bouvier, a student at Vassar and a graduate of George Washington University, excelled at horseback riding, was an avid reader, and a talented writer having a command of many languages. Her appearance was like that of a Dresden doll. John (Jack) Kennedy was the son of a rich businessman, Joe Kennedy, a former United States ambassador to Great Britain, had political ambitions for his son. As a young man, John was graduated from Harvard and then became a Naval skipper on a PT boat. He later entered the political arena in the state of Massachusetts. He enjoyed playing touch football and other sports with his brothers and sisters. He was as handsome as Jackie was glamorous.

Jack and Jacqueline (Jackie) first met at the home of Charlie and Martha Barlett in May 1951 when Jack was 34 and Jackie was 21. At that time Jackie was a university senior. Jack and Jackie did not actually relate to each other until their third meeting involving the persistent Barletts. By that time, Jackie was a photographer and article writer for the *Times-Herald* newspaper, and Jack was already enthusiastic about being elected Senator from Massachusetts.

When Jack finally invited Jackie to visit his family, his brothers and sisters were playing touch football. His sisters teased Jackie when they found out she was not an athlete; however, Jackie won the heart of Joe, Jack's father, with her humor, cleverness,

249

and intellect.

When Jackie attended the coronation of Queen Elizabeth in London, Jack, now 36, made a trans-Atlantic call to ask Jackie to marry him. Mr. and Mrs. Hugh D. Auchincloss, Jackie's mother and second husband, held an engagement party for the couple in Newport Beach. The Kennedy's held another party with family friends in Hyannisport on Cape Cod where the Kennedy family resided.

The bridal dinner was held at the Clambake Club where Jack gave Jackie a diamond bracelet. Before the wedding took place, Jack, his ushers, and his brothers played a game of touch football. At least 700 people were invited to the wedding ceremony, including United States senators, Congressmen, and John Kennedy's father, Joe's business associates. Six hundred more guests arrived at the reception.

Both political parties were represented, for Jackie's family members were Republican and the Kennedy family members were Democrat. About 3,000 people watched Jackie approach the Catholic church on her wedding day. The sanctuary was decorated with chrysanthemums and gladioli, and rays of morning sunshine illuminated the stained glass windows.

### ❤ The wedding

Jack and his brother Bobby, the best man, waited for the bride near the altar at the Catholic church.

Jackie's sister Lee was her matron of honor and others from her family, including Jackie's step-siblings took on related roles. Seven bridesmaids, wearing pink taffeta dresses and bandeaux, advanced slowly down the aisle before the bride's entrance. Then, Jackie, adorned with her grandmother's antique veil and a traditional ivory silk taffeta off-shoulder gown, entered. Her gown was made by an African-American society seamstress, Ann Lowe. Her bouquet consisted of orchids, stephanotis and gardenias. Jackie's step-father escorted her down the aisle. Jackie was so beautiful she made the crowd gasp.

John's father selected Cardinal Cushing to conduct the Nuptial High Mass. The Cardinal gave Pope Pius XII's Apostolic blessing and pronounced the couple man and wife.

The newlyweds then went to Hammersmith Farm where tents and umbrella tables were erected outdoors to serve food and champagne to 1200 or more guests. Servers wore black uniforms. The music for Jack and Jackie's first dance was "I Married an Angel."

The couple had two children: Caroline and John (John-John). Caroline is now married to Edwin A. Schlossberg and John Kennedy's wife is Carolyn Bessette Kennedy.

Unfortunately, the marriage of Jackie and President John F. Kennedy ended abruptly when their children were very young, for the President was assassinated on November 21, 1963.

**Reference:** *Jack and Jackie: Portrait of an American Marriage* **by Christopher Anderson.**

# Glossary

*Premarriage*

❤ *Matchmakers,* go-between, khatbeh, nakodo (Japan), portador (Mexico), magula kapuwa (Sri Lanka) kalyn (Russia), soa (Samoa), agwa (Mauritius), nkhoswe (Zaire). Throughout the globe, there are professional go-betweens whose business is to propose a match. Matchmakers broadly vary from professional matchmakers, astrologers, dating services to friends or family. In many Muslim countries and in China, matchmakers are used to assess the families' finances and social prestige as well as the characteristics and quality of the future spouse. In some cultures, matchmakers make the marriage proposal for the suitor and negotiate the payment for the bride.

❤ *Courtship or dating.* Courtship is the time during which a male and female are committed to become acquainted with each other more intimately after their initial attraction and before a formal engagement and marriage. It involves giving gifts to each other and their families, going to the theater, restaurant and parties together, and spending intimate time alone. Dating is mostly practiced in western European countries, in the United States and Canada, but has spread to other countries that have been influenced by Christianity.

❤ *Bundling.* This is the outmoded method of courtship where the couple is permitted by their parents to lie in bed together with their clothing on while they become acquainted. The Pennsylvania Dutch in the United States often placed a board between the couple. Bundling during courtship was the result of cold winters in which candlelight and fuel at night was to be conserved. It was a way for couples to stay warm under covers while getting to know each other in solitude. Bundling was accomplished successfully when the girls strategically knotted their petticoats at the bottom, provided they stayed tied. Margaret Baker's book *Wedding Customs and Folklore* disclosed that a Welsh mother produced a single-legged bundling stocking which fit the girl's body from the waist down. The bundling tradition was brought from Holland and England to colonial settlements in the United States.

❤ *Virginity or chastity* is the abstinence of sexual intimacy before marriage. Virginity of the woman especially, occasionally in men, in many religious cultures is considered their most prized possession. Sometimes, proof of virginity during the wedding night is required and severe punishment follows if the bride is not a virgin. Proof of female virginity often is a demanded in many Muslim countries and among the Ethiopian Jews in Africa. In some parts of the world, virginity is a negotiable part of the marriage contract..

❤ *Betrothal or engagement.* The engagement is formal declaration of impending marriage. Often rings or some form of material goods are exchanged. The engagement may last from a few days to several years and may be dependent on the duration of education, the couples' financial status, or the wealth of their parents. In many places, unborn children or newborn babies were betrothed and the marriage became binding when they reached puberty. In some cases, the young girl lived with the boy's family before puberty. Betrothal during infancy was prevalent in New Guinea, Northern Asia, and the Turk population of Central Asia as well as with some Eskimo and Alaskan Indian tribes. Early marriage prior to puberty was contracted by Hindus and Muslims to continue the line of male descendants and to make certain the daughter did not have indiscriminate sexual relations prior to marriage. Betrothal ceremonies are formally part of wedding ceremonies.

❤ *Brideprice.* Brideprice is called *bridewealth, roora, labola, mahr, emu aye,* or *mboya* (in African countries) or *sadaq* (Islamic), *sijak* (Bedouins and *daro* (European Gypsy) - meaning purchasing the bride. It is the gift of money, material goods, or livestock to the girl's parents for the man to obtain a bride. The brideprice is the amount given to the bride's parents by the groom and/or his family prior, at the marriage or signing of the contract, or after marriage. The brideprice is most often given to the parents to make up for the loss of work of their daughter. It also symbolizes the man's promise to support a wife. The brideprice is paid by some Islamic peoples to protect the wife should she be divorced or widowed. It was also established by Jewish law and was often provided for in the marriage deed, called the *Ketubah.* Today's Jewish brideprice is represented by a gold wedding ring. In some cultures, the brideprice is given in services or work for the bride's family, especially if the groom is not wealthy. The brideprice was or still is prevalent in some Buddhist communities in Asia and former American Indian culture. In some Islamic cultures, the brideprice is greater for a virgin than for a widow or divorcee.

❤ *Dowry or trousseau.* It is the property the bride and her family contributes to the marriage or to the groom's family. The dowry was common throughout countries of Europe, especially in Italy, Greece and France and still is prevalent in some areas. In certain Asian countries, a bride's family will pay for a home and the groom's professional office if their daughter marries a man who has the promise of a high financial position, like a doctor.

❤ *Bridal shower.* A party sponsored by a relative(s) or a friend(s) of the bride or groom before the wedding. At this get-together the bride is given gifts from friends, relatives, and acquaintances.

❤ *Banns.* A notice of future marriage given at a parish church, particularly in the Church of England or Catholic Church. The rector "published the banns," or announced a couple's impending marriage for three consecutive Sunday mornings. If no one were to "forbid the banns," permission was given and the couple could marry within the next three months.

❤ *Henna designs using mehndi paste.* Mehndi designs are usually applied to the hands and feet of Hindu, Muslim, The designs may be applied to Jewish brides-to-be in those regions. If the paste is left on the skin overnight, the orange-brown designs will remain on the skin for about three weeks before fading.

Reference: "Stars drawn to ornate body decoration" by Alona Wartofsky, *Washington Post* and the article "This & That" by Elisabeth Ashford in the newsletter *The Regency Plume.*

## Types of Marriages

❤ *Marriage* is the uniting of men and women under civil or religious law, usually through a wedding ceremony, though sometimes implied by living together for a prescribed number of years in a common law marriage or by the birth of a child. Marriage is a social institution sanctioned by custom and law throughout centuries of human existence. For many religions, marriage sanctions men's and women's sexual desire, permitting a man and woman to live together with the possibility of having children. Marriage involves economics of maintaining the family and property rights. Various types of marriages are monogamy, serial monogamy, polyandry, and polygamy. Occasionally, homosexual people are also married, but this practice is not legal everywhere. Monogamy, one husband to one wife, is by far the most prevalent type of marriage throughout the world.

❤ *Trial marriage.* It is usually defined as a temporary marriage which may either be terminated or later made into a legal marriage if a partner is found to be satisfactory and/or children are born.

❤ *Temporary marriage.* Temporary marriage for pleasure, based on a contractual agreement, is available to Muslim men in Iran. Temporary marriage is utilized by men who travel or for other reasons.

❤ *Handfasting* was the ancient Dane and Scottish custom that allowed for a trial marriage in which the couple lived together for one year and one day prior to their wedding.

### *Plural marriages*

❤ *Monogamy.* Monogamy is marriage involving one husband and one wife.

❤ *Serial monogamy.* Serial monogamy is when subsequent legitimate marriages occur after a spouse has been either divorced or widowed.

❤ *Polyandry.* Polyandry occurs when several brothers or various men share the wife simultaneously. It is the least common marriage throughout the globe. Polyandry was prevalent in Tibet and was also sometimes practiced among Seminole Indians in North America.

❤ *Polygamy* is the practice of a man having more than one wife simultaneously or the wives being married to one man simultaneously. Polygamy exists in Africa and in the Mideastern countries, and in the past, among the American Indians and Mormons. The Muslim religion permits men to have up to four wives. Some men are married to their sister-in-laws or to their brother's widow.

❤ *Outside wife.* In Nigeria, an outside wife is a woman with whom a man has sexual relations for several years or longer. The stipulations include that the man financially supports the wife on a regular basis or acknowledges having her children. The outside wife differs from one who has the respectability of being married in a church ceremony.

### *Other types of marriages*

❤ *Matriarchal marriage.* Matriarchy occurs when the husband lives with his wife and her family and the mother is considered the head of the family. Blood kinship is recognized in the mother line and more power is extended toward the mother than to the father. The maternal family, not commonly practiced throughout the world, has traditionally existed among the American Indians, including the Eskimos, and in specific African, Asiatic and Polynesian cultures. Over history, the matriarchal marriage has gradually changed to patriarchy.

❤ *Patriarchal marriage.* This is a form of marriage in which the husband takes the woman away from her parents and lives with her in his family home. The husband has superior authority over his wife and children.

❤ *Trial marriage.* This is a temporary marriage which may be terminated or later made into a legal marriage if a satisfactory partner is found and/or children are born.

❤ *Civil marriage.* This ia a legal form of marriage in which the couple registers with the state and is married by a state official. It is accepted as a governmental form of marriage in most European countries and in the United States. It often takes place prior to a church wedding in European countries. The civil marriage reduces the possibility of fraud and prevents polygamous unions where they are considered illegal.

### *Methods of acquiring of marital partners*

❤ *Marriage by capture.* Marriage by capture is taking a wife by force. It was an act that took place in every part of the world during primitive times and infrequently occurs at the present time. It was known to take place in antiquity in Ireland, by the Southern Slavs, in Tibet, and by the Hindu Aryans. In Africa, it occurred in Chad, the Ivory Coast, and in Cameroon. Pretend resistance and mock marriage by capture still take place as an amusing sham and is part of tradition in certain regions of Europe and in Chad. During the mock marriage by capture, arrangements for marriage are usually already made in advance. The seizure on the man's part and resistance by the woman is purely symbolic and is jolly fun for all.

❤ *Marriage by elopement* usually occurs when the couple runs away to be married in a civil ceremony with as witnesses. In the case of certain American Indian tribes in the past, a couple could elope by leaving for a few days and return as husband and wife. Couples may resort to elopement as a result of parental opposition, to avoid the brideprice or the high cost of the wedding ceremony and reception. Others simply do not wish to make plans and enjoy the spontaneous process of elopement.

❤ *Marriage by purchase.* The man purchases a wife from the father as if she is property. The selection of the wife is based on the reasons which tempt him to make a bid for his possession, like the right family financial and social background, age, and appearance. This type of marriage increases the power the husband has over his wife. In certain countries a girl is sold like merchandise to the highest bidder without permitting her to choose based on the quality of her purchaser.

❤ *Levirate marriage* is marriage of a widow to her husband's brother. Levirate marriages, done so that widows would be cared for, were particularly the traditions of the Jews, Hindus, Afghans, Mongols, and certain American Indian tribes.

❤ *Common law marriage.* After cohabiting together for a specified number of years in certain countries, states, or provinces, a couple is considered legally married.

# Bibliography

## Books

**Anderson, Christopher,** *Jack and Jackie: Portrait of an American Marriage*, William Morrow and Company, Inc., NY, 1996.

**Aridas, Rev. Chris,** *Your Catholic Wedding*, Doubleday and Co., Inc., New York, 1982.

**Baker, Margaret,** W*edding Customs & Folklore*, Rowman and Littlefield, New Jersey, U.S.A. and David and Charles Limited, Oxford, Great Britain, 1977.

**Bangura, Ph.D.,** Abdul Karim, *The Heritage Library of African Peoples: Kipsigis*, The Rosen Publishing Group Inc., NY, 1994.

**Barnavi, Eli,** *The Historical Atlas of the Jewish People*, Schocken Books, NY, 1992.

**Begley, Eve,** *Of Scottish Ways*, Dillon Press, Minnesota, 1977.

**Bennett, Linda A.,** *Encyclopedia of World Cultures: Europe*, Volume IV, G.K. Hall & Company, 1992.

**Bennett, Olivia,** *A Sikh Wedding*, Hamish Hamilton Children's Books, London, 1985.

**Birket-Smith, Dr.** Jaj, *Eskimos*, Crown Publishers, NY, 1971.

**Bledsoe, Caroline and Pison, Glles,** *Nuptiality in Sub-Saharan Africa*, Clarendon Press, Oxford, 1994.

**Boddy, Janice,** *Wombs and Alien Spirits: Women, Men and the Zar Cult in Northern Sudan*, The University of Wisconsin Press, 1989.

**Bradbury, R.E. and P.C. Lloyd,** *The Benin Kingdom*, International African Institute, London, 1950.

**Bray, Warwick,** *The Aztecs*, G.P. Putnam's Sons, NY, 1968.

**Biesanz, John and Mavis,** *The People of Panama*, Columbia University Press, 1955.

**Brown, Kerry and Joanne O'Brien,** *The Essential Teachings of Buddhism,* Rider, London, 1989.

**Brown, R. and Forde, D.,** *African System of Kinship and Marriage*, Oxford University Press, London, 1956.

**Broude, Gwen J.,** *Marriage Family Relationships*, ABC-CLIO Inc., Santa Barbra, California, 1994.

**Carrier, Achsah,** *Transformations in Oceanic Matrimony.*

**Cartland, Barbara,** *Romantic Royal Marriages*, Beaufort Books, New York and Toronto, 1981.

**Chadwick, Henry and Evans,** *G. R., Atlas of the Christian Church*, Facts on File Publications, New York, 1987.

**Chamratrithirong, Aphichat, Editor,** *Perspectives on the Thai Marriage*, Institute for Population and Social Research, Mahidol University, 1984.

**Charsley, Simon R.,** *Rites of Marrying: The Wedding Industry in Scotland*, Manchester University Press, 1991.

**Chatterjuee, Dr. Krishna Nath,** *Hindu Marriage Past and Present*, Tara Publications, 1972.

**Cheney, Patricia,** *The Land and People of Zimbabwe*, J.B. Lippincott, NY, 1990.

**Clifford, Mary Louise,** *The Land and People of Afghanistan*, J.P. Lippincott, NY, 1989.

**Combs-Schillng, M.E.,** *Sacred Performances*, Columbia University Press, New York, NY 1989.

**Compton, Anita,** *Marriage Customs*, Wayland Ltd, Thomson Learning, New York, 1993.

**Chondoka, Yizenge A.,** *Traditional Marriages in Zambia*, Mission Press, Ndola, 1988.

**Cole, Harriette,** *Jumping the Broom: The African-American Wedding Planner,* Henry Holt and Company, Inc. NY, 1993.

**Costa, Shu Shu,** *Wild Geese and Tea*, An Asian-American Wedding Planner, Riverhead Books, NY, 1997.

**Creighton, Colin and Omari, C.K.,** *Gender, Family and Household in Tanzania*, Avebury, Hamphire, England, 1995.

**Crystal, David,** *The Cambridge Factfinder*, Cambridge University Press, 1994.

**Cushing, Frank Hamilton,** *Zuni*, University of Nebraska Press, Lincoln and London, 1979.

**Danielsson, Bengt,** *Love in the South Seas*, George Allen and Unwin LTD, 1956.

**Davies, Nicholas,** *Queen Elizabeth II*, A Birch Lane Press Book published by Carol Publishing Group, New York, 1994.

**Davis, Deborah and Harrel Stevan, Editors,** *Chinese Families in the Post-Mao Era*, University of California Press, Berkeley, CA, 1993.

**Davis, Kingsley,** *Contemporary Marriage: Comparative Perspectives on a Changing Institution*, Russell Sage Foundation, New York, 1985.

**DeLancey, Mark W,** *Cameroon*, Westview Press, Boulder and San Francisco, 1989.

**Dundas, Charles,** *Kilimanjaro and its People*, Frank Cass and Company Ltd., 1968.

**Editors of B*ride's Magazine* with Antonia van der Meer,** *Bride's New Ways to Wed,* The Putnam Publishing Group, New York, 1990.

**Edwards, Walter Drew,** *Modern Japan Through Its Weddings*, Stanford University Press, 1989, California, 1989.

**Eliad, Mircea,** *The Encyclopedia of Religion,* Macmillan Publishing Company, New York, 1987.

**Elgin, Kathleen,** *The Quakers*, Van Rees Press, New York, 1968.

**Elliott, J.H.,** *The Spanish World*, Harry N. Abrams, Inc., New York, 1991.

**Episcopal Church, The,** *The Book of Common Prayer*, Oxford University Press, New York, February, 1990.

**Estermann, Carlos,** *The Ethnography of Southwest Angola*, Holmes and Meier Publishers, Africana Publishing Company, New York and London, 1976.

**Famighette, Robert,** *The World Almanac and Book of Facts*, 1995, Funk & Wagner Corporation, 1994.

**Fielding, William J.,** *Strange Customs of Courtship and Marriage*, The Blakiston Company, Philadelphia, U.S.A., 1942.

**Fixico, Donald L.,** *Urban Indians,* Chelsea House Publishers, New York, 1991.

**Fletcher, Alice C. and Francis L Flesche,** *The Omaha Tribe*, University of Nebraska Press, Lincoln, 1972.

**Forde, Daryll, Editor,** *Peoples of The Central Cameroons*, Takar by Merran McCulloch, Bamum and Bamilleke by Margaret Littlewood, and Banen, Bafia and Balom by I. Dugast, International African Institute, 1954.

**Fraser, Angus,** *The Gypsies*, Blackwell Publishers, Oxford, U.K., 1992.

**Freedman, Maurice,** *Family and Kinship in Chinese Society,* Stanford University Press, Stanford, CA, 1970.

**Fritts, Roger,** *For As Long As We Both Shall Live*, Avon Books, New York, 1993.

**Frolec, Vaclav; Bodi, Erzsebet; Kwaisniewicz, Krystyna;** Obrad, Svatebni; Strakova, Libuse; Musinka, Mikulas; and Navratilova, Alexandra, *Svatebni Obrad*, pp. 303-305, p. 278, p. 209, Block, 1983.

**Gabron, Kahlil,** *The Prophet,* Alfred A Knopf Inc., 1923.

**Genchev, Stoyan,** *The Wedding: Bulgarian Folk Feasts and Customs*, Septemvri Publishing House, Sofia, 1988.

**Gibran, Kahlil,** *The Prophet,* p. 15, Knopf, NY, 1969.

**Geller, Nan J.,** *Victorian Weddings,* Mark Publishing , Scotts Valley, CA, 1993.

**Gillies, John,** *The New Russia*, Dillon Press, New York, 1994.

**Glasse, Cyril,** *Concise Encylopaedia of Islam*, Stacey International, London, 1989.

**Goring, Rosemary,** *Dictionary of Beliefs and Religions*, W & R Chambers Publishing, New York, 1992.

**Grinnell, George Bird,** *The Cheyenne Indians: History and Society,* Volume I, A Bison Book, University of Nebraska, Lincoln and London, 1923, 1972.

**Gruen, Yetta Fisher,** *Your Wedding: Making It Perfect,* Penguin Books, NY, England, Canada, New Zealand, 1986.

**Grumwald, Henry Anatol, Editor-in-Chief,** *Brazil*, Time-Life Books, Inc., Alexandria, VA, 1988.

**Guerry, Vincent,** *Life With The Baoule,* Three Continents Press, 1975.

**Haegh, Christopher,** *The Cambridge Historical Encyclopedia of Great Britain and Ireland*, Cambridge University Press, 1985.

**Haeri, Shahla,** *The Law of Desire : Temporary Marriage in Shi'i Iran*, Syracuse University Press, 1989.

**Handy, E.S.** Craighill and Mary Kawena Pukui, The *Polynesian Society*, Wellington, 1958.

**Hecht, Leo,** *USSR Today,* Scholasticus Publishing, 1987.

### *Cultures of the World Books*

**Hew, Shirley, Editorial Director,** *Cultures of the World, Argentina, Marshall Ca*vendish Corporation, Times Editions Pte Ltd, p 54, 1991.

**Hew, Shirley, Editorial Director,** *Cultures of the World, Britain,* Marshall Cavendish Corporation, Times Editions Pte Ltd, pp. 60-61, 1994.

**Hew, Shirley, Editorial Director,** *Cultures of the World, Burma,* Marshall Cavendish Corporation, Times Editions Pte Ltd, pp. 60-61, 1990.

**Hew, Shirley, Editorial Director,** *Cultures of the World, Chile,* p. 63, Marshall Cavendish Corporation, Times Editions Pte Ltd, pp. 60-61, 1993.

**Hew, Shirley, Editorial Director,** *Cultures of the World, Columbia,* p. 57, Marshall Cavendish Corporation, Times Editions Pte Ltd, 1993.

**Hew, Shirley, Editorial Director,** *Cultures of the World, Egypt,* Marshall Cavendish Corporation, Times Editions Pte Ltd, 1993.

**Hew, Shirley, Editorial Director,** *Cultures of the World, Iceland,* Marshall Cavendish Corporation, Times Editions Pte Ltd, p. 66, 1996.

**Hew, Shirley, Editorial Director,** *Cultures of the World, Israel,* Marshall Cavendish Corporation, Times Editions Pte Ltd, pp. 70-71, 1993.

**Hew, Shirley, Editorial Director,** *Cultures of the World, Jamaica,* Marshall Cavendish Corporation, Times Editions Pte Ltd, pp. 68-72, 1993.

**Hew, Shirley, Editorial Director,** *Cultures of the World, Kenya,* Marshall Cavendish Corporation, Times Editions Pte Ltd, pp. 60-61, 1994.

**Hew, Shirley, Editorial Director,** The *Cultures of the World, Libya,* Marshall Cavendish Corporation, Times Editions Pte Ltd, pp. 70-71, 1993.

**Hew, Shirley, Editorial Director,** The *Cultures of the World, Malaysia,* Marshall Cavendish Corporation, Times Editions Pte Ltd, pp. 50-52, 1994.

**Hew, Shirley, Editorial Director, Reilly, Mary Jo,** *The Cultures of the World, Mexico,* Marshall Cavendish Corporation, Times Editions Pte Ltd, p. 56-7, 72, 1991.

**Hew, Shirley, Editorial Director,** The *Cultures of the World, Nepal,* Marshall Cavendish Corporation, Times Editions Pte Ltd, p. 53, 1991.

**Hew, Shirley, Editorial Director,** The *Cultures of the World, Nigeria,* Marshall Cavendish Corporation, Times Editions Pte Ltd, pp. 61-64, 1993.

**Hew, Shirley, Editorial Director,** The *Cultures of the World, Pakistan,* Marshall Cavendish Corporation, Times Editions Pte Ltd, pp. 56-57, 1994.

**Hew, Shirley, Editorial Director,** The *Cultures of the World, Poland,* Marshall Cavendish Corporation, Times Editions Pte Ltd, pp. 68-69, 1994.

**Hew, Shirley, Editorial Director,** The *Cultures of the World, Romania,* Marshall Cavendish Corporation, Times Editions Pte Ltd, pp. 62-63, 1994.

**Hew, Shirley, Editorial Director,** The *Cultures of the World, Saudi Arabia ,* Marshall Cavendish Corporation, Times Editions Pte Ltd, pp. 67-68, 1993.

**Hew, Shirley, Editorial Director,** The *Cultures of the World, Sri Lanka ,* Marshall Cavendish Corporation, Times Editions Pte Ltd, pp. 71-72, 1991.

**Hew, Shirley, Editorial Director,** The *Cultures of the World, Sweden,* Marshall Cavendish Corporation, Times Editions Pte Ltd, 1992.

**Hew, Shirley, Editorial Director,** The *Cultures of the World, Thailand,* Marshall Cavendish Corporation, Times Editions Pte Ltd, pp. 58-59, 1990.

**Hew, Shirley, Editorial Director,** The *Cultures of the World, Turkey,* Marshall Cavendish Corporation, Times Editions Pte Ltd, pp. 60-61, 1990.

**Hew, Shirley, Editorial Director,** The *Cultures of the World, Venezuela,* Marshall Cavendish Corporation, Times Editions Pte Ltd, pp. 69, 71, 75, 1991.

**Hew, Shirley, Editorial Director,** The *Cultures of the World, Zimbabwe,* Marshall Cavendish Corporation, Times Editions Pte Ltd, pp. 63-64, 1993.

**Hintz, Martin,** *Ghana,* Children's Press, Chicago, 1987.

**Hiroa, Te Rangi,** *Coming of the Maori*, Whitcombe and Tombs, 1952.

**Hoebel, E. Adamson,** *The Cheyennes: Indians of the Great Plains*, Holt, Rinehart and Winston, pp. 27-28, 1978.

**Holmes, Lowell D.,** *Quest for the Real Samoa,* Bergin and Garvey Publishers, Inc., 1987.

**Hostetler, John A.,** *Amish Society,* The Johns Hopkins University Press, 1993.

**Hsu, Francis L. K.,** *Under the Ancestors' Shadow: Kinship, Personality, and Social Mobility in China,* University Press, Stanford, CA, 1970.

**Huntington, Richard,** *Gender and Social Structure of Madagascar, Indiana,* University Press, Indianapolis, U.S.A., 1988.

**Hur, Ben Seunghwa and Sonja Vegdahl,** *Culture Shock,* Times Editions Pte. Lte., pp. 75 -85, 1993.

**Ishwaran, K.,** *The Canadian Family,* Holt, Rinehart and Winston of Canada, 1976.

**Jocano, Linda F.,** *The Hiligaynons: Philippines of Western Bisayas Regions*, Asian Center, University of Philippines Press, 1983.

**Jachim, Christian,** *Chinese Religions: A Cultural Perspective,*

Prentice-Hall, Englewood Cliffs, NY, 1986.

**Kapleaw, Philip,** *The Three Pillars of Zen: Teaching, Practice, and Enlightenment,* John Weatherly, Inc., Tokyo, 1965.

**Kendall, Laurel,** *Getting Married in Korea*, University of California Press, Berkeley, 1996.

**Keuneman, Herbert,** *Sri Lanka*, Apa Productions (Hong Kong) Ltd, 1983.

**Keshishian, Kevork K.,** *Romantic Cyprus*, 17th Edition, Romantic Cyprus Publications, 1992.

**Kiep, Walther Leisler,** *These Strange German Ways*, 16th Edition, Atlantik-Brucke Publication.

**Klausner, Abraham J.,** *Weddings: A Complete Guide to All Religious and Interfaith Marriage Services*, Apha Publishing Company, Columbus, Ohio, 1986.

**Krige, Eillen Jensen,** *The Social System of the Zulus*, Lohgmas Green and Co., 1957.

**Lacey, Robert,** *Grace, G.P. Putnam's* Sons, New York, 1994.

**Laman, Karl,** *The Congo,* Boktryckeri Aktiebolag, 1957.

**Lang, Robert,** *The Land and People of Pakistan*, J.B. Lipponcott Company, NY, 1968.

**Lam Ping-fai, Robert**, *Local Traditional Chinese Wedding*, Hong Kong Museum of History, Hong Kong, 1986.

**Lamm, Maurice,** *Jewish Way in Love and Marriage*, Harper and Row, New York, 1979.

**Layish, Aharon,** *Marriage, Divorce and Succession in the Druze Family*, E. J. Brill, Netherlands, 1982.

**Lee, Vera,** *Something Old, Something New*, Sourcebooks, Inc., Illinois, 1994.

**Lemennicier, Bertrand,** *Marche du Mariage et de la Famille*, Presses Universitaires de France, 1988.

**Lewin, Ted,** *The Reindeer People*, Macmillan Publishing Company, 1994.

**Leyburn, James G.,** *The Scotch-Irish Social History*, University of North Carolina, U.S.A. , 1962.

**Liegeois, Jean-Pierre,** *Gypsies: An Illustrated History*, Al Saqi Books, London, 1986.

**Locke, Raymond Friday,** *The Book of the Navajo*, Holloway House Publishing Company, Los Angeles, CA, USA. 1992.

**Luchetti, Cathy,** *"I Do!" Courtship, Love and Marriage on the American Frontier*, Crown Publishers, Random House, New York, 1996.

**Mackey, Sandra,** *Saudis: Inside the Desert Kingdom,* Signet, Penquin Group, November, pp. 160-169 & 205-209, 1990.

**Mails, Thomas E.,** *The Mystic Warriors of the Plains*, Marlowe and Company, New York, 1972.

**Mails, Thomas E.,** *The People Called Apache*, BBD Illustrated Books, New York, 1974, 1993.

**Marksbury, Richard A., Editor,** *The Business of Marriage: Transformations in Oceanic Matrimony,* University of Pittsburgh Press, Pittsburgh, PA, U.S.A., 1993.

**Marston, Elsa,** *Lebanon, New Light in an Ancient Land,* pp. 54, 56-57, Dillon Press, NY, 1994.

**Maxwell, James A.,** America's Fascinating Indian Heritage, Reader's Digest, Pleasantville, NY, Montreal, 1978.

**Mbiti, S. John,** *Introduction to African Religion, Second Edi*tion, Heinemann Education Books Ltd, Oxford, England, Portsmouth, New Hampshire and Gaborone, Botswana, 1991.

**McCollister, John C.,** *The Christian Book of Why,* Jonathan David Publishers, Inc., Middle Village, New York, 1983.

**McCulla, Patricia E.,** *Places and People of the World, Bahamas,* 1988.

**McCulloch, M.,** *Peoples of Sierra Leone, International African* Institute, London, 1950.

**McNeil, Jesse Jai,** *Ministers Service Book for Pulpit and Parish,* William B. Eerdmans Publishing Company, Grand Rapids, Michigan, 1961.

**Mead, Margaret,** *Coming of Age in Samoa,* William Morrow & Company, 1928.

**Mendez, Paz Policarpio, Jocano, Landa F., Rolda, Realidad Santico, Matela, Salvacion Bautista,** *The Filipino Family in Transition*, pp. 119-129, Centro Escolar University, Mendiola, Manila, 1984.

**Metrick, Sydney Barbara,** *I Do: A Guide to Creating Your Own Unique Wedding Ceremony*, Celestial Arts, Berkeley, California, 1992.

**Millar, Susan Bolyard,** *Bugis Weddings: Rituals of Social Location in Modern Indonesia,* Regents of the University of California at Berkeley, 1989.

**Murphy, Brian Michael,** *The World of Weddings*, Paddington Press Ltd., New York and London, 1978.

**Morgan, Kenneth W.,** The Path of *the Buddha*, The Ronald Press Company, NY, 1956.

**Morgan, Lewis Henry,** *League of the Iroquois*, Citadel Press, New Jersey, USA, 1962, 1990, 1993.

**Musil, Alois,** *The Manners and Customs of the Rwala Bedouins*, Czech Academy of Sciences and Arts, 1928.

**Musharhamina, Mulago Gua Cikala,** *Traditional African Marriage and Christian Marriage*, St. Paul Publications, Uganda, 1981. Original Tite: *Marriage Traditionnel Africain et Mariage Chretian* published by editions Saint Paul, Afrique Zaire, 1981.

**Novas, Himilce,** *Everything You Need To Know About Latino History*, A Plume/Penguin Book, New York, 1994.

**Oliver, Douglas L.,** *Oceania: The Native Cultures of Australia and the Pacific Islands*, Volume I, University of Hawaii Press, Honolulu, 1989.

**Ottenheimer, Ph.D. , Martin,** *Forbidden Relatives: The American Myth of Cousin Marraiges,* University of Illinois Press, Urbana and Chicago, 1996. *Marriage in Domoni,* Sheffield Publishing Company, Salem, Wisconsin, 1985.

**Packham, Jo,** *Wedding Ceremonies*, Sterling Publishing Company, New York, 1993.

**Parris, Ronald, Ph.D.,** *The Heritage Library of African Peoples: Rendille*, The Rosen Publishing Group Inc., New York, 1994.

**Parkin, David, Nyiamwaya, David,** *Transformations of African Marriage*, Manchester University Press in the United Kingdom for the International African Institute, 1987.

**Picken, Stuart D.B.,** *Shinto: Japan's Spiritual Roots*, Kodansha International Ltd, Tokyo, New York, San Francisco, 1980.

**Piljac, Pamela A.,** *The Bride-to-Bride Book: A Complete Wedding Planner for the Bride*, Bryce-Waterton Publications, 1989.

**Prickett, John,** *Living Faiths: Marriage and the Family,* Lutterworth Press, Cambridge, 1985.

**Quisumbing, Lourdes R.,** *Marriage Customs in Rural Cebu*, Series A: Humanities, Number 3, pp. 32-44, San Carlos Publications, *Daily Life in Rembrandt's Holland*, The Macmillan Company, 1963.

**Rashid, Ahmed,** The Resurgence of *Central Asia*, Oxford University Press, 1994.

**Riesman, Paul,** *Freedom in Fulani Social Life*, The University of Chicago Press, Chicago and London, 1977.

**Ross, J.,** *Royalty in Vogue*, Cangdon and Weed, New York and Chicago, 1989.

**Ross, Marion,** *How to Plan a Perfect Wedding* (video tape), World Vision Home Video Inc., 1986.

**Rouvelas, Marilyn,** A *Guide to Greek Traditions and Customs in*

255

*America*, pp. 47-59, Attica Press, 1992.

**Rugh, Andrea B.,** *Family in Contemporary Egypt*, Syracuse University Press, 1984.

**Scott, George Ryley,** *Curious Customs of Sex & Marriage*, (ancient), Senate, England, 1953, 1995.

**Sedeen, Margaret, Managing Editor,** *The Soviet Union Today*, National Graphic Society, Washington, D.C., 1990.

**Singleton, Esther,** *Dutch NY*, Dodd, Mead and Company, 1909.

**Skabelunt, Grant P.,** *Culturgrams: The Nations of the World*, David M. Kennedy Center for International Studies, Brigham Young University, Gerrett Park Press, 1991.

**Small, Meredith F.,** *What's Love Got to Do with It?*, Doubleday, NY, 1995.

**Sokappadu, Ramanaidoo,** *The Telugu Marriages in Mauritius*, Budget Officer, Ministry of Finance, Port Louis, 1992.

**Spada, James,** *Grace: The Secret Lives of a Princess*, Doubleday and Company, New York, 1987.

**Spink, Kathryn,** *Invitation to a Royal Wedding*, Crescent Books, New York.

**Spier, Leslie,** *Yuman Tribes of the Gila River*, pp. 219—225, Dover Publications, NY, 1978.

**Stein, R. Conrad,** *The Enchanted World: Kenya*, pp. 86-88, Regensteiner Publishing Enterprises, Inc., 1985.

**Stevens, John,** *Lust For Enlightenment: Buddhism and Sex*, Shambhala, Boston and London, 1990.

**Storer, Des, Editor-in-Chief,** *Ethnic Family Values in Australia*, Prentice Hall, 1989.

**Sutherland, Anne,** *Gypsies: The Hidden Americans*, The Free Press, New York, 1975.

**Swinimer, Ph.D., Ciarunji Chesaina,** *The Heritage Library of African Peoples: Pokot*, The Rosen Publishing Group Inc., New York, 1994.

**Tenenbaum, Barbara A.,** *Encyclopedia of Latin American History and Culture*, Charles Scribner and Sons, 1996.

**Tapper, Nancy,** *Bartered Brides: Politics, Gender and Marriage in an Afghan Tribal Society*, Cambridge University Press, Cambridge, 1991.

**Tegg, William,** *The Knot Tied*, Singing Tree Press, 1970. Reprint from the 1877 edition published by William Tegg & Co., London..

**Thornton, Arland and Lin, Hui-Shen,** *Social Change & the Family in Taiwan*, The University of Chicago Press, 1994.

**Tomassion, Richard F.,** *Iceland*, University of Minnesota, 1980.

**Too, Lillian,** *The Complete Illustrated Guide to Feng Shui*, Barnes and Noble, 1996.

**Townsend, Richard F.,** *The Aztecs*, pp. 164-65, Thames and Hudson, 1992.

**Urlin, Ethel L.,** *A Short History of Marriage*, W. Rider & Son, Ltd., London and Omnigraphics, Detroit, MI, U.S.A., 1913.

**University of San Carlos,** Cebu City, Philippines, 1965.

**Wallace, Ernest and Hoebel, E. Adamson,** *The Comanches*, University of Oklahoma Press, 1952.

**Waltz, Mitzi,** *The International Internet Directory*, Ziff-Davis Press, 1995.

**Warner, Diane,** *Complete Book of Wedding Vows*, Career Press, Franklin Lakes, NJ, 1996.

**Weaver, Thomas,** *Handbook of Hispanic Cultures in the United States: Anthropology,* 1994.

**Weber, Eugen, France,** The Belknap Press of Harvard University Press, Cambridge, MA and London, England, 1986.

**Weinrich, A.K.H.,** *African Marriage In Zimbabwe*, Mamo Press in Nyanda and Holmes McDougall in Edinburg, 1982.

**Welply, Michael & Georgia Makhlouf,** *The Rise of Major*

*Religions,* Silver Burdett Press, 1986.

**Waddell, L. Austine,** *Tibetan Buddhism,* Dover Publishers, New York, 1972.

**Whitehead, Sandra,** *Cultures of America: Lebanese Americans,* Benchmark Books, Marshall Cavendish Corp., 1996.

**Wilson, Terry P.,** *The Osage*, Chelsea House Publishers, New York and Philadelphia, 1941, 1972.

**Winchester, Simon,** *Korea,* Prentice Hall Press, NY, 1988.

**Wissler, Clark,** *Social Organization and Ritualistic Ceremonies of the Blackfoot Indians*, Volume VII, Part 1, Order of the Trusties of the American Museum of Natural History.

**Younkin, Paula,** *Indians of the Arctic and Subarctic*, Facts on Files, New York, 1991.

**Youssef, Hisham and Rodenbeck, John,** *Insight Guides: Egypt*, APA Productions, 1988.

**Zumthor, Paul, Vir, Dharam, Editor, and Hutchinson, H.N.,** *Marriage Customs of the World*, Crown Publications, New Delhi, 1989.

**Editors of Bride's Magazine**, *Bride's All New Book of Etiquette,* A Perigee Book, The Berkley Publishing Group, 1993.

**Women of China,** *New Trends in Chinese Marriage and the Family,* Women of China, Beijing, 1987.

**Church Education System Department of Seminaries and Institutes of Religion,** *Achieving a Celestial Marriage,* Church of Jesus Christ of Latter-day Saints, Salt Lake City, Utah, 1992.

*Countries of the World: Great Britain,* The Bookwright Press, New York & England, 1988.

**The Church of Jesus Christ of Latter-day Saints,** *For the Strength of Youth,* The Church of Jesus Christ of Latter-day Saints, Salt Lake City, Utah, 1990.

*Desk Reference Atlas,* Oxford University Press, 1996.

*Encyclopedia of World Cultures, Middle America and the Caribbean, South America,* G.K. Hall & Company, Boston, Massachusetts, U.S.A., 1995.

*Gale Encyclopedia of Mutlicultural America.*

*Life World Library: Turkey,* Time-Life Inc., 1965.

*Marriage and the Family in Rural Bukwaya* (Tanzania), University Press of Fribourg Switzerland, 1973.

*Handbook of North American Indians*, Number 5, Smithsonian, Washington, D.C., 1984.

*National Geographic on Indians of the Americas*, National Geographic Society, Washington D.C., 1955.

**Enchantment of the World Books**

**Carran, Betty,** *Enchantment of the World: Romania*, Children's Press, Chicago, pp. 83-86, 1988.

**Cross, Esther and Wilber,** *Enchantment of the World: Portugal,* Children's Press, 1986.

**Foster, Leil Merrel,** *Enchantment of the World: Jordan,* Children's Press, 1986 and 1991.

**Greenblatt, Miriam,** *Enchantment of the World: Cambodia,* Children's Press, Chicago, 1995.

**Larue, Jason,** *Enchantment of the World: Bangladesh,* *Children's Press,* Chicago, 1992.

**Morrison, Marin,** *Enchantment of the World: Jordan,* Children's Press, 1992.

**Stein, Conrad A,** *Enchantment of the World: Greece,* Children's Press, 1987.

**United States Government Country Studies**

*Afghanistan: A Country Study,* The American University, Washington, D.C., U.S.A. pp. 120-122, 1986.

*Algeria: A Country Study,* The American University, Washington, D.C., U.S.A. pp. 133-137, 1985.

*Bangladesh: A Country Study*, The American University, Washington, D.C., U.S.A., 1989.

**Wickman, Stephen B.,** *Belgium: A Country Study*, The American University, Washington, D.C., 1984.

**Hudson, Rex A. and Hanratty, Dennis M.,** *Bolivia: A Country Study*, Federal Research Division, Library of Congress, Washington, D.C., U.S.A., pp. 80-81, 1991.

**Collelo, Thomas,** *Chad: A Country Study,* The American University, Washington, D.C., U.S.A., 1990.

*Cote d'Ivoire: A Country Study*, Federal Research Division, Library of Congress, Washington, D.C., U.S.A. , 1962 and 1991.

*El Salvadore: A Country Study*, Library of Congress, 1990.

**Haggerty, Richard A.,** *Dominican Republic and Haiti: Country Studies*, Second Edition, Federal Research Division, Library of Congress, Washington, D.C., U.S.A., pp. 66 & 256, 1991.

**Hanratty, Dennis M.,** *Ecuador: A Country Study*, Federal Research Division, Library of Congress, Washington, D.C., U.S.A., 1991.

*Iraq: A Country Study*, Federal Research Division, Library of Congress, Washington, D.C., U.S.A. , p. 113, 1990.

**Metz, Helen Capin,** *Jordan: A Country Study*, Library of Congress, Washington, D.C., U.S.A., 1989.

**Collelo, Thomas,** *Lebanon: A Country Study*, Federal Research Division, Library of Congress, Washington, D.C., U.S.A. , 1989.

**Robert E. Handloff,** *Mauritania, A Country Study,* pp. 56-58, 68-69, Federal Research Division, Library of Congress, Washington, D.C., U.S.A., 1990.

**Handloff, Robert E.,** *Mauritania: A Country Study,* pp. 78, Federal Research Division, Library of Congress, Washington, D.C., U.S.A. , 1987.

*Nicaragua: A Country Study*, pp. 78-80, Federal Research Division, Library of Congress, Washington, D.C., U.S.A. , 1993.

*Panama: A Country Study*, Federal Research Division, Library of Congress, Washington, D.C., U.S.A., 1987.

**Martin, Ralph G.,** *Charles & Diana*, G.P. Putman's Sons, New York, 1985.

**Metz, Helen,** *Persian Gulf States: A Country Study,* Federal Research Division, Library of Congress, Washington, D.C., U.S.A., 1994.

*Romania: A Country Study,* Federal Research Division, Library of Congress, Washington, D.C., U.S.A., 1990.

**LePoer, Barbara Leitch,** *Singapore: A Country Study*, pp. 100-102, Federal Research Division, Library of Congress, Washington, D.C., U.S.A., 1991.

**Nyrop, Richard F.,** *The Yemens: A Country Study*, Federal Research Division, Library of Congress, Washington, D.C., U.S.A., 1985.

### United States Government Area Handbooks

*Area Handbook for Chile,* United States Government Printing Office, Washington, D.C., 1969.

*Area Handbook for the Democratic Republic of the Congo* (Congo Kinshosa), United States Government Printing Office, Washington, D.C., 1970.

*Area Handbook for Ghana*, American University, U.S. Government Printing Office, Washington, D.C., 1971.

**Nyrop, Richard F.,** *Area Handbook for Egypt*, pp. 91-93. The American University, U.S. Government Printing Office, Washington, D.C., U.S.A., 1976.

**Nena Vreeland,** *Area Handbook for the Philippines,* The American University, U.S. Government Printing Office, Washington, D.C., U.S.A., 1976.

*U.S. Army Handbook for Venezuela*, American University, Washington, D.C., 1964.

*Area Handbook for Zambia*, American University, U.S. Government Printing Office, Washington, D.C., 1974.

### Periodicals

**Adams, Bert N. and Mburugu, Edward,** "Kikuyu Bridewealth and Polygyny Today," *Journal of Comparative Family Studies,* pp. 159-166, Summer.

**Brooks, Geraldine,** "Nine Parts Desire" (Islamic Marriage Customs and Rites), *Cosmopolitan,* pp. 213-217, July 1995.

**Brown, Paul,** 'New Guinea: 'Carry-Leg' Courtship', *Faces,* p. 24, 1991.

**Daniels, Celia A,** "Zulu Love Beads", p. 30, Faces, Feb. 1991.

**Eades, David,** "Maria Teresa of Luxembourg, *Majesty*, Vol. 17, No. 6, U.K.

**Ellingsen, Peter,** "Lonely Hearts in Beijing," *World Press Review,* p. 68, March 1990.

***Wedding and Home*** magazine, *Wedding Planner,* SouthBank Publishing Group, London, England. April & May, 1996.

**Ferguson, Susan J.,** *"Marriage Timing of the Chinese American and Japanese American Women"*, Journal of Family Issues, May 1995.

**Ferraro, Gary P.,** "Marriage and Conjugal Roles in Swaziland: Persistence and Change", *International Journal of Sociology of the Family*, pp. 89-128, Autumn, 1991.

**Finnas, Fjalar,** "Entry into Consensual Unions and Marriage among Finnish Women Born between 1938 and 1967", *Population Studies,* March, 1995.

**Istroni, Giovanni,** "Italian Men staying home for mom's food, Comfort", *New York Times, The Arizona Republic,* March 3, 1996.

**Hedges, Chris,** "Looking for Love (Shh!) in Ads" (Algeria), *The New York Times,* May 9, 1993."

**Hendricksz, John;** Schreuder, Osmund, Utltee, Wouter, "Religious Assortive Marriages in Germany (1901 to 1989) and the Netherlands (1914 to 1986)", *Koner Zeitschrift fur Soziologie und Sozialpsychologie,* 1994.

**Hiebert, Murray,** "Vietnam's Husband Shortage,"*World Press Review,* p. 44, May 1994.

**Jacobozzie, Vivian,** "Italian Traditions," *Wedding Day,* pp. 40-41, Creative Publications, Spring/Summer 1986.

**Kendall, Laurel,** "The Matchmaker was a Computer", *Faces,* pp. 10 -13, 1991.

**Narayon, Shoba,** "Passage to Kerala (India)", *House Beautiful,* pp. 16, 19, 22, April, 1995.

**Oni, Bankole,** "Contemporary Courtship and Marriage Practices Among the Yoruba," *International Journal of Sociology of the Family,* pp. 144-159, Autumn.

**Otite, Onigu,** "Marriage and Family Systems in Nigeria," *International Journal of Sociology of the Family,* pp. 15-54, 1991, Autumn.

**Page, Jake,** Hopi: "Slinging Mud at their In-laws," *Marie Claire* (a British magazine), December 21, 1992.

**Peters, Ann,** "The Government as a Matchmaker," *World Press Review,* February 1987, excerpted from the weekly *Asia Magazine* of Hong Kong.

**Russell, Marge,** "Women, Children, and Marriage in Swaziland," *International Journal of Sociology of the Family,* pp. 43-57, 1993.

**Ruxian, Yan,** "Marriage and Family among China's Minority Nationalities as Viewed from Beijing," *Mankind Quarterly,* 1991, Summer.

**Seward, Ingsrid,** "King Bhumibol of Thailand," *Majesty,* Vol. 17, no., 12, December 1996, England.

257

Sinclair, Stephanie, "Polttarit: The Finnish Pre-Marriage Ritual," pp. 59-62, *L & EIF: Life and Education* in Finland, February, 1995.

Shenon, Philip, "A Chinese Bias Against Girls Creates Surplus of Bachelors," *The New York Times,* August 16, 1994.

Stanley, Alessandra, Bagir Journal, "In the Land of Arranged Wedlock, Love Steals In," *The New York Times,* Dec. 7, 1993.

Sun, Lena H., "Abduction, Sale of Chinese Women a Tragic Epidemic," *Washington Post,* 6/21/92.

Terrill, Ross, "China's Youth Wait for Tomorrow," *National Geographic,* p. 127, Vol. 180, No. 1, July 1991.

Thompson, A.E., "Dial-a-counselor," Far Eastern Economic Review, 12/92.

Turnbull, Colin M., "Mbuti Marriage," *Faces,* June, 1987.

Wartofsky, Alona, "Stars drawn to ornate body decorations," *Washington Post*, July 1997.

Wentzel, Volkmar, "Zulu King Weds a Swazi Princess," *National Geographic,* pp. 46-51, Vol. 153, No. 1, January 1978.

Whitman, Sylvia, "Tunisia: Arranging for Marriage," *Faces,* pp. 34-36, February 1991.

Whyte, Martin King, "Choosing Mates —The American Way,"*Society,* March/April 1992.

Wikan, Unni, "Behind the Veil in Arabia: Women in Oman," *The Johns Hopkins University Press,* Baltimore, USA, 1982.

Yusufali, Jabeen, *Pakistan: An Islamic Treasure,* page 78, Dillon Press, Minneapolis, Minnesota, 1990.

"The Family in Tanzania," *International Journal of Sociology of the Family,* Autumn, 1991.

"Brides of India," *New India Digest,* No. 31, Colour Supplement, pp. 41- 51.

"Rocking and Hopping in Beijing," Dateline, *U.S. News & World Report,* March 20, 1995.

"Couplings," *Life,* p. 20, April 1993.

"Indonesian leader's son marries in lavish ritual," Associated Press article in the *Arizona Republic,* May 1, 1997.

**Pamphlets and Newsletters**

**The Regency Plume,** *This & That* by Elisabeth Ashford, Sept./ Oct. issue, 1997.

**Israel Information Center,** *Facts About Israel: Society,* Hamakor Press, Jerusalem, Israel, 1993.

**The Royal Embassy of Saudi Arabia Information Office,** *History,* Washington, D.C.

**Museum Notes of the Museum of Northern Arizona,** *Hopi Courtship and Marriage,* Northern Arizona Society of Science and Art, Flagstaff, Arizona.

**The Royal Embassy of Saudi Arabia Information Office,** *Islam,* Washington, D.C.

**Fujimoto, Hogen,** *Embarking on a Successful Marriage,* Buddhist Churches of America.

**Hite, John,** *Self,* Midwest Buddhist Temple Bulletin, Mar. 1995.

**Royal Netherlands Embassy Press and Cultural Department government publications:** *The Kingdom of the Netherlands: The Monarchy* and *Holland Information.*

**Lectures and Television Talk Shows**

**Dr. Helen Fisher,** Anthropologist. *Straight Talk* with Derek McGinty, PBS, April 1997.

**Dr. May May Yi,** *The Rights Vested in Myanmar Women,* The Fourth World Conference on Women, 1995.

**World Wide Web**

*Ethiopian Jewry (Beta Israel, Falasha, Jews of Ethiopia): Halacha, Customs and Traditions*, North American Conference on Ethiopian Jewry.

*African Weddings:* Melanet Home Pages, New Perspective Technologies Company, A Jordan Family Enterprises Co., 1995.

*Wedding World, Themed Weddings,* Churchfield Cottage, Fawley, near Henley on Thames, Oxon, United Kingdom.

*Bermuda Wedding Associates,* 1995.

*Chinese Wedding Traditions.*

*Scottish Wedding Customs,* Continuum Internet Publishing Services Inc., 1997.

## *Chinese Feng Shui*
### *Methods for living in harmony to promote luck for romance and a happy marriage.*

❤ The southwest corner of a house or apartment is considered the place for romance and conjugal bliss. No kitchen, toilet, or storeroom should be there. Mirrors should also not be placed in that bedroom area; instead they should be hung in a bathroom or separate dressing room since they would suggest the illusion of third parties in a bedroom. All decorative elements, like photographs, pictures, and hangings are hung in pairs representing a devoted couple. Symbols of conjugal bliss, such as two mandarin ducks, peacocks, or love birds, should be placed in a corner since ducks, geese, and many other birds are mates for life.

❤ An aquarium or anything associated with water should never be placed on the right side of the entrance to the room.

❤ Red, the fire element, symbolizes romance in the Chinese tradition. Red roses may be placed in the bedroom as well as crystals which symbolize the earth element. Crystals tied with red ribbons may also be set in the corner of the room.

**Reference: *The Complete Illustrated Guide to Feng Shui* by Lillian Too.**

# Index

259

265